Databases
DeMYSTiFieD®

DeMYSTiFieD® Series

Advanced Statistics Demystified
Algebra Demystified, 2e
Alternative Energy Demystified
ASP.NET 2.0 Demystified
Astronomy Demystified
Biology Demystified
Biophysics Demystified
Biotechnology Demystified
Business Calculus Demystified
Business Math Demystified
Business Statistics Demystified
Calculus Demystified, 2e
Chemistry Demystified
College Algebra Demystified
Data Structures Demystified
Databases Demystified, 2e
Differential Equations Demystified
Digital Electronics Demystified
Earth Science Demystified
Electricity Demystified
Electronics Demystified
Environmental Science Demystified
Everyday Math Demystified
Forensics Demystified
Genetics Demystified
Geometry Demystified
HTML & XHTML Demystified
Java Demystified
JavaScript Demystified
Lean Six Sigma Demystified
Linear Algebra Demystified
Logic Demystified
Macroeconomics Demystified

Math Proofs Demystified
Math Word Problems Demystified
Mathematica Demystified
Matlab Demystified
Microbiology Demystified
Microeconomics Demystified
Nanotechnology Demystified
OOP Demystified
Operating Systems Demystified
Organic Chemistry Demystified
Pharmacology Demystified
Physics Demystified, 2e
Physiology Demystified
Pre-Algebra Demystified, 2e
Precalculus Demystified
Probability Demystified
Project Management Demystified
Quality Management Demystified
Quantum Mechanics Demystified
Relativity Demystified
Robotics Demystified
Signals and Systems Demystified
SQL Demystified
Statistical Process Control Demystified
Statistics Demystified
Technical Analysis Demystified
Technical Math Demystified
Trigonometry Demystified
UML Demystified
Visual Basic 2005 Demystified
Visual C# 2005 Demystified
Web Design Demystified
XML Demystified

The Demystified Series publishes more than 125 titles in all areas of academic study. For a complete list of titles, please visit www.mhprofessional.com.

Databases

DeMYSTiFieD®

Second Edition

Andy Oppel

New York   Chicago   San Francisco   Lisbon   London   Madrid   Mexico City
Milan   New Delhi   San Juan   Seoul   Singapore   Sydney   Toronto

The McGraw·Hill Companies

Cataloging-in-Publication Data is on file with the Library of Congress

Databases DeMYSTiFieD®, Second Edition

567890   DOC DOC   10987654

ISBN   978-0-07-174799-8
MHID   0-07-174799-0

Sponsoring Editor Roger Stewart	**Technical Editor** Aaron Davenport	**Composition** Glyph International
Editorial Supervisor Jody McKenzie	**Copy Editor** Jan Jue	**Illustration** Glyph International
Project Manager Vasundhara Sawhney, Glyph International	**Proofreader** Reed Editorial Services	**Art Director, Cover** Jeff Weeks
Acquisitions Coordinator Joya Anthony	**Indexer** Jack Lewis	**Cover Illustration** Lance Lekander
	Production Supervisor Jim Kussow	

To Laurie, Keith, and Luke

About the Author

Andrew J. (Andy) Oppel is a proud graduate of The Boys' Latin School of Maryland and of Transylvania University (Lexington, Kentucky), where he earned a BA in computer science in 1974. Since then, he has been continuously employed in a wide variety of information technology positions, including programmer, programmer/analyst, systems architect, project manager, senior database administrator, database group manager, consultant, database designer, data modeler, and data architect. In addition, he has served as a part-time instructor with the University of California, Berkeley, Extension for more than 25 years and received the Honored Instructor Award for the year 2000. His teaching work included developing three courses for UC Berkeley Extension: "Concepts of Database Management Systems," "Introduction to Relational Database Management Systems," and "Data Modeling and Database Design." He also earned his Oracle 9*i* Database Associate certification in 2003. He is currently employed as a lead data modeler for Blue Shield of California. In addition to computer systems, Andy enjoys music (guitar and vocals), amateur radio, and soccer (referee instructor, U.S. Soccer).

Andy has designed and implemented hundreds of databases for a wide range of applications, including medical research, banking, insurance, apparel manufacturing, telecommunications, wireless communications, and human resources. He is the author of *SQL Demystified* (McGraw-Hill Professional, 2005), *Databases: A Beginner's Guide* (McGraw-Hill Professional, 2009), and *Data Modeling: A Beginner's Guide* (McGraw-Hill Professional, 2009) and is co-author of *SQL: A Beginner's Guide, Third Edition* (McGraw-Hill Professional, 2008), and *SQL: The Complete Reference, Third Edition* (McGraw-Hill Professional, 2009). His database product experience includes IMS, DB2, Sybase ASE, Microsoft SQL Server, Microsoft Access, MySQL, and Oracle.

If you have any comments, please contact Andy at andy@andyoppel.com.

About the Technical Editor

Aaron Davenport is a principal and senior technical consultant at LCS Technologies Inc., a database and application consulting company based in Sacramento, California. Aaron has been working with RDBMS technologies for over 12 years, with a focus on Oracle and MySQL platforms. Prior to joining LCS, Aaron had tenures at IBM, Gap Inc., and Yahoo!

Contents

Acknowledgments

My thanks to all the people involved in the development of *Databases DeMYSTiFieD®, Second Edition.* First, the editors and staff at McGraw-Hill, many of whom I do not know by name, provided untold hours of support for this project. In particular, I thank Editorial Director Roger Stewart for all the useful guidance and encouragement, Editorial Supervisor Jody McKenzie for smoothing out the rough spots, and Acquisitions Coordinator Joya Anthony for keeping the processes moving. A special thanks to Technical Editor Aaron Davenport for all your input—it really helped to make this a better book. And it was wonderful to again work with Jan Jue, whose consistency and attention to detail proved once again that she is simply the best copy editor around. And thanks to Project Manager Vasundhara Sawhney and all the people at Glyph International who worked on production of the book. Finally, thanks to my family for their understanding and support.

Introduction

Thirty-five years ago, databases were found only in special research laboratories, where computer scientists struggled with ways to make them efficient and useful, publishing their findings in countless research papers. Today databases are a ubiquitous part of the information technology (IT) industry and of business in general. We directly and indirectly use databases every day—banking transactions, travel reservations, employment relationships, web site searches, online and offline purchases, and most other transactions are recorded in and served by databases.

As is the case with many fast-growing technologies, industry standards have lagged behind the development of database technology, resulting in myriad commercial products, each following a particular software vendor's vision. Moreover, a number of different database models have emerged, with the relational model being the most prevalent. *Databases DeMYSTiFieD®, Second Edition,* examines all of the major database models, including hierarchical, network, relational, object oriented, and object relational. This book concentrates heavily on the relational and object-relational models, however, because these are the mainstream of the IT industry and will likely remain so in the foreseeable future.

The most significant challenge in implementing a database is correctly designing the structure of the database. Without a thorough understanding of the problem the database is intended to solve, and without knowledge of the best practices for organizing the required data, the implemented database becomes an unwieldy beast that requires constant attention. *Databases DeMYSTiFieD®, Second Edition,* focuses on the transformation of requirements into a working data model with special emphasis on a process called *normalization*, which has proven

xvi DATABASES DeMYSTiFieD

to be an effective technique for designing relational databases. In fact, normalization can be applied successfully to other database models. And, in keeping with the notion that you cannot design an automobile if you have never driven one, you're introduced to the Structured Query Language (SQL) so that you can "drive" a database before delving into the details of designing one.

I've drawn on my extensive experience as a database designer, administrator, and instructor to provide you with this self-help guide to the fascinating and complex world of database technology. Examples are included using both Microsoft Access and MySQL. I included Microsoft Access because it offers an excellent graphical query tool and is widely used in both business and personal computing settings. For SQL examples, I chose MySQL because its SQL is the most compliant to the ISO/ANSI SQL standard, and because it can be run on Windows, Mac OS, Linux, and several versions of Unix.

chapter 1

Database Fundamentals

This chapter introduces fundamental concepts and definitions regarding databases, including properties common to databases, prevalent database models, a brief history of databases, and the rationale for focusing on the relational model.

CHAPTER OBJECTIVES

In this chapter, the reader should:

- Understand the properties of a database and terms commonly used to describe databases.
- Identify the prevalent database models.
- Understand the history of databases.
- Explain why a focus on relational databases makes sense.

Properties of a Database

A *database* is a collection of interrelated data items that are managed as a single unit. This definition is deliberately broad because there is so much variety across the various software vendors that provide database systems. Microsoft Access places the entire database in a single data file, so an Access database can be defined as the file that contains the data items. Oracle Corporation defines their database as a collection of physical files that are managed by an instance of their database software product. A *file* is a collection of related records that are stored as a single unit by an operating system. An *instance* is a copy of the database software running in memory. Microsoft SQL Server and Sybase define a database as a collection of data items that have a common owner, and multiple databases are typically managed by a single instance of the database management software. This can be quite confusing if you work with multiple products because, for example, a database as defined by Microsoft SQL Server and Sybase is exactly what Oracle calls a *schema*.

> A database is a collection of interrelated data items that are managed as a single unit.

? Still Struggling

Given the unfortunately similar definitions of *files* and *databases,* how can we make a distinction? A number of Unix operating system vendors call their password file a "database," yet database experts will quickly point out that it is not. Clearly, we need a bit more rigor in our definitions. The answer lies in an understanding of certain characteristics or properties that databases possess that ordinary files do not, including management by a database management system (DBMS), layers of data abstraction, physical data independence, and logical data independence. These characteristics are discussed in subsections of this chapter.

A *database object* is a named data structure that is stored in a database. The specific types of database objects supported in a database vary from vendor to vendor and from one database model to another. *Database model* refers to the way in which a database organizes its data to pattern the real world. The most common database models are presented in "Prevalent Database Models," later in this chapter.

The properties of databases are discussed in the following subsections.

The Database Management System (DBMS)

The *Database Management System (DBMS)* is software provided by the database vendor. Software products such as Microsoft Access, Oracle, Microsoft SQL Server, Sybase, DB2, Ingres, and MySQL are all DBMSs. (If it seems odd to you that the acronym used is "DBMS" instead of merely "DMS," keep in mind that the term "database" was originally written as two words and by convention has become a single compound word.)

The DBMS provides all the basic services required to organize and maintain the database, including the following:

- Moving data to and from the physical data files as needed
- Managing concurrent data access by multiple users including provisions to prevent simultaneous updates from conflicting with one another
- Managing transactions so that each transaction's database changes are an all-or-nothing unit of work. In other words, if the transaction succeeds, all database changes made by it are recorded in the database; if the transaction fails, none of the changes it made are recorded in the database
- Support for a *query language*, which is a system of commands that a database user employs to retrieve data from the database
- Provisions for backing up the database and recovering from failures
- Security mechanisms to prevent unauthorized data access and modification

Layers of Data Abstraction

What is unique about databases is that although they store the underlying data only once, they can present multiple users of the data with multiple distinct views of that data. These views are collectively called *user views*. A *user* in this context is any person or application that signs onto the database for the purpose of storing and/or retrieving data. An *application* is a set of computer programs designed to solve a particular business problem, such as an order-entry system, a payroll-processing system, or an accounting system.

TERMS: **User Views**

User views are abstractions provided by the DBMS that permit different users of the database to use customized presentations of the same data that are tailored to their exact needs. This property is one of the fundamental benefits that databases provide over simple file systems.

In contrast to a database, when an electronic spreadsheet application such as Microsoft Excel is used, all users must share a common view of the data that must match the way the data is physically stored in the underlying data file. If a user hides some columns in a spreadsheet, reorders the rows, and saves the spreadsheet, the next user who opens it will have the data presented in the manner in which the first user saved it. An alternative, of course, is for users to save their own copy in separate physical files, but then as one user applies updates, the other users' data becomes out of date. With database systems, we can present each user a view of the same data, but the views can be *tailored* to the needs of the individual users, even though the views all come from one commonly stored copy of the data. Because views store no actual data, they automatically reflect any data changes made to the underlying database objects. This is all possible through *layers of abstraction*, as shown in Figure 1-1.

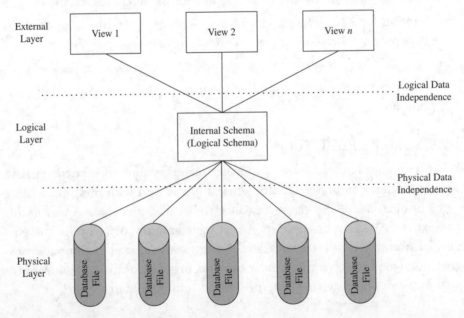

FIGURE 1-1 • Database layers of abstraction

The architecture shown in Figure 1-1 was first developed by ANSI/SPARC (American National Standards Institute Standards Planning and Requirements Committee) in the 1970s and quickly became a foundation for much of the database research and development efforts that followed. Most modern DBMSs follow this architecture, which is composed of three primary layers: the physical layer, the logical layer, and the external layer. The original architecture included a conceptual layer, which has been omitted here because none of the modern database vendors implemented it.

The Physical Layer

The *physical layer* contains the data files that hold all the data for the database. Nearly all modern DBMSs allow the database to be stored in multiple data files, which are usually spread out over multiple physical disk drives. With this arrangement, the disk drives can work in parallel for maximum performance. A notable exception is Microsoft Access, which stores the entire database in a single physical file. This arrangement limits the ability of the DBMS to scale to accommodate many concurrent users of the database, making it inappropriate as a solution for large enterprise systems, while simplifying database use on a single-user personal computer system.

The user of the database does not need to have any knowledge of how the data is actually stored within these files, or even which file contains the data item(s) of interest. In most organizations, a technician known as a *database administrator (DBA)* handles the details of installing and configuring the database software and data files and making the database available to the database users. The DBMS works with the computer's operating system to automatically manage the data files, including all file opening, closing, reading, and writing operations. The database user should not be required to refer to physical data files when using a database, which is in sharp contrast with spreadsheets and word processing, where the user must consciously save the document(s) and choose filenames and storage locations. Many of the personal computer-based DBMSs are exceptions to this tenet because the user is required to locate and open a physical file as part of the process of signing onto the DBMS. In contrast, with server-based DBMSs (such as Oracle, Sybase, Microsoft SQL Server, and so on), the physical files are managed automatically, and the database user never needs to refer to them when using the database.

The Logical Layer

The *logical layer* or *logical model* is the first of two layers of abstraction in the database. We say this because the physical layer has a concrete existence in the operating system files, whereas the logical layer exists only as abstract data structures assembled from the physical layer as needed. The DBMS transforms the data in the data files into a common structure. This layer is sometimes called the *schema*, a term used for the collection of all the data items stored in a particular database. (In some architectures, databases support multiple schemas. In this case, *schema* refers to all data items owned by a particular user account.) Depending on the particular DBMS, this can be a set of 2-D (two-dimensional) tables, a hierarchical structure similar to a company's organization chart, or some other structure. The "Prevalent Database Models" section later in this chapter describes the possible structures in more detail.

The External Layer

The *external layer* or *external model* is the second layer of abstraction in the database. This layer is composed of the user views discussed earlier, which are collectively called the *subschema*. This is the layer where users and application programs that access the database connect and issue queries against the database. Ideally, only the DBA deals with the physical layer, and only the DBA, developers, and other IT staff deal with the logical layers. The DBMS handles the transformation of selected items from one or more data structures in the logical layer to form each user view. The user views in this layer can be predefined and stored in the database for reuse, or they can be temporary items that are built by the DBMS to hold the results of a single ad hoc database query until no longer needed by the database user. By *ad hoc*, we mean a query that was not preconceived and one that is not likely to be reused. Views are discussed in more detail in Chapter 2.

Physical Data Independence

The ability to alter the physical file structure of a database without disrupting existing users and processes is known as *physical data independence*. As shown earlier in Figure 1-1, it is the separation of the physical layer from the logical layer that provides physical data independence in a DBMS. It is essential to understand that physical data independence is not a "have or have not" property, but rather one where a particular DBMS might have more or less data independence than another. The measure, sometimes called the *degree* of physical data independence, is how much change can be made in the file system without impacting the logical layer. Prior to systems that offered data independence, even the slightest change to the way data was stored required the programming staff to make changes to every computer program that used the data, an expensive and time-consuming process.

> ## TERMS: Physical Data Independence
>
> Physical data independence is the ability to alter the physical file structure of a database without disrupting existing users and processes; such as moving database objects from one physical file to another.

All modern computer systems have some degree of physical data independence. For example, a spreadsheet on a personal computer will continue to work properly if copied from a hard disk to a USB thumb drive or if burned onto a CD. The fact that the performance (speed) of these devices varies is not the point, but rather that the devices have entirely different physical construction. Yet the operating system on the personal computer will automatically handle the differences and present the data in the file to the application (that is, the spreadsheet program, such as Microsoft Excel), and therefore to the user, in exactly the same way. However, on most personal systems, users must still remember where they placed the file so they can locate it when they need it again.

DBMSs expand greatly on the physical data independence provided by the computer system in that they allow database users to access database objects (for example, tables in a relational DBMS) without having to reference the physical data files in any way. The DBMS *catalog* keeps track of where the objects are physically stored. Here are some examples of physical changes that may be made in a data-independent manner:

- Moving a database data file from one device or directory to another
- Splitting or combining database data files
- Renaming database files
- Moving a database object from one data file to another
- Adding new database objects or data files

Note that we have made no mention of deleting things. It should be obvious that deleting a database object will cause anything that uses that object to fail. However, everything else should be unaffected.

Logical Data Independence

The ability to make changes to the logical layer without disrupting existing users and processes is called *logical data independence*. Figure 1-1, earlier in the chapter, shows that it is the transformation between the logical layer and the external layer that provides logical data independence. As with physical data independence, there are degrees of logical data independence. It is important to understand that most logical changes also involve a physical change. For example, you cannot add a new database object (such as a table in a relational DBMS) without physically storing the data somewhere; hence, there is a corresponding change in the physical layer. Moreover, deletion of objects in the logical layer will cause anything that uses those objects to fail, but should not affect anything else.

TERMS: Logical Data Independence

Logical data independence is the ability to make changes to the logical layer without disrupting existing users and processes, such as adding a new database object or adding a column to an existing database table.

Here are some examples of changes in the logical layer that can be safely made thanks to logical data independence:

- Adding a new database object
- Adding data items to an existing object
- Any change where a view can be placed in the external model that replaces (and processes the same as) the original object in the logical layer, such as combining or splitting existing objects

Prevalent Database Models

A *database model* is essentially the architecture that the DBMS uses to store objects within the database and to relate them to one another. (Be careful not to confuse the term "database model" with the term *data model*, which refers to the design of a particular database. You may find it helpful to think of database models as architectures used by the DBMS to store data, while data models are designs of specific databases such as order entry and payroll systems.)

The most prevalent database models are presented here in the order of their evolution. A brief history of relational databases appears in the next section to help put things in a chronological perspective.

> ## ? Still Struggling
>
> A bit more elaboration may help you understand the difference between database models and data models. A database model defines the architecture used by the DBMS much like a building code contains the regulations for constructing buildings. A data model, on the other hand, is a description of the design of an individual database, using both diagrams and text definitions, much like the blueprint for an individual building.

Flat Files

Flat files are "ordinary" operating system files in that records in the file contain no information to communicate the file structure or any relationship among the records to the application that uses the file. Any information about the structure or meaning of the data in the file must be included in each application that uses the file or must be known to each human who reads the file. In essence, flat files are not databases at all because they do not meet any of the criteria previously discussed. However, it is important to understand them for two reasons. First, flat files are often used to store database information. In this case, the operating system is still unaware of the contents and structure of the files, but the DBMS has metadata that allows it to translate between the flat files in the physical layer and the database structures in the logical layer. *Metadata*, which literally means "data about data," is the term used for the information that the database stores in its catalog to describe the data stored in the database and the relationships among the data. The metadata for a customer, for example, might include a list of all the data items collected about the customer, along with the length, minimum and maximum data values, and a brief description of each data item. Second, flat files existed before databases, and the earliest database systems *evolved* from the flat file systems that preceded them.

Figure 1-2 shows a sample flat file system, a subset of the data in the Microsoft Northwind sample database in this case. Northwind Traders is a supplier of international food items. Keep in mind that the column titles (Customer ID, Company Name, and so on) are included for illustration purposes only—only the data records would be stored in the actual files. Customer data is stored in a Customer file, with each record representing a Northwind customer. Each employee of Northwind has a record in the Employee file, and each product sold by Northwind has a record in the Product file. Order data (orders placed with Northwind by its customers) is stored in two other flat files. The Order file contains one record for each customer order with data about the orders, such as the customer ID of the customer who placed the order and the name of the employee who accepted the order from the customer. The Order Detail file contains one record for each line item on an order (an order can contain multiple line items, one for each product ordered), including data such as the unit price and quantity.

An *application program* is a unit of computer program logic that performs a particular function within an application system. Northwind has an application program that prints a listing of all the orders. This application must correlate

Customer File

Customer ID	Company Name	Contact First Name	Contact Last Name	Job Title
6	Company F	Francisco	Pérez-Olaeta	Purchasing Manager
26	Company Z	Run	Liu	Accounting Assistant

Employee File

Employee ID	First Name	Last Name	Title
2	Andrew	Cencini	Vice President, Sales
5	Steven	Thrope	Sales Manager
9	Anne	Hellung-Larsen	Sales Representative

Product File

Product ID	Product Code	Product Name	Category	Quantity Per Unit	List Price
5	NWTO-5	Northwind Traders Olive Oil	Oil	36 boxes	$21.35
7	NWTDFN-7	Northwind Traders Dried Pears	Dried Fruit & Nuts	12 – 1 lb pkgs.	$30.00
40	NWTCM-40	Northwind Traders Crab Meat	Canned Meat	24 – 4 oz tins	$18.40
41	NWTSO-41	Northwind Traders Clam Chowder	Soups	12 – 12 oz cans	$9.65
48	NWTCA-48	Northwind Traders Chocolate	Candy	10 pkgs.	$12.75
51	NWTDFN-51	Northwind Traders Dried Apples	Dried Fruit & Nuts	50 – 300 g pkgs.	$53.00

Order File

Order ID	Customer ID	Employee ID	Order Date	Shipped Date	Shipping Fee
51	26	9	4/5/2010	4/5/2010	$60.00
56	6	2	4/3/2010	4/3/2010	$0.00
79	6	2	6/23/2010	6/23/2010	$0.00

Order Detail File

Order ID	Product ID	Unit Price	Quantity
51	5	$21.35	15
51	41	$9.65	21
51	40	$18.40	2
56	48	$12.75	20
79	7	$30.00	14
79	51	$53.00	8

FIGURE 1-2 · Flat file order system

the data between the five files by reading an order and performing the following steps:

1. Use the customer ID to find the name of the customer in the Customer file.

2. Use the employee ID to find the name of the related employee in the Employee file.

3. Use the order ID to find the corresponding line items in the Order Detail file.

4. For each line item, use the product ID to find the corresponding product name in the Product file.

This is rather complicated given that we are just trying to print a simple listing of all the orders, yet this is the best possible data design for a flat file system.

One alternative design would be to combine all the information into a single data file. Although this would greatly simplify data retrieval, consider the ramifications of repeating all the customer data on every single order line item. You might not be able to add a new customer until they have an order ready to place. Also, if someone deletes the last order for a customer, you would lose all the information about the customer. But the worst situation is when customer information changes, because you have to find and update every record where the customer data is repeated. We will explore these issues much more deeply when we explore logical database design in Chapter 7.

Another alternative approach often used in flat file–based systems is to combine closely related files, such as the Order file and Order Detail file, into a single file, with the line items for each order following each order header record, and a Record Type data item added to help the application distinguish between the two types of records. Although this approach makes correlating the order data easier, it does so by adding the complexity of mixing two different kinds of records into the same file, so there is no net gain in either simplicity or faster application development.

Overall, the worst problem with the flat file approach is that the definition of the contents of each file and the logic required to correlate the data from multiple flat files have to be included in every application program that requires those files, thus adding to the expense and complexity of the application programs. It was this problem that provided computer scientists of the day with the incentive to find a better way to organize data.

The Hierarchical Model

The earliest databases followed the hierarchical model. The model evolved from the file systems that the databases replaced, with records arranged in a hierarchy much like an organization chart. Each file from the flat file system became a *record type*, or *node* in hierarchical terminology, but we will use the term *record* here for simplicity. Records were connected using *pointers* that contained the address of the related record. Pointers told the computer system where the related record was physically located, much as a street address directs us to a particular building in a city or a URL directs us to a particular web page or file on the Internet. Each pointer establishes a parent-child relationship, also called a *one-to-many relationship*, where one parent may have many children, but each child may have only one parent. This is similar to the situation in a traditional business organization, where each manager may have many employees as direct reports, but each employee may have only one manager. The obvious problem with the hierarchical model is that there is data that does not exactly fit this strict hierarchical structure, such as an order that must have the customer who placed the order as one parent and the employee who accepted the order as another. Data relationships are presented in more detail in Chapter 2. The most popular hierarchical database was Information Management System (IMS) from IBM.

Figure 1-3 shows the hierarchical structure of the hierarchical model for the Northwind database. You will recognize the Customer, Employee, Product, Order, and Order Detail record types introduced previously. Comparing the hierarchical structure with the flat file system shown in Figure 1-2, note that the Employee and Product records are shown in the hierarchical structure with dotted lines because they cannot be connected to the other records via pointers. These illustrate the most severe limitation of the hierarchical model that was the main reason for its early demise: no record may have more than one parent. Therefore, we *cannot* connect the Employee records with the Order records because the Order records already have the Customer record as their parent. Similarly, the Product records cannot be related to

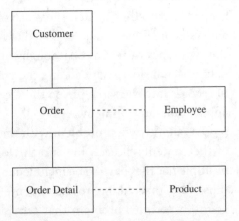

FIGURE 1-3 • Hierarchical model structure for Northwind

the Order Detail records because the Order Detail records already have the Order record as their parent. Database technicians had to work around this shortcoming either by relating the "extra" parent records in application programs, much as was done with flat file systems, or by repeating all the records under each parent, which of course was very wasteful of then-precious disk space. Neither of these was really an acceptable solution, so IBM modified IMS to allow for multiple parents per record. The resultant database model was dubbed the "Extended Hierarchical" model, which closely resembled the network database model in function, discussed in the next section.

Figure 1-4 shows the contents of selected records within the hierarchical model design for Northwind. For simplicity, only the identifiers of the records are shown, but a look back at Figure 1-2 should make the entire contents of each record clear to you. The record for Customer 6 has a pointer to its first order (ID 56), and that order has a pointer to the next order (ID 79). We know that Order 79 is the last order for the customer because it does not have a pointer to a subsequent order. Looking at the next layer in the hierarchy, Order 56 has a pointer to its only Order Detail record (for Product 48), while Order 79 has a pointer to its first Order Detail record (for Product 7), and that record has a pointer to the next detail record (for Product 51), and so forth. There is one additional important distinction between the flat file system and the hierarchical—the key (identifier) of the parent record is removed from the child records in the hierarchical model because the pointers handle the relationships among the records. Therefore, the Customer ID and Employee ID are removed from the Order record, and the Product ID is removed from the Order Detail record. Leaving them in is not a good idea because this could allow contradictory

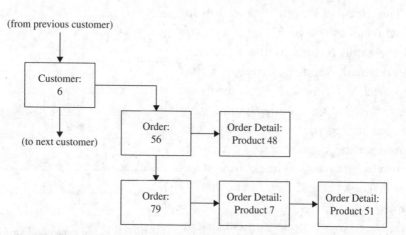

FIGURE 1-4 • Hierarchical model record contents for Northwind

information in the database, such as an order that is pointed to by one customer and yet contains the ID of a different customer.

The Network Model

The network database model evolved at around the same time as the hierarchical database model. A committee of industry representatives was formed to essentially build a better mousetrap. A cynic would say that a camel is a horse that was designed by a committee, and that may be accurate in this case. The most popular database based on the network model was the Integrated Database Management System (IDMS), originally developed by Cullinane (later renamed Cullinet). The product was enhanced with relational extensions, named IDMS/R, and eventually sold to Computer Associates.

As with the hierarchical model, record types (or simply "records") depict what would be separate files in a flat file system, and those records are related using one-to-many relationships, called *owner-member* relationships or *sets* in network model terminology. We'll stick with the terms *parent* and *child*, again for simplicity. As with the hierarchical model, physical address pointers are used to connect related records, and any identification of the parent record(s) is removed from each child record to avoid possible inconsistencies. In contrast with the hierarchical model, the relationships are named so the programmer can direct the database to use a particular relationship to navigate from one record to another in the database, thus allowing a record type to participate as the child in multiple relationships. The network model provided greater flexibility, but as is often the case with computer systems, at the expense of greater complexity.

The network model structure for Northwind, as shown in Figure 1-5, has all the same records as the equivalent hierarchical model structure that appeared in Figure 1-3. By convention, the arrowhead on the lines points from the parent record to the child record. Note that the Customer and Employee records now have solid lines in the structure diagram because they can be directly implemented.

In the network model contents example shown in Figure 1-6, each parent-child

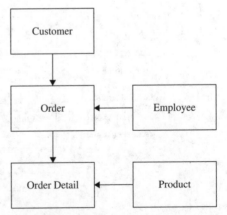

FIGURE 1-5 · Network model structure for Northwind

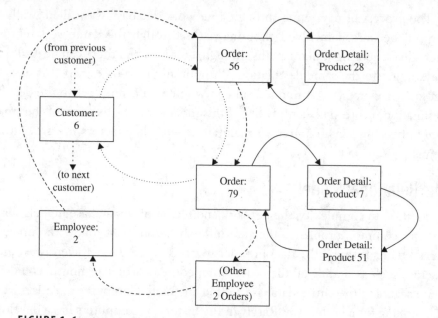

FIGURE 1-6 · Network model record contents for Northwind

relationship is depicted with a different type of line, illustrating that each has a different name. This difference is important because it points out the largest downside of the network model, which is complexity. Instead of a single path that may be used for processing the records, there are now many paths. For example, if we start with the record for Employee 2 and use it to find the first order (ID 56), we land in the chain of orders that belong to Customer 6. We happen to land on the first order belonging to Customer 6, but this is merely by chance—had there been orders for Customer 6 that were taken by other employees, we could have landed in the middle of the chain. To find all the other orders for this customer, there must be a way to work forward from where we are to the end of the chain and then wrap around to the beginning and forward from there until we return to the order from which we started. It is to satisfy this processing need that all pointer chains in network model databases are circular. As you might imagine, these circular pointer chains can easily result in an infinite loop (that is, a process that never ends) should database users not keep careful track of where they are in the database and how they got there. The structure of the Web loosely parallels a network database in that each web page has links to other related web pages, and circular references are not uncommon.

The process of navigating through a network database was called "walking the set" because it involved choosing paths through the database structure much like choosing walking paths through a forest when there can be multiple ways to get to the same destination. Without an up-to-date map, it is easy to get lost, or worse yet, to find a dead end where you cannot get to the desired destination record. The complexity of this model and the expense of the small army of technicians required to maintain it were key factors in its eventual demise.

The Relational Model

In addition to complexity, the network and hierarchical database models share another common problem—they are inflexible. You must follow the preconceived paths through the data in order to process the data efficiently. Ad hoc queries, such as finding all the orders shipped in a particular month, could require scanning the entire database to find them all. Computer scientists were still looking for a better way. Rarely in the history of computers has a development been truly revolutionary, but the research work of Dr. E.F. Codd that led to the relational model was clearly just that.

The relational model is based on the notion that any preconceived path through a data structure is too restrictive a solution, especially in light of ever-increasing demands to support ad hoc requests for information. Database users simply cannot think of every possible use of the data before the database is created; therefore, imposing predefined paths through the data merely creates a "data jail." The relational model therefore provides the ability to relate records *as needed* rather than predefining them when the records are first stored in the database. Moreover, the relational model is constructed such that queries can work with sets of data (for example, all the customers who have an outstanding balance) rather than one record at a time, as with the network and hierarchical models.

TERMS: Relational Model

The relational model is a database model that presents data in 2-D tables using common data to link tables. For example, a Customer ID stored in an order table can be used to link orders to the Customer table that contains information about the customers that placed the orders.

The relational model presents data in familiar 2-D tables, much like a spreadsheet does. Unlike with a spreadsheet, the data is not necessarily stored in tabular form, and the model also permits combining (*joining* in relational terminology) tables to form views, which are also presented as 2-D tables. In short, it follows the ANSI/SPARC model and therefore provides healthy doses of physical and logical data independence. Instead of linking related records together with physical address pointers, as is done in the hierarchical and network models, a common data item is stored in each table, just as was done in flat file systems.

Figure 1-7 shows the relational model design for Northwind. A look back at Figure 1-2 will confirm that each file in the flat file system has been mapped to a table in the relational model. As you will learn in Chapter 6, this one-to-one correspondence between flat files and relational tables will not always hold true, but it is quite common. In Figure 1-7, lines are drawn between the tables to show the one-to-many relationships, with the single-line end denoting the "one" side and the line end that splits into three parts (called a "crow's foot") denoting the "many" side. For example, merely by inspecting the lines that connect these tables, you can see that "one" customer is related to "many" orders and that "one" order is related to "many" order details. The diagramming technique shown here, called the *entity-relationship diagram* (ERD), will be covered in more detail in Chapter 7.

In Figure 1-8, three of the five tables have been represented with sample data in selected columns. In particular, note that the Customer ID column is stored in both the Customer table and the Order table. When the customer ID of a row in the Order table matches the customer ID of a row in the Customer table, you know that the order belongs to that particular customer. Similarly, the Employee ID

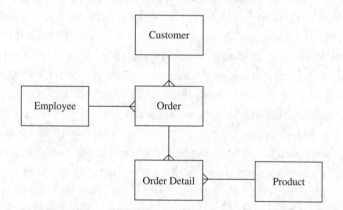

FIGURE 1-7 · Relational model structure for Northwind

Customer Table

Customer ID	Company Name	Contact First Name	Contact Last Name	Job Title
6	Company F	Francisco	Pérez-Olaeta	Purchasing Manager
26	Company Z	Run	Liu	Accounting Assistant

Order Table

Order ID	Customer ID	Employee ID	Order Date	Shipped Date	Shipping Fee
51	26	9	4/5/2010	4/5/2010	$60.00
56	6	2	4/3/2010	4/3/2010	$0.00
79	6	2	6/23/2010	6/23/2010	$0.00

Employee Table

Employee ID	First Name	Last Name	Title
2	Andrew	Cencini	Vice President, Sales
5	Steven	Thrope	Sales Manager
9	Anne	Hellung-Larsen	Sales Representative

FIGURE 1-8 · Relational table contents for Northwind

column is stored in both the Employee and Order tables to indicate the employee who accepted each order.

The elegant simplicity of the relational model and the ease with which people can learn and understand it has been the main factor in its universal acceptance. The relational model is the main focus of this book because it is ubiquitous in today's information technology systems and will likely remain so for many years to come.

The Object-Oriented Model

The object-oriented (OO) model actually had its beginnings in the 1970s, but it did not see significant commercial use until the 1990s. This sudden emergence came from the inability of then-existing RDBMSs (Relational Database Management Systems) to deal with complex data types such as images, complex drawings, and audio-video files. The sudden explosion of the Internet and the Web created a sharp demand for mainstream delivery of complex data.

An *object* is a logical grouping of related data and program logic that represents a real-world thing, such as a customer, employee, order, or product. Individual data items, such as customer ID and customer name, are called *variables* in the OO model and are stored within each object. In OO terminology, a *method* is a piece of application program logic that operates on a particular object and provides a finite function, such as checking a customer's credit limit or updating a customer's address. Among the many differences between the OO model and the models already presented, the most significant is that variables may *only* be accessed through methods. This property is called *encapsulation*.

The strict definition of *object* used here applies only to the OO model. The general term *database object*, as used earlier in this chapter, refers to any named item that might be stored in a non-OO database (for example, a table, index, or view). As OO concepts have found their way into relational databases, so has the terminology, although often with less precise definitions.

Figure 1-9 shows the Customer object as an example of OO implementation. The circle of methods around the central core of variables is to remind us of encapsulation. In fact, you can think of an object much like an atom with an electron field of methods and a nucleus of variables. Each customer for Northwind would have its own copy of the object structure, called an *object instance*, much as each customer has a copy of the customer record structure in the flat file system.

At a glance, the OO model looks horribly inefficient because it seems that each instance requires that the methods and the definition of the variables be redundantly stored. However, this is not at all the case. Objects are organized into a *class hierarchy* so that the common methods and variable definitions need only be defined once and then *inherited* by other members of the same class.

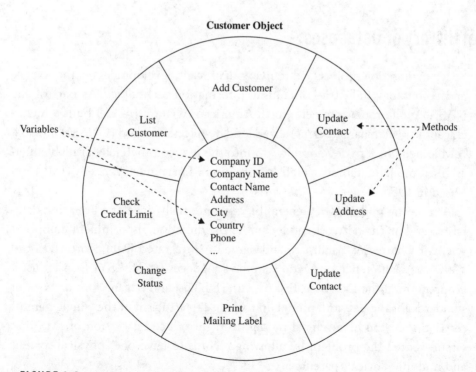

FIGURE 1-9 • The anatomy of an object

OO concepts have such benefit that they have found their way into nearly every aspect of modern computer systems. For example, the Microsoft Windows Registry has a class hierarchy.

The Object-Relational Model

Although the OO model provided some significant benefits in encapsulating data to minimize the effects of system modifications, the lack of ad hoc query capability has relegated it to a niche market where complex data is required, but ad hoc querying is not. However, some of the vendors of relational databases noted the significant benefits of the OO model and added object-like capability to their relational DBMS products with the hopes of capitalizing on the best of both models. The original name given to this type of database was "universal database," and although the marketing folks loved the term, it never caught on in technical circles, so the preferred name for the model became object-relational (OR). Through evolution, the Oracle, DB2, and Informix databases can all be said to be OR DBMSs to varying degrees.

To fully understand the OR model, a more detailed knowledge of the relational and OO models is required.

A Brief History of Databases

Space exploration projects led to many significant developments in the science and technology industries, including information technology. As part of the NASA Apollo moon project, North American Aviation (NAA) built a hierarchical file system named Generalized Update Access Method (GUAM) in 1964. IBM joined NAA to develop GUAM into the first commercially available hierarchical model database, called Information Management System (IMS), released in 1966.

Also in the mid-1960s, General Electric internally developed the first database based on the network model, under the direction of prominent computer scientist Charles W. Bachman, and named it Integrated Data Store (IDS). In 1967, the Conference on Data Systems Languages (CODASYL), an industry group, formed the Database Task Group (DBTG) and began work on a set of standards for the network model. In response to criticism of the "single parent" restriction in the hierarchical model, IBM introduced a version of IMS that circumvented the problem by allowing records to have one "physical" parent and multiple "logical" parents.

In June 1970, E.F. (Ted) Codd, an IBM researcher (later an IBM fellow), published a research paper titled "A Relational Model of Data for Large Shared Data Banks" in *Communications of the ACM*, the Journal of the Association for Computing Machinery, Inc. The publication can be easily found on the Internet. In 1971, the CODASYL DBTG published their standards, which were over three years in the making. This began five years of heated debate over which model was the best.

The CODASYL DBTG advocates argued the following:

- The relational model was too mathematical.
- An efficient implementation of the relational model could not be built.
- Application systems need to process data one record at a time.

The relational model advocates argued the following:

- Nothing as complicated as the DBTG proposal could possibly be the correct way to manage data.
- Set-oriented queries were too difficult in the DBTG language.
- The network model had no formal underpinnings in mathematical theory.

The debate came to a head at the 1975 ACM SIGMOD (Special Interest Group on Management of Data) conference. Ted Codd and two others debated against Charles Bachman and two others over the merits of the two models. At the end, the audience was more confused than beforehand. In retrospect, this happened because every argument proffered by the two sides was completely correct! However, interest in the network model waned markedly in the late 1970s. It was the evolution of database and computer technology that followed that proved the relational model was the better choice, including these significant developments:

- Query languages such as SQL emerged that were not so mathematical.
- Experimental implementations of the relational model proved that reasonable efficiency could be achieved, although never as efficient as an equivalent network model database. Also, computer systems continued to drop in price, and flexibility became more important than efficiency.
- Provisions were added to the SQL language to permit processing of a set of data using a record-at-a-time approach.
- Advanced tools made the relational model even easier to use.
- Codd's research led to the development of a new discipline in mathematics known as *relational calculus*.

In the mid-1970s, database research and development was at full steam. A team of 15 IBM researchers in San Jose, California, under the direction of Frank King, worked from 1974 to 1978 to develop a prototype relational database called System R. System R was built commercially and became the basis for HP ALLBASE and IDMS/SQL. Larry Ellison and a company that later became known as Oracle independently implemented the external specifications of System R. It is now common knowledge that Oracle's first customer was the CIA. With some rewriting, IBM developed System R into SQL/DS and then into DB2, which remains their flagship database to this day.

A pickup team of University of California, Berkeley, students under the direction of Michael Stonebraker and Eugene Wong worked from 1973 to 1977 to develop the Ingres DBMS. Ingres also became a commercial product and was quite successful. It is still available today as an open source solution.

In 1976, Dr. Peter Chen presented the entity-relationship (ER) model. His work bolstered the modeling weaknesses in the relational model and became the foundation of many modeling techniques that followed. If Ted Codd is considered the "father" of the relational model, then we must consider Peter Chen the "father" of the ER diagram. We explore ER diagrams in Chapter 7.

Sybase, which had a successful RDBMS deployed on Unix servers, entered into a joint agreement with Microsoft to develop the next generation of Sybase (to be called System 10) with a version available on Windows servers. For reasons not publicly known, the relationship soured before the products were completed, but each party walked away with all the work developed up to that point. Microsoft finished the Windows version and marketed the product as Microsoft SQL Server, whereas Sybase rushed to market with Sybase System 10. The products were so similar that instructors for Microsoft were known to use the more mature Sybase manuals in class rather than first-generation Microsoft documentation. The product lines have diverged considerably over the years, but Microsoft SQL Server's Sybase roots are still evident in the product.

Relational technology took the market by storm in the 1980s. Object-oriented databases, which first appeared in the 1970s, were also commercially successful during the 1980s. In the 1990s, object-relational systems emerged, with Informix being the first to market, followed relatively quickly by Oracle and IBM.

Not only did the relational technology of the day move around, but the people did also. Michael Stonebraker left UC Berkeley to found Illustra, an object-relational database vendor, and became chief science officer of Informix when it merged with Illustra. He is currently an adjunct professor at MIT, where he is involved in the development of a number of advanced database systems projects. Bob Epstein, who worked on the Ingres project with Stonebraker, moved to the commercial company along with the Ingres product. From there he went to Britton-Lee (subsequently absorbed by NCR) to work on early *database machines* (computer systems with hardware and software specialized to run only databases) and then to start up Sybase, where he was the chief science officer for a number of years. Database machines, incidentally, died on the vine because they were so expensive compared with the combination of an RDBMS running on a general-purpose computer system. However, several vendors, including Oracle, Teradata, and Netezza, currently market database machines that use specialized software for running databases, but with industry-standard hardware. The San Francisco Bay Area was an exciting place for database technologists in that era, because all the great relational products started there, more or less in parallel, with the explosive growth of "Silicon Valley." Others have moved on, but Oracle and Sybase are still largely based in the Bay Area.

Why Focus on Relational?

The remainder of this book will focus on the relational model, with some coverage of the object-oriented and object-relational models. Aside from the relational model being the most prevalent of all the database models in modern business systems, there are other important reasons for this focus, especially for those learning about databases for the first time:

- Definition, maintenance, and manipulation of data storage structures is easy.
- Data is retrieved through simple ad hoc queries.
- Data is well protected.
- Well-established ANSI (American National Standards Institute) and ISO (International Organization for Standardization) standards exist.
- There are many vendors from which to choose.
- Conversion between vendor implementations is relatively easy.
- RDBMSs are mature and stable products.

Summary

In this chapter, you learned the properties of databases, terms used to describe databases, the prevalent database models, a brief history of databases, and the reasoning behind a focus on relational databases. In Chapter 2, we will explore the components of relational databases.

QUIZ

Choose the correct responses in each of the multiple-choice questions. Note that there may be more than one correct response to each question.

1. **Some of the properties of a database are**
   A. It provides less logical data independence than the file systems it replaced.
   B. It provides both physical and logical data independence.
   C. Data items are stored exactly the way they are presented to the database user.
   D. It provides layers of database abstraction.
   E. Databases are always managed by a Database Management System.

2. **Flat file systems:**
   A. Require the user or application program to relate one file to another
   B. Require the user or application to know the contents of each file
   C. Are not really databases by themselves, even though some vendors call them that
   D. Provide no logical data independence when used directly by application programs
   E. Can be used to store the database objects for a database

3. **The hierarchical database model:**
   A. Stores data and methods together in the database
   B. Was first developed by Dr. Peter Chen
   C. In its pure form, permits only one parent for any given record
   D. Connects data in a hierarchical structure using physical address pointers
   E. Allows the processing of sets of database records

4. **The network database model:**
   A. Allows the processing of sets of database records
   B. Allows multiple parents for any given database record
   C. Was first proposed by Dr. E.F. Codd
   D. Is known for its simplicity of use
   E. Connects database records using physical address pointers

5. **The object-oriented model:**
   A. Was first invented in the 1980s
   B. Stores data as variables along with application logic modules called "methods"
   C. Restricts access to variables through encapsulation
   D. Provides for freeform ad hoc querying of variables
   E. Provides better support for complex data types than the relational model

6. **The physical layer of the ANSI/SPARC model:**
   A. Provides physical data independence
   B. Contains the physical files that comprise the database
   C. Contains files that are read and written by the DBMS independently of the computer's operating system
   D. Is normally invisible to the database user
   E. Supplies data to the logical layer

7. **The logical layer of the ANSI/SPARC model:**
   A. Contains database objects that are assembled by the DBMS from data in the physical layer
   B. Contains the database schema
   C. Lies between the physical and external layers
   D. Provides logical data independence
   E. Is referenced by the external layer

8. **According to advocates of the relational model, the problems with the CODASYL model are**
   A. Set-oriented queries are too difficult.
   B. An efficient implementation cannot be built.
   C. It is too mathematical.
   D. It is too complicated.
   E. It lacks generally accepted standards.

9. **According to the advocates of the network model, the problems with the relational model are**
   A. An efficient implementation cannot be built.
   B. Record-at-a-time processing is poorly supported.
   C. It has no formal mathematical underpinnings.
   D. It is too complicated.
   E. It lacks generally accepted standards.

10. **Important historic events in database development are**
    A. Early relational databases were built by both IBM and UC Berkeley.
    B. Nearly all the commercial relational databases are descendents of either System R or Ingres.
    C. GUAM was the first commercially available database.
    D. Dr. E.F. Codd published his famous research paper in 1970.
    E. General Electric's IDS was the first known network database.

chapter 2

Exploring Relational Database Components

In this chapter, we explore the conceptual, logical, and physical components that the relational model comprises. The processes involved in database design are covered in Chapter 5. In the sections that follow, we explore first the components of a conceptual database design, and then the components of a logical and physical design.

CHAPTER OBJECTIVES

In this chapter, the reader should:

- Understand conceptual database design components, including entities, attributes, relationships, and business rules.

- Understand logical/physical database design components, including tables, columns and data types, constraints, and views.

Conceptual Database Design Components

Conceptual database design involves studying and modeling the data in a technology-independent manner. The conceptual data model that results can be theoretically implemented on any database, or even on a flat file system. The person who performs conceptual database design is often called a *data modeler*.

> Conceptual database design is the process that creates a technology-independent data model that can be implemented on any database, or even on a flat file system.

Figure 2-1 shows part of the conceptual design for Northwind. The labeled items (Entity, Attribute, Relationship, Business Rule, and Intersection Data)

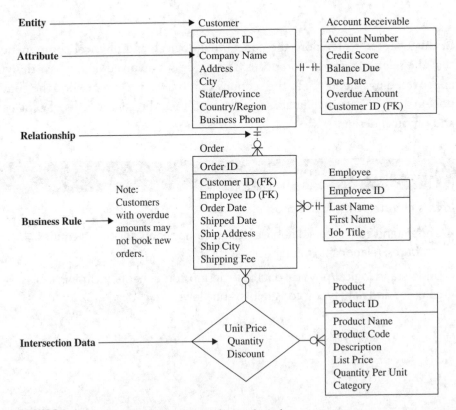

FIGURE 2-1 · Conceptual database design for Northwind

are the basic components that make up a conceptual database design. Each is presented in sections that follow, except for intersection data, which is presented in "Many-to-Many Relationships."

Entities

An *entity* is a person, place, thing, event, or concept about which data is collected. In other words, entities are the real-world things in which we have sufficient interest to capture and store data about them in a database. An entity is represented as a rectangle on the diagram. Just about anything that can be named with a noun can be an entity. However, to avoid designing everything on the planet into our database, we restrict ourselves to entities of interest to the people who will use our database. Each entity shown in the conceptual model represents the entire class for that entity. For example, the Customer entity represents the collection of all Northwind customers. The individual customers are called *instances* of the entity.

> An entity is a person, place, thing, event, or concept about which data is collected.

An *external entity* is an entity with which our database exchanges data (sending data to, receiving data from, or both), but about which we collect no data. For example, most businesses that set up credit accounts for customers purchase credit reports from one or more credit bureaus. They send a customer's identifying information to the credit bureau and receive back a credit report, but all this data is about the *customer* rather than the credit bureau itself. Assuming there is no compelling reason for the database to store data about the credit bureau, such as the mailing address of their office, the credit bureau will not appear in the conceptual database design as an entity. In fact, external entities are seldom shown in database designs, but they commonly appear in data flow diagrams as a source or destination of data. These diagrams are discussed in Chapter 7.

Attributes

An *attribute* is a unit fact that characterizes or describes an entity in some way. These are represented on the conceptual design diagram shown in Figure 2-1 as names inside the rectangle that represents the entity to which they belong. The attribute (or attributes) that appears at the top of the rectangle (above the horizontal line) is the *unique identifier* for the entity. A unique identifier, as the name suggests, provides a unique value for each instance of the entity. For example, the Customer ID attribute is the unique identifier for the Customer entity, so each customer must have a unique value for that attribute. Keep in mind that a unique identifier can be composed of multiple attributes, but when this happens, it is still considered just *one* unique identifier.

> *An attribute is a unit fact that characterizes or describes an entity in some way.*

We say attributes are a *unit* fact because they should be *atomic*, meaning they cannot be broken down into smaller units in any meaningful way. An attribute is therefore the smallest named unit of data that appears in a database system. In this sense, Address should be considered a suspect entity because it could easily be broken down into Address Line 1 and Address Line 2, as is commonly done in business systems. This change would add meaning because it makes it easier to print address labels, for example. On the other hand, database design is not an exact science, and judgment calls must be made. Although it is possible to break the Contact Name attribute into component attributes, such as First Name, Middle Initial, and Last Name, we must ask ourselves whether such a change adds meaning or value. There is no right or wrong answer here, so we must rely on the people who will be using the database, or perhaps those who are funding the database project, to help us with such decisions. Always remember that an attribute *must* describe or characterize the entity in some way (for example, size, shape, color, quantity, location).

Relationships

Relationships are the associations among the entities. Because databases are all about storing related data, the relationships become the glue that holds the database together. Relationships are shown on the conceptual design diagram (refer to Figure 2-1) as lines connecting one or more entities. Each end of a relationship line shows the *maximum cardinality* of the relationship, which is the maximum number of instances of one entity that can be associated with the entity on the opposite end of the line. The maximum cardinality may be *one* (where the line has no special symbol on its end) or *many* (where the line has a crow's foot on the end). Just short of the end of the line is another symbol that shows the *minimum cardinality*, which is the minimum number of instances of one entity that can be associated with the entity on the opposite end of the line. The minimum cardinality may be *zero*, denoted with a circle drawn on the line, or *one*, denoted with a short vertical line or tick mark drawn across the relationship line. Many data modelers use two vertical lines to mean "one and *only* one."

> Relationships are the associations among the entities. They can be considered the glue that binds the relational model's entities together.

Learning to read relationships takes practice, and learning to define and draw them correctly takes a *lot* of practice. The trick is to think about the association between the entities in one direction and then to reverse your perspective to think about it in the opposite direction. For the relationship between Customer and Order, for example, we must ask two questions: "Each customer can have how many orders?" followed by "Each order can have how many customers?" Relationships may thus be classified into three types: *one-to-one, one-to-many,* and *many-to-many,* as discussed in the following sections. Some people will say many-to-one is also a relationship type, but in reality, it is only a one-to-many relationship looked at with a reverse perspective. Relationship types are best learned by example. Getting the relationships right is *essential* to a successful design.

? Still Struggling

If you are having difficulty absorbing the different types of relationships, try writing out some examples of physical tables with rows of data in them. For example, if you draw tables for the Customer and Order entities like those shown in Figure 2-1 and include some sample data rows, it should be become clear that an order can belong to only one customer because the identifier of the customer is included in the order data and has only one value per order. Conversely, a customer row contains one value of the Customer ID, but that value can appear in multiple rows in the Order table. With some practice you will be able to visualize the physical tables without having to write out the examples.

One-to-One Relationships

A *one-to-one relationship* is an association where an instance of one entity can be associated with *at most* one instance of the other entity, and vice versa. In Figure 2-1, the relationship between the Customer and Account Receivable entities is one-to-one. This means that a customer can have *at most* one associated account receivable, and an account can have *at most* one associated customer. The relationship is also *mandatory* in both directions, meaning that a customer must have *at least* one account receivable associated with it, and an account receivable must have *at least* one customer associated with it. Putting this all together, we can read the relationship between the Customer and Account Receivable entities as "one customer has one and only one associated account receivable, and one account receivable has one and only one associated customer."

Another important concept is *transferability*. A relationship is said to be *transferable* if the parent can be changed over time—or, said another way, if the child can be reassigned to a different parent. In this case, the relationship between Customer and Account Receivable is obviously not transferable because we would never take one customer's account and transfer it to another customer (it would be horribly bad accounting practice to do so). Unfortunately, no widely accepted symbol is available for showing transferability on data models, but it is an important consideration in some cases, particularly with one-to-one relationships that are mandatory in both directions.

One-to-one relationships are surprisingly rare among entities. In practice, one-to-one relationships that are mandatory in both directions and not transferable represent a design flaw that should be corrected by combining the two entities. After all, isn't an account receivable merely more information about the customer? We're not going to collect data *about* an account receivable, but rather the information in the Account Receivable entity is data we collect *about* the customer. On the other hand, if we buy our financial software from an independent software vendor (a common practice), the software would almost certainly come with a predefined database that it supports, so we may have no choice but to live with this situation. We won't be able to modify the vendor's database design to add additional customer data of interest to us, and at the same time, we won't be able to get the vendor's software to recognize anything that we store in our own database.

Figure 2-2 shows a different "flavor" of one-to-one relationship, one that is *optional* (some say *conditional*) in both directions. Suppose we are designing the database for an automobile dealership. The dealership issues automobiles to some employees, typically sales

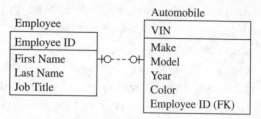

FIGURE 2-2 · Employee-to-automobile relationship

staff, for them to drive for a finite time. They obviously don't issue *all* the automobiles to employees (if they did, they would have none to sell). We can read the relationship between the Employee and Automobile entities as follows: "At any point in time, each employee can have zero or one automobile issued to him or her, and each automobile can be assigned to zero or one employee." Note the clause "At any point in time." If an automobile is taken back from one employee and then reassigned to another (that is, if the relationship is transferable), this would still be a one-to-one relationship. This is because when we consider relationships, we are always thinking in terms of a snapshot taken at an arbitrary point in time.

One-to-Many Relationships

A *one-to-many relationship* is an association between two entities where any instance of the first entity may be associated with one or more instances of the second, and any instance of the second entity may be associated with at most one instance of the first. Figure 2-1, shown earlier in this chapter, has two such relationships: the one between the Customer and Order entities, and the one between the Employee and Order entities. The relationship between Customer and Order, which is mandatory in only one direction, is read as follows: "At any point in time, each customer can have zero to many orders, and each order must have one and only one owning customer."

One-to-many relationships are quite common. In fact, they are the fundamental building block of the relational database model in that all relationships in a relational database are implemented as if they are one-to-many. It is rare for them to be optional on the "one" side and even more rare for them to be mandatory on the "many" side, but these situations do occur. Consider the examples shown in Figure 2-3. When a customer account closes, we record the reason it was closed using an account closure reason code. Because some accounts are open at any point in time, this is an optional code. We read the relationship this way: "At any given point in time, each account closure reason code value can have zero, one, or many customers assigned to it, and each customer can have either zero or one account closure reason code assigned to them." Let us next suppose that as a matter of company policy, no customer account can be opened without first obtaining a credit report, and that all credit reports are kept in the database, meaning that any customer may have more than one credit report in the database. This makes the relationship between the Customer and Credit Report entities one-to-many, and mandatory in both directions. We read the relationship thus: "At any given point in time, each customer can have one or many credit reports, and each credit report belongs to one and only one customer."

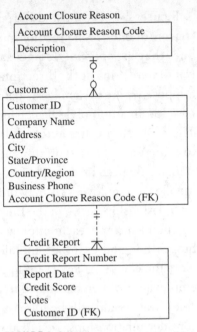

FIGURE 2-3 · One-to-many relationships

Many-to-Many Relationships

A *many-to-many relationship* is an association between two entities where any instance of the first entity may be associated with zero, one, or more instances of the second, and vice versa. Back in Figure 2-1, the relationship between Order and Product is many-to-many. We read the relationship thus: "At any given point in time, each order contains zero to many products, and each product appears on zero to many orders."

This particular relationship has data associated with it as shown in the diamond on the diagram. Data that belongs to a many-to-many relationship is called *intersection data*. The data doesn't make sense unless you associate it with both entities at the same time. For example, Quantity (the number of units ordered) doesn't make sense unless you know *who* (which customer) ordered *what* (which product). In Figure 2-4, you will recognize this data as the Order Detail table from Northwind's relational model, which was previously shown in Figure 1-7 in the last chapter. So, why isn't Order Detail just shown as an entity in the conceptual model shown in Figure 2-1? The answer is simple: It doesn't fit the definition of an entity. We are not collecting data about the line

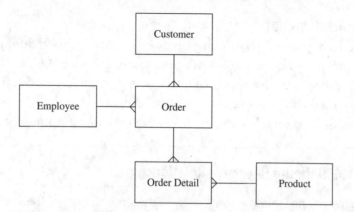

FIGURE 2-4 • Relational model structure for Northwind

items on the order, but rather the line items on the order are merely more data about the order.

Many-to-many relationships are quite common, and most of them will have intersection data. The bad news is that the relational model does not directly support many-to-many relationships. There is no problem with having many-to-many relationships in a conceptual design because such a design is independent of any particular technology. However, if the database is going to be relational, some changes have to be made as we map the conceptual model to the corresponding logical model. The solution is to map the intersection data to a separate table (an *intersection table*) and the many-to-many relationship to two one-to-many relationships, with the intersection table in the middle and on the "many" side of both relationships. Figure 2-4 shows this outcome. The process for recognizing and dealing with the many-to-many problem is covered in detail in Chapter 6.

TERMS: Intersection Table

An intersection table is placed in the middle of a many-to-many relationship to hold the data that is common to the intersection of the two entities. Once placed, the intersection table transforms the many-to-many relationships into two one-to-many relationships with the intersection table on the "many" side of both relationships.

Recursive Relationships

So far we have covered relationships between entities of two different types. However, relationships can exist between entity instances of the same type. These are called *recursive relationships*. Any one of the relationship types already presented (one-to-one, one-to-many, or many-to-many) can be a recursive relationship. Figure 2-5 and the following list show examples of each:

> ### TERMS: Defining Recursive Relationship
>
> A recursive relationship is a relationship between instances of the same entity such as an employee who reports to another employee or a product part composed of other product parts.

- **One-to-one**   If we were to track which employees have other employees as spouses, we would expect each to be married to either zero or one other employee.

- **One-to-many**   It is very common to track the employment "food chain" of who reports to whom. In most organizations, people have only one supervisor or manager. Therefore, we normally expect to see each employee reporting to zero or one other employee, and employees who are managers or supervisors to have one or more direct reports.

- **Many-to-many**   In manufacturing, a common relationship has to do with parts that make up a finished product. If you think about the CD-ROM drive in a personal computer, for example, you can easily imagine that it is made of multiple parts, and yet, it is only one part of your personal computer. So, any part can be made of many other parts, and at the same time, any part can be a component of many other parts.

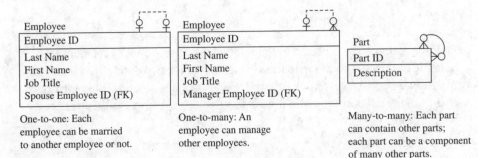

FIGURE 2-5 · Recursive relationship examples

Business Rules

A *business rule* is a policy, procedure, or standard that an organization has adopted. Business rules are *very* important in database design because they dictate
controls that must be placed upon the data. In Figure 2-1, we see a business
rule that states that orders will be accepted only from customers who do not
have a past-due balance. Most business rules can be enforced through manual
procedures that employees are directed to follow or through logic placed in the
application programs. However, each of these can be circumvented—employees
may forget or may choose not to follow a manual procedure, and databases can
be updated directly by authorized people, bypassing the controls included in
the application programs. The database can serve nicely as the last line of defense. Business rules can be implemented in the database as *constraints*, which
are formally defined rules that restrict the data values in the database in some
way. More information on constraints can be found in the "Constraints" section
later in this chapter. Note that business rules are not normally shown on a conceptual data model diagram, as was done in Figure 2-1 for easy illustration. It
is far more common to include them in a text document that accompanies the
diagram.

Logical/Physical Database Design Components

Logical database design is the process of translating, or *mapping*, the conceptual
design into a logical design that fits the chosen database model (relational,
object-oriented, object-relational, and so on). A specialist who performs logical
database design is called a *database designer*, but often the data modeler or database administrator (DBA) performs this design step. The final design step is
physical database design, which involves mapping the logical design to one or
more physical designs—each tailored to the particular DBMS that will manage
the database and the particular computer system on which the database will
run. The person who performs physical database design is usually the DBA.

   The logical database design is implemented in the logical layer of the ANSI/
SPARC model discussed in Chapter 1. The physical design is implanted in the
ANSI/SPARC physical layer. However, we work through the DBMS to imple-
ment the physical layer, making it difficult to separate the two layers. For exam-
ple, when we create a table, we can optionally include a clause in the CREATE
TABLE command that tells the DBMS where we wish to place it and how

much space to allocate for it. In most DBMS implementations, defaults are used if the location and space allocation are not explicitly specified. Because so much of the physical implementation is buried in the DBMS definitions of the logical structures, we have elected not to try to separate them here. During logical database design, physical storage properties (filename, storage location, and sizing information) may be assigned to each database object as we map them from the conceptual model, or they may be omitted at first and added later in a physical design step that follows logical design. For time efficiency, most data modelers and DBAs perform the two design steps (logical and physical) in parallel.

Tables

The primary unit of storage in the relational model is the *table*, which is a 2-D structure composed of rows and columns. Each row represents one occurrence of the entity that the table represents, and each column represents one attribute for that entity. The process of mapping the entities in the conceptual design to tables in the logical design is called *normalization* and is covered in detail in Chapter 6. Often, an entity in the conceptual model maps to exactly one table in the conceptual model, but this is not always the case. For reasons you will learn with the normalization process, entities are commonly split into multiple tables, and in rare cases, multiple entities may be combined into one table.

> A relational database table is a 2-D structure composed of rows and columns. It is the primary unit of storage in the relational model.

Figure 2-6 shows a listing of part of the Northwind Orders table.

It is important to remember that a relational table is a *logical* storage structure and usually does not exist in tabular form in the physical layer. In most DBMS products, the DBA assigns a table to a logical structure called a *tablespace*, and each tablespace is implemented using one or more operating system files in the physical layer. It is quite common for multiple tables to be placed in a single tablespace. However, large tables may be placed in their own tablespace or split across multiple tablespaces, which is called *partitioning*. This flexibility typically does not exist in personal computer–based RDBMSs such as Microsoft Access.

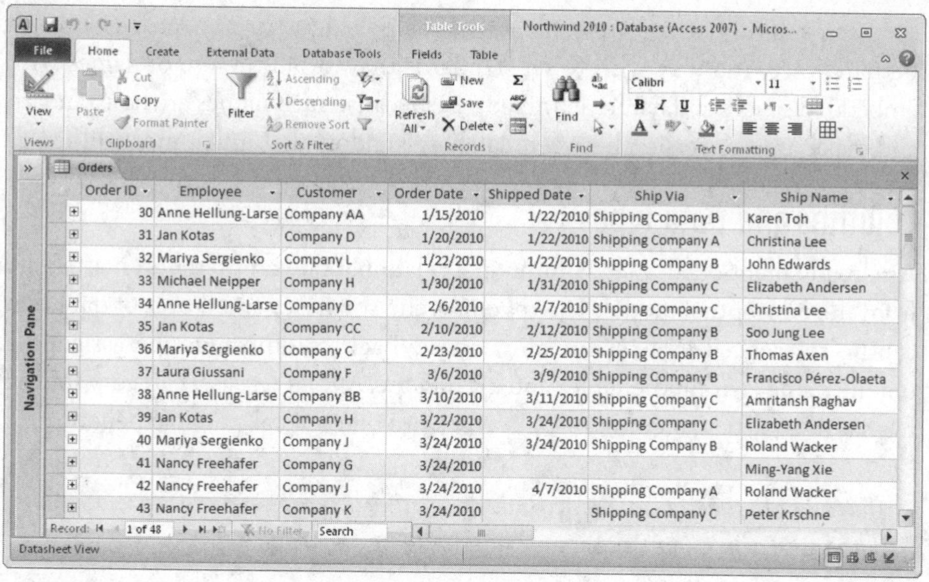

FIGURE 2-6 · Northwind Orders table (partial listing)

A tablespace is a logical structure used to store relational tables. It is usually implemented using one or more operating system files in the physical layer.

Each table must be given a unique name by the DBA who creates it. The maximum length for these names varies a lot among RDBMS products, from as few as 18 characters to as many as 255. Table names should be descriptive and should reflect the name of the real-world entity they represent. By convention, some DBAs always name entities in the singular and tables in the plural, and you will see this convention used in the Northwind database. I prefer that both be named in the singular, but obviously there are other learned professionals with counter opinions. It is essential to establish naming standards at the outset so that names are not assigned in a haphazard manner, which only leads to confusion later. As a case in point, Microsoft Access permits embedded spaces in table and column names, which is counter to industry standards. Moreover, Microsoft Access, Sybase, and Microsoft SQL Server allow mixed-case names, such as OrderDetails, whereas Oracle, DB2, and others force all names to be uppercase letters. Because table names such as ORDERDETAILS are not very readable, the use of an underscore to separate words per industry standards is a much better choice. You may wish to set standards that forbid the use of names with embedded spaces and names in mixed case because such names are nonstandard and make any conversion between database vendors that much more difficult.

Columns and Data Types

As already mentioned, each column in a relational table represents an attribute from the conceptual model. The *column* is the smallest named unit of data that can be referenced in a relational database. Each column must be assigned a unique name (within the table) and a data type. A *data type* is a category for the format of a particular column. Data types provide several valuable benefits:

> The column is the smallest named unit of data that can be referenced in a relational database. Each column must be assigned a name and a data type.

- Restricting the data in the column to characters that make sense for the data type (for example, all numeric digits or only valid calendar dates).
- Providing a set of behaviors useful to the database user. For example, if you subtract a number from another number, you get a number as a result; but if you subtract a date from another date, you get a number representing the elapsed days between the two dates as a result.
- Assisting the RDBMS in efficiently storing the column data. For example, numbers can often be stored in an internal numeric format that saves space, compared with merely storing the numeric digits as a string of characters.

Figure 2-7 shows the table definition of the Northwind Orders table from Microsoft Access (the same table listed in Figure 2-6). The data type for each column is listed in the second column from the left. The data type names are usually self-evident, but if you find any of them confusing, you can find definitions of each in the Microsoft Access help pages.

NOTE *If you compare Figure 2-6 with Figure 2-7, you will notice that Figure 2-6 shows the employee name (Employee), customer name (Customer), and shipping company name (Ship Via) instead of Employee ID, Customer ID, and Shipper ID, as shown in Figure 2-7. This is not an error, but rather a feature of Microsoft Access, as explained in the "Referential Constraints" section later in this chapter.*

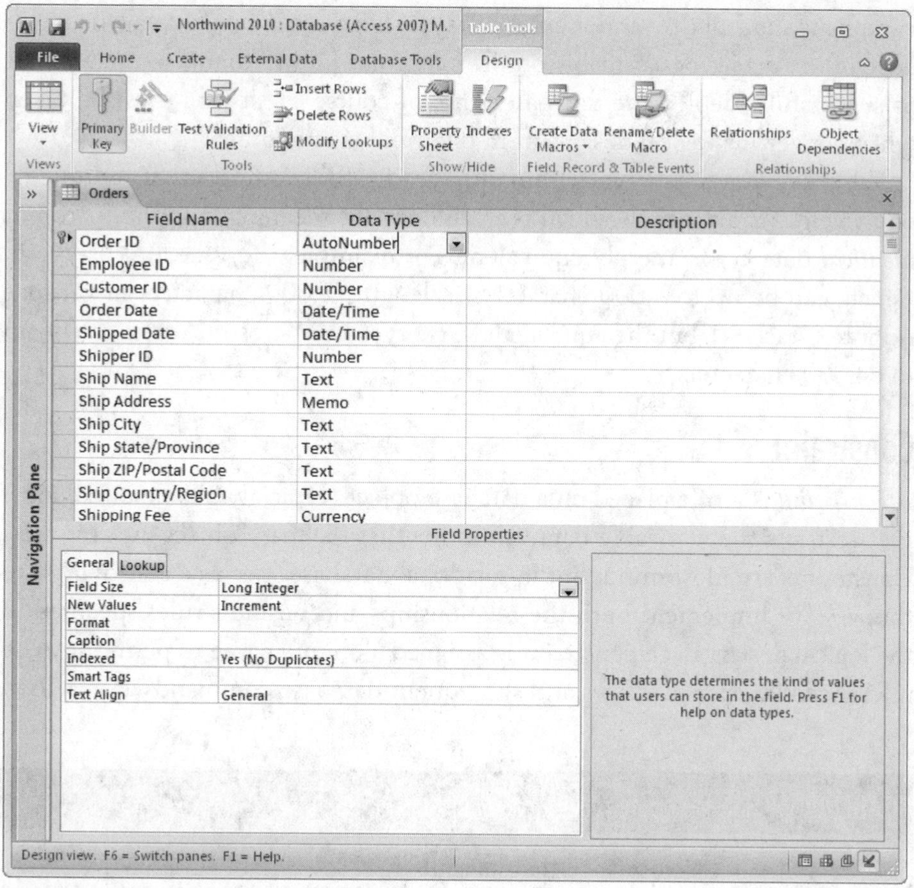

FIGURE 2-7 · Table definition of the Northwind Orders table (Microsoft Access)

It is most unfortunate that industry standards lagged behind RDBMS development. Most vendors did their own thing for many years before sitting down with other vendors to develop standards, and this is no more evident than in the wide variation of data type options across the major RDBMS products. Today there are ANSI standards for relational data types, and the major vendors support all or most of the standard types. However, each vendor has their own "extensions" to the standards, largely in support of data types they developed before there were standards. One could say (in jest) that the greatest thing about database standards is that there are so many from which to choose (each vendor having their own). In terms of industry standards for relational databases, Microsoft Access is probably the least compliant and MySQL the most compliant of the most popular products. Given the many levels of standards compliance and all the vendor extensions, the DBA must have a detailed knowledge of the data types available on the particular DBMS that is in use in order to successfully deploy the database. And, of course, great care must be taken when converting logical designs from one vendor to another.

Table 2-1 shows data types from different RDBMS vendors that are roughly equivalent. As always, the devil is in the details, meaning that these are not *identical* data types, merely equivalent. For example, the VARCHAR2 type in Oracle can be up to 4,000 characters in length (2,000 characters in versions prior to Oracle8*i*), but the equivalent MEMO type in Microsoft Access can be up to 64,000 characters.

Constraints

A *constraint* is a rule placed on a database object (typically a table or column) that restricts the allowable data values for that database object in some way. Constraints are most important in relational databases because constraints are the way we implement both the relationships and business rules specified in the logical design. Each constraint is assigned a unique name to permit it to be referenced in error messages and subsequent database commands. It is a good

TABLE 2-1 Equivalent Data Types in Major RDBMS Products

Data Type	Microsoft Access	Microsoft SQL Server	Oracle	MySQL
Fixed–length character	TEXT	CHAR	CHAR	CHAR
Variable–length character	MEMO	VARCHAR	VARCHAR2	VARCHAR
Long text	MEMO	TEXT	CLOB or LONG (deprecated)	TEXT or MEDIUMTEXT or LONGTEXT
Integer	INTEGER or LONG INTEGER	INTEGER or SMALLINT or TINYINT	NUMBER	INT or BIGINT or MEDIUMINT or SMALLINT or TINYINT
Decimal	NUMBER	DECIMAL or NUMERIC	NUMBER	DECIMAL or NUMERIC
Currency	CURRENCY	MONEY or SMALL-MONEY	None, use NUMBER	None, use DECIMAL or NUMERIC
Date/time	DATE/TIME	DATETIME or SMALLDATETIME	DATE or TIMESTAMP	DATE or DATETIME or TIMESTAMP

habit for DBAs to supply the constraint names because names generated automatically by the RDBMS are never very descriptive.

Primary Key Constraints

A *primary key* is a column or a set of columns that uniquely identifies each row in a table. A unique identifier in the conceptual design is thus implemented as a primary key in the logical design. The small icon that looks like a door key to the left of the Order ID field name in Figure 2-7 indicates that this column has been defined as the primary key of the Orders table. When we define a primary key, the RDBMS implements it as a *primary key constraint* to guarantee that no two rows in the table will ever have duplicate values in the primary key column(s). Note that for primary keys composed of multiple columns, each column by itself *may* have duplicate values in the table, but the *combination* of the values for the primary key columns must be unique among all rows in the table.

> *A primary key is a column or a set of columns that uniquely identifies each row in a table.*

Primary key constraints are nearly always implemented by the RDBMS using an *index*, which is a special type of database object that permits fast searches of column values. As new rows are inserted into the table, the RDBMS *automatically* searches the index to make sure the value for the primary key of the new row is not already in use in the table, rejecting the insert request if it is. Indexes can be searched much faster than tables; therefore, the index on the primary key is essential in tables of any size so that the search for duplicate keys on every insert doesn't create a performance bottleneck.

Referential Constraints

To understand how the RDBMS enforces relationships using referential constraints, we must first understand the concept of foreign keys. When one-to-many relationships are implemented in tables, the column or set of columns that is stored in the child table (the table on the "many" side of the relationship), to associate it with the parent table (the table on the "one" side), is called a *foreign key*. It gets its name from the column(s) copied from another (foreign) table. In the Orders table definition shown earlier in Figure 2-7, the Employee ID column is a foreign key to the Employees table, the Customer ID column is a foreign key to the Customers table, and the Shipper ID column is a foreign key to the Shippers table.

> *A foreign key is the column or set of columns that is stored in a child table (the table on the "many" side of the relationship), to associate it with its parent table (the table on the "one" side of the relationship).*

In most relational databases, the foreign key must either be the primary key of the parent table or a column or set of columns for which a unique index is defined. This again is for efficiency. Most people prefer that the foreign key column(s) have names identical to the corresponding primary key column(s), but again there are counter opinions, especially because like-named columns are a little more difficult to use in query languages. It is best to set some standards up front and stick with them throughout your database project.

Each relationship between entities in the conceptual design becomes a referential constraint in the logical design. A *referential constraint* (sometimes called a *referential integrity constraint*) is a constraint that enforces a relationship among tables in a relational database. By "enforces," we mean that the RDBMS automatically checks to ensure that each foreign key value in a child table always has a corresponding primary key value in the parent table.

Microsoft Access provides a very nice feature for foreign key columns, but it takes a bit of getting used to. When you define a referential constraint, you can define an automatic lookup of the parent table rows, as was done throughout the Northwind database. In Figure 2-7, the second column in the table is listed as Employee ID. However, in Figure 2-6, you will notice that the second column of the Orders table displays the employee name and is labeled "Employee." If you click in the Employee column for one of the rows, a pull-down menu appears to allow the selection of a valid employee (from the Employees table) to be the parent (owner) of the selected Orders table row. Similarly, the Customer column of the table displays the customer name, and the Ship Via column displays the shipping company name. This is a convenient and easy feature for the database user, and it prevents a nonexistent customer, employee, or shipper from being associated with an order. However, it hides the foreign key in such a way that Figure 2-6 isn't very useful for illustrating how referential constraints work under the covers. Figure 2-8 lists the Orders table with the lookups removed so you can see the actual foreign key values in the Employee ID, Customer ID, and Shipper ID columns.

	Order ID	Employee ID	Customer ID	Order Date	Shipped Date	Shipper ID	Ship Name
+	30	9	27	1/15/2010	1/22/2010	2	Karen Toh
+	31	3	4	1/20/2010	1/22/2010	1	Christina Lee
+	32	4	12	1/22/2010	1/22/2010	2	John Edwards
+	33	6	8	1/30/2010	1/31/2010	3	Elizabeth Andersen
+	34	9	4	2/6/2010	2/7/2010	3	Christina Lee
+	35	3	29	2/10/2010	2/12/2010	2	Soo Jung Lee
+	36	4	3	2/23/2010	2/25/2010	2	Thomas Axen
+	37	8	6	3/6/2010	3/9/2010	2	Francisco Pérez-Olaeta
+	38	9	28	3/10/2010	3/11/2010	3	Amritansh Raghav
+	39	3	8	3/22/2010	3/24/2010	3	Elizabeth Andersen
+	40	4	10	3/24/2010	3/24/2010	2	Roland Wacker
+	41	1	7	3/24/2010			Ming-Yang Xie
+	42	1	10	3/24/2010	4/7/2010	1	Roland Wacker
+	43	1	11	3/24/2010		3	Peter Krschne

FIGURE 2-8 · Northwind Orders table (with foreign key values displayed)

When we update the Orders table, as shown in Figure 2-8, the RDBMS must enforce the referential constraints we have defined on the table. The beauty of database constraints is that they are *automatic* and therefore cannot be circumvented unless the DBA disables or removes them. Here are the particular events that the RDBMS must handle when enforcing referential constraints:

- When we try to insert a new row into the child table, the insert request is rejected if the corresponding parent table row does not exist. For example, if we insert a row into the Orders table with an Employee ID value of 12345, the RDBMS must check the Employees table to see if a row for Employee ID 12345 already exists. If it doesn't exist, the insert request is rejected.

- When we try to update a foreign key value in the child table, the update request is rejected if the new value for the foreign key does not already exist in the parent table. For example, if we attempt to change the Employee ID for Order 30 from 9 to 12345, the RDBMS must again check the Employees table to see if a row for Employee ID 12345 already exists. If it doesn't exist, the update request is rejected.

- When we try to delete a row from a parent table, and that parent row has related rows in one or more child tables, either the child table rows must be deleted along with the parent row, or the delete request must be rejected. Most RDBMSs provide the option of automatically deleting the child rows, called a *cascading delete*. At first, you probably wondered why anyone would ever want automatic deletion of child rows. Consider the Orders and Order Details tables. If an order is to be deleted, why not delete the order and the line items that belong to it in one easy step? However, with the Employee table, we clearly would not want that option. If we attempt to delete Employee 9 from the Employee table (perhaps because he or she is no longer an employee), the RDBMS must check for rows assigned to Employee ID 9 in the Orders table and reject the delete request if any are found. It would make no business sense to have orders automatically deleted when an employee left the company.

In most relational databases, an SQL statement is used to define a referential constraint. SQL is introduced in Chapter 4. *SQL (Structured Query Language)* is the language used in relational databases to communicate with the database. Many vendors also provide GUI (graphical user interface) panels for defining database objects such as referential constraints. In Oracle and SQL Server, these GUI panels are located within their respective Enterprise Manager tools. For Microsoft Access, Figure 2-9 shows the Relationships panel that is used for defining referential constraints.

For simplicity, only the Orders table and its immediate parent and child tables are shown in Figure 2-9. The Customers, Shippers, and Employees tables are considered parent tables because they are on the "one" side of the one-to-many relationships with the Orders table. Conversely, the Order Details and Invoices table are considered child tables because they are on the "many" side to the one-to-many relationships with the Orders table. The referential constraints are shown as bold lines with the numeric symbol "1" near the parent table (the "one" side) and the mathematical symbol for "infinity" near the child table (the "many" side). These constraints are defined by simply dragging the name of the primary key in the parent table to the name of the foreign key in the child table. A pop-up window is then automatically displayed to allow the definition of options for the referential constraint, as shown in Figure 2-10.

At the top of the Edit Relationships panel, the two table names appear with the parent table on the left and the child table on the right. If you forget which is which, the Relationship Type field, near the bottom of the panel,

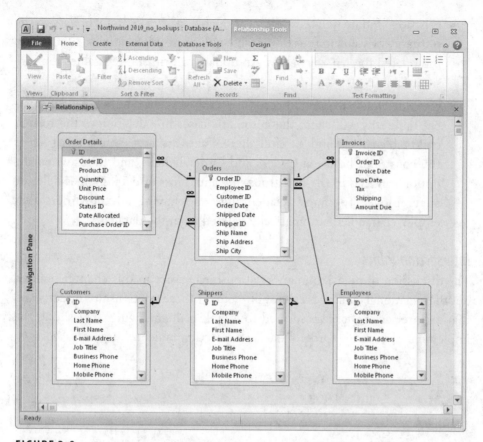

FIGURE 2-9 • Microsoft Access Relationships panel

should remind you. Under each table name, are rows for selection of the column names that constitute the primary key and the foreign key. Figure 2-10 shows the primary key column as ID in the Customers table and foreign key column as Customer ID in the Orders table. The check boxes provide some options:

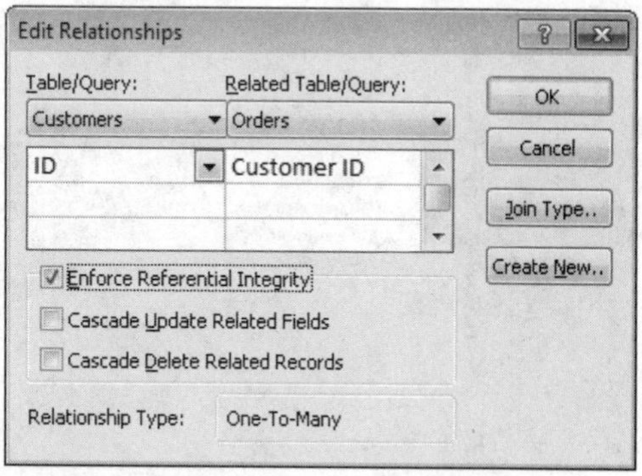

- **Enforce Referential Integrity** If the box is checked, the constraint is enforced; unchecking the box turns off constraint enforcement.

FIGURE 2-10 • Microsoft Access Edit Relationships panel

- **Cascade Update Related Fields**   If the box is checked, any update to the primary key value in the parent table will cause automatic like updates to the related foreign key values. An update of primary key values is a rare situation.

- **Cascade Delete Related Records**   If the box is checked, a delete of a parent table row will cause the automatic cascading deletion of the related child table rows. Think carefully here. There are times to use this, such as the constraint between Orders and Order Details, and times when the option can lead to the disastrous unwanted loss of data, such as deleting an employee (perhaps accidentally) and having all the orders that employee handled automatically deleted from the database.

Intersection Tables

The discussion of many-to-many relationships earlier in this chapter pointed out that relational databases cannot implement these relationships directly and that an intersection table is formed to establish them. Figure 2-11 shows the implementation of the Order Details intersection table in Microsoft Access.

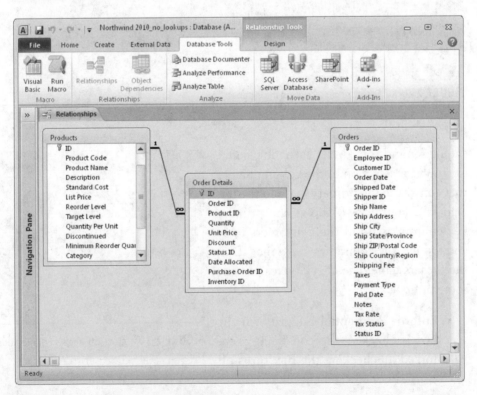

FIGURE 2-11 · Order Details intersection table (Microsoft Access)

The many-to-many relationship between orders and products in the conceptual design becomes an intersection table (Order Details) in the logical design. The relationship is then implemented as two one-to-many relationships with the intersection table on the "many" side of each. The Order ID column is the foreign key to the Orders table, and the Product ID column is the foreign key to the Products table. The combination of Order ID and Product ID should be unique, but the designer of this database chose to add a separate column, ID, as the primary key of the Order Details table.

? Still Struggling

Take a moment to examine the contents of the intersection table and the two referential constraints. Understanding this arrangement is fundamental to understanding how relational databases work. Here are some points to consider:

- Each row in the Order Details intersection table belongs to the intersection of one product and one order. It would not make sense to put Product Name in this table because that name is the same every time the product appears on an order. Also, it would not make sense to put Customer ID in the Order Details table because all line items on the same order belong to the same customer.

- Each Products table row may have many related Order Details rows (one for each order line item on which the product was ordered), but each Order Details row belongs to one and only one Products table row.

Each Orders table row may have many related Order Details rows (one for each line item for that particular order), but each Order Details row belongs to one and only one Orders table row.

Integrity Constraints

As already mentioned, business rules from the conceptual design become constraints in the logical design. An *integrity constraint* is a constraint (as defined earlier) that promotes the accuracy of the data in the database. The key benefit is that these constraints are invoked automatically by the RDBMS and cannot be circumvented (unless you are a DBA) no matter how you connect to the database. The major types of integrity constraints are NOT NULL constraints, CHECK constraints, and constraints enforced with triggers.

NOT NULL Constraints

As we define columns in database tables, we have the option of specifying whether null values are permitted for the column. A *null value* in a relational database is a special code that can be placed in a column that indicates that the value for that column in that row is unknown. A null value is not the same as a blank, an empty string, or a zero—it is indeed a special code that has no other meaning in the database.

A uniform way to treat null values is an ANSI standard for relational databases. However, there has been much debate over the usefulness of the option because the database cannot tell you *why* the value is unknown. If we leave the value for Job Title null in the Northwind Employees table, for example, we don't know whether it is null because it is truly unknown (we know employees must have a job title, but we do not know what it is), it doesn't apply (perhaps some employees do not get job titles), or it is unassigned (they will get a job title eventually, but their manager hasn't figured out which title to use just yet). The other dilemma is that null values are not equal to anything, including other null values, which introduces three-valued logic into database searches. With nulls in use, a search can return the condition *true* (the column value matches), *false* (the column value does not match), or *unknown* (the column value is null). The developers who write the application programs have to handle null values as a special case. You'll see more about nulls when SQL is introduced.

In Microsoft Access, the NOT NULL constraint is controlled by the Required option on the Table Tools | Design panel. Figure 2-12 shows the definition of the Order Date column of the Orders table. Note that the column is not required because the Required option is set to No. In SQL definitions of tables, we simply include the keyword NULL or NOT NULL with the column definition.

CHECK Constraints

A CHECK constraint uses a simple logic statement to validate a column value. The outcome of the statement must be a logical true or false, with an outcome of true allowing the column value to be placed in the table, and a value of false causing the column value to be rejected with an appropriate error message.

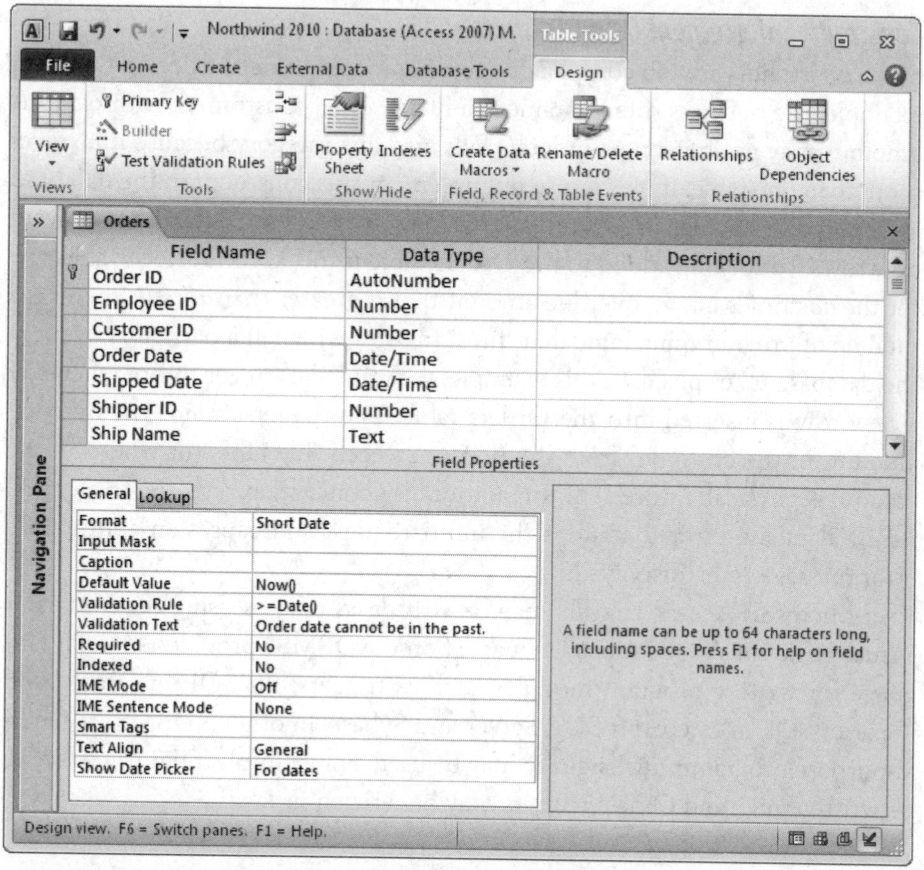

FIGURE 2-12 • Orders table definition panel, Order Date column

In Figure 2-12, notice that `>=Date()` appears in the Validation Rule option for the Order Date column. This rule prevents order dates from the past (dates earlier than the current date) from being entered by making sure that the value supplied for the column is greater than or equal to the current date. It is important to understand that CHECK constraints are tested only when the row is initially created or when the column's data value is modified. If this were not the case, a constraint like this one would cause error conditions anytime an old row was retrieved from the database.

Although the syntax of the option will vary for other databases, the concept remains the same. In Microsoft SQL Server SQL, it would be written this way:

```
CHECK (ORDER_DATE >= GETDATE() )
```

Constraint Enforcement Using Triggers

Some constraints are too complicated to be enforced using the declarations. For example, the business rule contained in Figure 2-1 ("Customers with overdue amounts may not book new orders") falls into this category because it involves more than one table. If we choose to implement this constraint in the database, as opposed to leaving it up to application logic, we need the database to prevent new rows from being added to the Orders table if the Account Receivable row for the customer has an overdue amount that is greater than zero. A *trigger* is a module of programming logic that "fires" (executes) when a particular event in the database takes place. In this example, we want the trigger to fire whenever a new row is inserted into the Orders table. The trigger obtains the overdue amount for the customer from the Account Receivable table (or wherever the column is physically stored). If this amount is greater than zero, the trigger will raise a database error that stops the insert request and causes an appropriate error message to be displayed.

In Microsoft Access, triggers may be written as macros using the Microsoft Visual Basic for Applications language. Some RDBMSs provide a special language for writing program modules such as triggers: PL/SQL in Oracle, and Transact SQL in Microsoft SQL Server and Sybase. In other RDBMSs, a general-purpose programming language may be used. For example, DB2 triggers may be written in C, and Oracle triggers may be written in Java.

Views

A *view* is a stored database query that provides a database user with a customized subset of the data from one or more tables in the database. Said another way, a view is a *virtual table* because it looks like a table and for the most part behaves like a table, yet it stores no data (only the defining query is stored). The user views form the external layer in the ANSI/SPARC model. During logical design, each view is created using an appropriate method for the particular database. In many RDBMSs, a view is defined using SQL. In Microsoft Access, views are called *queries* and are created using the Query panel. Figure 2-13 shows the Microsoft Access definition of a simple view (query) that lists active products.

The view defined in Figure 2-13 contains only four columns of a table that contains more than ten columns. Rows for discontinued products are not displayed in the view by virtue of the "No" in the criteria row for the Discontinued column. Furthermore, the Discontinued column will not appear in the query

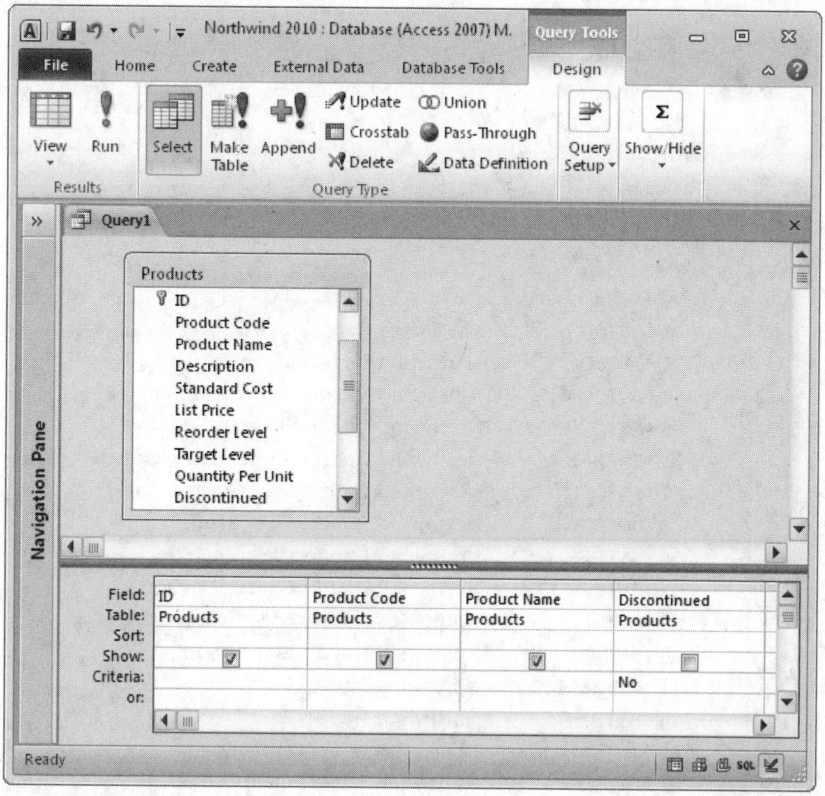

FIGURE 2-13 • Microsoft Access query, list of active products

results because the check box for the "Show:" line is unchecked. (If it were displayed, all the values would be "Yes", so displaying it is pointless.) Figure 2-14 shows a portion of the query results. We explore the Microsoft Access Query panel in detail in Chapter 3.

Views serve a number of useful functions:

- Hiding columns that the user does not need to see (or should not be allowed to see)

- Hiding rows from tables that a user does not need to see (or should not be allowed to see)

- Hiding complex database operations such as table joins

- Improving query performance (in some RDBMSs, such as Microsoft SQL Server)

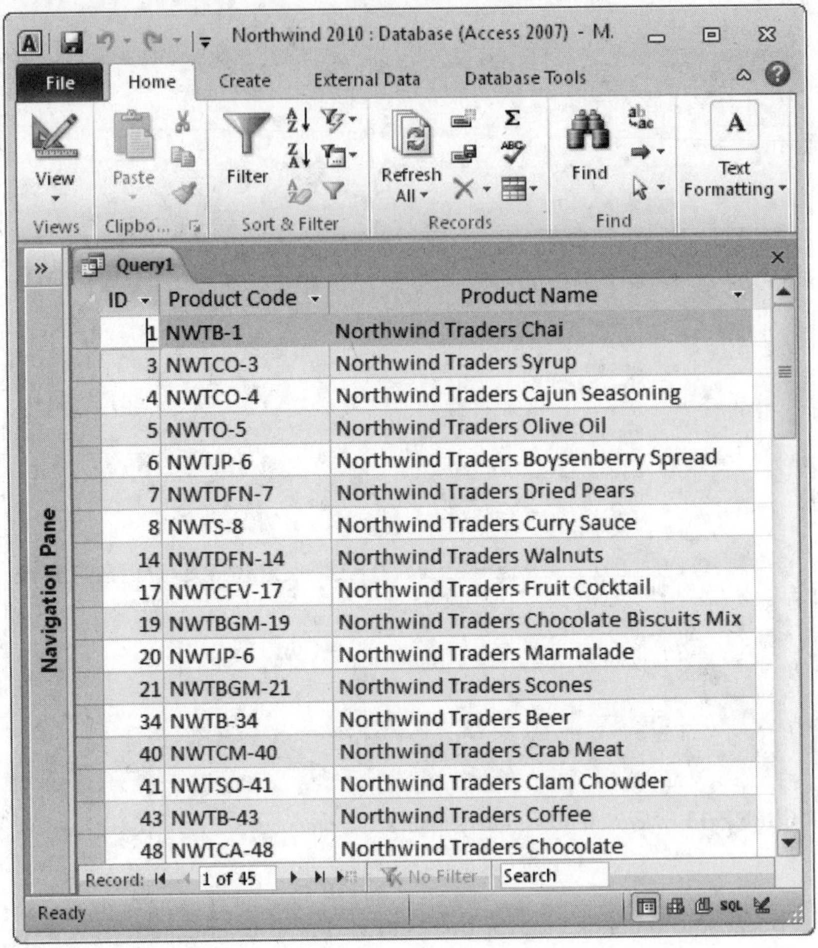

FIGURE 2-14 · Microsoft Access query results, list of active products

Summary

In this chapter, you learned about conceptual database components such as entities, attributes, relationships, and business rules. You also learned about logical/physical database components, including tables, columns and data types, constraints, and views. In Chapter 3, we'll look at how to query the database using a forms-based query tool.

QUIZ

Choose the correct responses to each of the multiple-choice questions. Note that there may be more than one correct response to each question.

1. An item in the external level of the ANSI/SPARC model becomes which type of database object in the logical model?
    A. Table
    B. Column
    C. View
    D. Referential constraint
    E. Index

2. A primary key constraint is implemented using which type of object in the logical design?
    A. Table
    B. Column
    C. View
    D. Referential constraint
    E. Index

3. On a relationship line, the cardinality of "zero, one, or more" is denoted as
    A. A circle and a vertical tick mark near the end of the line
    B. A circle near the end of the line and a crow's foot at the end of the line
    C. A vertical tick mark near the end of the line and a crow's foot at the line end
    D. Two vertical tick marks near the end of the line
    E. The mathematical symbol for "infinity" above the end of the line

4. Valid types of relationships among entities are
    A. One-to-one
    B. One-to-many
    C. One-to-many-to-one
    D. None-to-many
    E. Many-to-many

5. Examples of a business rule are
    A. An employee must be at least 18 years old.
    B. Employees below pay grade 6 are not permitted to modify orders.
    C. Every order may belong to only one customer, but each customer may have many orders.
    D. A referential constraint must refer to the primary key of the parent table.
    E. A database query that eliminates columns an employee should not see.

6. **A primary key constraint:**

   A. Must be defined for every database table
   B. Must reference one or more columns in a single table
   C. Guarantees that no two rows in a table have duplicate primary key values
   D. Is usually implemented using an index
   E. Enforces referential integrity constraints

7. **Major types of integrity constraints are**

   A. NOT NULL constraints
   B. CHECK constraints
   C. Indexes
   D. Constraints enforced with triggers
   E. One-to-one relationships

8. **A referential constraint is defined:**

   A. Using a database trigger
   B. Using the Relationships panel in Microsoft Access
   C. Using SQL in most relational databases
   D. Using the referential data type for the foreign key column(s)
   E. In a view

9. **A relational table:**

   A. Appears in the conceptual database design
   B. Is composed of rows and columns
   C. Is the primary unit of storage in the relational model
   D. Must be assigned a data type
   E. Must be assigned a unique name

10. **A data type:**

    A. May be selected based on business rules for an attribute
    B. Provides a set of behaviors for a column that assists the database user
    C. Restricts the data that may be stored in a view
    D. Assists the DBMS in storing data efficiently
    E. Restricts characters allowed in a database column

chapter 3

Forms-Based Database Queries

This chapter provides an overview of forming and running database queries using the forms-based query tool in Microsoft Access. Even if you never intend to use Microsoft Access or another forms-based database query product, at least give this chapter a quick read because it will help you visualize database concepts. Also keep in mind that Chapter 4 introduces SQL, the standard query language for all modern relational databases.

CHAPTER OBJECTIVES

In this chapter, the reader should:

- Understand the basics of forms-based queries.
- Be able to use Microsoft Access and the video store sample database to create and run queries.

QBE: The Roots of Forms-Based Queries

A *forms-based* query language uses a GUI panel for the creation of a query. The database user defines queries by entering sample data values directly into a query template to represent the result that the database is to achieve. An alternative query method uses a *command-based* query language, in which queries are written as text commands. SQL is the ubiquitous command-based query language for relational databases. The emphasis with both forms-based and command-based query languages is on *what* the result should be rather than *how* the results are achieved. The difference between the two is in the way the user describes the desired result—similar to the difference between using Microsoft Windows Explorer to copy a file versus using the MS-DOS `copy` command (in the DOS command window) to do the same thing.

> A command-based query language such as SQL requires queries to be entered by the database user as text commands.

The first well-known forms-based query tool was Query By Example (QBE), which was developed by IBM in the 1970s. Personal computers, Microsoft Windows, the mouse, and many other modern computing amenities were unheard of then, but the interface was still graphical in nature. A form was displayed, and database users typed sample data and simple commands in boxes, where today they would click an onscreen button using a mouse. SQL, also initially developed by IBM, was new in the 1970s. IBM conducted a controlled study to determine whether QBE or SQL was preferred by database users of the day. IBM learned that most users preferred to use the method they learned first— human nature, it seems.

TERMS: Forms-based Query Language

A forms-based query language uses a GUI panel on which database users define queries by entering sample data values directly into a query template to represent the result that the database query is to achieve.

Experience has shown us that both methods are useful to know. Forms-based queries lend themselves well to individuals who are more accustomed to GUI environments than to touch-typing commands. However, database users familiar with command syntax and possessing reasonable typing skills can enter command-based queries more quickly than their GUI equivalents, and command-based queries can be directly used within a programming language such as Java or C.

Getting Started in Microsoft Access

I am using Microsoft Access to present database query concepts that will provide a foundation for the database design theory that follows later in this book. I will provide enough basic information about using Access so you can follow along on your computer as you explore forms-based queries.

The queries used in this chapter all feature a video store sample database available from the McGraw-Hill web site, as explained in Appendix C. You will have the best learning experience if you try the queries presented in this chapter as you read. If you don't have Microsoft Access 2007 or 2010 available, you can download a free 60-day trial of Microsoft Access from the Access product page: **http://office.microsoft.com/en-us/access**. (As of this writing, Access 2010 is in beta testing and the beta version is available for download from **http://www.microsoft.com/office/2010**, but it should be available on the Access product page as soon as the beta test period is over.)

Getting Started with the Video Store Sample Database

This topic contains two sets of instructions: The first set is for using the sample database using Microsoft Access 2007; the second is for using the sample database using Microsoft Access 2010. Both versions of Access use the same format database (MDB) file, which is the same format used in Access 2000. Follow the steps in the procedure that applies to you.

Opening the Video Store Sample Database by Using Microsoft Access 2007

Follow this procedure if you have Microsoft Access 2007 installed.

1. If you have not already done so, follow the instructions in Appendix C for downloading the sample database file.

2. Start Microsoft Access 2007 from your Start menu with no databases open. The Getting Started panel, shown in Figure 3-1, is displayed.

3. Click the Office button in the upper-left corner of the Getting Started panel (the round button with the Microsoft Office 2007 logo on it), and then click Open.

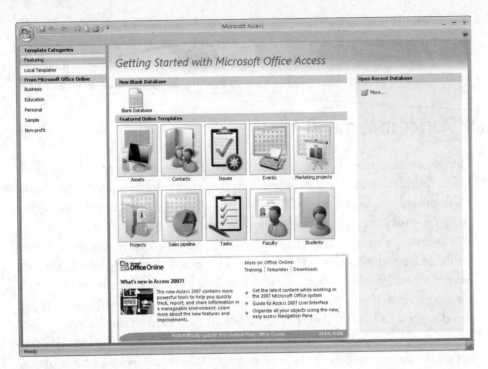

FIGURE 3-1 · Microsoft Access 2007 Getting Started panel

4. In the Open dialog box, navigate to where you stored the video store access database (the video_store_Access_2000.mdb file) and double-click it.

5. The Microsoft Access 2007 main panel is displayed with the video store database tables listed along the left margin, as shown in Figure 3-2. Note the following:

   • You must respond to the Security Warning shown on Figure 3-2. Microsoft Access automatically disables application code such as Visual Basic macros when a database is opened. The sample database does not contain any such code, so you can also simply close the message by clicking the Close button (the X) to the far right of the Security Warning message. (Do *not* click the X at the upper-right corner of your screen; that will close Microsoft Access, and you will have to start all over.) You will need to repeat this step every time you open the database.

   • An alternate way to start Microsoft Access and the video store database is to find the file using Windows Explorer (Start | Documents in Windows Vista and Windows 7) and to double-click the filename. Windows will then launch Microsoft Access and open the database file in one continuous operation.

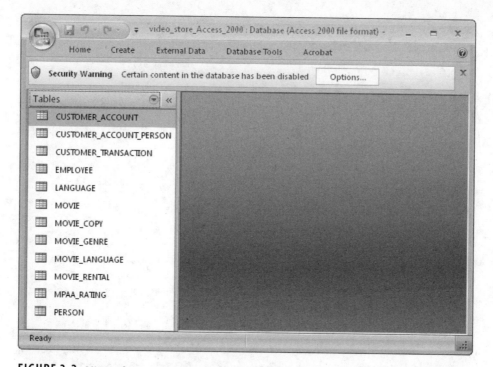

FIGURE 3-2 • Microsoft Access 2007 Main panel with video store database open

Opening the Video Store Sample Database by Using Microsoft Access 2010

Follow this procedure if you have Microsoft Access 2010 installed:

1. Start Microsoft Access from your Start menu with no databases open. The File panel is displayed as shown in Figure 3-3.

2. Along the left margin, click Open.

3. In the Open dialog box, navigate to where you stored the video store Access database (the video_store_Access_2000.mdb file) and double-click it.

4. Once connected to the database, a screen like the one shown in Figure 3-4 will be displayed. Note the following:

   • The first time you open the sample database, you must respond to the Security Warning like the one shown on Figure 3-4. Microsoft Access 2010 automatically disables content such as Visual Basic macros when databases are opened for the first time. The sample database has no such content, so it is safe to click the Enable Content button. A side benefit of doing this is that you will not have to repeat this step if you close the database and subsequently reopen it. Alternatively, you can click the

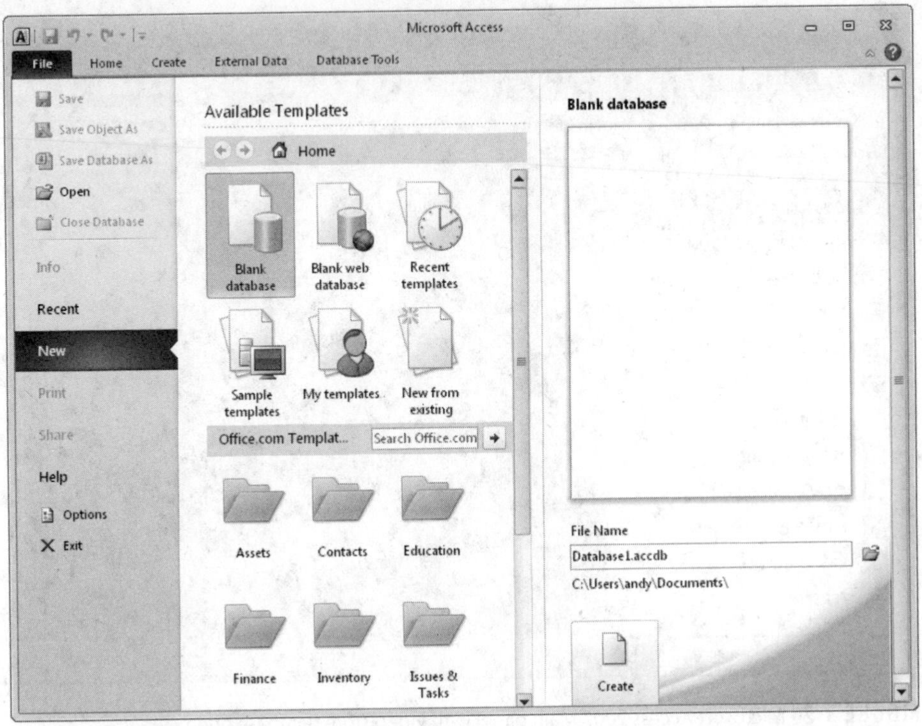

FIGURE 3-3 · Microsoft Access 2010 File panel

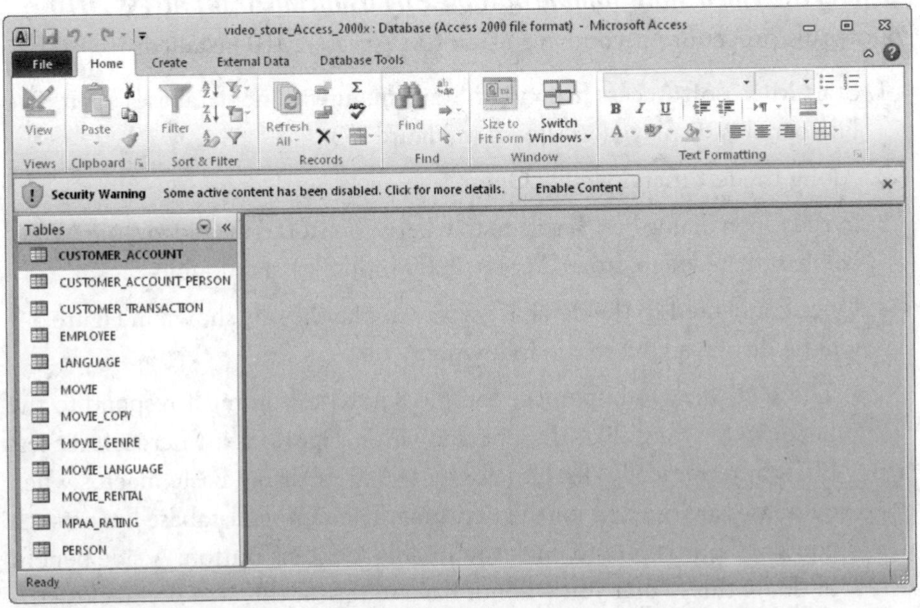

FIGURE 3-4 · Microsoft Access 2010 Main panel with video store database open

Close button (the X) to the far right of the Security Warning message. (Do *not* click the X at the upper-right corner of your screen; that will close Microsoft Access, and you will have to start all over.)

- An alternate way to start Microsoft Access and the video store database is to find the file using Windows Explorer (Start | Documents in Windows Vista and Windows 7) and to double-click the filename. Windows will then launch Microsoft Access and open the database file in one continuous operation.

Exploring Microsoft Access

Throughout the remainder of this chapter, I use Microsoft Access 2010. However, Access 2007 is similar enough that you should have no difficulty following along while using it. You will learn the most if you try the examples in this chapter as you read. Appendix C contains an overview of the video store sample database, including an ERD (entity-relationship diagram). I have also included a PDF file of the ERD so you can print it for easy reference as you work the examples.

Should you need to close Microsoft Access before completing this chapter, you can simply launch it later, and pick up where you left off. If you do so, you will see a startup screen like the one shown in Figure 3-1 or 3-3, and the video store database should be listed on it because you have previously opened it. For Access 2007, look for the database under the Open Recent Database heading on the right; for side of the panel Access 2010, look for it along the left side of the panel, or click the Recent option to display the Recent Databases panel. Simply click the listed filename to open the database. If the database is not listed, you can download it by following the procedure in the previous topic.

Keep in mind that it is easy to update the database accidentally when using Microsoft Access, and no simple "undo" function is available. However, if this happens, you can just download the database again.

Once you have started Access and connected to the video store database, the main panel is displayed with the Home ribbon selected, as shown in Figure 3-4.

NOTE *Like most PC-based database tools, Access provides not only a database, but also a complete programming environment that supports the creation of screens, reports, and application logic in the form of macros. The development of applications using Access is well beyond the scope of this book. This chapter focuses on those components that are directly related to defining data structures and to managing the data stored in them.*

The area along the top of the panel that contains all the options you can use in Access is called the *ribbon*. This user interface was new with Office 2007 (Access is part of the Office suite of applications) and is a radical departure from previous versions that used a series of drop-down menus. If you are accustomed to using the old interface, it takes a while to adapt to this new one. On the top line of the ribbon is the Quick Access Toolbar, which has options for Save, Undo Typing, and Repeat Typing. A final option allows you to customize the toolbar. The icons are reasonably intuitive, but you can allow your cursor pointer to hover over each one for a second or two, and see the names of the options. These options are common to most Microsoft Office applications.

Directly below the Quick Access Toolbar are tabs for the major groupings of ribbon options available within Access. In previous versions, these were used to open drop-down menus; in Access 2007 and beyond, they are tabs that change the ribbon of options that appears immediately below the tabs. Figure 3-5 shows the Home ribbon, for example. Many of the Home ribbon options are related to building application components within Access (forms, reports, and so forth), which are beyond the scope of database work. However, you will use the View option often, because it allows you to switch between the Design View, which shows the metadata that defines a database object, and the Datasheet View, which shows the data that is stored in the database object in rows and columns.

The Create ribbon, shown in Figure 3-6, provides options for creating templates, tables, forms, reports, and other types of objects. We won't be using templates, forms, or reports because these are application programming functions rather than database functions. As you can see, the Tables group of options allows you to create relational tables using various tools. The Macros & Code group at the right side of the ribbon contains options for queries. These options

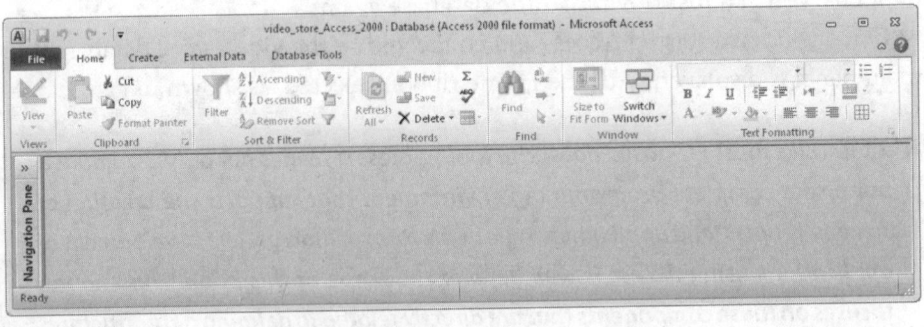

FIGURE 3-5 · Access main panel, Home ribbon

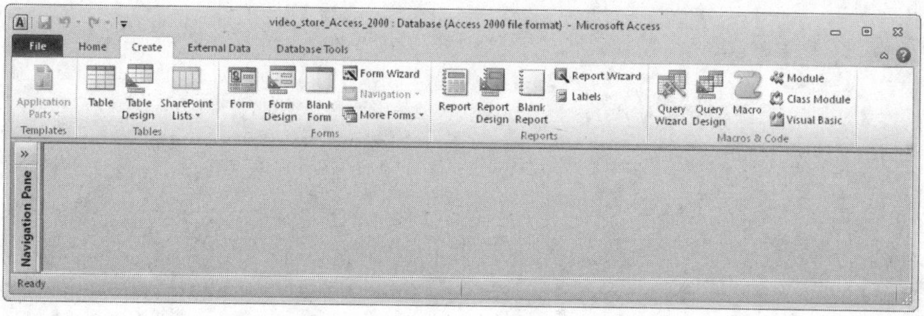

FIGURE 3-6 · Access main panel, Create ribbon

let you create, run, and store database queries, which closely resemble what most other DBMSs and the ISO/ANSI SQL standard call *views*.

Figure 3-7 shows the External Data ribbon, which contains options for importing or linking data from external sources, exporting to external file formats, including most of the other Office applications, collecting data from e-mail, and linking to data lists on web pages. While you will find these options very useful in practice, we won't need them for this tour of features because we are using a sample database that is already populated for us.

The Database Tools ribbon, shown in Figure 3-8, contains various tools that assist in managing the database. The most important of these in terms of database design is the Relationships option, which you will study in the next section. First, though, we need to cover another important navigation feature in Access.

You might have noticed the Navigation Pane along the left side of the panels we have examined thus far. This is an essential feature of Access because it provides a common method of organizing, listing, and opening (accessing) the objects stored in the database. If you need more real estate on your screen, you can shutter the Navigation Pane (minimize it to the left) by clicking the double

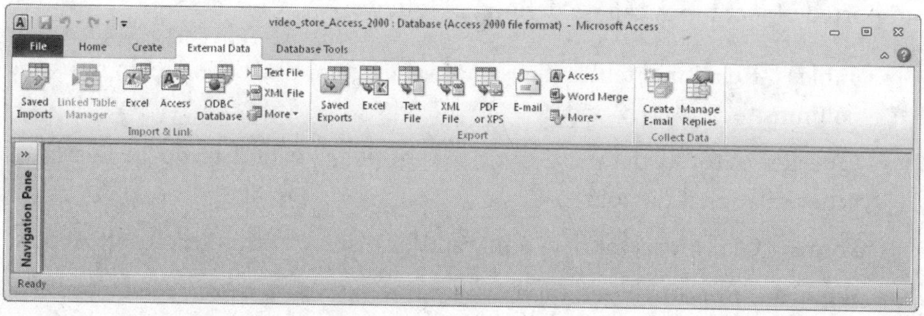

FIGURE 3-7 · Access main panel, External Data ribbon

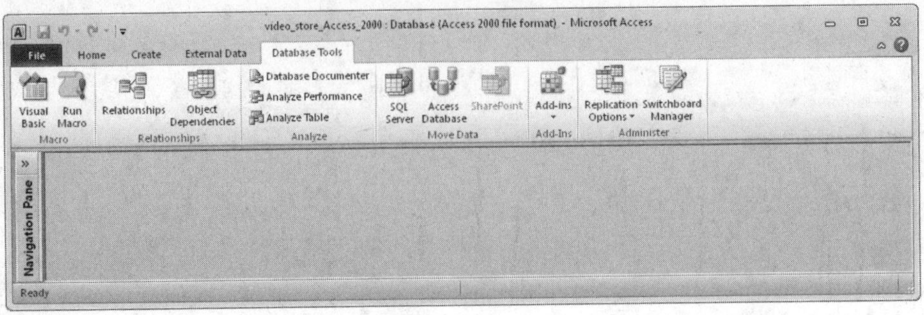

FIGURE 3-8 · Access main panel, Database Tools ribbon

arrowhead that points to the left, as shown in Figure 3-4. Once minimized, as shown in Figures 3-5 through 3-8, you can maximize it by again clicking the double arrowhead (pointing to the right this time).

You can right-click the top of the pane to change the way it organizes the listed objects. In the video store database, the default organization is Object Type, with only tables displayed. To switch to an organization other than Object Type, right-click the top of the pane, and click Category and then the organization you desire. The choices include Tables And Related Views, Object Type, Created Date, and Modified Date. However, you'll find the Object Type organization the most useful for database work, and I use it throughout this chapter. To show other object types, click the label "Tables," and then click the object type you wish to display. For the exercises in this chapter to make sense, you should select either Tables or All Access Objects. You can expand any category as needed to view the list of objects in that category, and of course, minimize the categories that are not of current interest. Note that Access does not display headings for categories that have no objects in them.

If you have used older versions of Access, the object types should be familiar because they appeared on the main panel of those older versions. Briefly, the supported object types can be defined as follows:

- **Tables**   Relational tables. These hold the actual database data in rows and columns.
- **Queries**   Stored database queries. These are called *views* in nearly all other relational databases.
- **Forms**   GUI forms for data entry and/or display within Microsoft Access.
- **Reports**   Reports based on database queries.

- **Macros** Sets of actions that each perform a particular operation, such as opening a form or printing a report.
- **Modules** Collections of Visual Basic for Applications (VBA) programming language components that are stored as a unit.

As noted earlier, Microsoft Access is not only a database, but also a complete development environment for building and running applications. The enterprise-class database products that usually run on larger, shared computer systems called *servers* typically do *not* come with application-development environments. Learning to build application programs is well outside the scope of this book, so we will not deal with the Forms, Reports, Macros, and Modules types at all. We will focus only on the Tables and Queries types in Microsoft Access.

Maintenance of the objects in the database can be performed from this panel, including the following tasks:

- To add a new object, use the Create ribbon and click the appropriate icon. For example, you can create a new table by clicking the Table or Table Design icon on the Create ribbon.
- To delete an existing object, right-click its name in the Navigation Pane and choose the Delete option.
- To open an object, double-click its name in the Navigation Pane.
- To display the definition (design) of an object, right-click its name in the Navigation Pane, and choose the Design View option.

The Microsoft Access Relationships Panel

Microsoft Access provides the Relationships panel, shown in Figure 3-9, for the definition and maintenance of referential constraints between the relational tables. To display this panel, click the Relationships option on the Database Tools ribbon.

NOTE *If you are following along with your own copy of the video store database, you will see that Figure 3-9 shows only part of the Relationships panel for the database.*

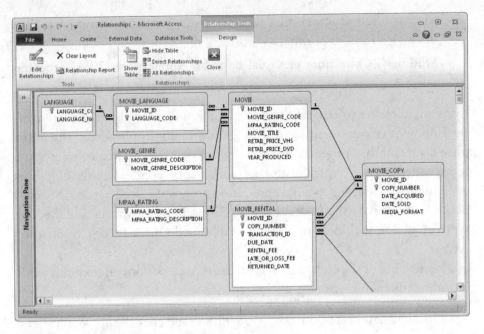

FIGURE 3-9 · The Microsoft Access Relationships panel

The Relationships panel graphically displays tables, shown as rectangles, and one-to-many relationships, shown as lines between the rectangles. Technically, these are referential constraints (*relationships* being only a conceptual term), but because Microsoft calls them relationships on this panel, I will also use this term for consistency. The number *1* shows the "one" side of each relationship, whereas the infinity symbol (similar to the number *8* on its side) shows the "many" side of each relationship.

The relationships can be maintained as follows:

- *To add tables that are not displayed,* click the Show Table icon (the table with a bold yellow plus sign) on the ribbon, and select the tables from the pop-up window.

- *To remove a table from the display,* click to select it, and then press DELETE (on your keyboard). Note that this does *not* delete the table or any relationships in which the table participates; it merely removes the table from the panel.

- *To add a relationship,* drag the primary key in one table to the matching foreign key in another. For recursive relationships, the table must be added to the display a second time, and the relationship must be created between one displayed copy of the table and the other. This looks odd at first, but it serves to facilitate the drag-and-drop method of creating the relationship. A table shown multiple times on the panel still exists only one time in the database. The video store database contains a recursive relationship defined on the EMPLOYEE table, but it is not shown in Figure 3-9. We'll have a closer look at this relationship later in the chapter.

- *To delete a relationship*, click the narrow part (the middle section) of its line and press DELETE. Selecting relationships can be tricky in Microsoft Access because clicking only the *narrow* part of the line will work, and you might have to stretch short lines by moving a table on the panel to expose the narrow part of the line.

- *To edit a relationship*, double-click the narrow part of its line. A pop-up window can be used to change various options about the relationship, including toggling enforcement of the relationship as a referential constraint on and off (that is, enabling and disabling the constraint).

? Still Struggling

Constraints can be a little confusing because they can be defined in the database and then toggled on (enabled) or off (disabled). When a referential constraint is disabled, the DBMS will allow inserts, updates, and deletes to create "orphan" foreign key values (foreign key values that have no matching primary key values in the parent table). The DBMS will not, however, permit a constraint to be enabled if orphan foreign key values exist in the child table.

To close the Relationships panel, you can either click the Close button (X) at the upper-right corner of the panel or right-click the Relationships tab and choose Close.

The Microsoft Access Table Design View

A table can be selected by double-clicking its name on the Navigation Pane. The default display, called the Datasheet View, is shown in Figure 3-10. (I shuttered the Navigation Pane so you can see more of the table data.) The data in the table is displayed in the familiar tabular form, and the data can be updated if

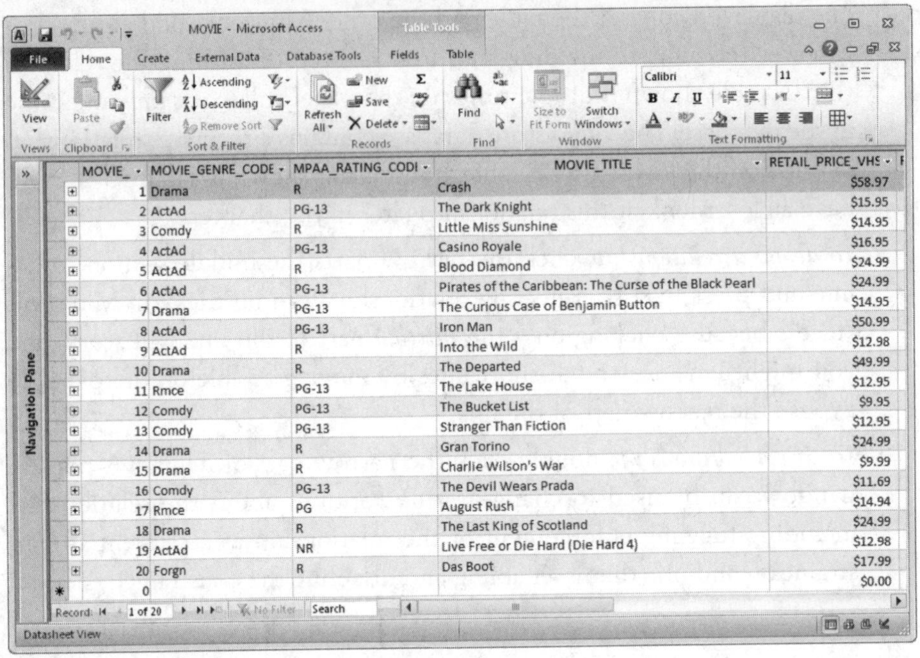

MOVIE_	MOVIE_GENRE_CODE	MPAA_RATING_CODE	MOVIE_TITLE	RETAIL_PRICE_VHS
1	Drama	R	Crash	$58.97
2	ActAd	PG-13	The Dark Knight	$15.95
3	Comdy	R	Little Miss Sunshine	$14.95
4	ActAd	PG-13	Casino Royale	$16.95
5	ActAd	R	Blood Diamond	$24.99
6	ActAd	PG-13	Pirates of the Caribbean: The Curse of the Black Pearl	$24.99
7	Drama	PG-13	The Curious Case of Benjamin Button	$14.95
8	ActAd	PG-13	Iron Man	$50.99
9	ActAd	R	Into the Wild	$12.98
10	Drama	R	The Departed	$49.99
11	Rmce	PG-13	The Lake House	$12.95
12	Comdy	PG-13	The Bucket List	$9.95
13	Comdy	PG-13	Stranger Than Fiction	$12.95
14	Drama	R	Gran Torino	$24.99
15	Drama	R	Charlie Wilson's War	$9.99
16	Comdy	PG-13	The Devil Wears Prada	$11.69
17	Rmce	PG	August Rush	$14.94
18	Drama	R	The Last King of Scotland	$24.99
19	ActAd	NR	Live Free or Die Hard (Die Hard 4)	$12.98
20	Forgn	R	Das Boot	$17.99
0				$0.00

FIGURE 3-10 • Datasheet View (MOVIE table)

desired, including the insertion and deletion of rows. Be careful because there is no undo feature—once you move the cursor from one row to another, any changes you have made cannot be easily reversed.

You can get to the Design View, which shows the definition of the table, in several ways. You can right-click the tab with the name of the table and choose Design View. Or you can select the Home ribbon (if not already selected), click the View icon, and choose the Design View option. Or you can right-click the table name in the Navigation Pane and select the Design View option. Finally, there is a Design View icon on the status bar near the bottom right of the panel. Figure 3-11 shows the Design View for the MOVIE table.

The Design View for a table displays information such as the following:

- **Field Name** The name of the column.
- **Data Type** The data type for the column.
- **Description** A description of the column, typically provided by a DBA.
- **Field Size** A subtype within the data type. For example, Integer and Long Integer apply to the more general Number data type.
- **Required** Indicates whether the column is optional (that is, whether it may have null values).

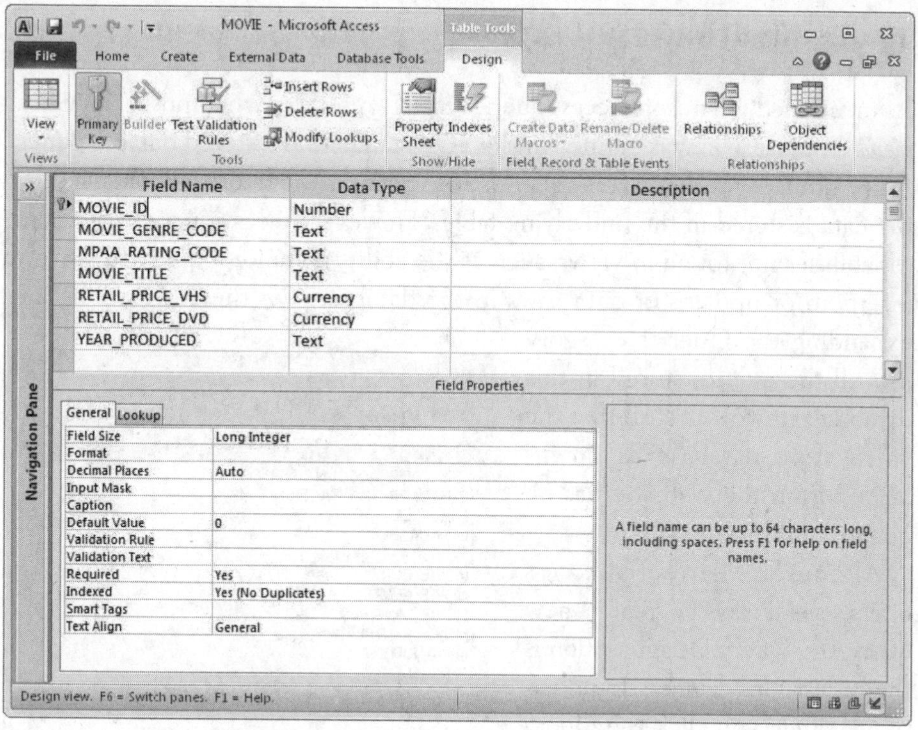

FIGURE 3-11 · Design View (MOVIE table)

- **Indexed**   Indicates whether the column has an index.
- **Primary Key**   Denoted with a small key icon next to the field name (or names) that make up the primary key.

Hopefully, you recognized that everything on this panel is *metadata*. Many more options are available but not noted here, and Microsoft Access is very clever about hiding and exposing options so that only the applicable ones are displayed. Notice that help text automatically displays in the blue area in the lower-right corner of the panel as you move the cursor from one option to another.

TERMS: Metadata

Metadata is a word adapted from Greek that literally means "data about data." The term applies to the information that describes the structure and contents of a database, but not to the actual business data stored in the database.

Creating Queries in Microsoft Access

As mentioned, Microsoft Access queries closely resemble what most DBMSs call *views*, because a view is defined in the SQL standard as a stored database query. A key similarity is that Access queries, like views, do not store any data; instead, the data is stored in the underlying tables. However, Access queries have some capabilities not found in views, such as the ability to tailor a query to perform inserts to or updates of data rows in the database. On the Navigation Pane, expanding the Queries category lists all the queries stored in this database. However, recall that the video store database as downloaded from the web site has no queries to display.

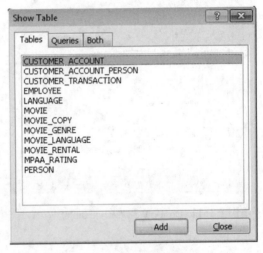

FIGURE 3-12 • Show Table dialog box

Although Microsoft Access offers several ways to create a new query, the Query Design option is the easiest for beginners to understand. When you click the Query Design icon (in the Macros & Code area of the Create ribbon), Access displays the Show Table dialog box, as shown in Figure 3-12.

For every new query, Access opens the Show Table dialog box to allow you to select the tables and/or queries on which the query will be based (that is, the tables or queries that are to be the source of the data that will be displayed). As tables and queries are added, they appear on the Query Design panel, which allows for the entry of the specification for the desired query. Figure 3-13 shows the Query Design panel with the MOVIE table added.

The Query Design panel has the following components:

- In the open area at the top of the panel (light blue background), a graphical representation of the query's source tables, queries, and their relationships for the query is shown. Any relationships defined for the tables are automatically inherited here.

- In the grid area in the lower part of the panel, each column represents a column of data that is to be returned in the result set when the query is executed. Lines (rows) in the grid area define various options to be applied

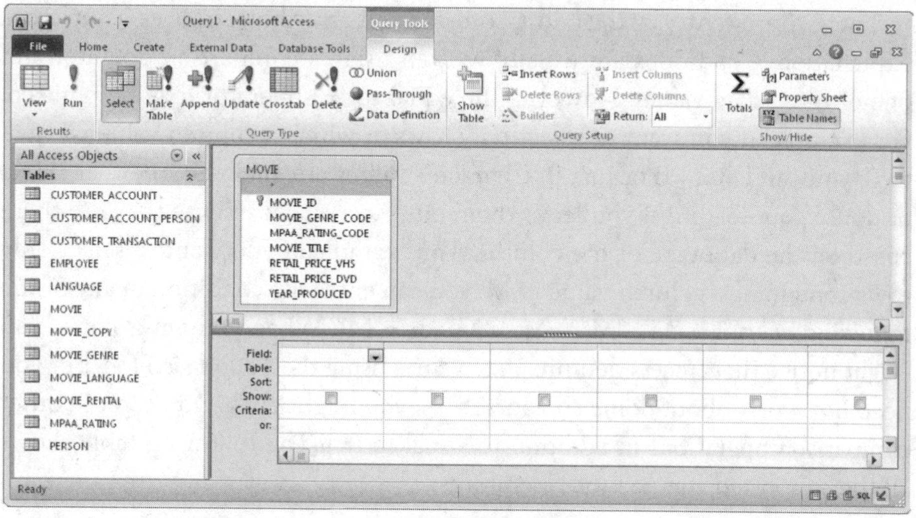

FIGURE 3-13 · Query Design panel (with MOVIE table added)

to the corresponding columns. Usage examples are provided in the sections that follow. The basic options available are

- **Field**   The specification for the source of the column. This is normally a table or query column name, but it can also be a constant or an expression similar to calculations used in spreadsheets.

- **Table**   The source table or query name for the column.

- **Sort**   The specification for any sort sequencing for the column (Ascending, Descending, or None).

- **Show**   A check box that controls display of the column. If the box is not checked, the column can be used in forming the query, but does not appear in the query results.

- **Criteria**   The specification that determines which rows of data are to appear in the query results. All conditions placed on the same line must be met for a row of data to be displayed in the query results. Conditions placed on subsequent lines (labeled "Or:" on the panel) are alternative sets of conditions that will also cause a matching data row to be displayed in the results. Use of these will likely not make sense until you see the examples that follow, but in short, conditions placed on one line are connected with a logical AND operator, and each new line of criteria is connected with all the other lines by using a logical OR operator. Said another way, any row that matches the specifications that appear on any one of the criteria lines will be displayed in the query results.

The Criteria entry is the most complicated and thus requires a bit more explanation. Conditions are usually written using a comparison operator and one or more data values. However, the equal to (=) operator may be omitted. For example, if you want to select only rows in which a column value is equal to 0, you can enter =0 or just 0. Character values are enclosed in either single or double quotes, but if you leave them out, Access will assume they are there based on the data type of the column. For example, if you want to select only rows containing a column value of M, you can enter the condition in any of the following ways: M, 'M', "M", =M, ='M', or ="M". When you enter dates, you might notice that Access delimits date values using the pound sign (#), but you need not worry about doing so yourself. As you might guess, you can use other comparison operations in addition to equal to (=). The following table shows all the supported comparison operators:

Operator	Description Values
=	Equal to
<	Less than
<=	Less than or equal to
>	Greater than
>=	Greater than or equal to
<>	Not equal to

Once the specification is complete, clicking the Run icon (the exclamation point in the Results group of the Design ribbon) runs the query and displays the results using the Datasheet View like the one shown in Figure 3-10. To go back to the Query Design panel, simply click the View icon (the ruler, pencil, and triangle icon in the Views group of the Home ribbon). For most queries, data updates can be entered directly in the Datasheet View table, and they are applied directly to the source tables for the query. If a column in the query results cannot be mapped to a single table column—perhaps because it was calculated in some way—then it cannot be updated in the query results.

If all this seems confusing, that's because the best way to learn how to create queries in Microsoft Access is by trying them for yourself. Therefore, the remainder of this chapter will use a series of examples to demonstrate the powerful features of the Microsoft Access Queries tool. To reduce the amount of work required to complete each one, these examples build on one another. Each example offers a description of the result desired and the steps required to create the specification for the query on the Query Design panel, along with a figure containing a screen shot showing the completed Query Design panel, and another figure showing the results when the query is executed.

Example 3-1: List All Movies

In this example, you will simply list the entire MOVIE table (all rows and all columns). Follow these steps:

1. On the Create ribbon, click Query Design.

2. Perform the following actions in the Show Table dialog box:
   - Click MOVIE to select the MOVIE table.
   - Click the Add button.
   - Click the Close button.

3. On the Query Design panel, double-click the asterisk in the MOVIE table template (near the top of the panel).

4. Click the Run icon on the ribbon (the exclamation point) to run your query. The completed panel is shown in Figure 3-14 with the query results shown in Figure 3-15.

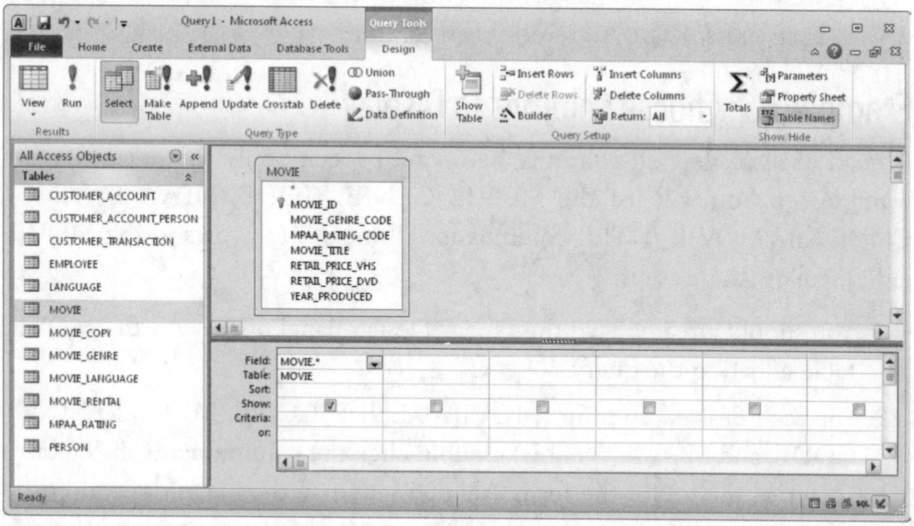

FIGURE 3-14 • Example 3-1 (List All Movies), query design

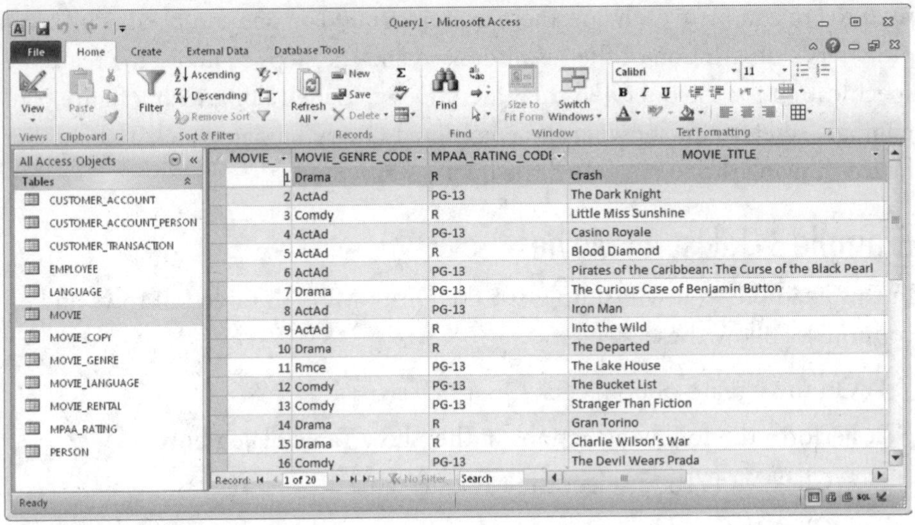

FIGURE 3-15 · Example 3-1 (List All Movies), query results

5. To get ready for the next exercise, do the following:

- Return to the Query Design panel by clicking the View icon (the triangle, ruler, and pencil) just below the File tab.

- On the Query Design panel (Figure 3-14), clear the existing query specification by clicking the slim gray strip just above the field name MOVIE.* (which changes the entire column to a black background). Then press DELETE to remove the column.

Example 3-2: Choose Columns to Display

Instead of displaying all columns, here you'll specify only the ones that you want to see. You will list the MOVIE_GENRE_CODE, MPAA_RATING_CODE, and MOVIE_TITLE columns for all movies (all rows in the MOVIE table). Follow these steps:

1. You should already have the Query Design panel open with the MOVIE table added to the query.

2. For each desired column (MOVIE_GENRE_CODE, MPAA_RATING_CODE, and MOVIE_TITLE), double-click the column name in the table shown at the top of the form. An alternative method is to drag-and-drop the column name from the table shown at the top of the form to the grid in the lower part of the form.

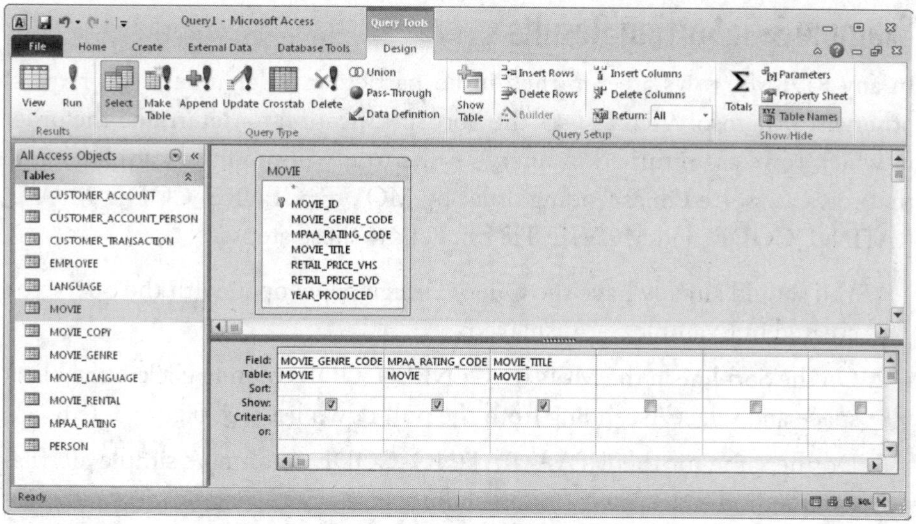

FIGURE 3-16 · Example 3-2 (Choose Columns to Display), query design

3. Click the Run icon on the ribbon to run your query. The completed panel is shown in Figure 3-16 with the query results shown in Figure 3-17.

4. To get ready for the next exercise, return to the Query Design panel by clicking the View icon (the triangle, ruler, and pencil) just below the File tab.

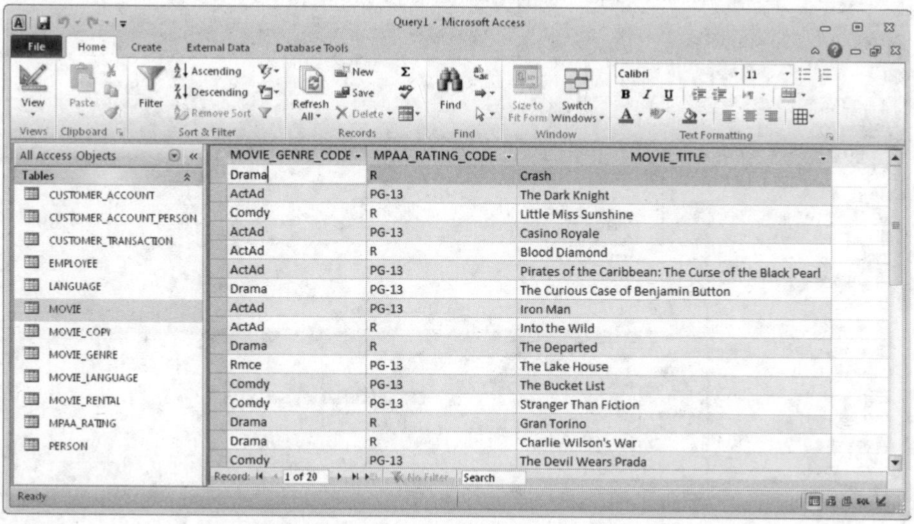

FIGURE 3-17 · Example 3-2 (Choose Columns to Display), query results

Example 3-3: Sorting Results

In any RDBMS, rows are returned in no particular order unless you request otherwise. Microsoft Access uses the Sort specification to determine the order in which rows are returned in query results. You will modify Example 3-2 so that rows are sorted in ascending order by MOVIE_GENRE_CODE, MPAA_RATING_CODE, and MOVIE_TITLE. Follow these steps:

1. You should already have the Query Design panel open with the query you created in Example 3-2 displayed.

2. On the Sort line in the MOVIE_GENRE_CODE column, click in the blank space and select Ascending from the pull-down list (see Figure 3-18).

3. Do the same for the MPAA_RATING_CODE column. A simple alternative method is to type **A** (for ascending) in the Sort specification and press ENTER.

4. Do the same for the MOVIE_TITLE column.

5. Click the Run icon on the ribbon to run your query. The completed panel is shown in Figure 3-18 with the query results shown in Figure 3-19.

6. To get ready for the next exercise, return to the Query Design panel by clicking the View icon (the triangle, ruler, and pencil) just below the File tab.

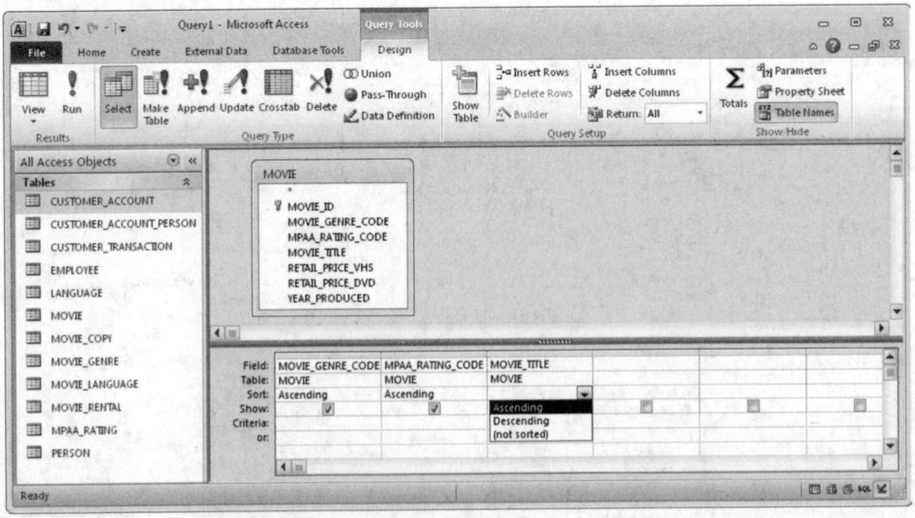

FIGURE 3-18 · Example 3-3 (Sorting Results), query design

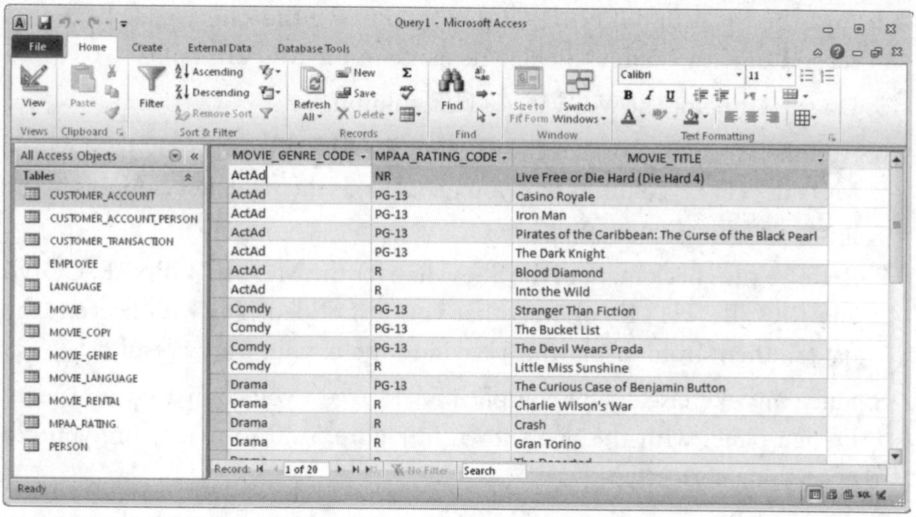

FIGURE 3-19 · Example 3-3 (Sorting Results), query results

Example 3-4: Advanced Sorting

Looking at the results of Example 3-3, suppose we have a requirement to produce the same result set, but sorted by MOVIE_RATING_CODE first, then by MOVIE_GENRE_CODE, and finally by MOVIE_TITLE. Another way to say this is sorting by MOVIE_TITLE *within* MOVIE_GENRE_CODE *within* MPAA_RATING_CODE. However, Access works from left to right when handling sort requests, so how can we accomplish our goal? We can place the MOVIE_GENRE_CODE and MOVIE_TITLE columns in the query a second time, use the second copies for sorting, but omit them from the query results by clearing the Show check box.

In this example, you modify Example 3-3 so that rows are sorted as discussed. Follow these steps:

1. You should already have the Query Design panel open with the query you created in Example 3-3 displayed.

2. Remove the Sort specifications on the existing MOVIE_GENRE_CODE column by doing the following:

   • Click in the Sort line of the query specification for the column.

   • Click the downward-facing arrow to display the pull-down menu.

   • Select the (Not Sorted) option from the list.

3. Do the same for the MOVIE_TITLE column.

4. Add the MOVIE_GENRE_CODE column to the query specification a second time by double-clicking its name in the MOVIE table.

5. Do the same for the MOVIE_TITLE column.

6. Add the ascending sort specification to the MOVIE_GENRE_CODE and MOVIE_TITLE columns that you just added (the *rightmost* columns in the query specification column).

7. Remove the check mark in the Show line for the MOVIE_GENRE_CODE and MOVIE_TITLE columns that you just added. This will prevent the data in them from displaying a second time in your query results.

8. Since this exercise is a bit complicated, I suggest you compare your Query Design panel with the one shown in Figure 3-20 to make sure you did everything correctly.

9. Click the Run icon on the ribbon to run your query. The completed panel is shown in Figure 3-20 with the query results shown in Figure 3-21. Note that most languages are read from left to right, so we naturally expect tabular listings to be sorted moving from left to right, starting with the leftmost column. It is unusual, and perhaps poor human engineering, to sort columns another way. But should you ever need to do so, you now know how.

10. To get ready for the next exercise, do the following:

   • Return to the Query Design panel by clicking the View icon (the triangle, ruler, and pencil) just below the File tab.

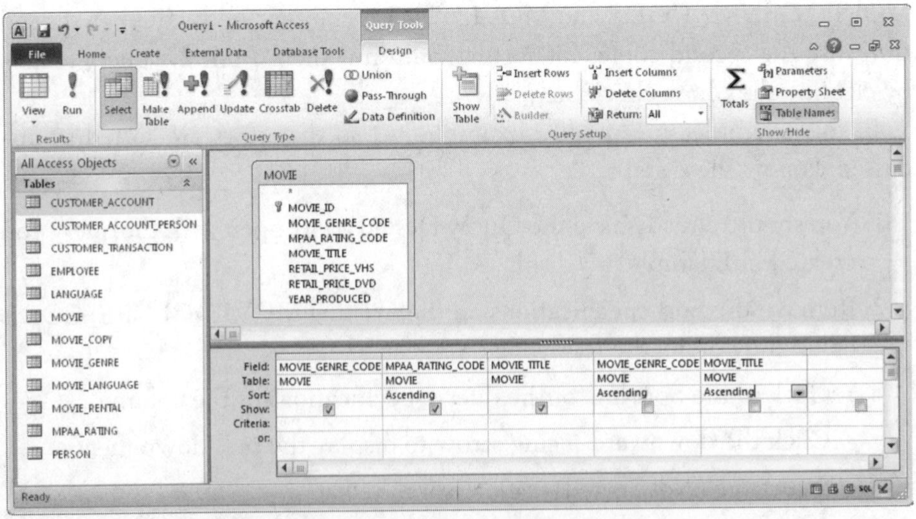

FIGURE 3-20 · Example 3-4 (Advanced Sorting), query design

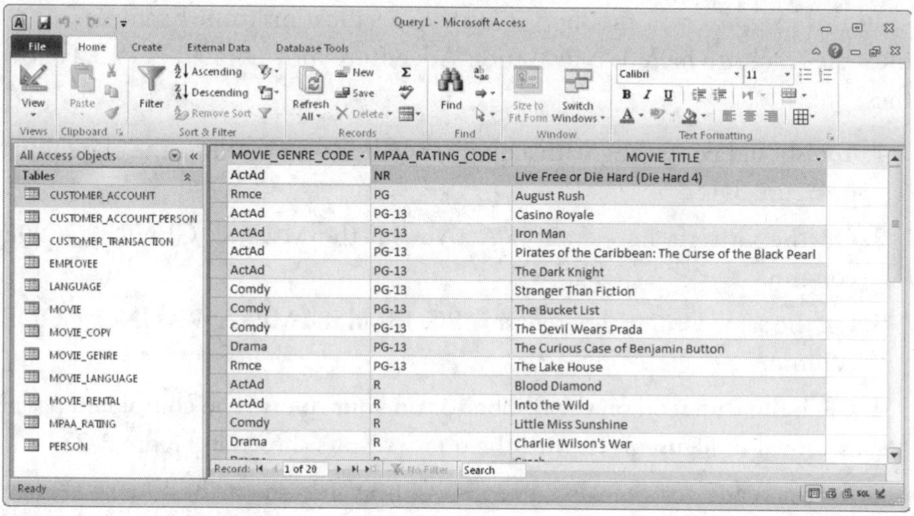

FIGURE 3-21 · Example 3-4 (Advanced Sorting), query results

- To simplify the upcoming examples, put the query specification back to the way it was at the end of Example 3-3.

- Remove the additional MOVIE_GENRE_CODE and MOVIE_TITLE columns you added to the sort specification by clicking the slim gray strip above the field name (which changes the entire column to a black background) and pressing DELETE to remove the column.

- Add the Ascending sort specification to the remaining MOVIE_GENRE_CODE and MOVIE_TITLE columns by clicking in the Sort line for each, typing the letter **A**, and pressing ENTER. This should add "Ascending" to each column.

Example 3-5: Choosing Rows to Display

Thus far you have been displaying all 20 rows in the MOVIE table in every query. However, displaying rows you do not need to see can be confusing and can waste system resources, especially if you are sorting them. Suppose you want to see rows only for movies where the movie genre is ActAd (Action-Adventure) and the rating is PG-13. You can add conditions using the Criteria line on the Query Design panel to filter the rows so that only those you want are included. Keep in mind that for a row to be displayed in the results, all the conditions on at least one of the Criteria lines need to evaluate to True.

In this exercise, you modify the query specification from Example 3-3 to filter the results to include only Action-Adventure movies rated PG-13. Follow these steps:

1. You should be starting with a query specification matching the one shown in Figure 3-18.

2. On the Criteria line, enter ="ActAD" in the MOVIE_GENRE_CODE column.

3. On the same Criteria line, enter ="PG-13" in the MPAA_RATING_CODE column.

4. Click the Run icon on the ribbon to run your query. The completed panel is shown in Figure 3-22 with the query results shown in Figure 3-23.

5. To get ready for the next exercise, simply return to the Query Design panel by clicking the View icon just below the File tab.

NOTE *Microsoft Access pays no attention to case when selecting data in queries. For example, in the preceding query, you could have used any of the following criteria in the MOVIE_GENRE_CODE column and achieved the same results: ="ACTAD", ="actad", ="AcTaD". Note that character constants used in an RDBMS are normally enclosed in quotation marks. However, Microsoft Access knows which columns have a character data type, and it will add the quotes automatically should you leave them out.*

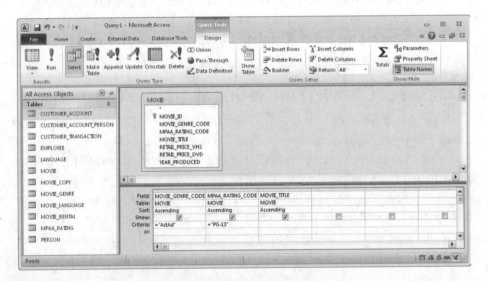

FIGURE 3-22 · Example 3-5 (Choosing Rows to Display), query design

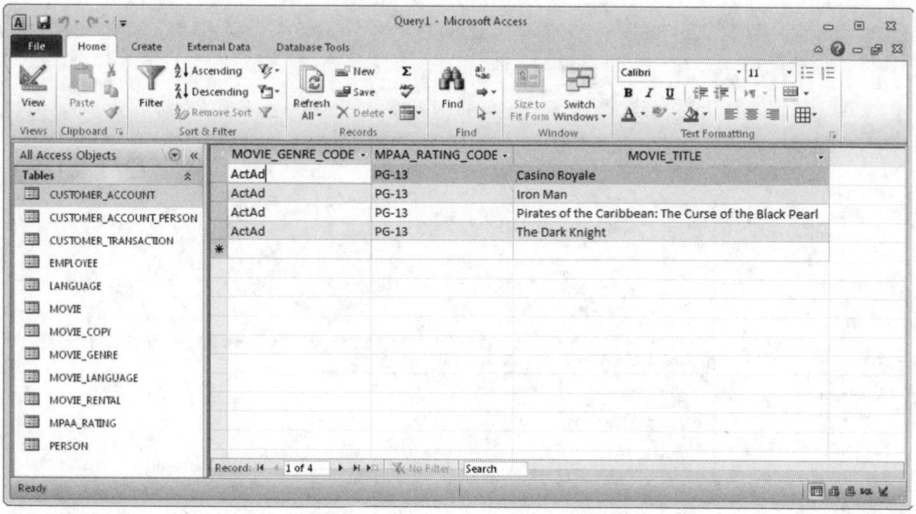

FIGURE 3-23 · Example 3-5 (Choosing Rows to Display), query results

Example 3-6: Compound Row Selection

Suppose you now want to select all movies rated PG in addition to the PG-13 action-adventure movies selected in the previous example. You must add the new criteria on a *different* line of the Query Design panel.

In this example, you modify Example 3-5 to include the additional movies. Follow these steps:

1. You should be starting with the query specification from Example 3-5, as shown in Figure 3-22.

2. On the Or line, enter **PG** in the MPAA_RATING_CODE column. (If you leave out the comparison operator, Access will assume the equal to [=] operator.) Note that for a row to appear in the query results, it must have a value of either PG-13 or PG in the MPAA_RATING_CODE column, and if the rating is PG-13, it must also have a value of ActAd in the MOVIE_GENRE_CODE column. Criteria on the same line are connected with a logical AND, while the criteria lines themselves are connected with a logical OR.

3. Click the Run icon on the ribbon to run your query. The completed panel is shown in Figure 3-24 with the query results shown in Figure 3-25.

4. To get ready for the next exercise, simply return to the Query Design panel by clicking the View icon just below the File tab.

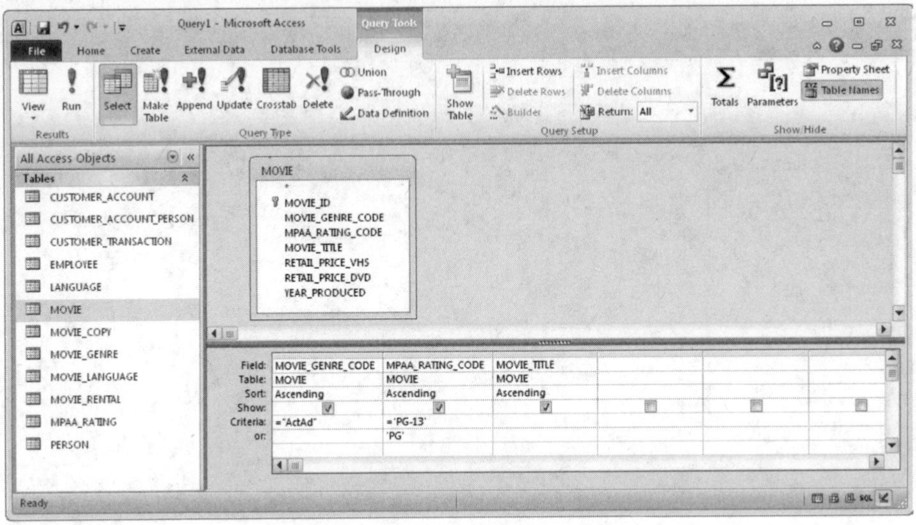

FIGURE 3-24 · Example 3-6 (Compound Row Selection), query design

Example 3-7: Using Not Equal To

Thus far we have looked at search criteria that assumes the equal to (=) comparison operator. However, several other comparison operators can be used, as shown earlier in this chapter. Suppose, for example, you want to list all the movies that are neither action-adventure (ActAd) nor comedy (Comdy). The easiest way to do this is to use the not equal to (<>) operator.

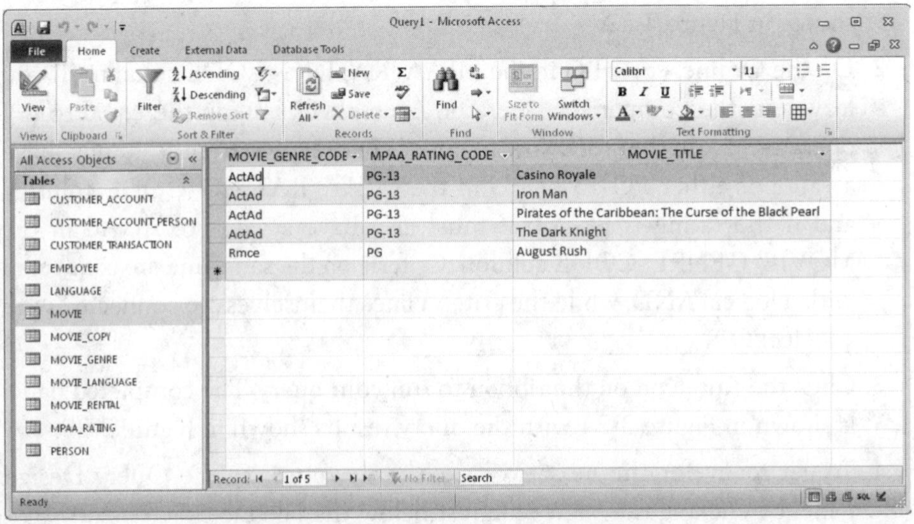

FIGURE 3-25 · Example 3-6 (Compound Row Selection), query results

As queries become more complex, you'll often find that you can write the same query specification multiple ways, and that is the case here. One way is to type **<>ActAd AND <>Comdy** in a single MOVIE_GENRE_CODE column. Another way is to add the MOVIE_GENRE_CODE column to the query a second time, unchecking the Show box like you did in Example 3-4, and typing **<>ActAd** in one of the MOVIE_GENRE_CODE columns and **<>Comdy** on the *same* Criteria line in the other MOVIE_GENRE_CODE column.

In this exercise, you will modify the query from Example 3-6 to find all the movies which are neither action-adventure (ActAd) nor comedy (Comdy). Follow these steps:

1. You should be starting with a query specification matching the one shown in Figure 3-24.

2. Clear all the existing conditions on the Criteria lines by selecting each one (dragging your cursor over them while holding down the left button on your mouse or other pointing device) and then pressing DELETE.

3. On one of the Criteria lines in the MOVIE_GENRE_CODE column, enter this condition: **<>ActAd AND <>Comdy**. Note that Access may reformat it somewhat if you select something else on the Query Design panel, but the result will still be logically the same.

4. Click the Run icon on the ribbon to run your query. The completed panel is shown in Figure 3-26 with the query results shown in Figure 3-27.

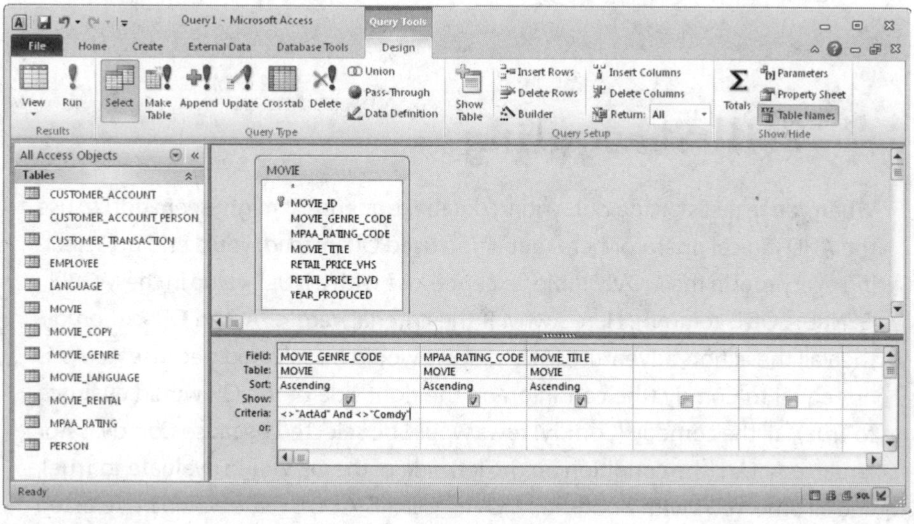

FIGURE 3-26 • Example 3-7 (Using Not Equal To), query design

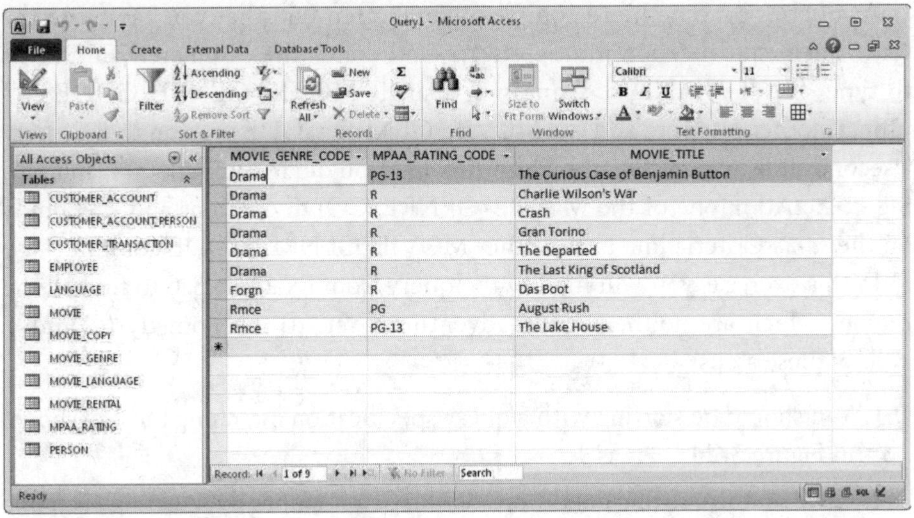

FIGURE 3-27 · Example 3-7 (Using Not Equal To), query results

5. To get ready for the next exercise, do the following:

- Return to the Query Design panel by clicking the View icon just below the File tab.

- Click the MOVIE table at the top of the Query Design panel (the rectangle that shows the table name along with a listing of some of the column names) and then press DELETE. This will clear out the form so it contains no tables, columns, or criteria.

? Still Struggling

When you're first starting out writing database queries, it might seem odd to use the AND logical operator here, but if you used OR instead, you'd end up selecting every row in the MOVIE table (except those with a NULL value in the MOVIE_GENRE_CODE column). Here's why. If the criteria were <>ActAd OR <>Comdy, then all the action-adventure (ActAd) rows would be selected because ActAd is not equal to Comdy (the condition on the right side of the OR would evaluate to True), all the comedy (Comdy) rows would be selected because Comdy is not equal to ActAd (the condition on the left side of the OR would evaluate to True), and all other rows with a non-null MOVIE_GENRE_CODE value would be selected because the conditions on both sides of the OR would evaluate to True.

Example 3-8: Joining Tables

In this exercise, you want to display two columns from the MOVIE table along with one column from the MOVIE_GENRE table, displaying the MOVIE_GENRE_DESCRIPTION with each movie instead of the MOVIE_GENRE_CODE that was displayed in the preceding examples. In relational databases, combining data from more than one table is called *joining*. Because the relationship between movie genres and movies is one-to-many, whenever a movie genre has multiple movies, the same information about the movie genre will be repeated in the query results for each row returned.

TERMS: Join

A join is a relational database operation that combines data from multiple tables by placing columns from each table side by side in the query results. Usually the primary key in one table and the foreign key in the other table are used to match up the rows of data. Joins are the fundamental building blocks for relational database queries.

Understanding joins is essential to understanding relational databases. Just as one-to-many relationships (implemented in the database as referential constraints) are the fundamental building blocks for relational databases, joins are the fundamental building blocks for relational database queries. Follow these steps:

1. You should be starting with an empty Query Design panel (no tables, columns, criteria, and so on, are displayed). If this is not the case, select (click) each table shown and press DELETE to remove it from the query.

2. Click the Show Table icon (with the yellow plus sign) to display the Show Table dialog box, like the one shown in Figure 3-12.

3. Select the name of the MOVIE table, and then click Add to add it to the query.

4. Do the same for the MOVIE_GENRE table, and then close the Add Table dialog box. Notice the line connecting the two tables on the Query Design panel. This tells you that Access already knows how to match up rows in these two tables (foreign key MOVIE_GENRE_CODE in the MOVIE table matched to primary key MOVIE_GENRE_CODE in the MOVIE_GENRE table) based on the metadata supplied by the database designer on the Relationships panel.

TERMS: Cartesian Product

A join that matches each row in one table with every row in the other table is called a Cartesian product, named after French mathematician René Descartes. Cartesian products are seldom the desired result and they can be avoided by carefully specifying the join conditions (also called *predicates*) that the DBMS uses to match rows between the tables being joined.

? Still Struggling

Avoiding Cartesian products can be challenging at first. Microsoft Access has a nice feature where a query *inherits* the relationship between the two tables from the one specified on the Relationships panel at a much earlier time. If the join condition were not included, you would get a *Cartesian product* as a result (every row in one table combined with every row in the other—the *product* of multiplying the two tables together) unless you add the condition by dragging your pointer from the foreign key column to the primary key column (the method in Access for manually adding a join condition). You clearly do not want your query results to look like every movie is assigned to every single genre (for example), so Microsoft Access helps you do the right thing by automatically inheriting the join condition.

---

5. In the MOVIE table, double-click the MOVIE_ID and MOVIE_TITLE columns to add them to the query specification.

6. In the MOVIE_GENRE table, double-click MOVIE_GENRE_DESCRIP-TION to add this column to the query specification. Notice that you don't have to select the MOVIE_GENRE_CODE column even though the join criteria will use it to find the matching row in the MOVIE_GENRE table.

7. Click the Run icon on the ribbon to run your query. The completed panel is shown in Figure 3-28 with the query results shown in Figure 3-29. Note the record count at the bottom of the query results. All 20 movies are displayed. However, if you scroll through the results, you will see that only 5 genre descriptions are displayed even though there are 16 rows in the MOVIE_GENRE description. When a genre is assigned to multiple movies, the genre

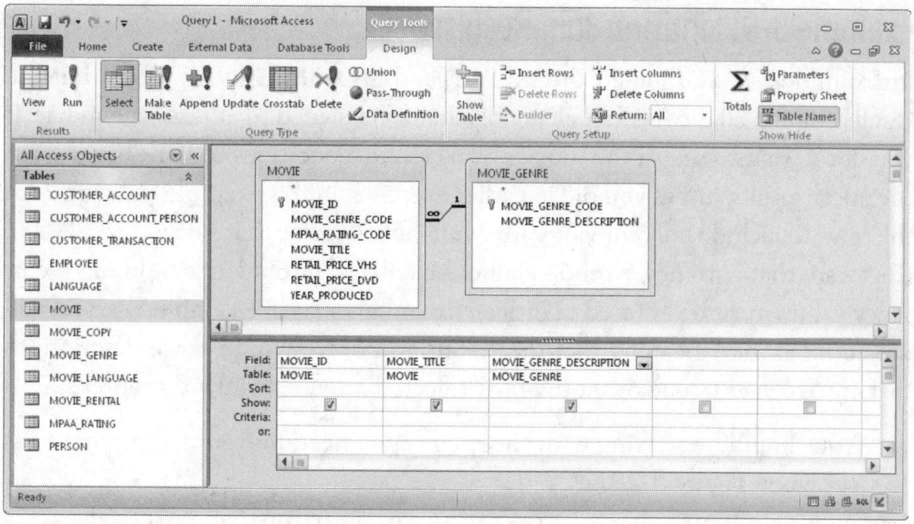

FIGURE 3-28 · Example 3-8 (Joining Tables), query design

description is repeated for each of those movies. However, if a genre is not used by any movies, it will not appear in the results because, by default, this query uses an *inner join*—where only matched rows are displayed. You'll try an *outer join*, where unmatched rows are included, in Example 3-10.

8. To get ready for the next exercise, simply return to the Query Design panel by clicking the View icon just below the File tab.

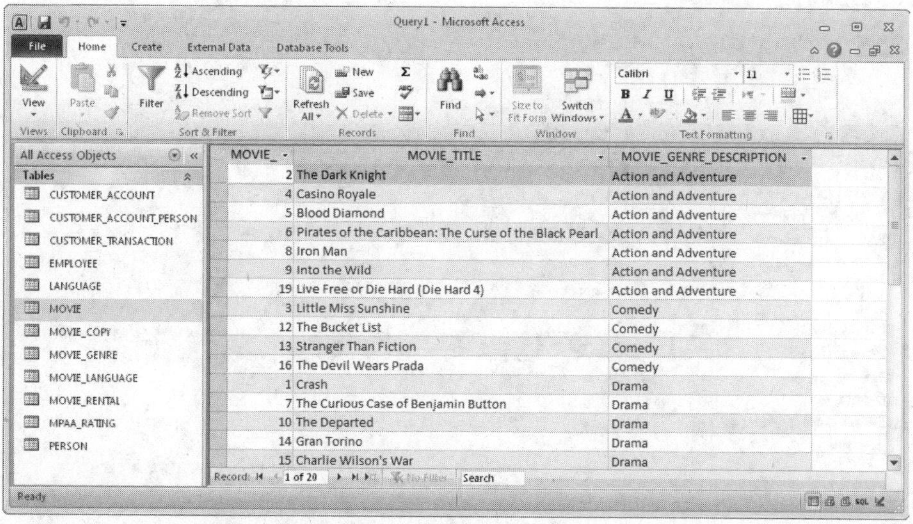

FIGURE 3-29 · Example 3-8 (Joining Tables), query results

Example 3-9: Limiting Join Results

In Example 3-8, you joined the MOVIE and MOVIE_GENRE tables, but the results contain all movies and all genres that are assigned to at least one movie. If you don't want to see all the movies, you can use conditions to limit the rows in the query results, just as you did in earlier exercises. In this example, you will limit the rows to include only movies with a retail DVD price that is less than $20.00. (Be aware that currency symbols cannot be entered into query conditions – currency values must be entered as ordinary numbers.) As in Example 3-8, you will use an inner join, meaning that the results will only include genre descriptions that are assigned to one or more of the selected movies. Follow these steps:

1. You should be starting with the query specification from Example 3-8, as shown in Figure 3-28.

2. In the MOVIE table, double-click the RETAIL_PRICE_DVD column to add it to the query results.

3. On the Criteria line, enter **<20** in the RETAIL_PRICE_DVD column. Note that RETAIL_PRICE_DVD is a numeric column, so literals like 20 in the selection criteria are not enclosed in quotes.

4. Click the Run icon on the ribbon to run your query. The completed panel is shown in Figure 3-30 with the query results shown in Figure 3-31.

5. To get ready for the next exercise, return to the Query Design panel by clicking the View icon just below the File tab.

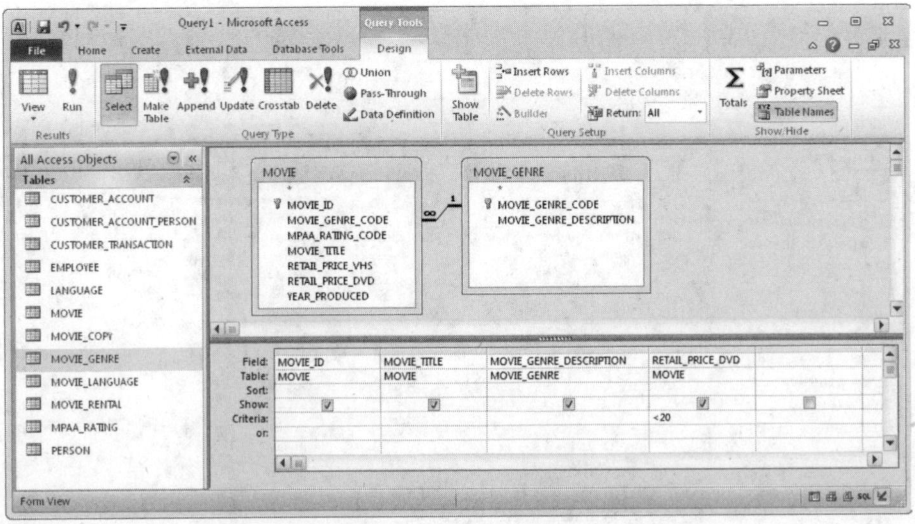

FIGURE 3-30 · Example 3-9 (Limiting Join Results), query design

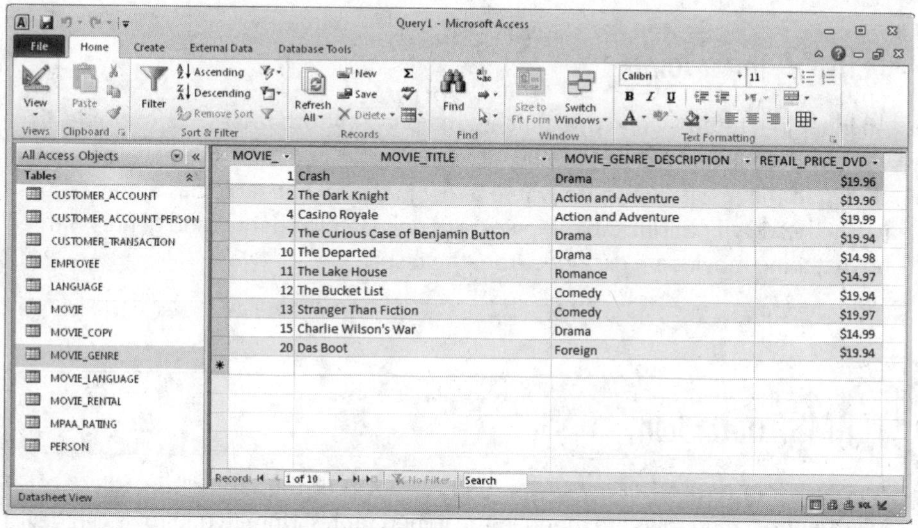

FIGURE 3-31 · Example 3-9 (Limiting Join Results), query results

Example 3-10: Outer Joins

As described in Example 3-9, the join technique you have used thus far is the *inner join*. As mentioned, some genres have no movies assigned to them, and thus data for those genres did not appear in the Example 3-9 results. If you want to include all genres in the results, regardless of whether they have movies assigned to them, you must use an *outer join* (also called an *inclusive join*). An outer join returns all rows from one (or both) of the tables, regardless of whether matching rows are found in the joined tables. Any data to be displayed from the table where no matching row is found is set to NULL in the query results. (For Microsoft Access, NULL columns appear blank, but if you click the column data, you will see that the column contains no characters of data.) For example, for the genre that has no matching movies, all the columns from the MOVIE table would be NULL in the results. Keep in mind that the returned data rows are still filtered by other search criteria (in this case, only movies with a DVD price under 20), but whether the filtering occurs before, during, or after the join operation is immaterial, so long as the unwanted rows are eliminated from the query results. Remember, you only describe the result you want, not how it is achieved.

TERMS: Inner Join

An inner join returns only rows that are matched in both tables. For example, if you join MOVIE and MOVIE_GENRE tables using an inner join, the only rows included in the results are those where a row in the MOVIE table has a matching row in the MOVIE_GENRE table. Movies with no matching genres and genres with no matching movies are excluded from the results.

TERMS: Outer Join

An outer join returns all rows from one (or both) of the tables, regardless of whether matching rows are found in the joined tables. Unmatched rows can be included from either the first table named in the join (a left outer join), the second table named in the join (a right outer join) or both tables (a full outer join).

Three types of outer joins can be used, and unfortunately, the industry has settled on potentially confusing names for them:

- **Left Outer Join** An outer join for which all rows are returned from the left-hand table in the join, and data from any matching rows found in the right-hand table is also returned.

- **Right Outer Join** An outer join for which all the rows are returned from the right-hand table in the join, and data from any matching rows found in the left-hand table is also returned.

- **Full Outer Join** An outer join for which all rows are returned from both tables, regardless of whether matching data is found between them. Microsoft Access does not currently support this type of join.

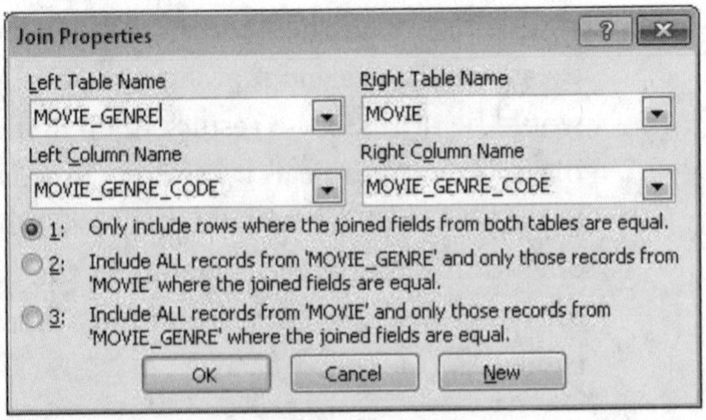

FIGURE 3-32 •Join Properties dialog box

Figure 3-32 shows the Join Properties dialog box that is used in Access to specify the desired type of join.

? Still Struggling

People are often confused by the use of *left* and *right* in the names of the join types. All you have to do is reverse the order of the tables in any existing query, and you are essentially switching it from a left outer join to a right outer join, or vice versa. However, Microsoft Access does not make this distinction, so all its joins are simply called *outer joins*. Instead, Access uses a dialog box named Join Properties, shown in Figure 3-32, to specify the type of join you want to use, with an inner join as the default.

In this example, you will change the query from Example 3-9 into an outer join so that all MOVIE_GENRE table rows are displayed, regardless of whether there are any matching movies in the query results. Follow these steps:

1. You should be starting with the query specification from Example 3-9, as shown in Figure 3-30.

2. To access the Join Properties dialog box (shown in Figure 3-32), double-click somewhere in the middle of the line between the two tables displayed on the Query Design panel, or as an alternative, right-click the line. As with the Relationships panel, it can be tricky to get the cursor pointer in exactly the right place on the line, but practice and a bit of patience always prevail.

3. In the Join Properties dialog box, select the option "Include ALL records from 'MOVIE_GENRE' and only those records from 'MOVIE' where the joined fields are equal." It is most likely option 2, but if you added the tables to the query in the reverse order, it could have ended up as option 3. Click OK to close the dialog box.

4. Since you have a condition on the RETAIL_PRICE_DVD column from the MOVIE table, you need to change it to allow for null values. For genres that have no matching movies, the value in the RETAIL_PRICE_DVD column will be null, and therefore the criteria on the column (<20) will filter those rows out of the results unless you change it to allow for null values. Add the condition **OR IS NULL** (which can also be written as Or Is Null) to the condition on the RETAIL_PRICE_DVD column to allow nulls to be included in the results.

5. Since you will be listing all genres regardless of whether matching movies are found, the results will be easier to read and understand if you move the MOVIE_GENRE_DESCRIPTION column to the leftmost column of the results and sort the results by genre. To do this, follow these steps:

   1. Clear the existing MOVIE_GENRE_DESCRIPTION column by dragging your mouse pointer over the slim gray strip above the column (just above the Field: label). The column will display as black (reverse video) as it is selected. Then press DELETE to remove it from the query.

   2. Drag the MOVIE_GENRE_DESCRIPTION column from the MOVIE_GENRE table in the upper part of the panel, and drop it on top of the MOVIE_ID column in the query specification in the lower part of the panel. This will cause all the existing columns in the specification to shift one position to the right and the MOVIE_GENRE_DESCRIPTION column to become the first (leftmost) column in the query results.

   3. In the Sort line under the MOVIE_GENRE_DESCRIPTION column, change the specification to sort it in Ascending sequence.

6. The completed panel is shown in Figure 3-33. Notice the arrow on the line between the two tables that points toward the MOVIE table. This is the way Access alerts you to the fact that the join is an outer join.

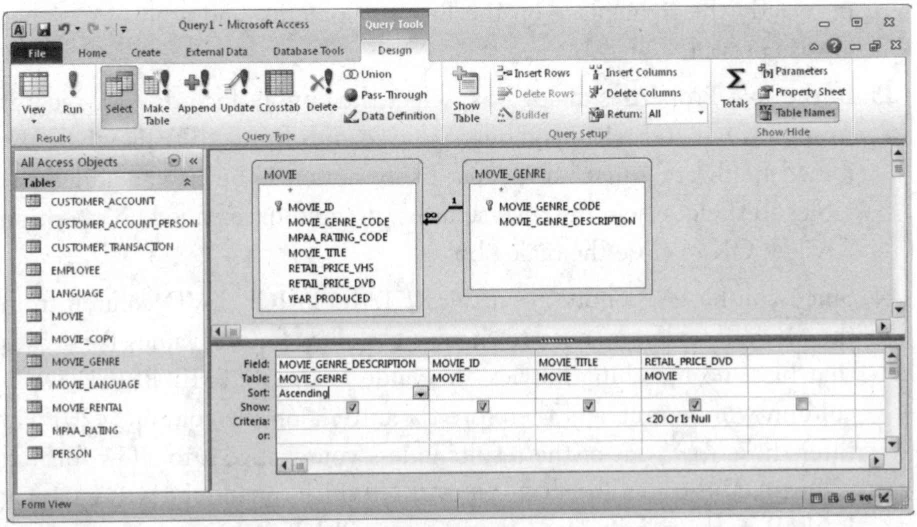

FIGURE 3-33 · Example 3-10 (Outer Joins), query design

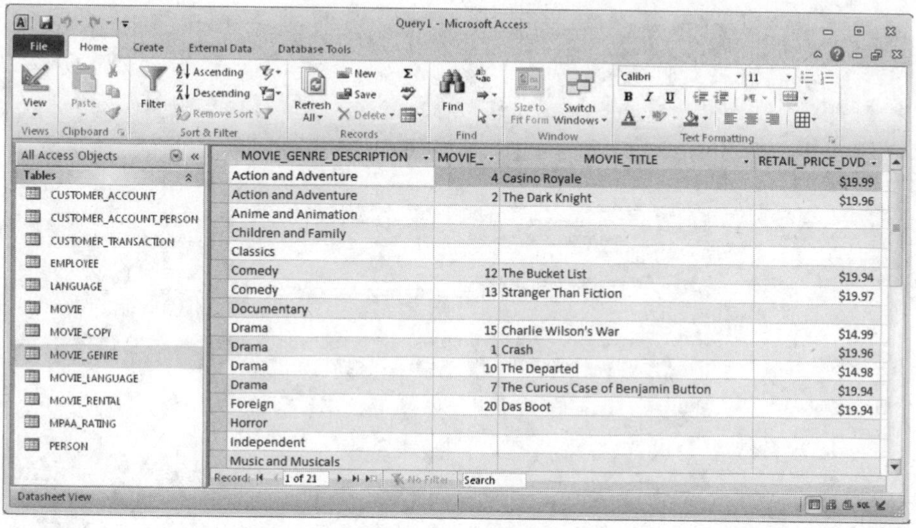

FIGURE 3-34 · Example 3-10 (Outer Joins), query results

7. Click the Run icon on the ribbon to run your query. The query results are shown in Figure 3-34.

8. To get ready for the next exercise, return to the Query Design panel by clicking the View icon just below the File tab.

Example 3-11: Microsoft Access SQL

SQL is discussed in Chapter 4; however, since Microsoft Access automatically generates SQL for queries defined on the Query Design panel, a quick preview of SQL is in order. In this example, you will display the SQL for the query created in Example 3-10. Follow these steps:

1. You should be starting with a query specification from Example 3-10, as shown in Figure 3-33.

2. On the Query Design panel, click the arrow below the View icon (under the File tab) to expand the options. Select the SQL View option, as shown in the top of Figure 3-35. Alternatively, you can click the SQL icon on the status bar at the lower-right corner of the panel.

3. The SQL for the current query will be displayed as shown in the lower part of Figure 3-36. The SELECT keyword is followed by a list of the columns to be displayed in the query results. The FROM keyword is followed by the two tables and their outer join condition. Next is the WHERE keyword, followed by the conditions that limit rows to movies with DVD

Query1 - Microsoft Access
Query Tools
File Home Create External Data Database Tools Design
MOVIE
MOVIE_ID
MOVIE_GENRE_CODE
MPAA_RATING_CODE
MOVIE_TITLE
RETAIL_PRICE_VHS
RETAIL_PRICE_DVD
YEAR_PRODUCED
MOVIE_GENRE
MOVIE_GENRE_CODE
MOVIE_GENRE_DESCRIPTION
Field: MOVIE_GENRE_DESCRIPTION MOVIE_ID MOVIE_TITLE RETAIL_PRICE_DVD
Table: MOVIE_GENRE MOVIE MOVIE MOVIE
Sort: Ascending
Criteria: <20 Or Is Null

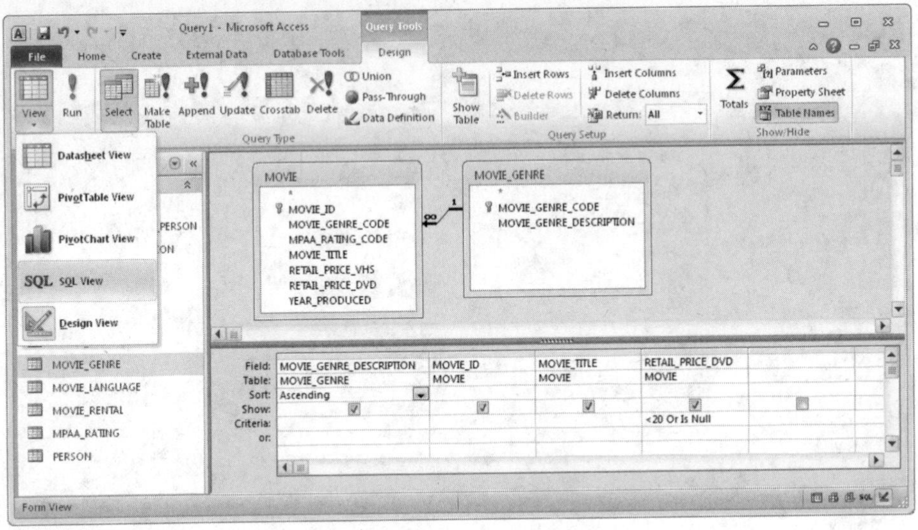

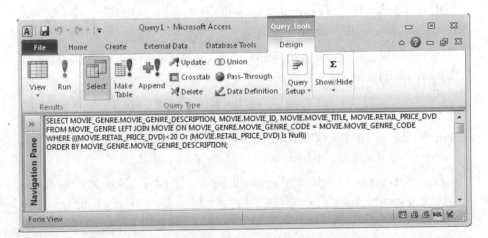

FIGURE 3-35 • Example 3-11 (Microsoft Access SQL), query design

retail prices that are either `NULL` or less than 20. And last is the `ORDER BY` clause that specifies the ordering of the rows in the result set. This is a great product feature because you can use it not only to help you learn SQL, but once you know SQL, you also can work back and forth between the Query Design View and the SQL View to develop your queries quickly. (Incidentally, Access SQL is the least standards-compliant of all the modern RDBMSs because object names can have embedded spaces.)

Query1 - Microsoft Access
Query Tools
File Home Create External Data Database Tools Design
SELECT MOVIE_GENRE.MOVIE_GENRE_DESCRIPTION, MOVIE.MOVIE_ID, MOVIE.MOVIE_TITLE, MOVIE.RETAIL_PRICE_DVD
FROM MOVIE_GENRE LEFT JOIN MOVIE ON MOVIE_GENRE.MOVIE_GENRE_CODE = MOVIE.MOVIE_GENRE_CODE
WHERE (((MOVIE.RETAIL_PRICE_DVD)<20 Or (MOVIE.RETAIL_PRICE_DVD) Is Null))
ORDER BY MOVIE_GENRE.MOVIE_GENRE_DESCRIPTION;
Navigation Pane
Form View

FIGURE 3-36 • Example 3-11 (Microsoft Access SQL), generated SQL query

4. To get ready for the next exercise, do the following:

- Return to the Query Design panel by clicking the View icon below the File tab.

- Clear all the selected columns and criteria by dragging your mouse pointer over the slim gray strips above each column (just above the Field: label). The columns will display as black (reverse video) as they are selected. Then press DELETE to remove them from the query.

- Change the join between the MOVIE and MOVIE_GENRE tables back to an inner join. To do this, double-click the thin part of the line between the two tables displayed on the Query Design panel to display the Join Properties dialog box. Then select option 1 and click OK.

Example 3-12: Multiple Joins and Calculated Columns

When you need information from more than two tables in the same query result, you can simply add more tables, and therefore more join operations, to the query. The beauty of relational databases is that you need not be concerned with which join is best processed first and other such implementation details. You can trust the RDBMS to make those decisions for you.

For this example, consider another scenario: The video store wants to liquidate all the VHS movie copies, and therefore you need to list all movies, sorted by genre, for which there are VHS copies in the inventory along with a sale price that is half of the list price. If you look at the Relationships panel (see Figure 3-9), the solution becomes obvious: you need the MOVIE_COPY to find the movies for which the store has VHS copies. It should be clear from this example that an overall diagram of all your tables and relationships is an *essential* document because it gives you the roadmap you need when forming queries.

TERMS: Calculated (Derived) Column

A calculated column (also called a derived column) is a column in the query results that is formed using some form of transformation or calculation. This can be as simple as supplying a literal value or a simple arithmetic calculation to more complex transformations using database functions. (Functions are introduced in Example 3-13 later in this chapter.)

This example also requires a *calculated column* (also called a *derived* column), which is formed by multiplying the values in the RETAIL_PRICE_VHS by 0.5 to calculate the sale price for each VHS copy. Just about any formula that you can use in a spreadsheet can be used in a relational database query. Follow these steps:

1. You should be starting with a query specification that joins the MOVIE and MOVIE_GENRE tables with a join specification (a line between them) and no other conditions, like the one shown in Example 3-8 (Figure 3-28), but with no columns included in the query results. Be certain that the join between MOVIE and MOVIE_GENRE is an inner join and that no columns are currently included in the query specification.

2. Add the MOVIE_COPY table to the query by clicking the Show Table icon and selecting the table from the list in the Show Table dialog box.

3. In the MOVIE_GENRE table, add the MOVIE_GENRE_DESCRIPTION column to the query by double-clicking its name. Alternatively, you can drag-and-drop the column name to the column in the query specification.

4. Change the Sort line for the MOVIE_GENRE_DESCRIPTION so that the query results will be sorted Ascending on the genre description.

5. In the MOVIE table, add the MOVIE_TITLE column to the query.

6. In the MOVIE_COPY table, add the COPY_NUMBER and MEDIA_FORMAT columns to the query by either double-clicking them or dragging and dropping them into the query specification.

7. On the Criteria line for the MEDIA_FORMAT column, enter **V** so that only VHS movie copies are selected. You should also uncheck the box on the Show line. (There is no point in displaying a column where every row in the results is guaranteed to have the same data value.)

8. To add the calculated column, enter the following into the Field line of the empty column to the right of the MEDIA_FORMAT column.

```
SALE_PRICE: Round((RETAIL_PRICE_VHS * 0.5), 2)
```

The first part of the entry (SALE_PRICE:) is a *label* for the new column. Every column in your results must have a unique name, and if you don't name it, Microsoft Access will. Default column names are usually not very

? Still Struggling

You may find it easier to enter complex specifications on the Field line if you expand the width of the column in the query form. To do so, place the cursor over the line that separates the column from the next column near the top of the column (where the gray strips over the columns are). The cursor will change to a vertical bar with left and right arrows protruding from it. Then click and drag the edge of the column to the right to expand the column to an appropriate size.

meaningful and sometimes are just plain ugly, so it is *always* best to supply a column label (name) for calculated columns. The Round function is used to round the results to two decimal places since the price is supposed to be in dollars and cents. Without it, the results would have additional decimal places, which would make the results more difficult to understand. To help you understand the syntax, here is how it would look with the multiplication operation removed:

```
Round(RETAIL_PRICE_VHS, 2)
```

Note that spaces on each side of the multiplication operator (*) in the field specifications do not matter, so you could have left them out. Chances are that Microsoft Access will rewrite your column specification by removing the spaces and placing square brackets around the other column name, so don't be surprised if you see what you entered change on the panel when you move the cursor to another location. The square brackets help Access deal with column names that contain spaces by marking the beginning and end of each name. The removal of spaces helps Access parse the statement for correct syntax.

9. Click the Run icon on the ribbon to run your query. The completed panel is shown in Figure 3-37 with the query results shown in Figure 3-38.

10. To get ready for the next exercise, return to the Query Design panel by clicking the View icon just below the File tab.

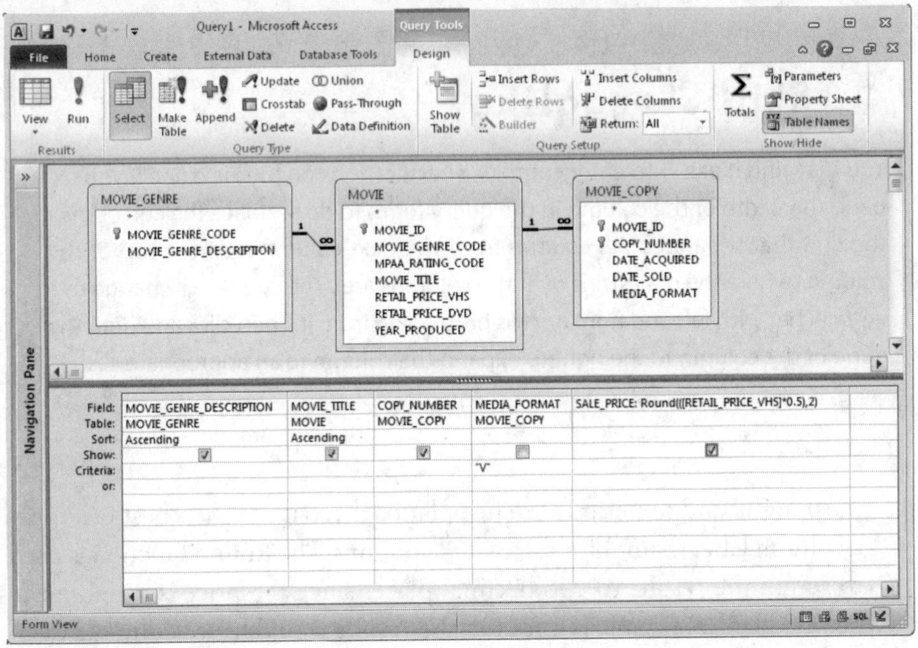

FIGURE 3-37 • Example 3-12 (Multiple Joins and Calculated Columns), query design

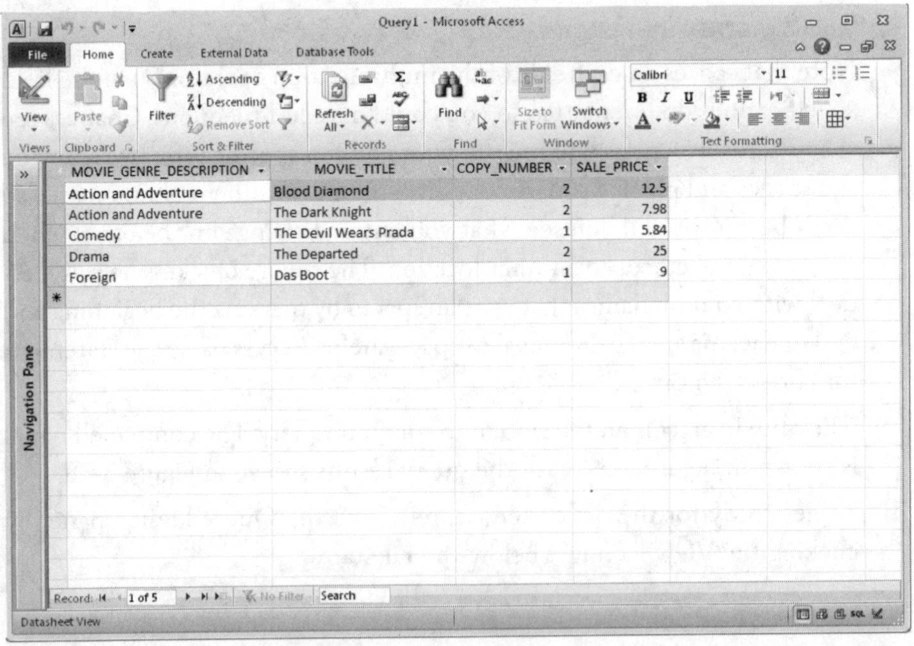

FIGURE 3-38 • Example 3-12 (Multiple Joins and Calculated Columns), query results

Example 3-13: Aggregate Functions

The Example 3-12 results contain five rows. All the details are here, but at a glance, it's not easy to get a sense of the *total* amount that the video store can expect to collect for each genre if all the VHS movie copies are sold at the sale price. (It would obviously be more difficult if the results contained many more rows.) If the store's accountant wants to know this, then what you really need to do is sum up the SALE_PRICE column for each customer. In relational databases, this is done with the SUM function.

> *A function is a special type of program that returns a single value each time it is invoked, named for the mathematical concept of a function.*

A *function* is a special type of program that returns a single value each time it is invoked, named for the mathematical concept of a function. (You saw the Round function used in Example 3-12.) Because you will use the function to operate on a column, it will be invoked for each row and therefore will return a single value for each row the query handles. Sometimes the term *column function* is used to remind you that the function is being applied to a table or view column. An example of an ordinary column function is ROUND (or Round), which can be used to round numbers in various ways. Special classes of functions that combine multiple rows together into one row are called *aggregate* functions. The following table shows aggregate functions that are commonly used in relational databases:

Function Name	Description
AVG	Calculates the average value for a column
COUNT	Counts the number of values found in a column
MAX	Finds the maximum value in a column
MIN	Finds the minimum value in a column
SUM	Sums (totals up) the values in a column

If you use an aggregate function by itself in a query, you get one row back for the entire query. This makes sense, because there is no way for the RDBMS to know what other result you might want. So, if you want the aggregate result to be for *groups* of rows in the query, you need to include a GROUP BY specification to tell the RDBMS to group the rows by the values in one or more columns, and to apply the aggregate function to each group. This is much like asking for subtotals instead of a grand total for a list of numbers.

For this exercise, you want the RDBMS to provide a total of the calculated column SALE_PRICE for each movie genre. In other words, you want to group the rows by genre, and for each group, display a single row containing the genre and the total sale price dollar amount.

The MOVIE_TITLE and COPY_NUMBER columns are unnecessary because we need a total for each genre regardless of which movie copies are included in the details. They illustrate an important concept that most new-comers to relational databases have a difficult time understanding:

PROBLEM 3-1

If you select the MOVIE_GENRE_DESCRIPTION, MOVIE_TITLE, COPY_NUM-BER, and calculated SALE_PRICE columns, telling the RDBMS the formula for calculating the total price and asking it to group the rows in the result by genre, there is a hidden logic problem that will cause an error to be returned by the RDBMS. You have essentially asked the RDBMS to return the values of MOVIE_TITLE and COPY_NUMBER for every row in the query results, but, at the same time, to aggregate rows by MOVIE_GENRE_DESCRIPTION and provide the calculated total for each aggregate. It is illogical to ask for some rows to be aggregated and others not. To make matters worse, the resulting error message is rather cryptic. Small wonder that we often hear aggregate functions called "aggravating" functions.

SOLUTION

Remember this rule: Whenever a query includes an aggregate function, then *every* column in the query results must either be formed using an aggregate function or be named in the GROUP BY column list.

In Microsoft Access, the Totals icon (Σ) on the ribbon toggles (hides and exposes) a line called Total on the Query View panel. It is the total line that lets you specify aggregate functions and groupings for our query. Follow these steps:

1. You should be starting with a query specification from Example 3-12 as shown in Figure 3-37.

2. Remove the MOVIE_TITLE and COPY_NUMBER columns by clicking in the slim gray strip above the field names and pressing DELETE.

3. Change the label on the SALE_PRICE column to TOTAL_SALE_PRICE. This column name will make more sense in the results.

4. Click the Totals icon on the ribbon to expose the Total line in the query specification. By default, each column will initially have Group By specified on that line.

5. In the TOTAL_SALE_PRICE column, click in the Total line and use the pull-down list to select the Sum function.

6. In the MEDIA_FORMAT column, click the Total line and use the pull-down list to select the Where specification. This tells Access that the column is only used to filter rows and will not appear in the query results.

7. Click the Run icon on the ribbon to run your query. The completed panel is shown in Figure 3-39 with the query results shown in Figure 3-40.

8. To complete this exercise, close the Query Design panel either by clicking the Close button in the upper-right corner of the panel (being careful *not* to click the button at the upper-right of your Microsoft Access screen, because that will completely close the Access database), or by right-clicking the tab that shows the query name (most likely Query1) and choosing Close. When asked about saving the query, click No.

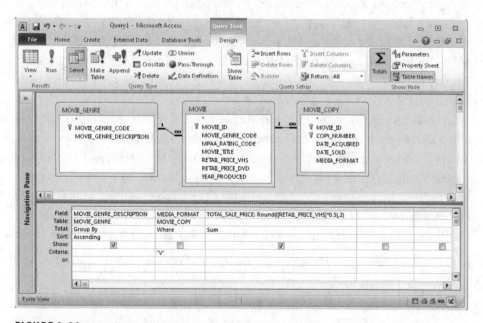

FIGURE 3-39 · Example 3-13 (Aggregate Functions), query design

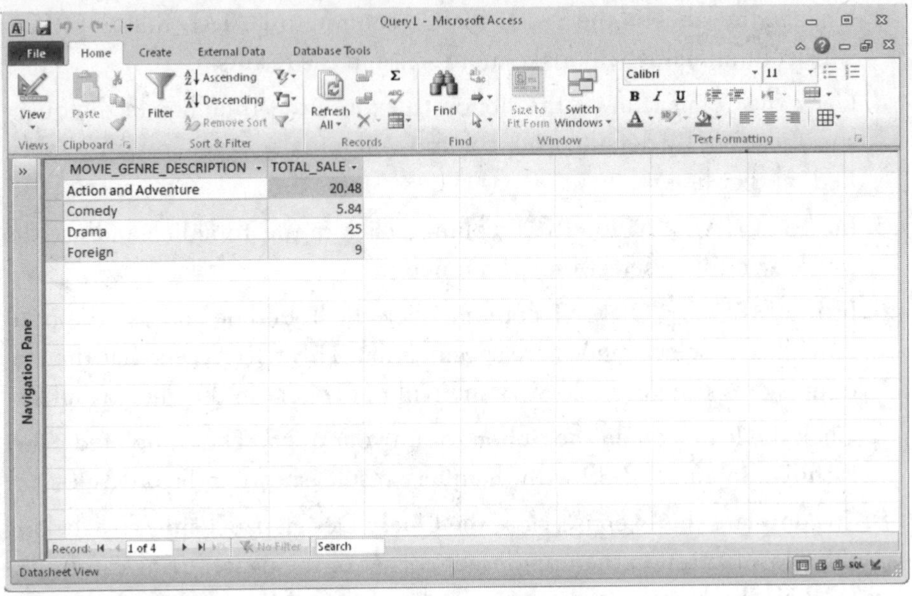

FIGURE 3-40 · Example 3-13 (Aggregate Functions), query results

Example 3-14: Self-Joins

When tables have a recursive relationship built into them, you must use a *self-join* (joining a table to itself) to resolve the relationship. In the video store database, the EMPLOYEE table contains such a relationship where SUPERVISOR_PER- SON_ID is a foreign key to the primary key PERSON_ID. The row for each employee can then contain the identifier of another row in the EMPLOYEE table which contains the information regarding their immediate supervisor.

In this example, suppose the store owner needs a report showing employees and a comparison of the hourly rate paid to employees and their supervisors. You will create a query that lists the ID, first name, last name, and hourly rate for each employee along with the manager's hourly rate. To get the manager's hourly rate, you will have to join the EMPLOYEE table to itself so that Access can match the SUPERVISOR_PERSON_ID (foreign key) to the row in the EMPLOYEE table that contains the manager's hourly rate. Follow these steps:

1. Create a new query by opening the Create ribbon and then clicking the Query Design icon.

2. When the Show Table dialog box opens, add the EMPLOYEE table to the query *twice*. This may seem odd at first, but this is the only way to tell Microsoft Access that you want to match each row in the EMPLOYEE

table with a different row (the manager's row) in the same table. Note that the tables are named EMPLOYEE and EMPLOYEE_1 on the panel, even though both are really two representations of the same table.

3. Also using the Show Table dialog box, add the PERSON table to the query. The PERSON table contains the names of all people associated with the video store, including employees.

4. You can minimize the Navigation Pane if you want (to reduce the visual clutter on the screen).

5. In the EMPLOYEE table, find the SUPERVISOR_PERSON_ID column. Click its name and (while holding down the mouse button) drag-and-drop the name onto the PERSON_ID column in the EMPLOYEE_1 table. This tells Access how to join the EMPLOYEE table to itself. The table on the left represents the employees, and the one on the right is where you will find each employee's manager. Don't be overly concerned if this still seems confusing—we will revisit recursive relationships in subsequent chapters in this book.

6. You want the supervisor's row to display, but since he has no manager in the table (this video store has only one supervisor), you need to change the join to an outer join to see his row. Double-click in the line between the two copies of the EMPLOYEE table, select option 2 in the Join Properties dialog box, and click OK.

7. From the PERSON table, select the PERSON_ID, PERSON_GIVEN_ NAME, and PERSON_FAMILY_NAME columns by double-clicking each.

8. From the EMPLOYEE table, select the EMPLOYEE_HOURLY_RATE column by double-clicking its name.

9. From the EMPLOYEE_1 table, select the EMPLOYEE_HOURLY_RATE column by double-clicking its name.

10. At this point, you have two columns in the query named EMPLOYEE_ HOURLY_RATE. You need to change one of them to avoid confusion and to comply with the RDBMS principle that every column have a unique name. In the EMPLOYEE_HOURLY_RATE column from the EMPLOYEE_1 table (the rightmost column in the query specification), click just to the left of the column name and enter **MANAGER_HOURLY_ RATE:**, which assigns an alias name to the query column.

11. Click the Run icon on the ribbon to run your query. The completed panel is shown on Figure 3-41 with the query results shown in Figure 3-42.

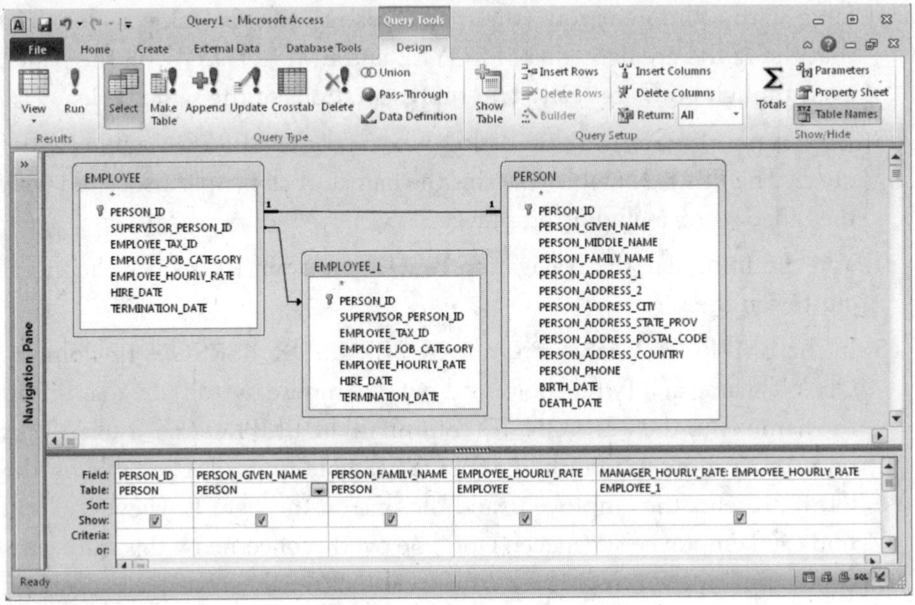

FIGURE 3-41 · Example 3-14 (Self-Joins), query design

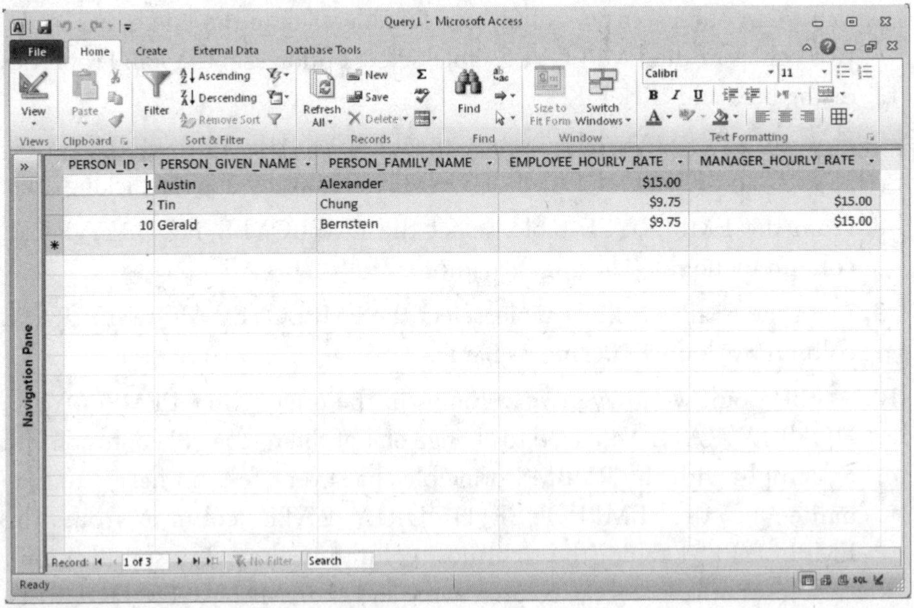

FIGURE 3-42 · Example 3-14 (Self-Joins), query results

Your results should be similar, but since you didn't specify a sort order, the order of rows in your results may be different.

12. To complete this exercise, close the Query Design panel either by clicking the Close box in the upper-right corner of the panel, or by right-clicking the tab that shows the query name (most likely Query1) and choosing Close. When asked about saving the query, click No. You can then close Microsoft Access if you want.

Summary

In the 14 examples in this chapter, you explored Microsoft Access queries in a manner intended to demonstrate the basic features that you will use the most. Obviously, there are many more features to explore. But it is time to move on to SQL, the topic of the next chapter.

QUIZ

Choose the correct responses to each of the multiple-choice and fill-in-the-blank questions. Note that there may be more than one correct response to each question.

1. **A forms-based query language:**
   A. Resembles SQL
   B. Describes how a query should be processed rather than what the results should be
   C. Was first developed by IBM in the 1980s
   D. Was shown to be clearly superior in controlled studies
   E. Uses a GUI (graphical user interface)

2. **The object types in Microsoft Access that relate strictly to database management (as opposed to application development) are**
   A. Modules
   B. Macros
   C. Forms
   D. Queries
   E. Tables

3. **When a table is deleted from the Microsoft Access Relationships panel, what happens next?**
   A. It is immediately deleted from the database.
   B. It remains unchanged in the database and is merely removed from the Relationships panel.
   C. It remains in the database, but all data rows are deleted.
   D. Relationships belonging to the table are also deleted.

4. **A column in the results of a Microsoft Access query can be formed from:**
   A. A table column
   B. A calculation
   C. A constant
   D. A query column
   E. All of the above

5. **Relationships on the Microsoft Access Relationships panel represent which object type in the database?**
   A. Queries
   B. Tables
   C. Primary keys
   D. Referential constraints
   E. Indexes

6. **A Cartesian product:**
   A. Results when a join between two tables in a query is not defined
   B. Results when a join between two tables in a query is incorrectly defined
   C. Results whenever a table is joined to itself
   D. Results when each row in one table is joined to every row in another table
   E. Can never happen in a Microsoft Access query

7. **In a query, the search criteria MPAA_RATING_CODE NOT = "PG" OR MPAA_RAT-ING_CODE NOT ="PG-13" will display:**
   A. An error message
   B. All the rows in the table except those in which the MPAA_RATING_CODE is "PG" or "PG-13"
   C. All the rows in the table
   D. All the rows in the table except those in which MPAA_RATING_CODE is NULL
   E. Only the rows in which MPAA_RATING_CODE is equal to "PG" or "PG-13"

8. **When an outer join is used, column data from tables (or views) in which no matching rows were found will contain:**
   A. Underscores (_)
   B. Asterisks (*)
   C. NULL values
   D. Spaces
   E. Xs

9. **The join connector between tables in a Microsoft Access query may:**
   A. Cause a Cartesian product if not defined between two tables or views in the query
   B. Be altered to define left, right, and full outer joins
   C. Be manually created by dragging a column from one table or view to a column of another table or view
   D. Be inherited from the metadata defined on the Relationships panel
   E. All of the above

10. **Criteria on different lines in a Microsoft Access query are connected with which logical operator?**
    A. GREATER THAN
    B. LESS THAN
    C. AND
    D. OR
    E. NOT

chapter 4

Introduction to SQL

This chapter introduces SQL, which has become the universal language for relational databases in that nearly every DBMS in modern use supports it. The reason for this wide acceptance is clearly the time and effort that went into the development of language features and standards, making SQL highly portable across different RDBMS products.

CHAPTER OBJECTIVES

In this chapter, the reader should:

- Understand the history of SQL.
- Learn how to write Data Query Language (DQL) statements in SQL to select data from database tables and views.
- Learn how to write Data Manipulation Language (DML) statements in SQL to update data in database tables.
- Understand how transactions support concurrent database access.
- Learn how to write Data Definition Language (DDL) statements in SQL to define, alter, and drop database objects.
- Learn how to write Data Control Language (DCL) statements to control database privileges.

> *SQL (Structured Query Language) is a computer language designed for managing data in relational database management systems (RDMSs).*

The video store database described in Appendix C is used to demonstrate SQL in this chapter. Appendix C also includes instructions for downloading the SQL statements required to create the video store database on MySQL, Microsoft SQL Server, and Oracle DBMSs, as well as an equivalent Microsoft Access 2000 database file. Throughout this chapter, I use MySQL to demonstrate SQL. The MySQL Community Server edition, with versions for Windows, Mac OS X, several versions of Linux, and several versions of Unix, is available free of charge from **http://www.mysql.com/downloads**. Except as noted in the examples, every command and feature demonstrated meets current SQL standards and therefore should work correctly in MySQL, SQL Server, Oracle, or any other DBMS that supports SQL. However, you may have to modify the downloaded SQL statements to run them on other DBMSs.

By convention, all the SQL statements are shown in uppercase. However, DBMS products are rarely case sensitive for SQL commands, so you may type the commands in uppercase, lowercase, or mixed case as you follow along on your own computer. However, do keep in mind that object names such as table names *are* case sensitive in some DBMS products. For example, MySQL is case sensitive for object names on platforms that are case sensitive, such as Linux and Unix. Moreover, data in many SQL DBMS implementations *is* case sensitive, so whenever you type a data value that is to be stored in the database or that is to be used to find data in the database, you must type it in the proper case.

As stated in the previous chapter, SQL is a command-based language. SQL statements are formed in clauses using keywords and parameters. The keywords used are usually reserved words for the DBMS, meaning they cannot be used for the names of database objects. The clauses usually have to be in a prescribed sequence. In most DBMS products, SQL statements must end with a semicolon (;). Although some RDBMSs are more forgiving, MySQL and Oracle, for example, will not run an SQL statement unless it ends with a semicolon. (Oracle allows a slash to be substituted for the semicolon.) Beyond these restrictions, the language is freeform, with one or more spaces separating language elements, and line breaks permitted between any two elements (but not in the middle of elements). SQL statements may be divided into the following categories:

- **Data Query Language (DQL)**   Statements that query the database but do not alter any data or database objects. This category contains the SE-LECT statement. Not all vendors make a distinction here; many lump DQL into DML, as defined next.

- **Data Manipulation Language (DML)**   Statements that modify data stored in database objects (that is, tables). This category contains the INSERT, UPDATE, and DELETE statements.

- **Data Definition Language (DDL)**   Statements that create and modify database objects. Whereas DML and DQL work with the data in the database objects, DDL works with the database objects themselves. Said another way, DDL manages the data *containers*, whereas DML manages the data *inside* the containers. This category includes the CREATE, ALTER, and DROP statements.

- **Data Control Language (DCL)**   Statements that manage privileges that database users have regarding the database objects. This category includes the GRANT and REVOKE statements.

Representative statements in each of these categories are presented in the sections that follow. But first, we'll cover a little bit of the history of the language.

The History of SQL

The forerunner of SQL, which was called SEQUEL (for Structured English Query Language), first emerged in the specifications for System R, IBM's experimental relational database, in the late 1970s. However, two other products, with various names for their query language, beat IBM to the marketplace with the first commercial relational database products: Relational Software's Oracle and Relational Technology's Ingres. IBM released SQL/DS in 1982, with the query language name shortened to "SQL" after IBM discovered that "SEQUEL" was a trademark of the Hawker-Siddeley Aircraft Company. When IBM released its next generation RDBMS, called DB2, the SQL acronym remained. To this day, you will hear the name pronounced as an acronym (*S-Q-L*) and as a word (*see-quel*), and both are considered correct pronunciations.

SQL standards committees were formed by ANSI (American National Standards Institute) in 1986 and ISO (International Organization for Standardization) in 1987. Fortunately, the two committees have collaborated well, so the ANSI and ISO standards are virtually identical. Two years later, the first standard specification, known as SQL-89, was published. The standard was expanded three years later into SQL-92, which weighed in at roughly 600 pages. The third generation was called SQL-99, or SQL3. Additional revisions were published in 2003 (SQL:2003), 2006 (SQL:2006), 2008 (SQL:2008), and work continues on the standard. The revisions published in 1999 and later incorporate many of the object features required for SQL to operate on an object-relational database, as well as language extensions to make SQL computationally complete (adding looping, branching, and case constructs) and additional features such as Extensible Markup Language (XML). Most current RDBMS products comply with the standard to one degree or another.

Nearly every vendor has added extensions to SQL, partly because they wanted to differentiate their products, and partly because market demands pressed them into implementing features before there were standards for them. One case in point is support for the DATE and TIMESTAMP data types. Dates are highly important in business data processing, but the developers of the original RDBMS products were computer scientists and academics, not business computing specialists, so such a need was unanticipated. As a result, the early SQL dialects did not have any special support for dates. As commercial products emerged, vendors responded to pressure from their biggest customers by hurriedly adding support for dates. Unfortunately, this led to each doing so in their own way. Whenever you migrate SQL statements from one vendor to another, beware of the SQL dialect differences. SQL is highly compatible and portable across vendor products, but complete database systems can seldom be moved without some adjustments.

Getting Started with MySQL

MySQL provides a simple command-line client tool for submitting SQL statements and viewing results. Other client tools are on the market, many requiring a license fee, but the command-line tool should work fine for our purposes.

The examples in this chapter focus on MySQL. However, if you are using a different RDBMS, there will be client tools for it as well, usually provided by the RDBMS vendor. For example, Sybase has a tool called iSQL, whereas Microsoft SQL Server has a GUI tool called Management Studio as well as a command-line tool called oSQL. Oracle has several GUI tools available as well as a command-line implementation called SQL*Plus. There are also a number of third-party query tools that work with popular RDBMS products. For example, Quest Software markets versions of Toad for Oracle, SQL Server, DB2, and MySQL, and also provides freeware versions that have reduced functionality (see **www.toadsoft.com**). If you are using a DBMS installed on a system other than a personal computer, you may require the assistance of a DBA or system administrator while properly setting up a database account so you can access a database and run the various SQL statements demonstrated in this chapter.

Follow this simple procedure to start the MySQL command-line query tool and connect to the database. (The procedure for installing the video store sample database on MySQL is located in Appendix C.)

1. Launch the MySQL Command Line Client. On Windows systems, you will find it on the Start menu under MySQL and then MySQL Server $x.y$ ($x.y$ being the version number, such as 5.1).

2. Enter the MySQL root password when prompted. (The root password is entered during the MySQL installation process.)

3. To connect to the video_store database, enter the following command. (As mentioned, on some platforms such as Windows, object names like VIDEO_STORE are not case sensitive.)

   ```
   use VIDEO_STORE
   ```

Figure 4-1 shows the MySQL command-line window after successful connection to the database.

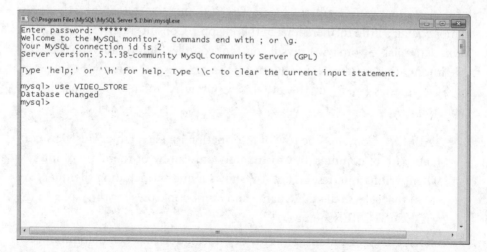

```
C:\Program Files\MySQL\MySQL Server 5.1\bin\mysql.exe
Enter password: ******
Welcome to the MySQL monitor.  Commands end with ; or \g.
Your MySQL connection id is 2
Server version: 5.1.38-community MySQL Community Server (GPL)

Type 'help;' or '\h' for help. Type '\c' to clear the current input statement.

mysql> use VIDEO_STORE
Database changed
mysql>
```

FIGURE 4-1 · MySQL command-line window after successful connection

Where's the Data?

You probably noticed that while command-line SQL clients help you format and run SQL statements, they don't provide an easy way for you to see the names and definitions of the database objects available to you. This is a typical arrangement for an RDBMS. If you are not familiar with the database schema you are using, you can obtain some basic information from one of three sources: documentation provided by the database designer or DBA, *catalog views* (special views provided by the RDBMS that present database metadata that describes the database contents), or a tool such as Toad for MySQL. You may have noticed that I included a PDF file of the ERD for the video store database in the ZIP file that you can download from the web site (see Appendix C) as a way of documenting the sample database.

> *Catalog views are special views provided by the RDBMS that present database metadata and describe database contents.*

Finding Database Objects Using Catalog Views

MySQL supports a set of catalog views called the information_schema (as defined in the ANSI/ISO SQL standard) that may be queried to show the names and definitions of all database objects available to a database user. Most other RDBMSs have a similar capability, but of course, the names of the views vary. By issuing a SELECT statement against any of these views, you may display information about your database objects. The SQL SELECT statement is described in more detail a little further along in this chapter. Consult the *MySQL Reference Manual* (available from **www.mysql.com**) for complete information on the available information_schema views. Here are the most useful ones for people writing SQL queries (many of the others are intended for use in managing the database):

- **TABLES**   Contains one row of information for each table. This view contains a lot of columns, but fortunately only a few of them are of interest when writing queries. Figure 4-2 shows a query (including the query results) that selects the table name and number of rows for the tables in the VIDEO_STORE schema.

- **COLUMNS**   Contains one row of information for each column in each database table. In addition to the schema name, table name, and column

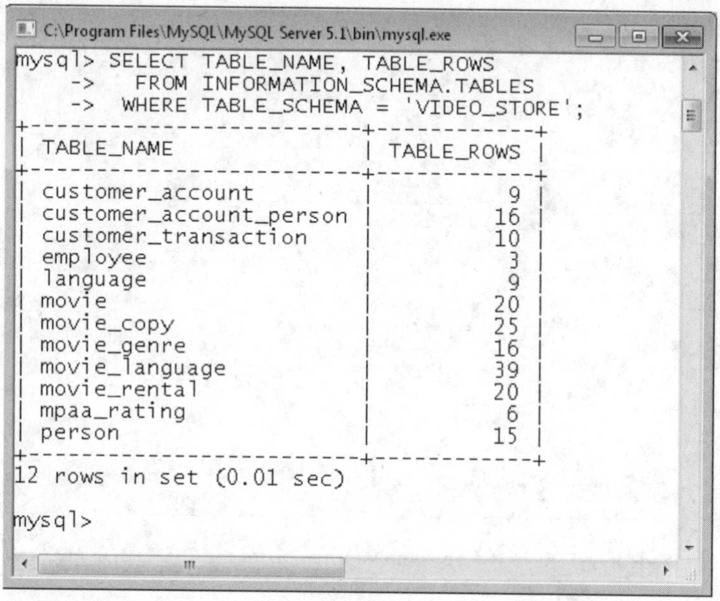

```
C:\Program Files\MySQL\MySQL Server 5.1\bin\mysql.exe
mysql> SELECT TABLE_NAME, TABLE_ROWS
    ->   FROM INFORMATION_SCHEMA.TABLES
    ->  WHERE TABLE_SCHEMA = 'VIDEO_STORE';
+-------------------------+------------+
| TABLE_NAME              | TABLE_ROWS |
+-------------------------+------------+
| customer_account        |          9 |
| customer_account_person |         16 |
| customer_transaction    |         10 |
| employee                |          3 |
| language                |          9 |
| movie                   |         20 |
| movie_copy              |         25 |
| movie_genre             |         16 |
| movie_language          |         39 |
| movie_rental            |         20 |
| mpaa_rating             |          6 |
| person                  |         15 |
+-------------------------+------------+
12 rows in set (0.01 sec)

mysql>
```

FIGURE 4-2 • Select table name and number of rows for the VIDEO_STORE schema

name, the information includes the column's data type, length, precision, scale, and so forth.

- **TABLE_CONSTRAINTS** Contains one row of information for each constraint placed on a table.
- **KEY_COLUMN_USAGE** Contains one row of information for each table column that participates in a unique or primary key constraint on that table.
- **VIEWS** Contains one row of information for each view defined in the database.

Viewing Database Objects Using Toad for MySQL

For those less inclined to type SQL commands, GUI tools are available from RDBMS vendors as well as from third parties. Although MySQL offers a free version of MySQL Workbench, I have found it more useful for database design than for viewing existing database objects. Therefore, I prefer Toad for MySQL (available from **www.toadsoft.com**) over MySQL Workbench for this purpose. It is also a very good GUI client for running SQL statements and viewing results.

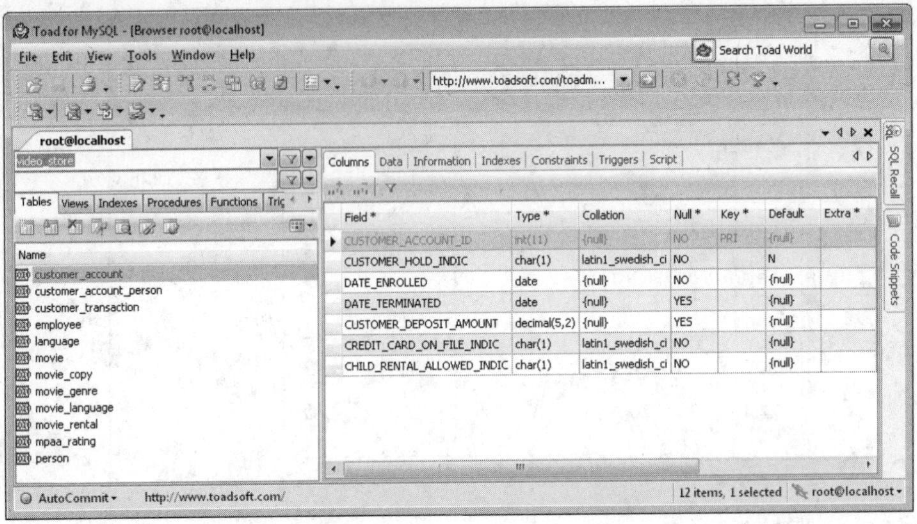

FIGURE 4-3 · Toad for MySQL showing column information for the CUSTOMER_ACCOUNT table

Figure 4-3 shows Toad for MySQL, listing the tables in the VIDEO_STORE database along the left margin and information about the columns in the CUSTOMER_ACCOUNT table to the right.

You've seen a little bit of the SQL SELECT statement so far. In the next section, we take a detailed look at SQL.

Data Query Language (DQL): The SELECT Statement

The SELECT statement retrieves data from the database. The clauses of the statement, as demonstrated in the following sections, are as follows:

- **SELECT**   Lists the columns that are to be returned in the results
- **FROM**   Lists the tables or views from which data is to be selected
- **WHERE**   Provides conditions for the selection of rows in the results
- **ORDER BY**   Specifies the order in which rows are to be returned
- **GROUP BY**   Groups rows for various aggregate functions

Although it is customary in SQL to write keywords in uppercase, this is not necessary in most implementations. The RDBMS SQL interpreter will usually recognize keywords written in uppercase, lowercase, or mixed case. As mentioned, MySQL is case sensitive on platforms that are case sensitive (Linux and Unix), but not on other platforms such as Windows. In fact, you may have noticed that even though I used uppercase names for all the database objects in the script that creates them, the names are shown as lowercase within MySQL. Be careful with other RDMS products, however. For example, Oracle is always case insensitive for object names (and it shifts all lowercase names to uppercase in its catalog tables—just the opposite of what MySQL has done on my Windows laptop), but both Sybase and MS SQL Server can be set to a case-sensitive mode where object names written in different cases are treated as *different* objects. In case-sensitive mode, the following names would be considered *different* tables: MOVIE, Movie, movie.

Example 4-1: Listing Everything in a Table

The asterisk (*) symbol may be used in place of a column list in order to select all columns in a table or view. This is a useful feature for quickly listing data, but it should be avoided in statements that will be reused—it compromises logical data independence because any new column will be automatically selected the next time the statement is run. Note also that in SQL syntax, tables, views, and *synonyms* (an alias for a table or view) are all referenced in the same way. It should follow that the names of these come for the same *namespace*, meaning that a name of a table, for example, must be unique among all tables, views, and synonyms defined in a particular schema. Figure 4-4 shows the query and query results using Toad.

Toad for MySQL - [Editor Untitled1*]

File Edit Editor Debug View Tools Window Help

http://www.toadsoft.com/toadm...

video_store

Editor Untitled1*

```
select * from movie;
```

Results

Result Sets | Messages | Explain Plan | Pivot & Chart

Set 1

MOVIE_ID *	MOVIE_GENRE_CODE *	MPAA_RATING_CODE *	MOVIE_TITLE *	RETAIL_PRICE_VHS	RETAIL_PRICE_DVD	YEAR_PROD
1	Drama	R	Crash	58.97	19.96	2005
2	ActAd	PG-13	The Dark Knight	15.95	19.96	2008
3	Comdy	R	Little Miss Sunshine	14.95	29.99	2006
4	ActAd	PG-13	Casino Royale	16.95	19.99	2006
5	ActAd	R	Blood Diamond	24.99	29.99	2006
6	ActAd	PG-13	Pirates of the Caribbean: The Curse of the Black Pearl	24.99	29.99	2003
7	Drama	PG-13	The Curious Case of Benjamin Button	14.95	19.94	2006
8	ActAd	R	Iron Man	50.99	29.98	2008
9	ActAd	R	Into the Wild	12.98	39.99	2007
10	Drama	R	The Departed	49.99	14.98	2006
11	Rmce	PG	The Lake House	12.95	14.97	2006
12	Comdy	PG-13	The Bucket List	9.95	19.94	2007

Record 1 of 20

AutoCommit | http://www.toad | Code | Ready | Ln 1 | Col 21 | Off 20 | Len 0 | root@localhost

FIGURE 4-4 · Query listing entire MOVIE table

I used Toad for this example because a command-line interface wraps query result lines when they are wider than the command window. This makes the results of a query like the one in this example very difficult to read.

Example 4-2: Limiting Columns to Display

To specify the columns to be selected, provide a comma-separated list following the SELECT keyword. Keep in mind that the list actually provides *expressions* that describe the columns desired in the query results, and although many times these expressions are merely column names from tables or views, they may also be any constant or formula that SQL can interpret and form into data values for the column. The examples that follow show you how to use formulas and constants to form query columns. Following is a query that selects only the MOVIE_ GENRE_CODE and MOVIE_TITLE columns from the MOVIE table.

```
SELECT MOVIE_GENRE_CODE, MOVIE_TITLE
  FROM MOVIE;
```

```
+-----------------+-----------------------------------------------------------+
| MOVIE_GENRE_CODE | MOVIE_TITLE                                              |
+-----------------+-----------------------------------------------------------+
| Drama           | Crash                                                     |
| ActAd           | The Dark Knight                                           |
| Comdy           | Little Miss Sunshine                                      |
| ActAd           | Casino Royale                                             |
| ActAd           | Blood Diamond                                             |
| ActAd           | Pirates of the Caribbean: The Curse of the Black Pearl|
| Drama           | The Curious Case of Benjamin Button                       |
| ActAd           | Iron Man                                                  |
| ActAd           | Into the Wild                                             |
| Drama           | The Departed                                              |
| Rmce            | The Lake House                                            |
| Comdy           | The Bucket List                                           |
| Comdy           | Stranger Than Fiction                                     |
| Drama           | Gran Torino                                               |
| Drama           | Charlie Wilson's War                                      |
| Comdy           | The Devil Wears Prada                                     |
| Rmce            | 13 Going on 30                                            |
| Drama           | Monster                                                   |
| ActAd           | Live Free or Die Hard (Die Hard 4)                        |
| Forgn           | Das Boot                                                  |
+-----------------+-----------------------------------------------------------+
20 rows in set (0.00 sec)
```

The last line shown in the result set, known as *feedback*, shows whether the SQL statement processed successfully along with other information such as row counts or error messages. The format varies from one RDBMS product to another.

Example 4-3: Sorting Results

Just as in Microsoft Access, SQL has no guarantee as to the sequence of the rows in the query results unless the desired sequence is specified in the query. In SQL, providing a comma-separated list following the ORDER BY keyword does this. In the previous example, the query results would be more useful if they were sorted by the movie genre and then the movie title. Following is a query that does just that.

```
SELECT MOVIE_GENRE_CODE, MOVIE_TITLE
  FROM MOVIE
 ORDER BY MOVIE_GENRE_CODE, MOVIE_TITLE;
```

```
+------------------+-----------------------------------------------------+
| MOVIE_GENRE_CODE | MOVIE_TITLE                                         |
+------------------+-----------------------------------------------------+
| ActAd            | Blood Diamond                                       |
| ActAd            | Casino Royale                                       |
| ActAd            | Into the Wild                                       |
| ActAd            | Iron Man                                            |
| ActAd            | Live Free or Die Hard (Die Hard 4)                  |
| ActAd            | Pirates of the Caribbean: The Curse of the Black Pearl|
| ActAd            | The Dark Knight                                     |
| Comdy            | Little Miss Sunshine                                |
| Comdy            | Stranger Than Fiction                               |
| Comdy            | The Bucket List                                     |
| Comdy            | The Devil Wears Prada                               |
| Drama            | Charlie Wilson's War                                |
| Drama            | Crash                                               |
| Drama            | Gran Torino                                         |
| Drama            | Monster                                             |
| Drama            | The Curious Case of Benjamin Button                 |
| Drama            | The Departed                                        |
| Forgn            | Das Boot                                            |
| Rmce             | 13 Going on 30                                      |
| Rmce             | The Lake House                                      |
+------------------+-----------------------------------------------------+
20 rows in set (0.00 sec)
```

Also note the following points:

- Ascending sequence is the default for each column named in the ORDER BY clause, but the keyword ASC may be added after the column name for ascending sequence, and DESC may be added for descending sequence.

- The column(s) named in the ORDER BY list do not have to be included in the query results (that is, the SELECT list). However, this is not the best human engineering.

- Instead of column names, the relative position of the columns in the results may be listed. The number provided has no correlation with the column position in the source table or view, however. This option is frowned upon in formal SQL (and no longer supported in the SQL standard) because someone changing the query at a later time might shuffle columns around in the SELECT list and not realize that, in doing so, they are changing the columns used for sorting results. In Example 4-3, the following ORDER BY clause achieves the same query results: ORDER BY 1, 2.

Choosing Rows to Display

SQL uses the WHERE clause for the selection of rows to display. Without a WHERE clause, all rows found in the source tables and/or views are displayed. When a WHERE clause is included, the rules of Boolean algebra, named for logician George Boole, are used to evaluate the WHERE clause for each row of data. Only rows for which the WHERE clause evaluates to a logical "True" are displayed in the query results.

As you will see in the examples that follow, individual tests of conditions must evaluate to either "True" or "False." The conditional operators supported are the same ones shown in Chapter 3 in Example 3-7 (=, <, <=, >, >=, and <>). If multiple conditions are tested in a single WHERE clause, the outcomes of these conditions can be combined together using logical operators such as AND, OR, and NOT. Parentheses may be (and should be) added to complex statements for clarity and to control the logical order in which the conditions are evaluated. A rather complicated order of precedence is used when multiple logical operators appear in one statement. However, it is far simpler to remember that conditions inside a pair of parentheses are always evaluated first, and to simply include enough sets of parentheses so there can be no doubt as to the order in which the conditions are evaluated.

Example 4-4: A Simple WHERE Clause

The following query shows a simple WHERE clause that selects only rows where RETAIL_PRICE_DVD is less than or equal to 20.00. Notice that the column(s) used to filter rows do not have to be included in the query results. However, in many cases it may be a good idea to include them so you can check your results for correctness.

```
SELECT MOVIE_GENRE_CODE, MOVIE_TITLE
  FROM MOVIE
 WHERE RETAIL_PRICE_DVD <= 20.00
```

```
ORDER BY MOVIE_GENRE_CODE, MOVIE_TITLE;
```

```
+-------------------+-------------------------------------+
| MOVIE_GENRE_CODE  | MOVIE_TITLE                         |
+-------------------+-------------------------------------+
| ActAd             | Casino Royale                       |
| ActAd             | The Dark Knight                     |
| Comdy             | Stranger Than Fiction               |
| Comdy             | The Bucket List                     |
| Drama             | Charlie Wilson's War                |
| Drama             | Crash                               |
| Drama             | The Curious Case of Benjamin Button |
| Drama             | The Departed                        |
| Forgn             | Das Boot                            |
| Rmce              | The Lake House                      |
+-------------------+-------------------------------------+
10 rows in set (0.00 sec)
```

Example 4-5: The BETWEEN Operator

SQL provides the BETWEEN operator to assist in finding ranges of values. The endpoints *are* included in the returned rows. The following query shows the use of the BETWEEN operator to find all rows where RETAIL_PRICE_DVD is greater than or equal to 15.00 and RETAIL_PRICE_DVD is less than or equal to 20.00:

```
SELECT MOVIE_GENRE_CODE, MOVIE_TITLE
  FROM MOVIE
 WHERE RETAIL_PRICE_DVD BETWEEN 15.00 AND 20.00
 ORDER BY MOVIE_GENRE_CODE, MOVIE_TITLE;
```

```
+-------------------+-------------------------------------+
| MOVIE_GENRE_CODE  | MOVIE_TITLE                         |
+-------------------+-------------------------------------+
| ActAd             | Casino Royale                       |
| ActAd             | The Dark Knight                     |
| Comdy             | Stranger Than Fiction               |
| Comdy             | The Bucket List                     |
| Drama             | Crash                               |
| Drama             | The Curious Case of Benjamin Button |
| Forgn             | Das Boot                            |
+-------------------+-------------------------------------+
7 rows in set (0.00 sec)
```

Here's an alternative way to write the equivalent WHERE clause:

```
WHERE RETAIL_PRICE_DVD >= 15.00
  AND RETAIL_PRICE_DVD <= 20.00
```

Example 4-6: The LIKE Operator

For searching character columns, SQL provides the LIKE operator, which compares the character string in the column to a pattern, returning a logical "True" if the column matches the pattern, and "False" if not. The underscore character (_) may be used as a positional *wildcard*, meaning it matches any character in that position of the character string being evaluated. The percent sign (%) may be used as a nonpositional wildcard, meaning it matches any number of characters for any length. Note that Microsoft Access has a similar feature, but the wildcard characters are different (they match those in DOS and Visual Basic): the question mark (?) is the positional wildcard, and the asterisk (*) is the nonpositional wildcard. The following table provides some examples:

Pattern	Interpretation
%Now	Matches any character string that ends with "Now"
Now%	Matches any character string that begins with "Now"
%Now%	Matches any character string that contains "Now" (whether at the beginning, the end, or in the middle)
N_w	Matches any string of exactly three characters, where the first character is "N" and the third character is "w"
%N_w%	Matches any string that contains the character "N" followed by any character, which is in turn followed by the character "w" and continues with any number of characters

Suppose we are searching for a person named Steven, but we are not sure if his first name is written as Steve, Steven, or Stephen in the database. The following query finds all persons whose first name begins with "Ste".

```
SELECT PERSON_ID, PERSON_GIVEN_NAME, PERSON_FAMILY_NAME
  FROM PERSON
 WHERE PERSON_GIVEN_NAME LIKE 'Ste%';
```

```
+-----------+--------------------+--------------------+
| PERSON_ID | PERSON_GIVEN_NAME  | PERSON_FAMILY_NAME |
+-----------+--------------------+--------------------+
|        12 | Steven             | Bernstein          |
+-----------+--------------------+--------------------+
1 row in set (0.00 sec)
```

Example 4-7: Compound Conditions Using OR

As stated earlier, multiple conditions may be combined using the OR operator. The following query shows a WHERE clause that selects rows having either a PERSON_GIVEN_NAME column beginning with "Ste" *or* a PERSON_ADDRESS_CITY column equal to "Los Angeles".

```
SELECT PERSON_GIVEN_NAME, PERSON_FAMILY_NAME, PERSON_ADDRESS_CITY
  FROM PERSON
 WHERE PERSON_GIVEN_NAME LIKE 'Ste%'
    OR PERSON_ADDRESS_CITY = 'Los Angeles';
+--------------------+--------------------+---------------------+
| PERSON_GIVEN_NAME  | PERSON_FAMILY_NAME | PERSON_ADDRESS_CITY |
+--------------------+--------------------+---------------------+
| Gerald             | Bernstein          | Los Angeles         |
| Rose               | Bernstein          | Los Angeles         |
| Steven             | Bernstein          | Los Angeles         |
+--------------------+--------------------+---------------------+
3 rows in set (0.00 sec)
```

The next query changes the OR operator from Example 4-7 to the AND operator. Note that only one row is returned now because both conditions must be true for a row to appear in the query results.

```
SELECT PERSON_GIVEN_NAME, PERSON_FAMILY_NAME, PERSON_ADDRESS_CITY
  FROM PERSON
 WHERE PERSON_GIVEN_NAME LIKE 'Ste%'
   AND PERSON_ADDRESS_CITY = 'Los Angeles';

+--------------------+--------------------+---------------------+
| PERSON_GIVEN_NAME  | PERSON_FAMILY_NAME | PERSON_ADDRESS_CITY |
+--------------------+--------------------+---------------------+
| Steven             | Bernstein          | Los Angeles         |
+--------------------+--------------------+---------------------+
1 row in set (0.00 sec)
```

Example 4-8: The Subquery

A very powerful feature of SQL is the *subquery* (or *subselect*), which, as the name implies, refers to a SELECT statement that contains a subordinate SELECT statement. This can be a very flexible way of selecting data.

> A subquery refers to a query (SELECT statement) that is contained in, and thus is subordinate to, another query.

Let's assume that we want to list the customer account ID for Steven Bernstein, but we don't know his Person ID. We could run one query to find his Person ID (the primary key of the PERSON table) and then run another one to find the CUSTOMER_ACCOUNT table rows that include his Person ID. However, it's much simpler to do both steps in a single query like the following. Note that SQL syntax requires the subquery to be enclosed in a pair of parentheses.

```
SELECT CUSTOMER_ACCOUNT_ID
  FROM CUSTOMER_ACCOUNT_PERSON
 WHERE PERSON_ID =
   (SELECT PERSON_ID
      FROM PERSON
     WHERE PERSON_GIVEN_NAME = 'Steven'
       AND PERSON_FAMILY_NAME = 'Bernstein');


+----------------------+
| CUSTOMER_ACCOUNT_ID |
+----------------------+
|                  7 |
+----------------------+
1 row in set (0.00 sec)
```

The main query is sometimes called the *outer* query, and the subquery (the one enclosed in parentheses) is sometimes called the *inner* query. For this query, the SQL engine will run the inner query first and then use its result set to filter rows when it runs the outer query. Note that I used the equal-to operator in the outer query to compare the PERSON_ID in the CUSTOMER table with the result from the inner query. This works fine if the inner query never returns more than a single value. However, if the inner query returns multiple values, the SQL statement will fail with an error condition. Given that people's names are never guaranteed to be unique, it's safer in a situation like this to use the IN operator instead of the equal-to operator. The difference is that IN returns a Boolean "True" if any value in the result set returned by the inner query matches whatever we are comparing it with in the outer query. Here is the same query changed to use the IN operator:

```
SELECT CUSTOMER_ACCOUNT_ID
  FROM CUSTOMER_ACCOUNT_PERSON
 WHERE PERSON_ID IN
   (SELECT PERSON_ID
      FROM PERSON
     WHERE PERSON_GIVEN_NAME = 'Steven'
       AND PERSON_FAMILY_NAME = 'Bernstein');
```

This subquery is called a *noncorrelated* subquery because the inner query does not refer to any values from the outer query. This is why the SQL engine can run the inner query just once to obtain the result set and then can use that result set to run the outer query. Let's look at another query using a subquery. The video store manager is looking at the effect of a recent price increase, and needs a list of transactions (TRANSACTION_IDs) where the customer paid more than the average fee (RENTAL_FEE) for a movie. Here is the query:

```
SELECT DISTINCT TRANSACTION_ID
  FROM MOVIE_RENTAL
 WHERE RENTAL_FEE >
   (SELECT AVG(RENTAL_FEE)
     FROM MOVIE_RENTAL);
```

```
+----------------+
| TRANSACTION_ID |
+----------------+
|              9 |
|             10 |
+----------------+
2 rows in set (0.00 sec)
```

The inner query finds the average rental fee and then the outer query finds all rows in the MOVIE_RENTAL table with a RENTAL_FEE that exceeds the average. Hopefully you recognized the AVG function, which was introduced in Example 3-12 in Chapter 3. We will review using aggregate functions in an upcoming SQL example. While IN and NOT IN are the most common operators used to connect subqueries to outer queries, in this case the subquery returns only one row, and therefore we can use the greater than (>) operator for comparison. The DISTINCT keyword eliminates any duplicate transaction IDs.

Unlike a noncorrelated subquery, a *correlated subquery* is a subquery where the inner select refers to values provided by the outer select. These are far less efficient than noncorrelated subqueries because the inner query must be invoked for each row found by the outer query. Recall that with a noncorrelated subquery, the inner query is only run once.

A correlated subquery is a subquery where the inner select refers to values provided by the outer select.

Suppose the video store wishes to mail a discount coupon to any customer who paid more than $15 in rental fees in any single rental transaction. To do this we must find the transactions in the CUSTOMER_TRANSACTION table where the sum of rental fees for the transaction in the MOVIE_RENTAL table is greater than 15. Here is the query:

```
SELECT DISTINCT CUSTOMER_ACCOUNT_ID
  FROM CUSTOMER_TRANSACTION A
 WHERE 15 <
   (SELECT SUM(RENTAL_FEE)
      FROM MOVIE_RENTAL B
     WHERE A.TRANSACTION_ID = B.TRANSACTION_ID);
```

```
+---------------------+
| CUSTOMER_ACCOUNT_ID |
+---------------------+
|                   2 |
|                   7 |
|                   9 |
+---------------------+
3 rows in set (0.00 sec)
```

Note the aliases (A and B) assigned to the table names in the inner and outer queries and the use of them in the WHERE clause in the inner query. This is the hallmark of a correlated subquery. (Table aliases are explained fully in Example 4-12 later in this chapter.) The outer select finds a distinct list of CUSTOMER_ACCOUNT_ID values in the CUSTOMER_TRANSACTION_TABLE. For each value found, the value is passed to the inner query, which is run to find the sum of rental fees for that transaction. If the sum of rental fees is greater than 15 (actually expressed in the query as "if 15 is less than the sum of rental fees"), then the WHERE clause in the outer select evaluates to "True," and the corresponding CUSTOMER_ID is added to the result set.

Joining Tables

Example 4-9: The Cartesian Product

As you learned previously in Example 3-8 in Chapter 3, we need to join tables (or views) whenever we need data from more than one table in our query results. In SQL, you specify joins by listing the tables or views to be joined in a comma-separated list in the FROM clause of the SELECT statement. However, SQL is not going to remind you to tell the RDBMS how to match rows in the tables (or views) being joined. If you forget, you will get a Cartesian product, as shown in the following query:

```
SELECT MOVIE_ID, MOVIE_GENRE_DESCRIPTION, MOVIE_TITLE
  FROM MOVIE, MOVIE_GENRE
```

```
ORDER BY MOVIE_ID;
```

```
+-----------+------------------------------+------------------+
| MOVIE_ID  | MOVIE_GENRE_DESCRIPTION      | MOVIE_TITLE      |
+-----------+------------------------------+------------------+
|         1 | Children and Family          | Crash            |
|         1 | Music and Musicals           | Crash            |
|         1 | Foreign                      | Crash            |
|         1 | Thrillers                    | Crash            |
|         1 | Comedy                       | Crash            |
|         1 | Science Fiction and Fantasy  | Crash            |
|         1 | Anime and Animation          | Crash            |
|         1 | Independent                  | Crash            |
|         1 | Drama                        | Crash            |
|         1 | Sports                       | Crash            |
|         1 | Classics                     | Crash            |
|         1 | Romance                      | Crash            |
|         1 | Action and Adventure         | Crash            |
|         1 | Horror                       | Crash            |
|         1 | Documentary                  | Crash            |
|         1 | Special Interest             | Crash            |
|         2 | Comedy                       | The Dark Knight  |
|         2 | Science Fiction and Fantasy  | The Dark Knight  |
|         2 | Anime and Animation          | The Dark Knight  |
|         2 | Independent                  | The Dark Knight  |
|         2 | Drama                        | The Dark Knight  |
|         2 | Sports                       | The Dark Knight  |
|         2 | Classics                     | The Dark Knight  |
|         2 | Romance                      | The Dark Knight  |
|         2 | Action and Adventure         | The Dark Knight  |
|         2 | Horror                       | The Dark Knight  |
|         2 | Documentary                  | The Dark Knight  |
|         2 | Special Interest             | The Dark Knight  |
|         2 | Children and Family          | The Dark Knight  |
|         2 | Music and Musicals           | The Dark Knight  |
|         2 | Foreign                      | The Dark Knight  |
|         2 | Thrillers                    | The Dark Knight  |
    . . .       . . .                            . . .
+-----------+------------------------------+------------------+
320 rows in set (0.00 sec)
```

PROBLEM 4-1

Whenever you write a new query, you should apply a "reasonableness" test to the results. Example 4-9 looks fine on the surface, but when you consider that there are only 20 movies in the sample database, you realize something is horribly wrong. How could we possibly get 320 rows simply by joining the MOVIE and MOVIE_GENRE tables?

SOLUTION

We failed to include a join specification, so the RDBMS created a Cartesian product for us, joining each movie with *every* genre, and 20 movies × 16 genres = 320 rows. Oops!

Example 4-10: The Inner Join of Two Tables

The following query shows the correction, which involves adding a JOIN clause that tells the DBMS to match the MOVIE_GENRE_CODE column in the MOVIE table (the foreign key) to the MOVIE_GENRE_CODE column in the MOVIE_GENRE table (the primary key). Now we get a much more reasonable result with 20 rows.

```
SELECT MOVIE_ID, MOVIE_GENRE_DESCRIPTION AS GENRE, MOVIE_TITLE
  FROM MOVIE JOIN MOVIE_GENRE
       ON MOVIE.MOVIE_GENRE_CODE = MOVIE_GENRE.MOVIE_GENRE_CODE
  ORDER BY MOVIE_ID;
```

```
+----------+----------------------+-------------------------------------+
| MOVIE_ID | GENRE                | MOVIE_TITLE                         |
+----------+----------------------+-------------------------------------+
|        1 | Drama                | Crash                               |
|        2 | Action and Adventure | The Dark Knight                     |
|        3 | Comedy               | Little Miss Sunshine                |
|        4 | Action and Adventure | Casino Royale                       |
|        5 | Action and Adventure | Blood Diamond                       |
|        6 | Action and Adventure | Pirates of the Caribbean: The Curse of|
|        7 | Drama                | The Curious Case of Benjamin Button |
|        8 | Action and Adventure | Iron Man                            |
|        9 | Action and Adventure | Into the Wild                       |
|       10 | Drama                | The Departed                        |
|       11 | Romance              | The Lake House                      |
|       12 | Comedy               | The Bucket List                     |
|       13 | Comedy               | Stranger Than Fiction               |
|       14 | Drama                | Gran Torino                         |
|       15 | Drama                | Charlie Wilson's War                |
|       16 | Comedy               | The Devil Wears Prada               |
|       17 | Romance              | 13 Going on 30                      |
|       18 | Drama                | Monster                             |
|       19 | Action and Adventure | Live Free or Die Hard (Die Hard 4)  |
|       20 | Foreign              | Das Boot                            |
+----------+----------------------+-------------------------------------+
20 rows in set (0.14 sec)
```

You may see queries where the join logic is included in the WHERE clause. This is an older way of writing joins in SQL that predates the introduction of the JOIN clause. I prefer the JOIN clause because it separates the join logic from *predicates* (row selection conditions) in the WHERE clause intended to filter (eliminate) rows from the result set. Also, as you will see shortly, the JOIN clause permits us to write outer joins using the same syntax as inner joins—this had to be done using vendor proprietary syntax in the days before the introduction of the JOIN clause.

> *An inner join is a join of two tables where the query results contain only rows that were matched in both of the tables being joined.*

Example 4-11: Outer Join

In the previous example, notice that of the 16 different genres, only 5 of them show up in the query results. The explanation for this lies in the fact that we performed an inner (or standard) join. Rows were returned only when a matching movie row was found for a genre—and there are 11 movie genres for which the sample database has no movies listed. We can correct this problem by changing our inner join to an outer join. In this case, we want all rows from the MOVIE_GENRE table, even if no matching row is found in the MOVIE table for some employees.

> *An outer join is a join between two tables where the query results contain both matched and unmatched rows.*

The following query lists all the movie genre descriptions, along with movies that match them. For genres that have no matching movies, any data selected from the MOVIE table for that row will have no value and thus be set to NULL in the query results.

```
SELECT MOVIE_GENRE_DESCRIPTION AS GENRE, MOVIE_TITLE
   FROM MOVIE_GENRE LEFT OUTER JOIN MOVIE
       ON MOVIE_GENRE.MOVIE_GENRE_CODE = MOVIE.MOVIE_GENRE_CODE
   ORDER BY MOVIE_GENRE_DESCRIPTION;
```

GENRE	MOVIE_TITLE
Action and Adventure	The Dark Knight
Action and Adventure	Casino Royale
Action and Adventure	Blood Diamond
Action and Adventure	Pirates of the Caribbean: The Curse of the
Action and Adventure	Iron Man
Action and Adventure	Into the Wild
Action and Adventure	Live Free or Die Hard (Die Hard 4)
Anime and Animation	NULL
Children and Family	NULL
Classics	NULL
Comedy	Little Miss Sunshine
Comedy	The Bucket List
Comedy	Stranger Than Fiction
Comedy	The Devil Wears Prada
Documentary	NULL
Drama	Crash
Drama	The Curious Case of Benjamin Button
Drama	The Departed
Drama	Gran Torino
Drama	Charlie Wilson's War
Drama	Monster
Foreign	Das Boot
Horror	NULL
Independent	NULL
Music and Musicals	NULL
Romance	The Lake House
Romance	13 Going on 30
Science Fiction and Fantasy	NULL
Special Interest	NULL
Sports	NULL
Thrillers	NULL

31 rows in set (0.00 sec)

Notice that the MySQL command-line client displays the word "NULL" whenever null values appear in query result sets. However, always keep in mind that nulls have no value whatsoever and are not equal to anything else, including other null values.

There are actually three types of outer joins:

- **LEFT OUTER JOIN**   Returns all rows in the left-hand table (the one named first, or leftmost in the JOIN clause) along with any rows in the right-hand table that can be matched.

- **RIGHT OUTER JOIN**   Returns all rows in the right-hand table (the one named second, or rightmost in the JOIN clause) along with any rows in the left-hand table that can be matched. Essentially, a left outer join may be rewritten as a right outer join simply by reversing the order of the table names and changing the keyword "LEFT" to "RIGHT". For example, the following two JOIN clauses are logically equivalent:

```
MOVIE_GENRE LEFT OUTER JOIN MOVIE
      ON MOVIE_GENRE.MOVIE_GENRE_CODE = MOVIE.MOVIE_GENRE_CODE

MOVIE RIGHT OUTER JOIN MOVIE_GENRE
      ON MOVIE_GENRE.MOVIE_GENRE_CODE = MOVIE.MOVIE_GENRE_CODE
```

• **FULL OUTER JOIN**   Returns all rows from both tables. This join is the least likely to be supported by your SQL implementation because the standard syntax for it is newer than the other two. It is essential to understand that this is not the same as a Cartesian product, which joins *every* row in one table with *every* row in the other. A full outer join, on the other hand, joins each row in one table with either *no* rows or all *matching* rows in the other table. In reality, you won't find an occasion to use a full outer join very often, but it can come in handy if there is a relationship between two tables that is optional in both directions.

Example 4-12: Limiting Join Results

Additional conditions can easily be added to the WHERE clause to limit rows returned from a query that also involves joins. Therefore, we can add conditions to the previous query that will filter out some of the movies or some of the genres or both. One interesting twist is to use the fact that unmatched genres in the previous example return null values for all the columns in the movie table. We can use that to filter out the matched rows, leaving only the genres for which there are no matching movies in the result set. Here is the query:

```
SELECT MOVIE_GENRE_DESCRIPTION AS GENRE
  FROM MOVIE_GENRE A LEFT OUTER JOIN MOVIE B
      ON A.MOVIE_GENRE_CODE = B.MOVIE_GENRE_CODE
 WHERE B.MOVIE_ID IS NULL
 ORDER BY MOVIE_GENRE_DESCRIPTION;
```

```
+--------------------------------+
| GENRE                          |
+--------------------------------+
| Anime and Animation            |
| Children and Family            |
| Classics                       |
| Documentary                    |
| Horror                         |
| Independent                    |
```

```
| Music and Musicals          |
| Science Fiction and Fantasy |
| Special Interest            |
| Sports                      |
| Thrillers                   |
+-----------------------------+
11 rows in set (0.00 sec)
```

Note the following:

- I used table aliases in the FROM clause, assigning the MOVIE_GENRE table an alias of A and the MOVIE table an alias of B. These aliases are then used instead of the table names in all other places in the query. They don't change the logic of the query in any way, but they reduce the amount of typing required because each table name is only spelled out one time. In fact, whenever you define a table alias in a query, you *must* use the alias instead of the table name everywhere else in that query. However, remember that you have to qualify only column names that are ambiguous.

- I removed the MOVIE_TITLE column from the query results. There is no point in displaying anything from the MOVIE table in the results because all of it will be null.

- I used the primary key (MOVIE_ID) to test for null values because it cannot possibly be null in a real table row. When finding unmatched rows in joins, you must be sure to always test for null values using a column that cannot be null in a real row of data in the table. Otherwise your results could be incorrect.

- Note that you cannot use the equal-to condition when testing for null values. A value of NULL is never equal to anything, so we must use the keywords IS NULL or IS NOT NULL to test for the presence or absence of null values.

Example 4-13: The Self-Join

When a table has a recursive relationship, we need to join the table to itself in order to follow the relationship in our query results. The EMPLOYEES table has such a relationship in that the SUPERVISOR_PERSON_ID column contains the PERSON_ID value of the employee to whom each employee reports.

The following query shows the values of PERSON_ID and SUPERVISOR_PERSON_ID in the EMPLOYEE table:

```
SELECT PERSON_ID, EMPLOYEE_HOURLY_RATE, SUPERVISOR_PERSON_ID
  FROM EMPLOYEE;
```

```
+-----------+----------------------+----------------------+
| PERSON_ID | EMPLOYEE_HOURLY_RATE | SUPERVISOR_PERSON_ID |
+-----------+----------------------+----------------------+
|         1 |                15.00 |                 NULL |
|         2 |                 9.75 |                    1 |
|        10 |                 9.75 |                    1 |
+-----------+----------------------+----------------------+
3 rows in set (0.00 sec)
```

Only three employees are in the sample database. Person 1 is the owner of the store and thus has no supervisor (SUPERVISOR_PERSON_ID is NULL), and the other two employees report to Person 1. Suppose we need to produce a report showing the pay difference between employees and their supervisors. With so few employees, we could obviously do the calculation in our heads, but let's assume that we want to use this at other stores that have more employees. The easiest way to do the calculation is to join each employee in the EMPLOYEE table to their supervisor's row in the EMPLOYEE table. This will seem confusing at first, but it's really just like any other join, except the primary key and foreign key used in the join logic happen to be columns in the same table. Here is the previous query with the self-join and the calculated column added. Notice that I used an inner (standard) join because we don't need to see the data for employees that have no supervisor.

```
SELECT A.PERSON_ID, A.EMPLOYEE_HOURLY_RATE AS HOURLY_RATE,
       B.EMPLOYEE_HOURLY_RATE AS SUPV_HOURLY_RATE,
       (B.EMPLOYEE_HOURLY_RATE - A.EMPLOYEE_HOURLY_RATE)
         AS RATE_DIFFERENCE
  FROM EMPLOYEE A JOIN EMPLOYEE B
       ON A.SUPERVISOR_PERSON_ID = B.PERSON_ID;
```

```
+-----------+-------------+------------------+-----------------+
| PERSON_ID | HOURLY_RATE | SUPV_HOURLY_RATE | RATE_DIFFERENCE |
+-----------+-------------+------------------+-----------------+
|         2 |        9.75 |            15.00 |            5.25 |
|        10 |        9.75 |            15.00 |            5.25 |
+-----------+-------------+------------------+-----------------+
2 rows in set (0.05 sec)
```

Aggregate Functions

Example 4-14: Simple Aggregate Functions

As you will recall from Example 3-12 in the previous chapter, aggregate functions combine multiple rows. The following table lists aggregate functions that are available in most SQL implementations:

Function Name	Description
AVG	Calculates the average value for a column or expression.
COUNT	Counts the number of values found in a column. The DISTINCT keyword can be used to count the number of unique values instead of the total number of values (rows) in a column.
MAX	Finds the maximum value in a column.
MIN	Finds the minimum value in a column.
SUM	Sums (totals up) the values in a column.

In the following query, aggregate functions are used to find the minimum, maximum, and average rental fee for all movie rentals along with a count of the total number of rentals. Because there is no GROUP BY clause to group rows (discussed in the next example), the entire table is considered one group, so only one row is returned in the result set.

```
SELECT MIN(RENTAL_FEE) AS MINIMUM, MAX(RENTAL_FEE) AS MAXIMUM,
       AVG(RENTAL_FEE) AS AVERAGE, COUNT(*) AS NUM_RENTALS
  FROM MOVIE_RENTAL;


+---------+---------+----------+-------------+
| MINIMUM | MAXIMUM | AVERAGE  | NUM_RENTALS |
+---------+---------+----------+-------------+
|    6.00 |    6.25 | 6.075000 |          20 |
+---------+---------+----------+-------------+
1 row in set (0.00 sec)
```

Example 4-15: Mixed Aggregate and Normal Columns (Error)

The following query is an attempt to count the number of movies in the MOVIE table by genre:

```
SELECT MOVIE_GENRE_CODE, COUNT(*) AS NUM_MOVIES
  FROM MOVIE;
+------------------+------------+
| MOVIE_GENRE_CODE | NUM_MOVIES |
+------------------+------------+
| ActAd            |         20 |
+------------------+------------+
1 row in set (0.00 sec)
```

PROBLEM 4-2

The result set produced by MySQL 5.1 is incorrect. The results fail the reasonableness check I suggested earlier. We know that we have 20 movies, but we also know that only some of them are in the ActAd (Action-Adventure) genre. Every other RDBMS I have used (Sybase, Oracle, SQL Server, DB2, etc.) would have returned an error in this situation, but MySQL allows it by default. The result is basically worthless because the value selected for each named column that is not part of the GROUP BY is indeterminate (that is, there is no way of predicting the row from which the value will be taken). You can change the default behavior in MySQL using the ONLY_FULL_GROUP_BY parameter.

SOLUTION

The problem with the query is that our request is illogical. We asked the SQL engine to list all the genre codes and to give us a single count of all the rows in the MOVIE table. What we wanted was a count of the number of movies in each genre, but we didn't tell the SQL engine to do that. The following example shows the corrected query.

Example 4-16: Aggregate Functions with GROUP BY

To remedy the situation, we must tell the RDBMS that we wish to *group* the rows by MOVIE_GENRE_CODE, and for each *group* display the

MOVIE_GENRE_CODE along with the aggregate column results (the count of the number of movies for the genre). The corrected statement follows:

```
SELECT MOVIE_GENRE_CODE, COUNT(*) AS NUM_MOVIES
  FROM MOVIE
 GROUP BY MOVIE_GENRE_CODE;
```

```
+------------------+------------+
| MOVIE_GENRE_CODE | NUM_MOVIES |
+------------------+------------+
| ActAd            |          7 |
| Comdy            |          4 |
| Drama            |          6 |
| Forgn            |          1 |
| Rmce             |          2 |
+------------------+------------+
5 rows in set (0.00 sec)
```

The GROUP BY clause causes returned rows to be automatically ordered by the columns listed because the DBMS must perform a sort in order to group the rows. However, an ORDER BY may also be included to return the rows in an alternate sequence. If the ORDER BY clause must include calculated columns, just use the expression for the column—you cannot use any alias name for the column because the alias is assigned to the column in the query results and therefore does not exist at the time the query runs. (However, there are SQL implementations that can handle sorting by a column alias.) Here is a version of the query that sorts descending on the number of movies:

```
SELECT MOVIE_GENRE_CODE, COUNT(*) AS NUM_MOVIES
  FROM MOVIE
 GROUP BY MOVIE_GENRE_CODE
 ORDER BY COUNT(*) DESC;
```

```
+------------------+------------+
| MOVIE_GENRE_CODE | NUM_MOVIES |
+------------------+------------+
| ActAd            |          7 |
| Drama            |          6 |
| Comdy            |          4 |
| Rmce             |          2 |
| Forgn            |          1 |
+------------------+------------+
5 rows in set (0.00 sec)
```

? **Still Struggling**

Mixing regular column expressions with aggregate functions in the same query takes some getting used to. Whenever you use an aggregate function in a query, remember that every column expression listed in the SELECT clause must be either an aggregate function or named in the GROUP BY clause.

Data Manipulation Language (DML)

The DML statement types in SQL are INSERT, UPDATE, and DELETE. These commands allow you to add, change, and remove rows of data in the tables. Before we look at each of these statement types, you first need to understand the concept of transactions and how the RDBMS supports them.

Transaction Support (COMMIT and ROLLBACK)

In terms of the RDBMS, a *transaction* is a series of one or more SQL statements that are treated as a single unit. A transaction must completely work or completely fail, meaning that any database changes a transaction makes must be made permanent when the transaction successfully completes. On the other hand, these changes must be entirely removed from the database if the transaction fails before completion. For example, we could start a transaction at the beginning of a process that creates a new order and then, at the end of the process when all the order information has been entered, complete the transaction. It is important that other database users not see fragments of an incomplete order until it has been completely entered and confirmed.

> In an RDBMS, a transaction is a series of SQL statements that are treated as a single unit that must completely work or completely fail.

SQL provides support for transactions with the COMMIT and ROLLBACK statements. Some variation occurs in the syntax and handling of these commands across different RDBMS vendors. Most vendors require no argument with the COMMIT or ROLLBACK statement, so the statement is just the keyword followed by the semicolon that ends every SQL statement.

In Oracle, a transaction is automatically started for each database user session as soon as the user connects to the database. At any time, the database user can issue a COMMIT, which makes all the database changes completed up to that point permanent and therefore visible to any other database user. The user can also issue a ROLLBACK, which reverses any changes made to the database. The COMMIT and ROLLBACK statements not only end one transaction, but they also begin a new one. There is one more wrinkle to remember: in Oracle, an *automatic* commit occurs before any DDL statement. (DDL statements are covered later in this chapter.)

By contrast, in Sybase and Microsoft SQL Server, transaction support is not as automatic. The database user must issue a BEGIN TRANSACTION statement to start a transaction. Once a transaction is started, changes made to the database can be made permanent with a COMMIT TRANSACTION statement, or they can be reversed using a ROLLBACK TRANSACTION statement. As of version 5.1, MySQL supports the COMMIT and ROLLBACK statements, but it takes no action when it processes them unless you first set autocommit=0 and then use the START TRANSACTION statement to begin a new transaction. Some RDBMSs, such as Microsoft Access, provide no transaction support at all.

The INSERT Statement

The INSERT statement in SQL is used to add new rows of data to tables. An INSERT statement may also insert rows via a view, provided the following conditions are met:

- If the view joins multiple tables, the columns referenced by the INSERT statement must all be from the same table. Said another way, an INSERT can only affect one table.

- The view must include all the mandatory table columns in the base table. If there are columns with NOT NULL constraints (and without default values) that do not appear in the view, it is impossible to provide values for those columns and therefore impossible to use the view to perform an insert.

The INSERT statement takes two basic forms: one where column values are provided in the statement itself, and the other where values are selected from a table or view using a subquery. Let's have a look at those two forms.

Example 4-17: INSERT with VALUES Clause

The INSERT with VALUES clause form of the INSERT statement can create only one row each time it is run because the values for that one row of data are provided in the statement itself. Here is an example of an INSERT statement from the sample database script:

```
INSERT INTO CUSTOMER_ACCOUNT
 (CUSTOMER_ACCOUNT_ID, CUSTOMER_HOLD_INDIC, DATE_ENROLLED,
  DATE_TERMINATED, CUSTOMER_DEPOSIT_AMOUNT,
  CREDIT_CARD_ON_FILE_INDIC, CHILD_RENTAL_ALLOWED_INDIC)
 VALUES (1, 'N', '2010-01-01', null, null ,'N', 'N');
```

Note the column list following the INSERT keyword. This comma-separated list is optional, but if provided must always be enclosed in a pair of parentheses. If you omit the list, the column values must be provided in the correct order (that is, in the same order as the columns are physically ordered in the table), and you cannot skip any column values. The statement may malfunction if anyone adds columns to the table, even optional ones, so it is *always* a good idea to provide the column list, even though it is more work to do so. Following the column list is the keyword VALUES and then a list of the values for the columns. This comma-separated list must also be enclosed in a pair of parentheses. The items in the VALUES list have a one-to-one correspondence with the column list (if one was provided) or with the columns defined in the table or view (if a column list was not provided). The keyword NULL (or null) may be used to assign null values to columns in the list.

Example 4-18: INSERT with Subquery

The INSERT with subquery form of the INSERT statement creates one row in the target table for each row retrieved from the source table or view. A subquery is used to retrieve the information that will be inserted. In the example that follows, rows in an imaginary table called MOVIE_INPUT are used to insert data into the MOVIE table:

```
INSERT INTO MOVIE
 (MOVIE_ID, MOVIE_GENRE_CODE, MPAA_RATING_CODE, MOVIE_TITLE,
  RETAIL_PRICE_VHS, RETAIL_PRICE_DVD, YEAR_PRODUCED)
    SELECT MOVIE_ID, MOVIE_GENRE_CODE, MPAA_RATING_CODE, MOVIE_TITLE,
           null, RETAIL_PRICE_DVD, YEAR_PRODUCED
      FROM MOVIE_INPUT;
```

If you wish to try this INSERT statement, you can find the statements used to create the MOVIE_INPUT table in the Data Definition Language (DDL) section later in this chapter. Notice that the RETAIL_PRICE_VHS column in MOVIE is set to null because the literal null is used in the subquery instead of a column name. This is necessary because the MOVIE_INPUT table does not have a RETAIL_PRICE_VHS column. (VHS movies are being discontinued.)

The UPDATE Statement

Example 4-19: The UPDATE Statement

The UPDATE statement in SQL is used to update the data values for table (or view) columns listed in the statement. A WHERE clause may be included to limit the scope of the statement to rows matching its conditions; otherwise, the statement attempts to update every row in the table (or view) named in the statement. Here is an UPDATE statement that increases an employee's hourly rate by 5 percent, rounded to two decimal places:

```
UPDATE EMPLOYEE
   SET EMPLOYEE_HOURLY_RATE =
       ROUND((EMPLOYEE_HOURLY_RATE * 1.05),2)
WHERE PERSON_ID = 2;
```

For each column to be updated, a SET clause is used to name the column and the new value for the column. The new value provided may be a constant, another column name, or any other expression that SQL can resolve to a column value. If the SET clause references multiple columns, the column names and values must be in a comma-separated list. The UPDATE statement may include a WHERE clause to limit the rows affected by the statement. If the WHERE clause is omitted, the UPDATE statement will attempt to update every row in the table (or view). If you forget this key point, remember our friend the ROLLBACK statement, which can back out the results of the update in SQL implementations that support it.

The DELETE Statement

The DELETE statement removes one or more rows from a table. The statement may also reference a view, but only if the view is based on a single table (in other words, views that join multiple tables cannot be referenced). A DELETE statement does not reference columns because the statement automatically clears all column data for any rows deleted. A WHERE clause may be included to limit the rows affected by the DELETE statement; if the WHERE clause is omitted, the statement attempts to delete all the rows in the referenced table. This statement deletes all the rows in the EMPLOYEE table that have been terminated.

(It's safe to run this statement because there are no terminated employees in the sample database.)

```
DELETE FROM EMPLOYEE
 WHERE TERMINATION_DATE IS NOT NULL;
```

Data Definition Language (DDL) Statements

Data Definition Language (DDL) statements define the database objects but do not insert or update any data stored within those objects (DML statements serve that function). In SQL, there are three basic commands within DDL:

- **CREATE** Creates a new database object of the type named in the statement
- **DROP** Drops (destroys) an existing database object of the type named in the statement
- **ALTER** Changes the definition of an existing database object of the type named in the statement

In the sections that follow, we look at the most commonly used DDL statement types. DDL statements vary a lot across RDBMS vendors, so consult the vendor's documentation for more details.

The CREATE TABLE Statement

The CREATE TABLE statement adds a new table to the database. Here is an example using the MOVIE_INPUT table:

```
CREATE TABLE MOVIE_INPUT (
MOVIE_ID               INTEGER            NOT NULL,
MOVIE_GENRE_CODE       CHAR(5)            NOT NULL,
MPAA_RATING_CODE       CHAR(5)            NOT NULL,
MOVIE_TITLE            VARCHAR(100)       NOT NULL,
RETAIL_PRICE_DVD       NUMERIC(5,2)       NULL,
YEAR_PRODUCED          CHAR(4)            NULL,
PRIMARY KEY (MOVIE_ID) );
```

Note that a comma-separated list of columns is provided, along with the data type and NULL or NOT NULL specification for each. You may recall that data types were discussed in Chapter 2 and that there is a wide variation in supported data types across RDBMS vendors. The data types shown here apply to MySQL and other databases that are fully compliant with the ANSI/ISO SQL standard. The NULL / NOT NULL specification is optional, but if you omit it, be sure you know the default that your SQL engine will assume. In most RDBMSs, including MySQL and Oracle, NULL is the default. However, in others, such as Sybase and Microsoft SQL Server, NOT NULL is the default unless the default is changed at the database or server level. It is therefore safer, but of course more work, to always specify either NULL or NOT NULL. Incidentally, most RDBMSs require that primary key columns be explicitly specified as NOT NULL. You'll see how to create a primary key constraint on the EMPLOYEE_ID column of this table in the "Primary Key Constraints" section a little further along in this chapter.

This example shows the ANSI/ISO standard components of the CREATE TABLE statement. There are many vendor extensions. For example, in Oracle, the STORAGE clause may be included to specify the amount of physical space that is to be allocated to the table, and a TABLESPACE clause may be included to specify the tablespace that will hold the table's data.

The ALTER TABLE Statement

The ALTER TABLE statement may be used to change many aspects of the definition of a database table. Again, there is a wide variation in implementation across RDBMS vendors, but generally speaking, the following types of changes may be made using the ALTER TABLE statement:

- Adding columns to the table
- Removing columns from the table
- Altering the data type for existing table columns
- Changing physical storage attributes of the table
- Adding, removing, or altering constraints

Because the implementation of constraints is the way we enforce business rules in the database, we will take a closer look at them here. In many RDBMS products, it is important to name the constraints because the names appear in any error messages generated when constraint violations take place.

Referential Constraints

Here is an example of a referential constraint definition using the ALTER TABLE statement:

```
ALTER TABLE MOVIE_INPUT
    ADD CONSTRAINT FK_MOVIE_INPUT_GENRE
    FOREIGN KEY (MOVIE_GENRE_CODE)
    REFERENCES MOVIE_GENRE (MOVIE_GENRE_CODE);
```

In this example, a referential constraint named FK_MOVIE_INPUT_GENRE is added to the MOVIE_INPUT table to define the MOVIE_GENRE_CODE column as a foreign key to the primary key column (MOVIE_GENRE_CODE) of the MOVIE_GENRE table. This is the way we implement the relationships we've identified in the logical database design.

In most SQL implementations, you can drop the foreign key constraint using this syntax:

```
ALTER TABLE MOVIE_INPUT
 DROP CONSTRAINT FK_MOVIE_INPUT_GENRE;
```

However, MySQL uses a slightly different syntax:

```
ALTER TABLE MOVIE_INPUT
 DROP FOREIGN KEY FK_MOVIE_INPUT_GENRE;
```

Primary Key Constraints

Primary key constraints ensure that the column(s) designated as the primary key for the table never have duplicate values. Nearly all RDBMSs create a unique index to assist in enforcement of primary key constraints. An *index* is a special database object containing the key value from one or more table columns and pointers to the table rows that match the key value. Indexes can be used for fast searching of a table based on the key value. Here is the definition of the primary key constraint for the MOVIE_INPUT table:

```
ALTER TABLE MOVIE_INPUT
   ADD CONSTRAINT PK_EMPLOYEE_INPUT
   PRIMARY KEY (MOVIE_ID);
```

> *An index is a special database object containing the key value from one or more table columns and pointers to the table rows that match the key value.*

If you try to run this statement, it will fail because a primary key was already defined in the CREATE TABLE statement for the MOVIE_INPUT table. However, if you wish to drop the existing primary key so you can run this statement, you can do so using this statement:

```
ALTER TABLE MOVIE_INPUT
 DROP PRIMARY KEY;
```

Unique Constraints

In addition to using primary keys, we can force uniqueness of other column(s) in a table using a unique constraint. A table may have only one primary key constraint, but in addition it may have as many unique constraints as necessary. Most RDBMSs use a unique index to assist with the enforcement of unique constraints. For example, we can use a unique constraint to ensure that no two employees have the same tax ID as follows:

```
ALTER TABLE EMPLOYEE
   ADD CONSTRAINT UNQ_EMPLOYEE_TAX_ID
   UNIQUE (EMPLOYEE_TAX_ID);
```

In most SQL implementations, you can drop the constraint using this syntax:

```
ALTER TABLE EMPLOYEE
 DROP CONSTRAINT UNQ_EMPLOYEE_TAX_ID;
```

However, in MySQL, you must use the DROP INDEX option of the ALTER TABLE statement to drop a unique constraint:

```
ALTER TABLE EMPLOYEE
 DROP INDEX UNQ_EMPLOYEE_TAX_ID;
```

Check Constraints

Check constraints can be used to enforce any business rule that can be applied to a single column in a table. The condition included in the constraint must always be true whenever a new row is added or the column data in an existing row is updated, or else an error message is displayed. The following example implements a check constraint that ensures that the EMPLOYEE_HOURLY_ RATE column in the EMPLOYEE table is always greater than zero:

```
ALTER TABLE EMPLOYEE
   ADD CONSTRAINT EMPLOYEE_CHK_RATE_MIN
   CHECK (EMPLOYEE_HOURLY_RATE > 0);
```

You can drop the check constraint using this syntax:

```
ALTER TABLE EMPLOYEES
 DROP CONSTRAINT EMPLOYEE_CHK_RATE_MIN;
```

NOTE *As of version 5.1, MySQL supports the syntax for adding a check constraint as shown here, but it doesn't actually create the constraint. Therefore, MySQL 5.1 provides no syntax support for dropping check constraints.*

The CREATE VIEW Statement

Because a view is merely a stored query, any query that can be run using a SE-LECT statement can be saved as a view in the database. View names must be unique among all the tables, views, and synonyms in the database schema. In Oracle, the OR REPLACE option may be included so that an existing view of the same name will be replaced. The following example creates a view for the movies with G, PG, and PG-13 ratings.

```
CREATE VIEW TAME_MOVIES AS
  SELECT MOVIE_ID, MOVIE_TITLE, MOVIE_GENRE_CODE
    FROM MOVIE
   WHERE MPAA_RATING_CODE IN ('G','PG','PG-13');
```

Running the following SQL statement will select the data from the view:

```
SELECT MOVIE_TITLE
  FROM TAME_MOVIES;
```

The CREATE INDEX Statement

The CREATE INDEX statement creates an index on one or more table columns. As previously mentioned, indexes provide fast searching of a table based on one or more key columns. Indexes on foreign keys can also greatly improve the performance of joins. The RDBMS automatically maintains the index when rows are added to or deleted from the database or when indexed column values are updated. However, indexes take storage space and their maintenance takes processing resources. The following example creates an index on the CUS-TOMER_ACCOUNT_ID column in the CUSTOMER_TRANSACTION table:

```
CREATE INDEX CUSTOMER_TRANSACTION_CUST_ID
  ON CUSTOMER_TRANSACTION (CUSTOMER_ACCOUNT_ID);
```

If the column values in the index will always be unique, the UNIQUE keyword may be placed between the CREATE and INDEX keywords. As an alternative, a unique constraint may be added to the table, which indirectly creates the unique index. Unique indexes are usually more efficient than non-unique ones.

The DROP Statement

The DROP statement is used to remove database objects from the database when they are no longer necessary. For table deletions, the CASCADE CONSTRAINTS clause may be added in most SQL implementations to automatically remove any referential constraints in which the table participates. When a table is dropped, most objects depending on the table (indexes and constraints) are also dropped. In most RDBMSs, however, views dependent on a dropped table remain, but are marked invalid so they cannot be used until the table is re-created. Here are the DROP statements that remove the TAME_MOVIES view and the MOVIE_INPUT table:

```
DROP VIEW TAME_MOVIES;
DROP INDEX CUSTOMER_TRANSACTION_CUST_ID;    -- except MySQL
DROP INDEX CUSTOMER_TRANSACTION_CUST_ID
        ON CUSTOMER_TRANSACTION;            -- MySQL syntax
DROP TABLE MOVIE_INPUT;
```

Data Control Language (DCL) Statements

A database *privilege* is the authorization to do something in the database. The database user granting the privilege is called the *grantor*, and the database user receiving the privilege is called the *grantee*.

> A database privilege is the authorization to do something in the database.

Privileges fall into two broad categories:

- **System privileges**   Permit the grantee to perform a general database function, such as creating new user accounts or connecting to the database
- **Object privileges**   Permit the grantee to perform specific actions on specific objects, such as selecting from the EMPLOYEE table or updating the MOVIE table

To reduce the tedium of managing privileges, most RDBMSs support storing a group of privilege definitions as a single named object called a *role*. Roles may then be granted to individual users, who then inherit all the privileges contained in the role. RDBMSs that support roles also typically come with a number of predefined roles. Oracle, for example, has a role called DBA that contains all the high-powered system and object privileges a database user needs in administering a database. System privileges vary widely across SQL implementations, but object privileges are defined in a relatively common manner. Therefore I will limit the examples in this topic to object privileges.

NOTE *Privileges are granted to database user accounts. The SQL statements in this topic will run successfully only if the user account TEST exists in the DBMS. The creation of user accounts varies widely across SQL implementations and therefore cannot be covered here.*

The GRANT Statement

The following statement grants the select, insert, and update privileges on the EMPLOYEE table to user TEST:

```
GRANT SELECT, INSERT, UPDATE ON EMPLOYEE TO TEST;
```

If an object referenced in an SQL statement exists in a schema other than the one to which we are currently connected, we must qualify the object name with the schema name. Here is the same statement qualified with the schema name VIDEO_STORE:

```
GRANT SELECT, INSERT, UPDATE ON VIDEO_STORE.EMPLOYEE TO TEST;
```

Most RDBMSs that support privileges also provide syntax for giving the grantee permission to grant the privilege to others. Most SQL implementations support the `WITH GRANT OPTION` clause for object privileges. Oracle, however, uses the `WITH ADMIN OPTION` clause for system privileges, but still uses the `WITH GRANT OPTION` for object privileges.

TIP *Even though most SQL products support giving grantees the privilege of granting their privileges to others, I strongly recommend against doing so. It is simply too easy to lose control of privileges when you allow people who have a privilege to in turn grant it to others.*

The REVOKE Statement

Granted privileges can be withdrawn using the `REVOKE` statement. For object privileges, if `WITH GRANT OPTION` is exercised by the user, the revoke cascades and everyone downstream loses the privilege as well. This is not necessarily true for system privileges—consult your RDBMS manuals for details. Better yet, if you never use the `WITH GRANT OPTION` and `WITH ADMIN OPTION` clauses, you will never have to worry about this problem. The privileges shown in the previous section can be revoked with these commands:

```
REVOKE SELECT, INSERT, UPDATE ON EMPLOYEE FROM TEST;
```

Summary

In this chapter, you learned the history of SQL and the details of writing SQL statements to select data (DQL); to modify data in database tables (DML); to define, drop, and alter database objects (DDL); and to control database privileges (DCL). In the next several chapters, you will learn how to design databases.

QUIZ

Choose the correct responses to each of the multiple-choice questions. Note that there may be more than one correct response to each question.

1. **SQL was first developed:**
    A. In the 1970s
    B. In 1982
    C. By IBM
    D. By ANSI
    E. Based on ANSI specifications

2. **A SELECT without a WHERE clause:**
    A. Always outputs results to a log file
    B. Results in an error message
    C. Selects all columns in the source table or view
    D. Selects all rows in the source table or view
    E. Lists only the definition of the table or view

3. **A join without a WHERE clause or JOIN clause:**
    A. Results in an outer join
    B. Results in an error message
    C. Returns no rows in the result set
    D. Returns only the rows in the first table
    E. Results in a Cartesian product

4. **An UPDATE statement without a WHERE clause:**
    A. Updates no rows in a table
    B. Updates every row in a table
    C. Results in an error message
    D. Updates every column in a table
    E. Results in a Cartesian product

5. **An INSERT statement:**
    A. May contain a subquery
    B. Must contain a VALUES list
    C. Must contain a column list
    D. May create multiple table rows
    E. Creates a new table

6. **The LIKE operator:**
   A. Uses question marks as nonpositional wildcards
   B. Uses underscores as nonpositional wildcards
   C. Uses percent signs as nonpositional wildcards
   D. Uses percent signs as positional wildcards
   E. Uses underscores as positional wildcards

7. **A self-join:**
   A. Can be either an inner or outer join
   B. Resolves recursive relationships
   C. May use a subquery to further limit returned rows
   D. Involves two different tables
   E. Can never result in a Cartesian product

8. **An SQL statement containing an aggregate function:**
   A. Must contain a GROUP BY clause
   B. May also include ordinary columns
   C. May include either the GROUP BY clause or the ORDER BY clause, but not both
   D. May also include calculated columns
   E. Must not involve joining multiple tables

9. **A COMMIT in Oracle:**
   A. Is automatic just before any DDL statement is run
   B. Begins a new transaction
   C. Ends a transaction
   D. Causes changes made by a transaction to become permanent
   E. Makes changes effected by a transaction visible to all users

10. **The WITH GRANT OPTION of the GRANT statement:**
    A. Is highly recommended because it reduces the tedium of granting privileges
    B. Is not recommended because of security risks
    C. Is supported by most SQL implementations
    D. Allows users to grant the privilege to other users
    E. Can only be used with system privileges

chapter 5

The Database Life Cycle

Before we delve into the particulars of database design, it is useful to understand the framework in which the design takes place. The *life cycle* of a database (or computer system) is the term we use for all the events that take place between the time we first recognize a need for a database, continuing through its development and deployment, and finally ending with the day it is retired from service.

CHAPTER OBJECTIVES

In this chapter, the reader should:

- Understand the framework (database life cycle) in which database design takes place.

- Learn about the traditional development life cycle as well as nontraditional methods, including prototyping, Rapid Application Development (RAD), and agile development.

Most businesses that develop computer systems have a formal process they follow. The process ensures that development runs smoothly, is cost-effective, and that the outcome is a complete computer system that meets expectations. Databases are never designed and implemented in a vacuum—other components of the complete system are always developed along with the database, such as the user interface, application programs, and reports. All the work to be accomplished over the long term is typically divided into projects, with each project having its own finite list of goals (sometimes called *deliverables)*, an expected timeframe for completion, and a project manager or leader who will be held accountable for delivery of the project. To understand the database life cycle, you must also understand the life cycle of the entire systems-development effort and the way projects are organized and managed. In this chapter, we take a look at both traditional and nontraditional systems-development processes.

Not all databases are built by businesses using formal projects and funding. However, the disciplines outlined in this chapter can assist you in thinking through your database project, asking the tough questions, before you embark on an extended effort.

The Traditional Method

The traditional method for developing computer systems follows a process called the *system development life cycle (SDLC)*, which divides the work into phases similar to the ones shown in Figure 5-1. There are perhaps as many variations of the SDLC as there are authors, project management software vendors, and companies that have elected to create their own methodology. However, they all have the basic components, and in that sense, are all cut from the same cloth. I could argue the merits of one variation versus another, but that would merely confuse matters when all we need is a basic overview. A good textbook on systems analysis can provide greater detail should you need it. Figure 5-1 shows the traditional SDLC steps in the left column, the basic project activities in the middle column, and the database steps that support the project activities in the right column. We will explore each step further in the sections that follow. Note that the process is not always unidirectional—sometimes missing or incomplete information is discovered that requires you to go back one phase and adjust the work done there. The dotted lines pointing back to prior phases in Figure 5-1 serve as a reminder that a certain amount of rework is normal and expected during a project following the SDLC methodology.

A systems development life cycle (SDLC) is a defined process for the development and maintenance of computer systems.

Phases	Project Activities	Database Activities
Planning	Feasibility Study Form Project Team	Review DBMS Options Assign Database Specialist to Team
Requirements Gathering	Collect Requirements Analyze Requirements	Collect and Analyze User Views Identify Preliminary Entities
Conceptual Design	Design Screens/forms/reports Document Business Rules Design Storyboards or Screen Flows	Develop Conceptual Data Model Update Enterprise Conceptual Model
Logical Design	Specify Logical System Software Specify Logical Hardware	Develop Logical Data Model Perform Normalization
Physical Design	Specify Physical System Software Specify Physical Hardware	Physical Database Design
Construction	Construct Application Software Build Application Development and Test Environments	Create Development and Test Databases Test any Required Data Conversion
Implementation and Rollout	Create Production Environment Install Application Components Train Users Rollout to Users	Create Production Databases Perform Required Data Conversion
Ongoing Support	Respond to Reported Problems Apply Mandated Changes Respond to Change Requests	Database Performance Tuning Database Software Patches Schema Changes to Support Application Changes

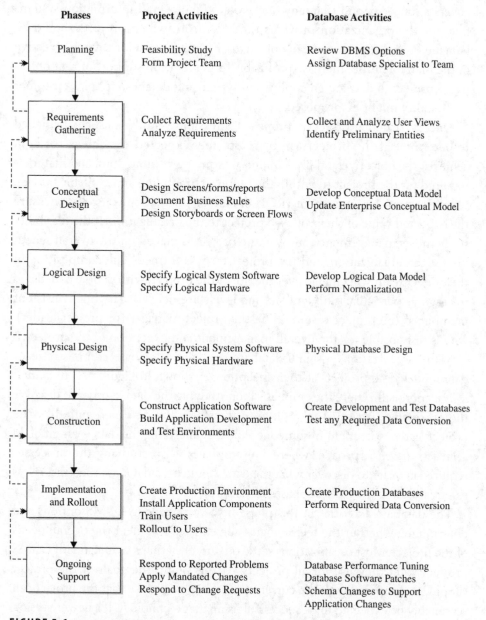

FIGURE 5-1 · Traditional system development life cycle (SDLC)

Planning

During the planning phase, the organization must reach a high-level understanding of where they are, where they want to be, and how they will reasonably approach or plan for getting from one place to the other. Planning often covers a longer period than any one project. The overall information-systems plan for the organization provides the basis from which projects should be launched to achieve the overall objectives. For example, a long-range objective in the plan might be "Increase profits by 15 percent." In support of that objective, a project to develop an application system and database to track customer profitability might be proposed.

Once a particular project is proposed, a feasibility study is usually launched to determine if the project can be reasonably expected to achieve (or help achieve) the objective and if preliminary estimates of time, staff, and materials required for the project fit within the required timeframe and available budget. Often a return on investment (ROI) or similar calculation is used to measure the expected value of the proposed project to the organization. If the feasibility study meets management approval, the project is placed on the overall schedule for the organization, and the project team is formed. The composition of the project team will change over the life of the project, with people added and released as particular skill and staffing levels are needed. The one consistent member of the project team will be the project manager (or project leader), who is responsible for the overall management and execution of the project.

Many organizations assign a database specialist (database administrator or data modeler) to projects at their inception, as shown in Figure 5-1. In a *data-driven* approach, where the emphasis is on studying the data in order to discover the processing that must take place to transform the data as required by the project, early assignment of someone skilled at analyzing the data is essential. In a *process-driven* approach, where the emphasis is on studying the processes required in order to discover what the data should be, a database specialist is less essential during the earliest phases of the project.

The database activities in this phase involve reviewing DBMS options and determining whether the technologies currently in use meet the overall needs of the project. Most organizations settle on one, or perhaps two, standard DBMS products that they use for all projects. At this point, the goals of the project should be compared with the current technology to ensure that the project can reasonably be expected to be successful using that technology. If a newer version

?

Still Struggling

There has been much debate over whether a process-driven or data-driven approach works best. Industry experience suggests that the very best results are obtained by applying *both* a process-driven and a data-driven approach. However, there is seldom time and staff to do so, so the next-best results for a project involving databases come from the data-driven approach. Processes still need to be designed, but if we study the data first, the required processes become apparent. For example, in designing our customer profitability system, if we have customer sales data and know that customers who place fewer, larger orders are more profitable, then we can conclude that we need a process to rank customers by order volume and size. On the other hand, if all we know is that we need a process that ranks customers, it may take considerably more work to arrive at the criteria we should use to rank them. Moreover, the data-driven approach is much more likely to produce data structures that can be shared by other current and future processes.

of the DBMS is required, or if a completely different DBMS is required, now is the time to find out so the acquisition and installation of the DBMS can be started.

Requirements Gathering

During the requirements-gathering phase, the project team must gather and document a high-level, yet precise, description of what the project is to accomplish. The focus must be on *what* rather than *how*; the "how" is developed during the subsequent design phases. It is important for the requirements to include as much as can be known about the existing and expected business processes, business rules, and entities. The more work that is done in the early stages of a project, the more smoothly the subsequent stages will proceed. On the other hand, without some tolerance for the unknown (that is, those gray areas that have no solid answers), *analysis paralysis* may occur, wherein the entire project stalls while analysts spin their wheels looking for answers and clarifications that are not forthcoming.

From a database design perspective, the items of most interest during requirements gathering are user views. Recall that a *user view* is the method employed for presenting a set of data to the database user in a manner tailored to the needs of that person or application. At this phase of development, user views take the form of existing or proposed reports, forms, screens, web pages, and the like.

Many techniques may be used in gathering requirements. The more commonly used ones are compared and contrasted here: interviews, a survey, observation, and document review. No particular technique is clearly superior to another, and it is best to find a blend of techniques that works well for the particular organization rather than to rely on one over the others. For example, whether it is better to conduct a survey and follow up with interviews with key people, or to start with interviews and use the interview findings to formulate a survey, is often a question of what works best given the organization's culture and operating methods. The following subsections detail each technique, listing some advantages and disadvantages to assist in decision making.

Conduct Interviews

Interviewing key individuals who have information about what the project is expected to accomplish is a popular approach. One of the common errors, however, is to interview only management. If representatives of the people who are actually going to use the new application(s) and database(s) are not included, the project may end up delivering something that is not practical because management may not fully understand the details of what is required to run the business of the organization.

The advantages of requirements gathering by using interviews include

- The interviewer can receive answers to questions that were not asked. Side topics often come up that provide additional useful information.
- The interviewer can learn a lot from the body language of the interviewee. It is far easier to detect uncertainty and attempts at deception in person rather than in written responses to questions.

The disadvantages include

- Interviews take considerably more time than other methods.
- Poorly skilled interviewers can "telegraph" the answers they are expecting by the way they ask the questions or by their reaction to the answers received.

Conduct a Survey

Another popular approach is to write a survey seeking responses to key questions regarding the requirements for a project. The survey is sent to all the decision makers and potential users of the application(s) and database(s) the project is expected to deliver, and responses are analyzed for items to be included in the requirements.

The advantages of requirements gathering by using surveys include

- A lot of ground can be covered in a short time. Once the survey is written, it takes little additional effort to distribute it to a wider audience if necessary.

- Questions are presented in the same manner to every participant.

The disadvantages include

- Surveys typically have very poor response rates. Consider yourself fortunate if 10 percent respond without having to be prodded or threatened with consequences.

- Unbiased survey questions are surprisingly difficult to compose.

- The project team does not get the benefit of the nonverbal clues that an interview provides.

Observation

Observing the business operation and the people who will be using the new application(s) and database(s) is another popular technique for gathering requirements.

The advantages of requirements gathering through observation include

- Assuming you watch in an unobtrusive manner, you get to see people following normal processes in everyday use. Note that these may not be the processes that management believes are being followed, or even the ones in existing documentation. Instead, you may observe adaptations that were made so that the processes actually work or so they are more efficient.

- You may observe events that people would not think (or dare) to mention in response to questionnaires or interview questions.

The disadvantages include the following:

- If the people know they are being watched, behavior changes, and you may not get an accurate picture of their business processes. This is often termed the *Hawthorne effect* after a phenomenon first noticed in the

Hawthorne Plant of Western Electric, where production improved not because of improvements in working conditions but rather because management demonstrated interest in such improvements.

- Unless enormous time is dedicated to observation, you may never see the exceptions that subvert existing business processes. To bend an old analogy, you end up paving the cow path while cows are wandering on the highway on the other side of the pasture due to a hole in the fence.
- Travel to various business locations can add to project expense.

Document Review

This technique involves locating and reviewing all available documents for the existing business units and processes that will be affected by the new program(s) and database(s).

The advantages of requirements gathering through document review include

- Document review is typically less time-consuming than any of the other methods.
- Documents often provide an overview of the system that is better thought out compared with the introductory information you receive in an interview.
- Pictures and diagrams really are worth a thousand words each.

The disadvantages are

- The documents may not reflect actual practices. Documents often deal with what should happen rather than what really happens.
- Documentation is often out of date.

Conceptual Design

The conceptual design phase involves designing the externals of the application(s) and database(s). In fact, many methodologies use the term *external design* for this project phase. The layout of reports, screens, forms, web pages, and other data entry and presentation vehicles is finalized during this phase. In addition, the flow of the external application is documented in the form of a flowchart, storyboard, or screen flow diagram. This helps the project team understand the logical flow of the system. Process-diagramming techniques are discussed further in Chapter 7.

During this phase, the database specialist (DBA or data modeler) assigned to the project updates the enterprise conceptual data model, which is usually maintained in the form of an entity-relationship diagram (ERD). New or changed entities discovered are added to the ERD, and any additional or changed business rules are also noted. The user views, entities, and business rules are essential for the successful logical database design that follows in the next phase.

Logical Design

During logical design, the bulk of the technical design of the application(s) and database(s) included in the project is carried out. Many methodologies call this phase *internal design* because it involves the design of the internals of the project that the business users will never see.

The work to be accomplished by the application(s) is segmented into *modules* (individual units of application programming that will be written and tested together), and a detailed specification is written for each unit. The specification should be complete enough that any programmer with the proper programming skills can write the module and test it with little or no additional information. Diagrams such as data flow diagrams or flowcharts (an older technique) are often used to document the logic flow between modules. Process modeling is covered in more detail in Chapter 7.

From the database perspective, the major effort in this phase is *normalization*, a technique developed by Dr. E.F. Codd for designing relational database tables that are best for transaction-based systems (that is, those that insert, update, and delete data in the relational database tables). Normalization is covered in great detail in Chapter 6. Normalization is the single most important topic in this entire book. Once normalization is completed, the overall logical data model for the enterprise (assuming one exists) is updated to reflect any newly discovered entities.

> *Normalization is a technique developed by Dr. E.F. Codd for designing relational database tables that are best for transaction-based systems.*

Physical Design

During the physical design phase, the logical design is mapped or converted to the actual hardware and systems software that will be used to implement the application(s) and database(s). From the process side, there may be little or nothing to do if the application specifications were written in a manner that can be directly implemented. However, there is much work to be done in specifying the hardware on which the application(s) and database(s) will be installed, including capacity estimates for the processors, disk devices, and network bandwidth on which the system will run.

On the database side, the normalized relations that were designed in the prior logical design phase are implemented in the relational DBMS(s) to be used. In particular, DDL is coded or generated to define the database objects, including the SQL clauses that define the physical storage of the tables and indexes. Preliminary analysis of required database queries is conducted to identify any additional indexes that may be necessary to achieve acceptable database performance. An essential outcome of this phase is the DDL for creation of the development database objects that the developers will need for testing the application programs during the construction phase that follows. Physical database design is covered in more detail in Chapter 8.

Construction

During the construction phase, the application developers code and test the individual programming units. Tested program units are promoted to a system test environment where the entire application and database system is assembled and tested from end to end. Figure 5-2 shows the environments that are typically used as an application system is developed, tested, and implemented. Each environment is a complete hardware and software environment that includes all the components necessary to run the application system. Once system testing is completed, the system is promoted to a quality assurance (QA) environment. Most medium and large organizations have a separate QA department that tests the application system to ensure that it conforms to the stated requirements. Some organizations also have business users test the system to make sure

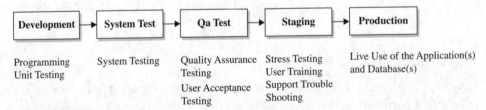

FIGURE 5-2 · Development hardware/software environments

it also meets their needs. The sooner errors are found in a computer system, the less expensive they are to repair. After QA has passed the application system, it is promoted to a staging environment. It is important that the staging environment be as near a duplicate of the production environment as possible. In this environment, stress testing is conducted to ensure that the application and database will perform reasonably when deployed into live production use. Often final user training is conducted here as well because it will be most like the live environment they will soon use.

> *Quality Assurance (QA) is a program for the systematic monitoring and evaluation of a computer system to ensure that standards of quality are being met.*

Again, the environments and usages shown in Figure 5-2 are typical, but there are often variances from one organization to another. For example, stress testing is sometimes called performance testing, and in some organizations, it is conducted in the QA environment or in a separate environment dedicated to performance testing.

The major work of the database designer is already complete by the time construction begins. However, as each part of the application system is migrated from one environment to the next, the database components needed by the application must also be migrated, so the DBA is still involved. Hopefully, a script is written that deploys the database components to the development environment, and that script is reused in each subsequent environment. However, it is more complicated when an existing database is being enhanced or an older data storage system is being replaced, because data must be converted from the old storage structures to the new. Data transcends systems. Therefore, data conversion between old and new versions of systems is quite commonplace, ranging from simply adding new tables and columns, to complex conversions that require extensive programming efforts in and of themselves.

Implementation and Rollout

Implementation is the process of installing the new application system's components (application programs, forms or web pages, reports, database objects, and so on) into the live system and carrying out any required data conversions. *Rollout* is the process of placing groups of business users on the new application.

Sometimes a new project is implemented *cold turkey*, meaning everyone is placed on the new version at the same time. However, with more complicated applications or those involving large numbers of users, a phased implementation is often used to reduce risk. The old and new versions of the application must run in parallel for a time while groups of users—often partitioned by physical work location or by department—are trained and migrated over to the new application. This method is often humorously referred to as the *chicken method* (in contrast to the cold turkey method).

Ongoing Support

Once a new application system and database have been implemented in a production environment, support of the application is often turned over to a production support team. This team must be prepared to isolate and respond to any issues that may arise, which could include performance issues, abnormal or unexpected results, complete failures, or the inevitable requests for enhancements. With enhancements, it is best to categorize and prioritize them and then fold them into future projects. However, genuine errors found in the existing application or database (called *bugs* in IT slang) must be fixed more immediately. Each bug fix becomes a mini-project, where all the SDLC phases must be revisited. At the very least, documentation must be updated as changes are made. As noted in Figure 5-2, the staging environment provides an ideal place for verifying errors and the fixes for them, and makes it possible to fix errors in parallel with the next major enhancement to the application system, which may have already been started in the development environment.

?

Still Struggling

There is often confusion when business users encounter problems with a computer system regarding which are defects versus enhancement requests. You must go back to the requirements for the system to make the determination. If the system does not perform to the stated requirements, then a defect has been found; else the solution to the problem should be classified as an enhancement request.

Assuming no gross errors were made during database design, the database support required during this phase is usually minor. Here are some of the tasks that may be required:

- Patches must be applied when the problems turn out to be bugs in the vendor's RDBMS software.

- Performance tuning, such as moving data files or adding indexes, may be necessary to circumvent performance problems.

- Space must be monitored and storage added as the database grows.

- Some application bug fixes may require new table columns or alterations to existing columns. If testing was done well, gross errors that require extensive database changes simply will not occur. Some application changes are required by statutory or regulatory changes beyond the control of the organization, and those changes can lead to extensive modifications to application(s) and database(s).

Nontraditional Methods

In response to the belief that SDLC projects take too much time and too many resources, some nontraditional methods have come into routine use in some organizations. The most prevalent of these are prototyping, Rapid Application Development (RAD), and agile software development.

Prototyping

Prototyping involves rapid development of the application by using iterative sets of design, development, and implementation steps to determine user requirements. Extensive business user involvement is required throughout the development process. In its extreme form, a meeting is held during the business day to review the latest iteration of the application, followed by a development team working through the evening and often late into the night. The next iteration is then reviewed during the following workday.

Some prototyping techniques carry all the way through to a production version of the application and database. In this variation, iterations have increasing levels of detail added to them until they become completely functional applications. If this path is chosen, prototyping never ends, and even after implementation and rollout, any future enhancements fall right back into more prototyping.

The most common downside to this implementation technique is development team burnout. Other common downsides include application code quality issues and poor performance.

Another variation of prototyping restricts the effort to only the definition of requirements. Once requirements and the user-facing parts of the conceptual design (that is, user views) are determined, a traditional SDLC methodology is used to complete the project. IBM introduced a version of this methodology called *Joint Application Design (JAD)*, which was highly successful in situations where user requirements could not be determined using more traditional techniques. The biggest exposure for this variant of prototyping is in not setting and maintaining expectations with the business sponsors of the project. The prototype is more or less a façade, much like a movie set where the buildings look real from the front, but have no substance beyond that. Nontechnical audiences have no understanding of what it takes to develop the logic and data storage structures that form the inner workings of the application, and they become most disappointed when they realize that what looked like a complete, functional application system was really just an empty shell. However, when done correctly, this technique can be remarkably successful in determining user requirements that describe precisely the application system the business users want and need.

> *Joint Application Design (JAD) is a prototyping process used to collect business requirements for new information systems.*

Rapid Application Development (RAD)

Rapid Application Development (RAD) is a software development process that allows functioning application systems to be built in as little as 60–90 days. Compromises are often made using the 80/20 rule, which assumes that 80 percent of the required work can be completed in 20 percent of the time. Complicated exception handling, for example, can be omitted in the interest of delivering a working system sooner. If the process is repeated on the same set of requirements, the system is ultimately built out to meet 100 percent of the requirements in a manner similar to prototyping.

RAD is not useful in controlling project schedules or budgets, and in fact, requires a project manager who is highly skilled at managing schedules and controlling costs. It is most useful in situations where a rapid schedule is more important than product quality (measured in terms of conforming to all known requirements).

Agile Software Development

Agile software development methodologies prescribe a disciplined project management process for iterative development where requirements and solutions evolve through the collaborative efforts of cross-functional teams with emphasis placed on face-to-face communication among team members. The methodology promotes frequent review of completed work, rapid adaptation of changes, teamwork, individual accountability, and a business philosophy that aligns development with the needs and goals of the organization and its business partners.

While many agile methodologies are available, one of the common themes is to break tasks down into small increments with minimal planning. Iterations are short periods that typically span one to four weeks. Each iteration consists of a full software development cycle, including planning, requirements, analysis, design, construction, and testing. Iterations usually conclude with the demonstration of a working product for the business stakeholders. Feedback from demonstrations must be segregated into both bug fixes, which must be resolved for the iteration to be considered complete, and enhancement requests, which will be considered for inclusion in subsequent iterations. The emphasis on working software as the most important measure of progress reduces the need to document requirements and designs prior to construction.

Summary

In this chapter, you learned about the systems development life cycle, including traditional and nontraditional methods. In the next chapter, you will learn about logical database design using the normalization process.

QUIZ

Choose the correct responses to each of the multiple-choice questions. Note that there may be more than one correct response to each question.

1. **During the planning phase of an SDLC project:**
   A. Prototyping takes place.
   B. A database specialist may be assigned to the project.
   C. The database design is normalized.
   D. A feasibility study is often conducted.
   E. Interviews are conducted.

2. **The advantages of conducting interviews are**
   A. Interviews take less time than other methods.
   B. Entities are more easily discovered.
   C. A lot can be learned from nonverbal responses.
   D. Questions are presented more objectively compared with survey techniques.
   E. Answers may be obtained for unasked questions.

3. **During the conceptual design phase:**
   A. New entities may be discovered.
   B. Web pages may be designed.
   C. The conceptual data model is updated.
   D. Application program modules are specified.
   E. Normalization takes place.

4. **During the logical design phase:**
   A. Program modules are written.
   B. Program specifications are written.
   C. The internal components of the application are designed.
   D. System testing takes place.
   E. Normalization takes place.

5. **During the physical design phase:**
   A. DDL is written or generated to define database objects.
   B. Hardware capacity planning takes place.
   C. Additional hardware is added as the database grows.
   D. Additional database indexes may be added.
   E. Application programs are written.

6. **During the construction phase:**

   A. Data conversion for production deployment takes place.
   B. DBA work may be limited to merely running deployment scripts.
   C. Application programs are tested.
   D. Quality assurance testing takes place.
   E. New entities are discovered.

7. **During implementation and rollout:**

   A. Quality assurance testing takes place.
   B. Users are placed on the live system.
   C. Enhancements are designed.
   D. The old and new applications may be run in parallel.
   E. User training takes place.

8. **During ongoing support:**

   A. The staging environment is no longer required.
   B. Bug fixes may take place.
   C. Patches may be applied if needed.
   D. Enhancements are immediately implemented.
   E. Storage for the database may require expansion.

9. **The database is initially constructed in the:**

   A. Development environment.
   B. System test environment.
   C. Quality assurance environment.
   D. Staging environment.
   E. Production environment.

10. **Agile software development includes**

    A. Iterations that run from 7 to 14 days.
    B. Frequent review of completed software.
    C. Thorough project planning before construction begins.
    D. Expanded requirements gathering.
    E. Face-to-face communication among team members.

chapter **6**

Logical Database Design Using Normalization

In this chapter, you will learn how to perform logical database design using a process called *normalization*. In terms of understanding relational database technology, this is the most important topic in this book because it is normalization that teaches you how to best organize your data into tables.

CHAPTER OBJECTIVES

In this chapter, the reader should:

- Understand the normalization process.
- Apply the normalization process during logical database design.
- Build normalization skills using two practice design problems.

171

Overview of Normalization

Normalization is a technique for producing a set of relations that possess certain properties. Dr. E.F. (Ted) Codd, the father of the relational database, developed the process in 1972, introducing three normal forms. The name was a bit of a political gag at the time. President Nixon was "normalizing" relations with China, so Codd figured if you could normalize relations with a country, you should be able to "normalize" data relations as well. Additional normal forms were added later, as discussed toward the end of this chapter.

The normalization process is shown in Figure 6-1. On the surface, it is quite simple and straightforward to understand, but it takes considerable practice to execute the process consistently and correctly. Briefly, we take any *relation* (data represented logically in a two-dimensional [2-D] format using rows and columns) and choose a unique identifier for the entity that the relation represents. Then, through a series of steps that apply various rules, we reorganize the relation into continuously more progressive normal forms. The definitions of each of these normal forms and the process required to arrive at each one are covered in the sections that follow.

Throughout the normalization process, we will use the *logical* terms for everything. For example, Codd used the term *tuple* for a collection of related data items that form one logical record. The more familiar physical term is a

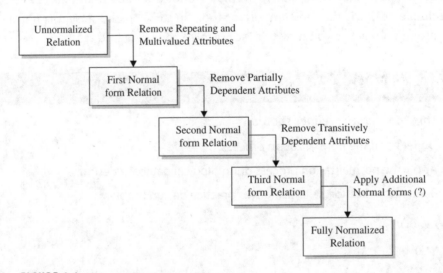

FIGURE 6-1 · The normalization process

? Still Struggling

For beginners, it is often easier to think in terms of the physical objects that will eventually be created from our logical design. This is because learning to think of databases at the conceptual and logical levels of abstraction instead of the physical level is, in fact, a very difficult discipline for your mind to master. If you find yourself thinking of tables instead of relations, and primary keys instead of unique identifiers, you need to break the habit as soon as possible. Those who think only physically while attempting to normalize tables run into difficulties later because there is not necessarily a one-to-one correspondence between normalized relations and tables. In fact, it is physical database design that transforms the normalized relations into relational tables, and there is some latitude in mapping normalized relations to physical tables.

row of data. The following table may help you remember the correspondence between the logical and physical terms:

Logical Term	Physical Term
Relation	Table
Unique identifier	Primary key
Attribute	Column
Tuple	Row

The Need for Normalization

In his early work with relational database theory, Codd discovered that unnormalized relations presented certain problems when attempts were made to update the data in them. He used the term *anomalies* for these problems. The reason we normalize the relations is to *remove* these anomalies from the data. These anomalies are essential to understand because they also tell us when it is acceptable to bend the rules during physical design by "denormalizing" the relations. Denormalization is covered in a section near the end of this chapter. To bend the rules, you have to understand why the rules exist in the first place.

Acme Industries
INVOICE

Customer Number: 1454837
Customer: W.Coyote
     General Deliver
     Falling Rocks, AZ 84211
     (599) 555-9345y

Terms: Net 30
Ship Via: USPS

Order Date: 09/01/2010

Product No.	Description	Quantity	Unit Price	Extended Amount
SPR-2290	Super Strength Springs	2	24.00	$48.00
STR-67	Foot Straps,leather	2	2.50	$ 5.00
HLM-45	Deluxe Crash Helmet	1	67.88	$67.88
SFR-1	Rocket, solidfuel	1	128,200.40	$ 128,200.40
ELT-1	Emergency Location Transmitter	1	79.88	** FREE GIFT **
TOTAL ORDER AMOUNT:				$ 128,321.28

FIGURE 6-2 • Invoice from Acme Industries

Figure 6-2 shows an invoice from Acme Industries, a fictitious company. The invoice contains attributes that are typical for a printed invoice from a supply company. Conceptually, the invoice is a user view. We will use this invoice example throughout our exploration of the normalization process.

Insert Anomaly

The term *insert anomaly* refers to a situation where you cannot insert a new tuple into a relation because of an artificial dependency on another relation. The error that has caused the anomaly is that attributes of two different entities are mixed into the same relation. Referring to Figure 6-2, we see that the number (identifier), name, and address of the customer are included in the invoice view. Were we to merely make a relation from this view as it is, and eventually make a table from the relation, we would soon discover that we could not insert a new customer into the database unless they had bought something. This is because all the customer data is embedded in the invoice.

> An insert anomaly is a situation where you cannot insert a new tuple into a relation because of an artificial dependency on another relation.

Delete Anomaly

The *delete anomaly* is just the opposite of the insert anomaly. It refers to a situation where a deletion of data about one particular entity causes unintended loss of data that characterizes another entity. In the case of the Acme Industries invoice, if we delete the last invoice that belongs to a particular customer, we lose all the data related to that customer. Again, this is because data from two entities (customers and invoices) would be incorrectly mixed into a single relation if we merely implemented the invoice as a table without applying the normalization process to the relation.

> *A delete anomaly is a situation where a deletion of data about one particular entity causes unintended loss of data that characterizes another entity.*

Update Anomaly

The *update anomaly* refers to a situation where an update of a single data value requires multiple tuples (rows) of data to be updated. In our invoice example, if we wanted to change the customer's address, we would have to change it on every single invoice for the customer. This is because the customer address would be redundantly stored in every invoice for the customer. To make matters worse, redundant data provides the golden opportunity to update many copies of the data, but to miss a few of them, which results in inconsistent data. The mantra of the skilled database designer is, For each attribute, capture it once, store it once, and use that one copy everywhere.

> *An update anomaly is a situation where an update of a single data value requires multiple tuples (rows) of data to be updated.*

Applying the Normalization Process

The normalization process is applied to each user view collected during earlier design stages. Some people find it easier to apply the first step (choosing a primary key) to each user view, then to apply the next step (converting to first normal form), and so forth. Other people prefer to take the first user view and apply all the normalization steps to it, then the next user view, and so forth. With practice, you'll know which one works best for you, but whichever you do, you must be *very* systematic in your approach, lest you miss something. Our example has only one user view (the Acme Industries invoice), so this may seem a moot point, but two practice problems toward the end of the chapter contain several user views each, so you will be able to try this out soon enough. Using dry-erase markers or chalk on a wall-mounted board is most helpful because you can easily erase and rewrite relations as you go.

We start with each user view being a relation, which means we represent it as if it is a 2-D table. As you work through the normalization process, you will be rewriting existing relations and creating new ones. Some find it useful to draw the relations with sample tuples (rows) of data in them to assist in visualizing the work. If you take this approach, be certain that your data represents real-world situations. For example, you might not have thought of two customers having exactly the same name in our invoice example, so then your normalization results could be incorrect. Therefore, *always* think of as many possibilities as you can when using this approach. Figure 6-3 shows the information from our invoice example (Figure 6-2) represented in tabular form. Only one invoice is shown here, but many more could be filled in to show examples of multiple invoices per customer, multiple customers, the same product on multiple invoices, and so on.

You probably noticed that each invoice has many line items. This will be essential information when we get to first normal form. In Figure 6-3, multiple values are placed in the cells for the columns that hold data from the line items. We call these *multivalued attributes* because they have multiple values for at least some tuples (rows) in the relation. If we were to construct an actual database table in this manner, our ability to use a language such as SQL to query those columns would be very limited. For example, finding all orders that contained a particular product would require us to parse the column data with a LIKE operator. Updates would be equally awkward because SQL was not designed to handle multivalued columns. Worst of all, a delete of one product from an invoice would require an SQL UPDATE instead of a DELETE because

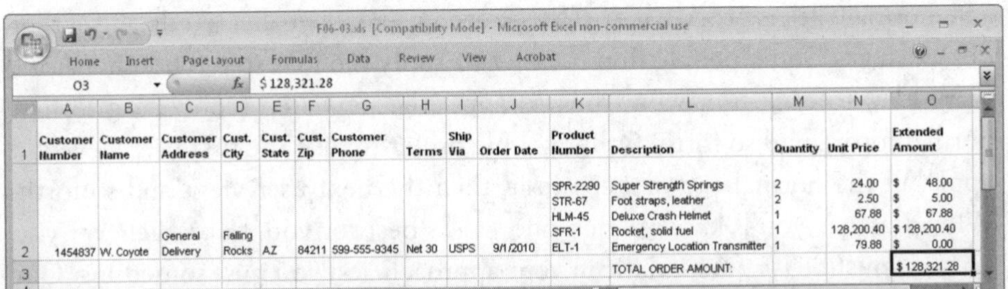

FIGURE 6-3 · Acme Industries invoice represented in tabular form

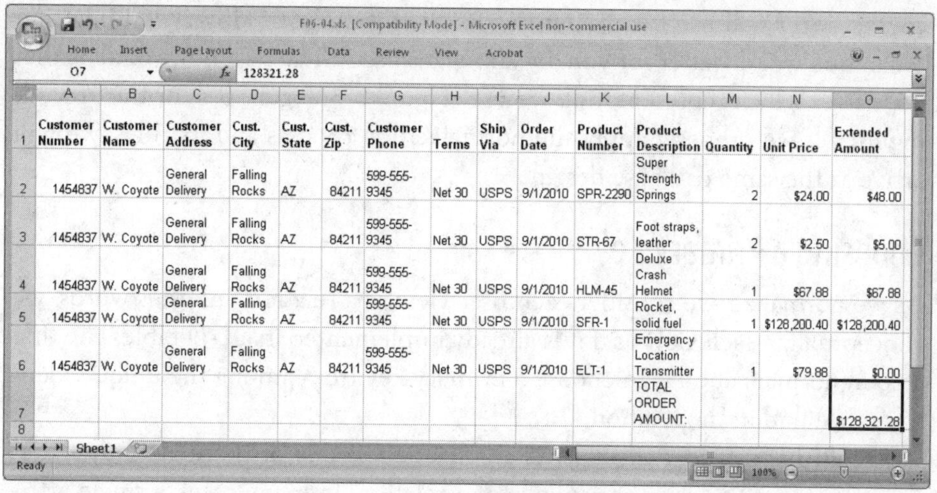

	A	B	C	D	E	F	G	H	I	J	K	L	M	N	O
1	Customer Number	Customer Name	Customer Address	Cust. City	Cust. State	Cust. Zip	Customer Phone	Terms	Ship Via	Order Date	Product Number	Product Description	Quantity	Unit Price	Extended Amount
2	1454837	W. Coyote	General Delivery	Falling Rocks	AZ	84211	599-555-9345	Net 30	USPS	9/1/2010	SPR-2290	Super Strength Springs	2	$24.00	$48.00
3	1454837	W. Coyote	General Delivery	Falling Rocks	AZ	84211	599-555-9345	Net 30	USPS	9/1/2010	STR-67	Foot straps, leather	2	$2.50	$5.00
4	1454837	W. Coyote	General Delivery	Falling Rocks	AZ	84211	599-555-9345	Net 30	USPS	9/1/2010	HLM-45	Deluxe Crash Helmet	1	$67.88	$67.88
5	1454837	W. Coyote	General Delivery	Falling Rocks	AZ	84211	599-555-9345	Net 30	USPS	9/1/2010	SFR-1	Rocket, solid fuel	1	$128,200.40	$128,200.40
6	1454837	W. Coyote	General Delivery	Falling Rocks	AZ	84211	599-555-9345	Net 30	USPS	9/1/2010	ELT-1	Emergency Location Transmitter	1	$79.88	$0.00
7												TOTAL ORDER AMOUNT:			$128,321.28
8															

FIGURE 6-4 • Acme Industries invoice represented without multivalued attributes

we would not want to delete the entire invoice. As we look at first normal form later in this chapter, you will see how to mitigate this problem.

Figure 6-4 shows another way we could organize a relation using the invoice shown in Figure 6-2. Here, the multivalued column data has been placed in separate rows, and the other columns' data has been repeated to match. The obvious problem here is all the repeated data. For example, the customer's name and address are repeated for each line item on the invoice, which is not only wasteful of resources, but also exposes us to inconsistencies whenever the data is not maintained in the same way (for example, we update the city for one line item but not all the others).

Rewriting user views into tables with representative data is a tedious and time-consuming process. For this reason, we'll simply write the attributes as a list and visualize them in our minds as 2-D tables. This takes some practice and some training of the mind, but once mastered, it speeds your ability to normalize relations several-fold over writing out exhaustive examples. Here is the list for the invoice example from Figure 6-2:

```
INVOICE: Customer Number, Customer Name, Customer Address,
         Customer City, Customer State, Customer Zip Code,
         Customer Phone, Terms, Ship Via, Order Date,
         Product Number, Product Description, Quantity,
         Unit Price, Extended Amount, Total Order Amount
```

For clarity, a name for the relation has been added, with the relation name in all capital letters and separated from the attributes with a colon. This is the convention I will use for the remainder of this chapter. However, if another technique works better for you, by all means use it. The best news of all is that no matter which representation we use (Figure 6-3, Figure 6-4, or the preceding list), if we properly apply the normalization process and its rules, we will arrive at the same database design.

Choosing a Primary Key

As we normalize, we consider each user view as a relation. In other words, we conceptualize each view as if it is already implemented in a 2-D table. The first step in normalization is to choose a primary key from among the unique identifiers we find in the relation.

Recall that a *unique identifier* is a collection of one or more attributes that uniquely identifies each occurrence of a relation. In many cases, a single attribute can be found. In our example, the customer number on the invoice uniquely identifies the customer data within the invoice, but because a customer may have multiple invoices, it is inadequate as an identifier for the entire invoice.

When no single attribute can be found to use for a unique identifier, we can concatenate several attributes to form the unique identifier. You will see this happen with our invoice example when we split the line items from the invoice as we normalize it. It is very important to understand that when a unique identifier is composed of multiple attributes, the attributes themselves are not combined—they still exist as independent attributes and will become individual columns in the table(s) created from our normalized relations.

In a few cases, there is no reasonable set of attributes in a relation that can be used as the unique identifier. When this occurs, we must invent a unique identifier, often with values assigned sequentially or randomly as we add entity occurrences to the database. This technique (some might say "act of desperation") is the source of such unique identifiers as social security numbers, employee IDs, and vehicle identification numbers. We call unique identifiers that have real-world meaning *natural* identifiers and call those that do not (which of course includes the ones we must invent) *surrogate* or *artificial* identifiers. Our invoice example appears to have no natural unique identifier for the relation. We could try using customer number combined with order date, but if a customer has two invoices on the same date, this would not be unique. Therefore, it would be much better to invent one, such as an invoice number.

A surrogate identifier is an identifier that has no real-world meaning and is used in place of the natural identifier.

Whenever we choose a unique identifier for a relation, we must be *certain* that the identifier will *always* be unique. If there is only *one* case where it is not unique, we cannot use it. People's names, for example, make lousy unique identifiers. You may have never met someone with exactly your name, but other people out there have completely identical names. As an example of the harm poorly chosen unique identifiers cause, consider the case of the Brazilian government when it started registering voters in 1994 to reduce election fraud. Father's name, mother's name, and date of birth were chosen as the unique identifier. Unfortunately, this combination is only unique for siblings born on *different* dates, so as a result, when siblings born on the same date (twins, triplets, and so on) tried to register to vote, the first one that showed up was allowed to register, and the rest were turned away. Sound impossible? It's not—this really happened. And to make matters worse, citizens are *required* to vote in Brazil and sometimes have to prove they voted in order to get a job. Someone should have spent more time thinking about the uniqueness of the chosen "unique" identifier.

Sometimes a relation will have more than one possible unique identifier. When this occurs, we call each possibility a *candidate*. Once we have identified all the possible candidates for a relation, we must choose one of them to be the primary key for the relation. Choosing a primary key is *essential* to the normalization process because all the normalization rules refer to the primary key. The criteria for choosing the primary key from among the candidates is as follows (in order of precedence, most important first):

- *If there is only one candidate, choose it.*
- *Choose the candidate least likely to have its value change.* Changing primary key values once we store the data in tables is a complicated matter because the primary key can appear as a foreign key in many other tables. Incidentally, surrogate keys are almost always less likely to change compared with natural keys.
- *Choose the simplest candidate.* The one that is composed of the fewest attributes is considered the simplest.

- *Choose the shortest candidate.* This is purely an efficiency consideration. However, when a primary key can appear in many tables as a foreign key, it is often worth it to save some space with each one.

> When there are multiple possible unique identifiers for a relation, we call each a candidate identifier.

For our invoice example, we have elected to add a surrogate primary identifier called Invoice Number. This gives us a simple primary key for the Acme Industries invoices that is guaranteed unique because we can have the database automatically assign sequential numbers to new invoices as they are generated. This will likely make Acme's accountants happy at the same time, because it gives them a simple tracking number for the invoices. There are many conventions for signifying the primary key as we write the contents of relations. Using capital letters causes confusion because we tend to write acronyms such as DOB (date of birth) that way, and those attributes are not always the primary key. Likewise, underlining and bolding the attribute names can be troublesome because these may not always display in the same way. Therefore, we'll settle on the use of a pound sign (#) preceding the attribute name(s) of the primary key. Rewriting our invoice relation in list form with the primary key added, we get the following:

```
INVOICE: # Invoice Number, Customer Number, Customer Name,
         Customer Address, Customer City, Customer State,
         Customer Zip Code, Customer Phone, Terms,
         Ship Via, Order Date, Product Number,
         Product Description, Quantity, Unit Price,
         Extended Amount, Total Order Amount
```

First Normal Form: Eliminating Repeating Data

A relation is said to be in *first normal form* when it contains no multivalued attributes. That is, every intersection of a row and column in the relation must contain *at most* one data value (saying "at most" allows for missing or null values). Sometimes, we will find a group of attributes that repeat together, as with the line items on the invoice. Each attribute in the group is multivalued, but several attributes are so closely related that their values repeat together. This is called a *repeating group*, but in reality, it is just a special case of the multivalued attribute problem.

> *A relation is said to be in first normal form when it contains no multivalued attributes.*

By convention, we enclose repeating groups and multivalued attributes in pairs of parentheses. Rewriting our invoice in this way to show the line item data as a repeating group, we get this:

```
INVOICE: # Invoice Number, Customer Number, Customer Name,
         Customer Address, Customer City, Customer State,
         Customer Zip Code, Customer Phone, Terms,
         Ship Via, Order Date, (Product Number,
         Product Description, Quantity, Unit Price,
         Extended Amount), Total Order Amount
```

It is essential to understand that although we know there are many customers of Acme Industries, there is only one customer for any given invoice, so the customer data on the invoice is *not* a repeating group. You may have noticed that the customer data for a given customer is repeated on every invoice for that customer, but this is a problem that we will address when we get to third normal form. Because there is only one customer per invoice, the problem is not addressed when we transform the relation to first normal form.

To transform unnormalized relations into first normal form, we must move multivalued attributes and repeating groups to new relations. Because a repeating group is a set of attributes that repeat *together*, all attributes in a repeating group should be moved to the same new relation. However, a multivalued attribute (individual attributes that have multiple values) should be moved to its own new relation rather than combined with other multivalued attributes in the new relation. As you will see later, this technique avoids fourth normal form problems. The procedure for moving a multivalued attribute or repeating group to a new relation is as follows:

1. Create a new relation with a meaningful name. Often, it makes sense to include all or part of the original relation's name in the new relation's name.

2. Copy the primary key from the original relation to the new one. The data depended on this primary key in the original relation, so it must still depend on this key in the new relation. The copied primary key now becomes a *foreign key* to the original relation. As you apply normalization to

a database design, always keep in mind that eventually you will have to write SQL to reproduce the original user view from which you started. So, having foreign keys to join things back together is essential.

3. Move the repeating group or multivalued attribute to the new relation. (The word "move" is used because these attributes are "removed" from the original relation.)

4. Make the primary key (as copied from the original relation) unique by adding attributes from the repeating group to it. If you move a multivalued attribute, which is basically a repeating group of only one attribute, it is that attribute that is added to the primary key. This will seem odd at first, but the primary key attribute (or set of attributes) that you copied from the original table is a *foreign key* in the new relation. It is quite normal for part of a primary key to also be a foreign key. One additional point: It is perfectly acceptable to have a relation where all the attributes are part of the primary key (that is, there are no "non-key" attributes). This is relatively common in intersection tables.

5. Optionally, you may choose to replace the primary key with a single surrogate key attribute. If you do so, you must keep the attributes that make up the natural primary key formed in steps 2 and 4.

For our Acme Industries invoice example, here is the result of converting the original relation to first normal form:

```
INVOICE: # Invoice Number, Customer Number, Customer Name,
         Customer Address, Customer City, Customer State,
         Customer Zip Code, Customer Phone, Terms,
         Ship Via, Order Date, Total Order Amount

INVOICE LINE ITEM: # Invoice Number, # Product Number,
         Product Description, Quantity, Unit Price,
         Extended Amount
```

Note the following:

- The Invoice Number attribute was copied from INVOICE to INVOICE LINE ITEM, and Product Number was added to it to form the primary key of the INVOICE LINE ITEM relation.

- The entire repeating group (Product Number, Product Description, Quantity, Unit Price, and Extended Amount) was removed from the INVOICE relation.

- Invoice Number is still the primary key in INVOICE, and it now also serves as a foreign key in INVOICE LINE ITEM as well as being *part* of the primary key of INVOICE LINE ITEM.

- There are no repeating groups or multivalued attributes in the relations, so they are therefore in first normal form.

An interesting consequence of composing a natural primary key for the INVOICE LINE ITEM relation is that we cannot put the same product on a given invoice more than one time. While preventing a product from appearing on an invoice more than once might be desirable, it could also restrict Acme Industries. We have to understand their business rules to know. If Acme Industries wants the option of putting multiple line items on the same invoice for the same product (perhaps with different prices), we should make up a surrogate key instead. Moreover, some believe that primary keys composed of multiple attributes are undesirable, along with software products that simply do not support them. The alternative is to make up a surrogate primary key for the INVOICE LINE ITEM relation. If we choose to do so, the relation may be rewritten this way:

```
INVOICE LINE ITEM: # Invoice Line Item Number,
                   Invoice Number, Product Number,
                   Product Description, Quantity,
                   Unit Price, Extended Amount
```

I am going to use the previous form (the one with the compound primary key made up of Invoice Number and Product Number, often called the *natural key*) as we continue with normalization.

Second Normal Form: Eliminating Partial Dependencies

Before we explore second normal form, you must understand the concept of *functional dependence.* For this definition, we'll use two arbitrary attributes, cleverly named "A" and "B." Attribute B is *functionally dependent* on attribute A if at any moment in time no more than one value of attribute B is associated with a given value of attribute A. Lest you wonder what planet I lived on before this one, let me try to make the definition more understandable. First, if we say that attribute B is functionally dependent on attribute A, what we are also saying is that attribute A *determines* attribute B, or that A is a *determinant* (unique identifier) of attribute B. Second, let's look again at the first normal form relations in our Acme Industries example:

```
INVOICE: # Invoice Number, Customer Number, Customer Name,
         Customer Address, Customer City, Customer State,
         Customer Zip Code, Customer Phone, Terms,
         Ship Via, Order Date, Total Order Amount

INVOICE LINE ITEM: # Invoice Number, # Product Number,
         Product Description, Quantity, Unit Price,
         Extended Amount
```

> *Functional dependence is the term used when an attribute (or set of attributes) determines another attribute.*

In the INVOICE relation, we can easily see that Customer Number is functionally dependent on Invoice Number because at any point in time, there can be only one value of Customer Number associated with a given value of Invoice Number. The very fact that the Invoice Number uniquely identifies the Customer Number in this relation means that, in return, the Customer Number is *functionally dependent* on the Invoice Number.

In the INVOICE LINE ITEM relation, we can also say that Product Description is functionally dependent on Product Number because, at any point in time, there is only one value of Product Description associated with the Product Number. However, the fact that the Product Number is only part of the key of the INVOICE LINE ITEM is the very issue addressed by second normal form.

A relation is said to be in *second normal form* if it meets both the following criteria:

- The relation is in first normal form.
- All non-key attributes are functionally dependent on the *entire* primary key.

> *A relation is in second normal form if it is in first normal form and all non-key attributes are functionally dependent on the entire primary key.*

If we look again at Product Description, it should be easy to see that Product Number *alone* determines the value. Said another way, if the same product appears as a line item on many different invoices, the Product Description is the same *regardless* of the Invoice Number. Or we can say that Product Description is functionally dependent on only *part of* the primary key, meaning it depends only on Product Number and not on the *combination* of Invoice Number *and* Product Number.

It should also be clear by now that second normal form only applies to relations where we have concatenated primary keys (that is, those made up of multiple attributes). If we have a primary key composed of only a single attribute, as we do with the first normal form version of the INVOICE relation, and the primary key is atomic (that is, has no subparts that make sense by themselves), as all attributes should be, then it is simply not possible for anything to depend on *part* of the primary key. It follows, then, that any first normal form relation that has only a single attribute for its primary key is *automatically* in second normal form.

Looking at the INVOICE LINE ITEM relation, however, second normal form violations should be readily apparent: Product Description and Unit Price depend only on the Product Number instead of the *combination* of Invoice Number and Product Number. But not so fast! What about price changes? If Acme decides to change their prices, how could we possibly want that change to be retroactive for every invoice we have ever created? After all, an invoice is an official record that we must maintain for seven years, per current tax laws. This is a common dilemma with fast-changing attributes such as prices. Either we must be able to recall the price at any point in time, or we must store the price with the invoice so we can reproduce the invoice as needed (that is, when the friendly tax auditors come calling). For simplicity, we have elected to store the price in two places, one being the current selling price, and the other being the price at the time the sale was made. Because the latter is a snapshot at a point in time that is not expected to change, there are no anomalies to this seemingly redundant storage. An alternative would be to store a date-sensitive price history somewhere that we could use to reconstruct the correct price for any invoice. That is a practical alternative here, but you would never be able to do that with stock or commodities market transactions, for example. The point is that while the sales price *looks* redundant, there are no *anomalies* to the additional attribute, so it does no harm. Notice that we adjusted the attribute names so their meaning is abundantly clear.

Once we find a second normal form violation, the solution is to move the attribute (or set of attributes) that is partially dependent to a new relation where it depends on the *entire* key instead of *part* of the key. Here is our invoice example rewritten into second normal form:

```
INVOICE: # Invoice Number, Customer Number, Customer Name,
         Customer Address, Customer City, Customer State,
         Customer Zip Code, Customer Phone, Terms,
         Ship Via, Order Date, Total Order Amount

INVOICE LINE ITEM: # Invoice Number, # Product Number,
         Quantity, Sale Unit Price, Extended Amount

PRODUCT:  # Product Number, Product Description,
          List Unit Price
```

The improvement from our first normal form solution is that maintenance of the Product Description now has no anomalies. We can set up a new product independent of there being an invoice for the product. If we wish to change the Product Description, we may do so by merely changing one value in one row of data. Also, should the last invoice for a particular product be deleted from the database for whatever reason, we won't lose its description (it will still be in the row in the Product relation). *Always* remember that the reason we are normalizing is to eliminate these anomalies.

Third Normal Form: Eliminating Transitive Dependencies

To understand third normal form, you must first understand transitive dependency. An attribute that depends on another attribute that is not the primary key of the relation is said to be *transitively dependent*. Looking at our INVOICE relation in second normal form, you can clearly see that Customer Name is dependent on Invoice Number (each Invoice Number has only one Customer Name value associated with it), but at the same time, Customer Name is also dependent on Customer Number. The same can be said of the rest of the customer attributes as well. The problem here is that attributes of another entity (Customer) have been included in our INVOICE relation.

A relation is said to be in *third normal form* if it meets both the following criteria:

- The relation is in second normal form.
- There is no transitive dependence (that is, all the non-key attributes depend *only* on the primary key).

A relation is in third normal form if it is in second normal form and has no transitive dependence.

To transform a second normal form relation into third normal form, simply move any transitively dependent attributes to relations where they depend only on the primary key. Be careful to leave the attribute on which they depend in the original relation as a foreign key. You will need it to reconstruct the original user view via a join.

If you have been wondering about easily calculated attributes such as Extended Amount in the INVOICE LINE ITEM relation, it is actually third normal form that forbids them, but it takes a subtle interpretation of the rule. Because the Extended Amount is calculated by multiplying Sale Unit Price by Quantity, it follows that Extended Amount is *determined by* the combination of Sale Unit Price and Quantity and therefore is *transitively dependent* on those two attributes. Thus, it is third normal form that tells us to remove easily calculated attributes. And in this case, they are simply removed. Using similar logic, we also removed the Total Order Amount from the INVOICE relation because we can simply sum the INVOICE LINE ITEM relation to reproduce the value. A good designer will make a note in the documentation specifying the formula for the calculated attribute so that its value can be reproduced when needed. Another effective alternative is to always write the SQL that reproduces the original views when you complete a normalization process. It's an excellent way to *test* your normalization because you can use the SQL to *prove* that the original user views can be easily reproduced.

Here is the Acme Industries invoice data rewritten into third normal form:

```
INVOICE: # Invoice Number, Customer Number, Terms,
         Ship Via, Order Date

INVOICE LINE ITEM: # Invoice Number, # Product Number,
         Quantity, Sale Unit Price

PRODUCT: # Product Number, Product Description,
         List Unit Price

CUSTOMER: # Customer Number, Customer Name,
         Customer Address, Customer City, Customer State,
         Customer Zip Code, Customer Phone
```

Did you notice one more possible third normal form violation? If we have the complete nine-digit ZIP code for the customer, doesn't that determine the Customer City and State? Yes, but it must be the *complete* nine-digit ZIP code (called "zip plus 4" by the U.S. Postal Service). In the past there have been five-digit ZIP codes in the United States that actually cross state lines. Moreover, there are thousands of examples of different cities and towns sharing the same five-digit ZIP codes. So be careful when you assume things. The U.S. Postal Service will be the first to tell you that they are not responsible for aligning their zoning system with political boundaries. By the way, ZIP is actually an acronym for Zone Improvement Plan, introduced in 1963.

Should we then make a Zip Code relation and normalize the City and State out of all our addresses? Or would that be considered overdesign? The question can be answered by going back to the anomalies, because removal of the insert, update, and delete anomalies is the entire reason we normalize data in the first place:

- If a new city is formed, do we need to add it to our database even if we have no customers located there? (This is an insert anomaly.)
- If a city is dissolved, do we need to delete its information without losing other data? (This is a delete anomaly.)
- If a city changes its name (this rarely occurs, but it has happened), is it a burden to us to find all the customers in that city and to change their address accordingly?

If you answered yes to any of the above, then you should normalize the City and State attributes into a table with a primary key of Zip Code. In fact, you can purchase that data on a regular basis from the U.S. Postal Service or other sources. Furthermore, if you maintain other data by ZIP code, such as shipping rates, you have all the more reason to normalize it. But if not, the Zip Code example is a valuable lesson in why we normalize and when it may not be as important. Common sense must prevail at all times.

? Still Struggling

Here is an easy way to remember the rules of first, second, and third normal form: In a third normal form relation, every non-key attribute must depend on the key, the whole key, and nothing but the key, so help me Codd.

Beyond Third Normal Form

Since the original introduction of normalization, various researchers and authors have offered advanced versions. Third normal form will cover well over 90 percent of the cases you will see in business information systems, and it's considered the "gold standard" in business systems. Once you have mastered third normal form, additional normal forms are worth knowing.

Boyce-Codd Normal Form

Boyce-Codd normal form (BCNF) is a stronger version of third normal form. It addresses anomalies that occur when a non-key attribute is a *determinant* of an attribute that is part of the primary key (that is, when an attribute that is part of the primary key is functionally dependent on a non-key attribute).

As an example, let's assume that Acme Industries assigns multiple product support specialists to each customer, and each support specialist handles only one particular product line. Following is a relation that assigns specialists to customers. In reality, we would use Customer ID and Support Specialist (Employee) ID instead of the customer and support specialist names, but their names are used here for better illustration of the issue.

Customer	Product Line	Support Specialist
W. Coyote	Springs	R. E. Coil
W. Coyote	Straps	B. Brown
W. Coyote	Helmets	C. Bandecoot
W. Coyote	Rockets	R. Goddard
USAF	Rockets	R. Goddard
S. Gonzalez	Springs	R. E. Coil
S. Gonzalez	Straps	B. Brown
S. Gonzalez	Rockets	E. John
L. Armstrong	Helmets	S. D. Osborne

In this example, we must concatenate the Customer and Product Line attributes to form a primary key. However, because a given support specialist only supports one product line, it is also true that the Support Specialist attribute determines the Product Line attribute. If we had chosen a surrogate primary key instead of combining Customer and Product Line for the primary key, the third normal form violation—a non-key attribute determining another non-key attribute (Support Specialist determining Product Line in this case)—would be obvious. However, we masked the normalization error by making Product Line part of the primary key. This is why BCNF is considered a *stronger* version of third normal form.

The Boyce-Codd normal form has two requirements:

- The relation must be in third normal form.
- No determinants exist that are not either the primary key or a candidate key for the table. That is, a non-key attribute may not uniquely identify (determine) any other attribute, including one that participates in the primary key.

The solution is to split the unwanted determinant to a different table, just as you would with a third normal form violation. The BCNF version of this relation is shown here:

```
SUPPORT SPECIALIST ASSIGNMENT: # CUSTOMER ID,
                                 SUPPORT SPECIALIST ID

SUPPORT SPECIALIST SPECIALTY: # SUPPORT SPECIALIST ID,
                                PRODUCT LINE
```

In tabular form, the relations and data look like this (again, names have been substituted for the IDs to make the data easier to visualize):

Customer	Support Specialist
W. Coyote	R. E. Coil
W. Coyote	B. Brown
W. Coyote	C. Bandecoot
W. Coyote	R. Goddard
USAF	R. Goddard
S. Gonzalez	R. E. Coil
S. Gonzalez	B. Brown
S. Gonzalez	E. John
L. Armstrong	S. D. Osborne

Support Specialist	Product Line
B. Brown	Straps
C. Bandecoot	Helmets
E. John	Rockets
R. E. Coil	Springs
R. Goddard	Rockets
S. D. Osborne	Helmets

Fourth Normal Form

An additional anomaly surfaces when two or more multivalued attributes are included in the same relation. Suppose, for example, that we wish to track both office skills and language skills for our employees. We might come up with a relation such as this one:

Employee ID	Office Skill	Language Skill
1001	Typing, 40 wpm	Spanish
1001	10 key	French
1002	Spreadsheets	Spanish
1002	10 key	German

We can form a primary key for this relation by choosing the combination of either Employee ID and Office Skill, or Employee ID and Language Skill. That leaves us with either of these two alternatives for third normal form relations:

```
EMPLOYEE SKILL: # EMPLOYEE ID, # OFFICE SKILL,
        LANGUAGE SKILL

EMPLOYEE SKILL: # EMPLOYEE ID, # LANGUAGE SKILL,
        OFFICE SKILL
```

Both the alternatives shown are in third normal form, and in fact, both pass Boyce-Codd normal form as well. The problem, of course, is that there is an implied relationship between office skills and language skills. Does the first tuple for employee 1001 imply that he or she can only type in Spanish? And does the second tuple imply he or she can only work a French 10-Key pad?

Relations such as these are rare in real life because when experienced designers resolve multivalued attribute problems to satisfy first normal form, they move each multivalued attribute to its own relation rather than combining them as shown here. So, with some strict interpretation of first normal form procedures, this can be avoided altogether. However, should you encounter a fourth normal form violation, the remedy is simply to put each multivalued attribute in a separate relation, such as these:

```
EMPLOYEE OFFICE SKILL: # EMPLOYEE ID, # OFFICE SKILL

EMPLOYEE LANGUAGE SKILL: # EMPLOYEE ID, # LANGUAGE SKILL
```

Fifth Normal Form

Fifth normal form is very easy to understand. You simply keep splitting relations, stopping only when one of the following conditions is true:

- Any further splitting would lead to relations where the original view cannot be reconstructed with joins.
- The only splits left are trivial. *Trivial splits* occur when resulting relations have a primary key consisting only of the primary key or candidate key of the other relation.

While fifth normal form seems to forbid all three-way relationships, some of these are legitimate. Problems arise only when the entities can be split into simpler, more fundamental relationships.

To most practitioners, fifth normal form is synonymous with *fully normalized*. However, in recent years, database management guru C.J. (Chris) Date has proposed a sixth normal form that deals with temporal and interval data. It remains to be seen whether it will be widely adopted.

Domain-Key Normal Form (DKNF)

Ron Fagin introduced domain-key normal form (DKNF) in a research paper published in 1981. The theory is that a relation is in DKNF if and only if every constraint on the relation is a result of the definitions of domains and keys. Although Fagin was able to prove that relations in DKNF have no modification anomalies, he provided no procedure or step-by-step rules to achieve it. The dilemma then is that designers have no solid indication of when DKNF has been achieved for a relation. This is likely why DKNF is not in widespread use and is not generally expected in the design of databases for business applications.

Denormalization

As you have seen, normalization leads to more relations, which translates to more tables and more joins. When database users suffer performance problems that cannot be resolved by other means, such as tuning the database or upgrading the hardware on which the RDBMS runs, then denormalization may be required. Most database experts consider denormalization a last resort, if not an act of desperation. With continuous improvements in hardware and RDBMS efficiencies, denormalization has become far less necessary than in the earlier days of relational databases. The most essential point is that denormalization is not the same as not bothering to normalize in the first place. Once a normalized database design has been achieved, adjustments can be made with the potential consequences (anomalies) in mind. Possible denormalization steps include the following:

- Recombining relations that were split to satisfy normalization rules
- Storing redundant data in tables
- Storing summarized data in tables

Note also that normalization is intended to remove anomalies from databases that are used for online transaction-processing systems. Databases that store historical data used solely for analytical purposes are not as subject to insert, update, and delete anomalies. Chapter 12 contains more information on databases that hold historical information.

Practice Problems

This section contains two practice problems with solutions so you can try normalization for yourself. These are very narrow, scaled-down case problems that most readers should be able to solve in about an hour each. As you work them, you will be more successful if you focus just on the views presented and do not worry about other business processes and data that might be needed. For each case problem, the intent is for you to produce third normal form relations that support the views presented and then to draw an ERD for the normalized relations. As you draw the ERDs, keep in mind that they are quite easy to do once normalization is complete—you simply create a rectangle for each normalized relation and then draw relationships everywhere the entire primary key in one relation is used as a foreign key in another (or the same) relation. These should all be one-to-many relationships, and the foreign key must always be on the *many* side of the relationship. Each problem concludes with the author's solution.

TLA University Academic Tracking

The University of Three-Letter Acronyms (UTLA) is a small academic facility offering undergraduate and continuing adult education. Most of the recordkeeping is either manual or done by individuals using personal tools such as spreadsheets. A modernization effort is underway, which includes building integrated application and database systems to perform basic business functions.

The User Views

UTLA wishes to construct a system to track their academic activities, including course offerings, instructor qualifications for the courses, course enrollment, and student grades. The following illustrations show the desired output reports with sample data (these are the user views that should be normalized):

Student report:

Student Report:

ID	Name	Mailing Address				Home Phone
4567	Helen Wheels	127 Essex Drive	Hayward	CA	94545	510-555-2859
4953	Barry Bookworm	P.O. Box45	Oakland	CA	94601	510-555-9403
6758	Carla Coed	South Hall #23	Berkeley	CA	94623	510-555-8742

Course report:

Course Report:

ID	Title	No. Credits	Prerequisite Courses	Description
X100	Concepts of Data Proc.	4	None	This course...
X301	C Programming I	4	X100	Students learn...
X302	C Programming II	6	X301	Continuation of...
X422	Systems Analysis	6	X301	Introduction to...
X408	Concepts of DBMS	6	X301,X422	The main focus...

Instructor report:

Instructor Report:

ID	Name	Home Address	Home Phone	Office Phone	Courses
756	Werdna Leppo	12 Main St. Alameda CA 94501	510-555-1234	x-7463	X408, X422
795	Cora Coder	32767 Binary Way Abend CA 21304	510-555-1010	x-5328	X301, X302
801	Tillie Talker	123Forms Rd. Paperwork CA 95684	510-555-2829	408-555-2047	X100, X422

Section report:

Section Report:

Year: 2010 **Semester:** Spr **Building:** Evans **Room:** 70 **Day(s):** Tu **Time(s):** 7-10

Instructor: 756, Werdna Leppo **Course:** X408 **Credits:** 6

Student ID	Student Name	Grade
4567	Helen Wheels	A
6758	CarlaCoed	B+

Year: 2010 **Semester:** Spr **Building:** SFO **Room:** 7 **Day(s):** We **Time(s):** 7-10

Instructor: 756, Werdna Leppo **Course:** X408 **Credits:** 6

Student ID	Student Name	Grade
4973	Barry Bookworm	B+
6758	CarlaCoed	A-

Year: 2010 **Semester:** Spr **Building:** Evans **Room:** 70 **Day(s):** M,Fr **Time(s):** 7-9

Instructor: 801, Tillie Talker **Course:** X100 **Credits:** 4

Student ID	Student Name	Grade

We cannot design a database without some knowledge of the business rules and processes of an organization. Here are a few such items to keep in mind:

- Only one mailing address and one contact phone number are kept for each student.

- Each course has a fixed number of credits (that is, there are no variable-credit courses).

- Each course may have one or more prerequisite courses. The list of all prerequisite courses for each course is shown in the Course report.

- Only one mailing address, one home phone number, and one office phone number are kept for each instructor.

- A qualifications committee must approve instructors before they are permitted to teach a particular course. The qualifications (that is, the courses that the committee has determined the instructor is qualified to teach) are then added to the instructor's records, as shown in the Instructor report. The list of qualified courses does not imply that the instructor has ever actually taught the course, only that he or she is qualified to do so.

- Based on demand, any course may be offered multiple times, even in the same year and semester. Each offering is called a "section," as shown in the Section report.

- A section exists even if no students have enrolled in it, as shown in the last section in the Section report.

- Students enroll in a particular section of a course and receive a grade for their participation in that course offering. Should they take the course again later, they receive another grade, and both grades are part of their permanent academic record.

- Although the day, time, building, and room for each section are noted in the Section report, this is done merely to facilitate registering students. The scheduling of classrooms is out of scope for this project.

- The day(s) and time(s) attributes on the Section report are merely text descriptions of the meeting schedule. The building of a meeting calendar for sections is out of scope for this project.

As a convenience, here are the attributes rewritten using our relation-listing method, with repeating groups and multivalued attributes enclosed in parentheses:

```
STUDENT REPORT: # ID, NAME, STREET ADDRESS, CITY, STATE,
                ZIP CODE, HOME PHONE

COURSE REPORT: # ID, TITLE, NUMBER OF CREDITS,
               (PREREQUISITE COURSES), DESCRIPTION

INSTRUCTOR REPORT: # ID, NAME, STREET ADDRESS, CITY, STATE,
                   ZIP CODE, HOME PHONE, OFFICE PHONE,
                   (QUALIFIED COURSES)

SECTION REPORT: YEAR, SEMESTER, BUILDING, ROOM, DAYS,
                TIMES, INSTRUCTOR ID, INSTRUCTOR NAME,
                COURSE ID, NUMBER OF CREDITS,
                (STUDENT ID, STUDENT NAME, GRADE)
```

Author's Solution

Database design is not an exact science, so there is some latitude for alternative solutions. However, all must meet the criteria for third normal form. Here are the normalized relations, with the pound sign (#) denoting primary key attributes:

```
COURSE: # COURSE ID, TITLE, DESCRIPTION, NUMBER OF CREDITS

INSTRUCTOR: # INSTRUCTOR ID, NAME, HOME ADDRESS STREET,
            HOME ADDRESS CITY, HOME ADDRESS STATE,
            HOME ADDRESS ZIP CODE, HOME PHONE, OFFICE PHONE

COURSE SECTION: # SECTION ID, YEAR, SEMESTER, COURSE ID,
                BUILDING, ROOM, MEETING DAY, MEETING TIME,
                INSTRUCTOR ID

STUDENT: # STUDENT ID, NAME, HOME ADDRESS, CITY, STATE,
         ZIP CODE, PHONE

STUDENT SECTION: # STUDENT ID, # SECTION ID, GRADE

COURSE PREREQUISITE: COURSE ID, PREREQUISITE COURSE ID

COURSE INSTRUCTOR QUALIFIED: INSTRUCTOR ID, COURSE ID
```

A few notes on this particular solution are in order:

- There was no simple natural key for the Course Section relation, so a surrogate key was added.
- The Course Prerequisite relation can be quite confusing. This is the intersection relation for a many-to-many recursive relationship. A course can

have many prerequisites, which may be found by joining COURSE ID in the COURSE relation with COURSE ID in the COURSE PREREQUISITE relation. At the same time, any course may be a prerequisite for many other courses. These may be found by joining COURSE ID in the COURSE relation with PREREQUISITE COURSE ID in the COURSE PREREQUISITE relation. This means that there are *two* relationships between the COURSE and COURSE PREREQUISITE: one where COURSE ID is the foreign key and another where PREREQUISITE COURSE ID is the foreign key. Comparing the upcoming illustrations for the COURSE and COURSE_PREREQUISITE tables should help make this point clear.

To assist you in visualizing how all this works, the following illustrations show each of the tables as implemented in a Microsoft Access database, each loaded with the data from the original user view (report) examples. The last illustration shows the ERD for the solution, using the Microsoft Relationships panel as the presentation media.

COURSE table:

INSTRUCTOR table:

COURSE_SECTION table:

STUDENT table:

STUDENT_ID	STUDENT_NAME	HOME_ADDRESS	HOME_ADDRESS_CITY	HOME_ADDRESS_STATE	HOME_ADDRESS_ZIP_CODE	HOME_PHONE
4567	Helen Wheels	127 Essex Drive	Hayward	CA	94545	510-555-2859
4973	Barry Bookworm	P.O. Box 45	Oakland	CA	94601	510-555-9403
6758	Carla Coed	South Hall #23	Berkeley	CA	94623	510-555-8742

STUDENT_SECTION table:

STUDENT_ID	SECTION_ID	GRADE
4567	1	A
4973	2	B+
6758	1	B+
6758	2	A-

COURSE_PREREQUISITE table:

COURSE_ID	PREREQUISITE_COURSE_ID
X301	X100
X302	X301
X408	X301
X408	X422
X422	X301

COURSE_INSTRUCTOR_QUALIFIED table:

COURSE_ID	INSTRUCTOR_ID
X100	801
X301	795
X302	795
X408	756
X422	756
X422	801

UTLA ERD:

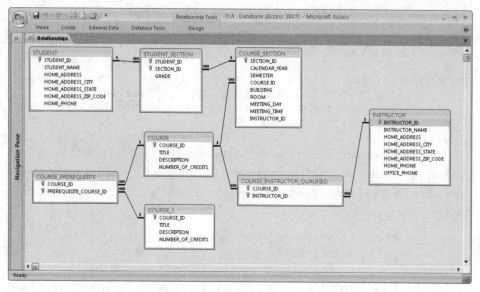

Computer Books Company

The Computer Books Company (CBC) buys books from publishers and sells them to individuals via mail and telephone orders. They are looking to expand their services by offering online ordering via the Internet, and in doing so, have a compelling need to build a database to hold their business information.

The User Views

Throughout these user views, "sale" and "price" refer to the retail sale of a book to a CBC customer, whereas "purchase" and "cost" refer to the purchase of books from a publisher (CBC supplier). Each user view is described briefly with a list of the attributes in the view following each description. Per our convention, multivalued attributes and repeating groups are enclosed in parentheses.

The Book Catalog lists all the books that CBC has for sale. Each book is uniquely identified by its International Standard Book Number (ISBN). Although an ISBN uniquely identifies a book, it is essentially a surrogate key, so there is no way to tell what edition a particular book is simply by looking at the ISBN. When new editions come out, CBC typically has leftover stock of prior editions and offers them at a reduced price. The previous edition code in the Book Catalog is intended to help the buyer find the prior edition, if there is one. Books are organized by subject, with each book having only one subject.

Any book may have multiple authors. (Although the catalog shows only author names, keep in mind that people's names are seldom unique, and nothing would stop two people with the same name from both writing books.) Here is the information in the Book Catalog:

```
BOOK CATALOG: SUBJECT CODE, SUBJECT DESCRIPTION, BOOK TITLE,
              BOOK ISBN, BOOK PRICE, PREVIOUS EDITION ISBN,
              PREVIOUS EDITION PRICE, (BOOK AUTHORS),
              PUBLISHER NAME
```

The Book Inventory Report helps the warehouse manager control the inventory in the warehouse. The Recommended Quantity is the reorder point, meaning when on-hand inventory falls below the recommended quantity, it is time to order more books of that title.

```
BOOK INVENTORY REPORT: BOOK ISBN, BOOK EDITION CODE, COST,
                       SELLING PRICE, QUANTITY ON HAND,
                       QUANTITY ON ORDER, RECOMMENDED QUANTITY
```

The Customer Book Orders view shows the orders placed by CBC customers for purchases of books:

```
CUSTOMER BOOK ORDERS: CUSTOMER ID, CUSTOMER NAME,
                      STREET ADDRESS, CITY, STATE,
                      ZIP CODE (ISBN, BOOK EDITION CODE,
                      QUANTITY, PRICE), ORDER DATE,
                      TOTAL PRICE
```

CBC bills customers as books are shipped. An invoice is created for each shipment. (An order can have zero, one, or more invoices, but each invoice belongs to only one order.) The Book Sales Invoice looks like this:

```
BOOK SALES INVOICE: SALES INVOICE NUMBER, CUSTOMER ID,
                    CUSTOMER NAME, CUSTOMER STREET ADDRESS,
                    CUSTOMER CITY, CUSTOMER STATE,
                    CUSTOMER ZIP CODE, (BOOK ISBN, TITLE,
                    EDITION CODE, (BOOK AUTHORS), QUANTITY,
                    PRICE, PUBLISHER NAME),
                    SHIPPING CHARGES, SALES TAX
```

The Master Billing Report helps the Collections and Customer Service departments manage customer accounts. A system for recording customer payments against invoices is out of scope for the current project, but the CBC project sponsors do want to keep a running balance showing what each customer owes CBC. As invoices are generated, a database trigger will be used to add invoice totals to the Balance Due. As payments are received, the CBC staff will manually adjust the Balance Due. The Master Billing Report attributes are as follows:

```
MASTER BILLING REPORT: CUSTOMER ID, NAME, STREET ADDRESS,
                       CITY, STATE, ZIP CODE, PHONE,
                       BALANCE DUE
```

Each time CBC buys books from a publisher, the publisher sends an invoice to CBC. To assist in managing inventory cost, CBC wishes to store the Purchase Invoice information and report it using this view:

```
PURCHASE INVOICE: PUBLISHER ID, PUBLISHER NAME,
                  STREET ADDRESS, CITY, STATE, ZIP CODE,
                  PURCHASE INVOICE NUMBER, INVOICE DATE,
                  (BOOK ISBN, EDITION CODE, TITLE,
                  QUANTITY, COST EACH, EXTENDED COST),
                  TOTAL COST
```

NOTE *Extended Cost is calculated as Cost Each × Quantity.*

Author's Solution

As before, there is some room for alternative solutions, provided all relations are in third normal form. The normalized relations in this solution follow, with primary keys noted with a pound sign (#):

```
BOOK: # ISBN, BOOK TITLE, SUBJECT CODE, PUBLISHER ID,
      EDITION CODE, COST, SELLING PRICE, QUANTITY ON HAND,
      QUANTITY ON ORDER, RECOMMENDED QUANTITY,
      PREVIOUS EDITION ISBN

CUSTOMER ORDER: # CUSTOMER ORDER NUMBER, CUSTOMER ID,
      ORDER DATE

CUSTOMER ORDER BOOK: # CUSTOMER ORDER NUMBER, # ISBN,
      QUANTITY, BOOK PRICE

SUBJECT: # SUBJECT CODE, DESCRIPTION

AUTHOR: # AUTHOR ID, AUTHOR NAME

BOOK-AUTHOR: # AUTHOR ID, # ISBN

CUSTOMER: # CUSTOMER ID, NAME, STREET ADDRESS, CITY, STATE,
      ZIP CODE, PHONE, BALANCE DUE
```

```
PUBLISHER: # PUBLISHER ID, NAME, STREET ADDRESS, CITY,
       STATE, ZIP CODE, AMOUNT PAYABLE

RECEIVABLE (SHIPPED) ORDER: # SALES INVOICE NUMBER,
       CUSTOMER ORDER NUMBER, SALES TAX, SHIPPING CHARGES

RECEIVABLE ORDER BOOK: # SALES INVOICE NUMBER, # ISBN,
       QUANTITY

PAYABLE (PURCHASES): # PURCHASE INVOICE NUMBER,
       PUBLISHER ID, INVOICE DATE, INVOICE AMOUNT

PAYABLE BOOK: # PURCHASE INVOICE NUMBER, # ISBN, QUANTITY,
       COST EACH
```

The following illustration shows the complete design implemented in Microsoft Access:

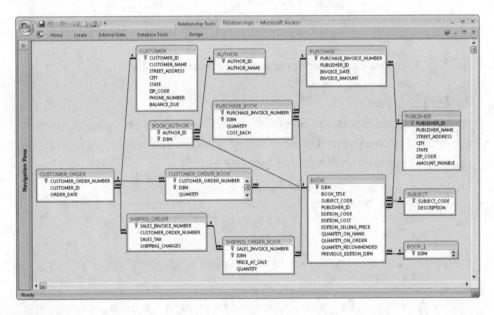

Summary

In this chapter, you learned about the normalization process and various normal forms. You also honed your normalization skills using two practice problems. In the next chapter, we look at data and process modeling.

QUIZ

Choose the correct responses to each of the multiple-choice questions. Note that there may be more than one correct response to each question.

1. **Normalization:**
   A. Was developed by E.F. Codd
   B. First appeared in 1972
   C. Provides a set of rules for each normal form
   D. Provides a procedure for converting relations to each normal form
   E. Was first introduced with five normal forms

2. **The insert anomaly refers to a situation where:**
   A. Data must be inserted before it can be deleted.
   B. Data must be deleted before it can be inserted.
   C. Too many inserts cause the table to fill up.
   D. A required insert cannot be done due to duplicate data.
   E. A required insert cannot be done due to an artificial dependency.

3. **The update anomaly refers to a situation where:**
   A. Data cannot be updated because it does not exist in the database.
   B. Data cannot be updated due to lack of privileges.
   C. Data cannot be updated due to an existing referential constraint.
   D. A simple update requires updates to multiple rows of data.
   E. Data cannot be updated due to an existing unique constraint.

4. **Writing sample user views with representative data in them is**
   A. A tedious and time-consuming process
   B. An effective way to understand the data being normalized
   C. The only way to successfully normalize the user views
   D. A widely used normalization technique
   E. Only as good as the examples shown in the sample data

5. **First normal form resolves anomalies caused by:**
   A. Join dependencies
   B. Multivalued attributes
   C. Repeating groups
   D. Partial dependency on the primary key
   E. Transitive dependencies

6. **Third normal form resolves anomalies caused by:**

    A. Join dependencies
    B. Multivalued attributes
    C. Repeating groups
    D. Partial dependency on the primary key
    E. Transitive dependencies

7. **Boyce-Codd normal form deals with anomalies caused by:**

    A. Join dependencies
    B. Multivalued attributes
    C. Determinants that are not primary or candidate keys
    D. Constraints that are not the result of the definitions of domains and keys
    E. Transitive dependencies

8. **Fourth normal form deals with anomalies caused by:**

    A. Join dependencies
    B. Multivalued attributes
    C. Determinants that are not primary or candidate keys
    D. Constraints that are not the result of the definitions of domains and keys
    E. Transitive dependencies

9. **Fifth normal form deals with anomalies caused by:**

    A. Multivalued attributes
    B. Determinants that are not primary or candidate keys
    C. Transitive dependencies
    D. Constraints that are not the result of the definitions of domains and keys
    E. Join dependencies

10. **Domain key normal form deals with anomalies caused by:**

    A. Multivalued attributes
    B. Determinants that are not primary or candidate keys
    C. Transitive dependencies
    D. Constraints that are not the result of the definitions of domains and keys
    E. Join dependencies

chapter 7

Data and Process Modeling

As you saw in Chapter 5, data and process modeling are major undertakings that are part of the logical design stage of an application system development project. You have seen the rudiments of data modeling when you used entity-relationship diagrams (ERDs) in preceding chapters. In this chapter, we will look at ERDs and data modeling in more detail. Process modeling, on the other hand, is less important to a database designer because application processes are designed by application designers and seldom directly involve the database designer. However, because the database designer must work closely with the application designer in gathering data requirements and in supplying a database design that will support the processes being designed, the database designer should at least be familiar with the basic concepts. For this reason, the second part of this chapter includes a high-level survey of process design concepts and diagramming techniques.

CHAPTER OBJECTIVES

In this chapter, the reader should:

- Understand the fundamentals of entity-relationship modeling, including Chen's format, the relational format, the information engineering (IE) format, the IDEF1X format, Unified Modeling Language (UML), and methods of depicting supertypes and subtypes.

- Understand basic process-modeling techniques, including the flowchart, the function hierarchy diagram, the swim lane diagram, the data flow diagram, and UML process-modeling diagrams.

- Know how to correlate entities with processes using the CRUD (Create, Read, Update, and Delete) matrix.

Entity Relationship Modeling

Entity relationship modeling is the process of visually representing entities, attributes, and relationships to produce the ERD. The process is iterative in nature because entities are discovered throughout the design process. The chief advantage of ERDs is that they can be understood by nontechnical people while still providing great value to technical people. Done correctly, ERDs are platform independent and can even be used for nonrelational databases if desired.

ERD Formats

Peter Chen developed the original ERD format in 1976. Since then, vendors, computer scientists, and academics have developed many variations, all of them conceptually the same. You should understand the most commonly used variations because you are likely to encounter them actively used in IT organizations. Here are the elements common to all ERD formats:

- Entities are represented as rectangles or boxes.
- Relationships are represented as lines.
- Line ends (or symbols next to them) indicate the maximum cardinality of the relationship (that is, one or many).

- Symbols near the line ends (in most ERD formats) indicate the minimum cardinality of the relationship (that is, whether participation in the relationship is mandatory or optional).

- Attributes may be optionally included (the format for displaying attributes varies quite a bit).

Chen's Format

For simplicity, we'll use the normalized solution for the Acme Industries invoice application from Chapter 6 for the examples in this chapter. Figure 7-1 shows the ERD using Chen's format.

Here are the particulars of the Chen format:

- Relationship lines contain a diamond in which a word or short phrase describes the relationship. For example, the relationship between Invoice and Product may be read as "An invoice *contains* many products." Some variations permit another word or phrase, separated with a slash, to be used in reading the relationship in the other direction. If the diamond read "Contains/Appears on," then the relationship from Product to Invoice would be read as "A product *appears on* many invoices."

- For many-to-many relationships that require an intersection table in an RDBMS, such as the one between Invoice and Product, a rectangle is often drawn around the diamond.

- Maximum cardinality of each relationship is shown using the symbol *1* for "one" or *M* for "many."

- Minimum cardinality is not shown.

- Attributes, when shown, appear in ellipses (elongated circles) connected with a line to the entity or relationship to which they belong.

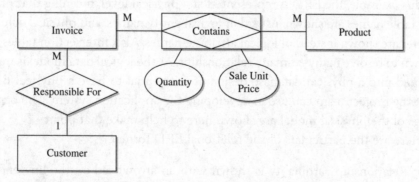

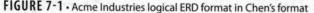

FIGURE 7-1 · Acme Industries logical ERD format in Chen's format

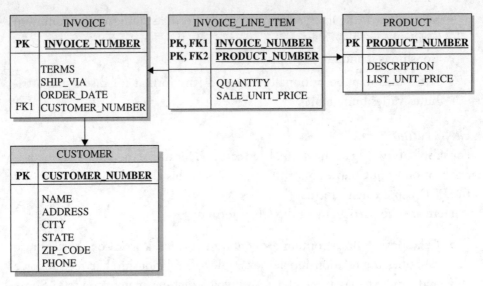

FIGURE 7-2 · Acme Industries physical ERD, relational format

In practice, Chen ERDs are cumbersome for complicated data models. The diamonds take up a lot of space on the diagrams for the little added value they provide. Also, any ERD that includes many attributes becomes very difficult to read. Notwithstanding, we owe Chen a lot for his pioneering work, which laid the foundation for the techniques that followed.

The Relational Format

Over time, an ERD format known generically as the *relational format* evolved. It is available as an option in several of the better-known data modeling software tools, including PowerDesigner from Sybase and ER/Studio from Embarcadero Technologies, and in popular general drawing tools such as Visio from Microsoft. Figure 7-2 shows the ERD from Figure 7-1 converted to the relational format. In this example, the ERD is represented at a physical level, meaning that physical table names are shown instead of logical entity names, and physical column names are shown instead of logical attribute names. Also, intersection tables are shown to resolve many-to-many relationships. As the logical data model is transformed into a physical database design, it is essential to have a physical ERD that the project team can use in developing the application system. The beginnings of the physical model are shown here to help make that point.

Here are the particulars of the relational ERD format:

- Relationship cardinality is shown with an arrowhead on the line end to signify "one" and nothing on the line end to signify "many." This will seem odd at first, but it aligns nicely with object diagrams, so this format is favored by object-oriented designers and developers.

- Attributes are shown inside the rectangle that represents each entity.
- Unique identifier attributes are shown above a horizontal line within the rectangle and are usually also shown with *PK* in bold type (for primary key) in the margin to the left of the attribute name.
- Attributes that are foreign keys are shown with *FK* and a number in the margin to the left of the attribute name.

The Information Engineering Format

The information engineering (IE) format was originally developed by Clive Finkelstein in Australia in the late 1970s. In the early 1980s he collaborated with James Martin to publicize it in the United States and Europe, including coauthoring the Savant Institute Report titled *Information Engineering*, published in 1981. Martin went on to be highly associated with the format, and in collaboration with Carma McClure, published a book on the subject in 1984 (*Diagramming Techniques for Analysis and Programmers*, Prentice-Hall). Finkelstein later published his own version in 1989 (*An Introduction to Information Engineering*, Addison-Wesley), which has some minor notation variations compared with Martin's version. Figure 7-3 shows our sample ERD converted to IE notation. You will notice that except for relationship lines, it is strikingly similar to the relational format.

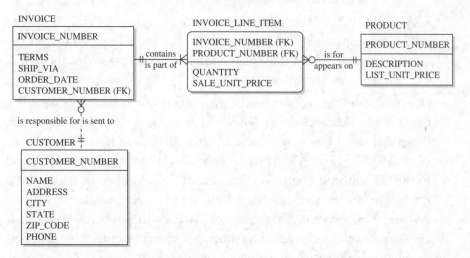

FIGURE 7-3 · Acme Industries physical ERD, IE format

Here are some of the ways that IE notation varies from the relational format:

- **Identifying relationships**   Shown with a solid line are those for which the foreign key is part of the child entity's primary key.

- **Non-identifying relationships**   Shown with a dotted line are those for which the foreign key is a non-key attribute in the child entity. In Figure 7-3, the relationship between PRODUCT and INVOICE_LINE_ITEM is identifying, but the one between CUSTOMER and INVOICE is non-identifying.

- **Maximum relationship cardinality**   Shown with a short perpendicular line across the relationship near its line end to signify "one" and with a "crow's foot" on the line end to signify "many." This is best understood in combination with minimum cardinality, described next.

- **Minimum relationship cardinality**   Shown with a small circle near the end of the line to signify "zero" (participation in the relationship is optional) or with a short perpendicular line across the relationship line to signify "one" (participation in the relationship is mandatory). Figure 7-3 shows a few combinations of minimum and maximum cardinality. For example:

  - **A PRODUCT**   May have zero to many associated INVOICE_LINE_ITEM occurrences (shown as a circle and a crow's foot); an INVOICE_LINE_ITEM must have one and only one associated PRODUCT (shown as two vertical bars).

  - **An INVOICE**   Must have one or more associated INVOICE_LINE_ITEM occurrences (shown as a vertical bar and a crow's foot); an INVOICE_LINE_ITEM must have one and only one associated INVOICE (shown as two vertical bars).

- **Dependent entities**   Shown with the corners of the rectangle rounded, they have an existence dependency on one or more other entities (that is, those that cannot exist without the existence of another). For example, the INVOICE_LINE_ITEM entity depends on both the PRODUCT and INVOICE entities. Therefore, you cannot delete either an invoice or a product unless you somehow deal with any related invoice line items. This is valuable information during physical database design because you must consider the options for handling situations when the application attempts to delete table rows when dependent entities exist.

? Still Struggling

You may have noticed the two short perpendicular lines at some of the line ends in Figure 7-3. The one nearest the line end indicates a maximum cardinality of 1 while the one just to the left indicates a *minimum* cardinality of 1. Therefore, when used together in this way, the pair of short perpendicular lines can be read to mean "one and only one."

The IE format is by far the most popular. Therefore, I use it for the majority of the diagrams in this book.

The IDEF1X Format

The Computer Systems Laboratory of the National Institute of Standards and Technology (NIST) released the IDEF1X standard for data modeling in FIPS Publication 184, first published in December 1993. The standard covers both a method for data modeling as well as the format for the ERDs produced during the modeling effort. It is widely used and understood across the information technology industry and is the mandatory standard for many branches of the U.S. government. Thanks to its underlying standard, it has few variants. Figure 7-4 shows our sample ERD converted to the IDEF1X standard format.

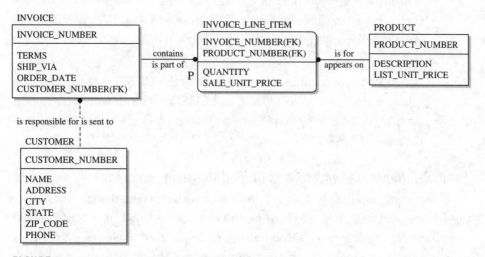

FIGURE 7-4 · Acme Industries physical ERD, IDEF1X format

The differences between IE and IDEF1X notation are largely isolated to relationships. Here are some key points:

- As in the IE format, a solid line indicates that the foreign key is part of the dependent entity's primary key, while a broken line indicates that the foreign key will be a non-key attribute.

- A solid circle next to an entity generally means zero, one, or more occurrences of that entity, as shown on the "many" end of the line between PRODUCT and INVOICE_LINE_ITEM. However, there are exceptions:

  - Adding the symbol *P* near the solid circle makes the relationship mandatory, signifying that the cardinality must be one or more. In Figure 7-4, the relationship from INVOICE to INVOICE_LINE_ITEM is one-to-many and mandatory, meaning that every invoice must have at least one line item.

  - Adding the symbol *1* also makes the relationship mandatory. However, this changes the cardinality of the relationship to *one*. Said another way, it changes the meaning of the solid circle from "may be one or more" to "must be one and only one."

- Absence of a solid circle at the end of the relationship line means that only one occurrence of the entity is involved. For example, the absence of any symbol on the end of the line next to CUSTOMER means "one and only one." It may be modified for optionality as well:

  - If no symbol appears next to the entity at that end of the line, the entity is mandatory in the relationship. Therefore an INVOICE_LINE_ITEM must be related to one and only one PRODUCT.

  - If a small diamond symbol appears next to the entity, the entity is optional. Were we to add a diamond next to the CUSTOMER end of the relationship between INVOICE and CUSTOMER, it would mean that each INVOICE *may* have zero or one related CUSTOMER occurrences.

Entity Relationship Modeling with Unified Modeling Language

With the rising popularity of object programming languages, the *Unified Modeling Language (UML)* has also become more popular. UML is a standardized visual specification language for object modeling that includes a graphical notation used to create an abstract model of a system, which is known as

?

Still Struggling

Many beginners to database design find the IDEF1X format confusing. Unlike other formats, relationship symbols in IDEF1X are asymmetrical. Each set of symbols describes a combination of optionality and cardinality, and thus the symbols used for optionality vary depending on the cardinality of the relationship. Said another way, optionality is shown differently for the "many" and "one" sides of a relationship.

a UML model. The Rational Unified Process (RUP), developed by Rational Software Corporation (now a division of IBM), uses UML exclusively. UML has 13 types of diagrams that can be used to model the behavior and structure of the system. However, the one of interest to data modelers is the class diagram. Figure 7-5 shows our sample model converted to a UML class diagram.

While the differences in notation are strikingly obvious, an individual skilled in reading ER diagrams can easily adapt. I have used so-called *camelcase* names in the diagram, meaning names with the first letter of each word capitalized

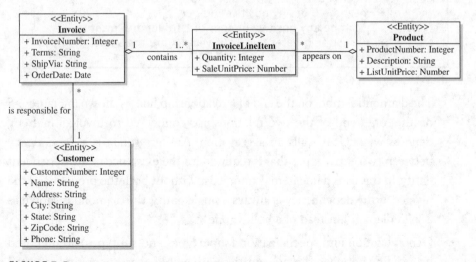

FIGURE 7-5 • UML class diagram for Acme Industries

and no delimiters between words, because nearly all UML modelers do so. Here are some key points regarding modeling entities using UML class diagrams:

- Each entity is shown as an object class in a rectangle. The symbol *<<Entity>>* is included with the class name to denote the type of class.
- Unique identifiers (primary keys) are not shown in class diagrams; they are specified elsewhere within the UML model.
- Foreign keys are not shown because they are not used in object-oriented systems. I discuss object-oriented technology in Chapter 13.
- Attributes are shown with a name and a type (separated with a colon). The type is very much like a relational data type. Attributes in entities are preceded by the symbol +, which means they are public (visible throughout the entire model).
- Relationships are shown with lines.
- Cardinality and optionality are shown with a combined symbol near the end of the line. Available symbols include those shown in the following table:

Symbol	Meaning
1	One and only one
*	Zero, one, or more
1..*	One or more
x..y	Between *x* and *y* occurrences. Also • *x* can be 0 or any positive integer • *y* can be any positive integer or * to denote "or more" • *y* must be greater than *x* (if *y* and *x* are the same, then *y* is simply omitted)

- The diamond symbol on the end of a relationship line, as shown in Figure 7-5 on the "one" end of the two relationships connected to InvoiceLineItem, denotes what UML calls an aggregation. An *aggregation* is a dependency between two entity types that is required for the existence of the dependent entity. In this case, a line item cannot exist without both the product and the invoice. If the dependency is always a single entity, the diamond is shown as a solid diamond instead of a hollow one.
- Generalization and specialization (supertypes and subtypes) are denoted using a line between the two entities with a hollow arrow pointing toward the general class (the supertype).

In UML models, an aggregation is a dependency between two entity types that is required for the existence of the dependent entity.

Supertypes and Subtypes

Some entities can be broken down into more specific categories or types. When this occurs, we call the more detailed entities *subtypes* and the more general entity to which they belong a *supertype*. In object terminology, the supertype is called a *superclass* or *base class*, and the subtypes are called *subclasses* of the superclass. It is essential that you understand that subtypes break down entities by type rather than by *state*, meaning their mode or condition. An easy way to distinguish between the two is to realize that existing entities can change state, but they seldom, if ever, change type. For example, a motor vehicle entity can logically be broken down by type into automobile, bus, truck, motorcycle, and so on. However, the distinction between vehicles that are new or used, or between those that are operable or inoperable, is one of *state* rather than *type* because new vehicles become used once they are sold, and vehicles change between inoperable and operable states as they break down and are subsequently repaired.

TERMS: Supertype and Subtype

Supertypes and subtypes always go together—you can't have one without the other. A supertype is a more general classification that is broken down into two or more subtypes. For example, circle, square and rectangle are subtypes of a supertype called geometric shape.

The decisions involved in which entities should be broken down into subtypes and how detailed the subtypes should be revolve around the trade-off between specialization and generalization. Unfortunately, there are no firm rules for resolving the trade-off. Therefore, generalization versus specialization becomes one of the topics that prevent database design from becoming an exact science. The physical design trade-offs involved are addressed in Chapter 8. Here, we will focus on the logical design trade-offs.

? Still Struggling

If you are having difficulty deciding when to specialize or generalize a database design (that is when to split an entity into subtypes versus when to combine subtypes into a supertype), you are not alone. This topic has been the source of many debates (some of the heated) among even seasoned professionals. The general guideline to follow (in addition to common sense) is that the more the various subtypes share common attributes and relationships, the more the designer should be inclined to combine the subtypes into the supertype.

Let's look at an example. Assume for a moment that the database design shown in Figure 7-3 has been implemented, and now the Customer Service Department at Acme Industries has requested database and application enhancements that will allow it to record and track more information about customers. In particular, the department is interested in knowing the type of customer (such as individual person, sole proprietorship, partnership, or corporation) so that correspondence can be addressed appropriately for each type. Figure 7-6 shows the logical data model that was developed based on the new requirements.

In IE notation, the type or category is shown using a symbol that looks like a circle with a line under it. Therefore, you know that Individual Customer and Commercial Customer are subtypes of Customer because of the symbol that appears in the line that connects them. Also note that they share the same primary key and that in the subtypes, the primary key of the entity is also a foreign key to the supertype entity. This makes perfect sense when you consider that an Individual Customer entity *is* a Customer, meaning that any occurrence of the Individual Customer entity would have a tuple in the Customer relation as well as a matching tuple in the Individual Customer entity. Usually, an attribute in the supertype entity indicates which subtype is assigned to each entity occurrence (tuple). Once this is implemented in tables, database users can use the type attribute to know where to look for (that is, which subtype table contains) the remainder of the information about each entity

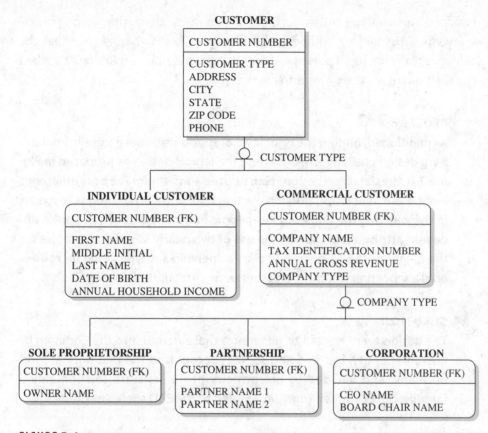

FIGURE 7-6 · Customer subclasses

occurrence (each row). Such an attribute is called the *type discriminator* and is named next to the type symbol on the ERD. Therefore, Customer Type is the type discriminator that indicates whether a given Customer is an Individual Customer or a Commercial Customer. Similarly, Company Type is the type discriminator that indicates whether a given Commercial Customer is a sole proprietorship, partnership, or corporation.

> *A type discriminator is an attribute in a supertype entity that indicates which subtype applies to each entity occurrence (row).*

As you might imagine, this IE notation is not the only format used in ERDs for supertypes and subtypes. However, it is the most commonly used method. Another popular format is to draw the subtype entities within the supertype entity (that is, subtype entity rectangles drawn inside the corresponding super-type entity's rectangle). Although this format makes it visually clear that the subtypes really are just a part of the supertype, it has practical limitations when the entities are broken down into many levels.

PROBLEM 7-1

As mentioned, finding the right level of specialization is a significant data-base design challenge. In reviewing the logical design as proposed in Fig-ure 7-6, the database design team noticed something: The only difference among the Sole Proprietorship, Partnership, and Corporation subtypes is in the way that the names of key people in those types of companies ap-pear as attributes. Moreover, the use of two nearly identical attributes for the names of the co-owners in the Partnership subtype could be consid-ered a repeating attribute, and therefore a first normal form violation.

SOLUTION

The design team elected to generalize these names into the Commercial Customer entity, but in doing so, they recognized the first normal form problems and decided to place them into a separate relation called Commercial Customer Principal. This led to the ERD shown in Figure 7-7.

Clearly, this is a simpler design that will result in fewer tables when it is physically implemented. It offers a very big win because not only is there no loss of function when you consolidate the subtypes into the supertype, but also you actually have *more* function available because you can add as many names as you want to any type of commercial customer.

PROBLEM 7-2

Further study by the design team helped them realize the similarity between the name attributes now contained in the Commercial Customer Principal entity and those contained in the Individual Customer entity. In discussing options further with the Customer Service Department, the design team uncovered a few cases for which it would be desirable for mul-tiple contact names to be recorded for individual customers as well as for commercial customers. For example, customers that have legal disputes often request that all contact go through an attorney.

✔ SOLUTION

Based on the preceding information, the design team decided to generalize these names and move Commercial Customer Principal up to be a child of Customer and to name it Customer Contact so that it could be used to hold the information about either a principal (owner, co-owner, partner, officer) of the customer or any other contact person for the customer that the Customer Service Department might find useful. The design team further realized that contact names would be more useful if a phone number were included. The Phone attribute was left in the Customer entity because it is intended to hold the general phone number for the customer. The phone number in the Customer Contact entity is intended to hold the phone for an individual contact person. The resultant logical design is shown in Figure 7-8.

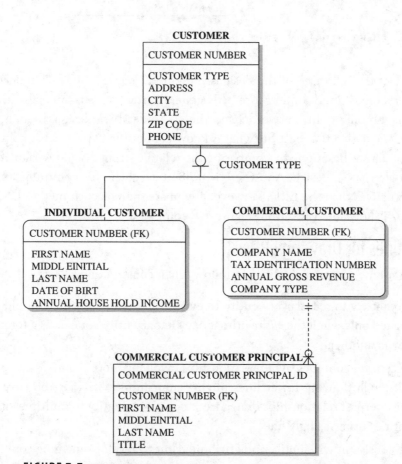

FIGURE 7-7 • Customer subtypes, version 2

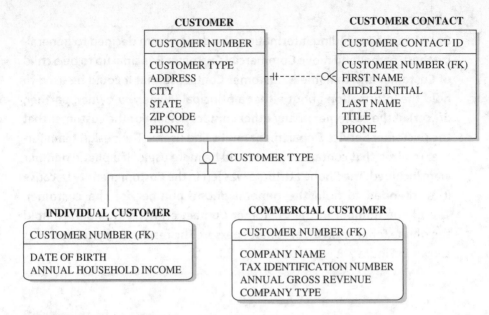

FIGURE 7-8 · Customer subtypes, version 3

The fact that all three of the designs presented (Figures 7-6, 7-7, and 7-8) are workable should underscore the generalization-versus-specialization dilemma: no one "right" answer exists. The art to database design, then, is to arrive at the design that best fits what is known about the expected uses of the database. This is best done by comparing the relative strengths and weaknesses of each alternative design. And there is no better vehicle for communicating the alternatives than the ERD. However, if you are more accustomed to UML, Figure 7-9 shows the ERD from Figure 7-8 converted to UML.

Guidelines for Drawing ERDs

Here are some general guidelines to follow when constructing ERDs:

- Do not try to relate every entity to every other entity. Entities should be related only when the *entire* primary key in one entity appears as a foreign key in another.

- Except for subtypes, avoid relationships involving more than two entities. Although drawing fewer lines might seem simpler, it is far too easy to misinterpret relationships drawn from one parent entity to multiple child entities using a single line.

- Be consistent with entity and attribute names. Develop a naming convention and stick with it.

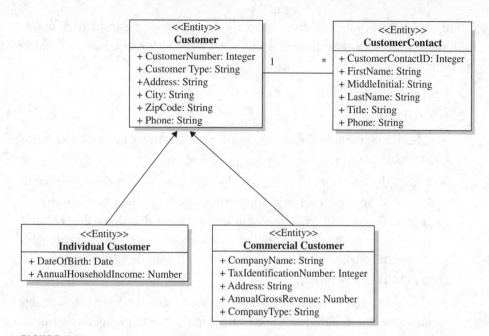

FIGURE 7-9 · Customer subtypes, version 3, converted to UML

- Use abbreviations in names only when absolutely necessary, and in those cases, use a standard list of abbreviations.

- Name primary keys and foreign keys consistently. Most experts prefer that the foreign key attributes (columns) have exactly the same name as the corresponding primary key attributes (columns).

- When relationships are named, strive for action words, avoiding nondescriptive terms such as "has," "belongs to," "is associated with," and so on.

Process Models

As mentioned, process design is seldom the responsibility of the database designer or DBA, but understanding the basics helps the DBA communicate with the process designers and ensure that the database design supports the process design. Therefore, this section presents a brief survey of common process-model-diagram techniques. If you want more detail about these or other process model techniques, find a good book on systems analysis and design.

Throughout, this section uses as an example the Acme Industries order-fulfillment process, a very simple business process. This process has the following steps:

1. Find all unshipped orders in the database.

2. For each order, do the following:

   - Check for available inventory. If sufficient inventory for the order is not available, skip to the next order.

   - Check the customer's credit to make sure they are not over their credit limit and do not have some other credit problem, such as overdue payments. This would typically occur at the time the order is entered, but it needs to occur again here because a customer's credit status with Acme Industries can change at any time. If a credit problem is found, skip to the next order.

   - Generate the documents required to pack and ship the order (packing slip, shipping labels, and so on), and route them to the Shipping Department.

   - When the Shipping Department has finished with the order, create the invoice for the order and bill the customer accordingly.

Obviously, this process could be a lot more complicated in a large company, but here it has been reduced to the basics to make it easier to illustrate process models.

The Flowchart

The flowchart (or structure chart) is probably the oldest form of computer systems documentation. Some believe that flowcharts are so old that anyone who still uses them is a dinosaur. Levity aside, flowcharts are often considered outmoded, but they still have much to offer in certain circumstances and are still widely used. Figure 7-10 shows the flowchart for our sample order-fulfillment process.

Here are the basic components of the flowchart:

- Process steps are shown with rectangles.

- Decision points are shown with diamonds. At each decision point, the logic branches are based on the outcome of the decision. For example, a decision might be "Is today Friday?" with a "Yes" outcome going in one direction and a "No" outcome going in another.

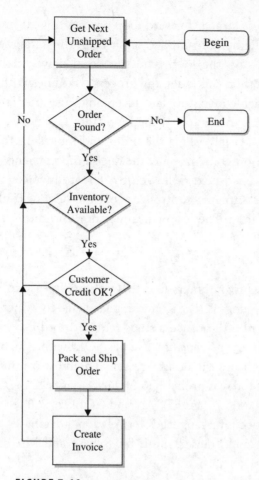

FIGURE 7-10 · Flowchart of Acme Industries order-fulfillment process

- Lines with arrows show the flow of control through the diagram. When one process completes, it hands over control to the next process or decision point.

- Start and endpoints are shown with either ellipses or rounded rectangles. Flowcharts can be used to show perpetual processes that have no start and no end, but more often they are used to show finite processes with specific beginning and ending points.

- Connector symbols that look like home plates on a baseball diamond (not shown in Figure 7-10) can be used to connect lines to processes or decision points on the same or another page. Usually these are given a reference letter, with a control flow line assumed between any two connectors that have the same reference letter.

Figure 7-10 shows a very straightforward loop process flow. It begins with a process step that gets the next unshipped order from the database. A decision is added after it to stop the loop (end the flow) if we don't find an unshipped order. If we do find the order, the process continues with decision points that check for available inventory and acceptable customer credit, with a "No" outcome going back to the top of the loop (the "Get next unshipped order" process), which essentially skips the order and moves on to find the next one. If we get a "Yes" outcome from all the decision points, the "Pack and ship order" process is invoked next, followed by "Create invoice." After the "Create invoice" process completes, control goes back to "Get next unshipped order," at the top of the loop. The loop continues until no more unshipped orders are found.

Flowcharts have the following strengths:

- Procedural language programmers find them naturally easy to learn and use. A *procedural language* is a programming language by which the programmer must describe the process steps required to do something, as opposed to a *nonprocedural language*, such as SQL, with which the programmer merely describes the desired results. The most commonly used procedural language today is probably C and its variants (C++, C#, and so on), but others, such as PL/1, FORTRAN and COBOL, still see some use. Also, specialized procedural languages for relational databases, including PL/SQL for Oracle and Transact SQL for Sybase and Microsoft SQL Server, are heavily used.

- Flowcharts are applicable to procedures outside of a programming context. For example, flowcharts are often used to walk repair technicians through troubleshooting procedures for the equipment they service.

- Flowcharts are useful for spotting reusable (common) components. The designer can easily find any process that appears multiple times in the flowcharts for a particular application system.

- Flowcharts may be easily modified and can evolve as requirements change.

On the other hand, flowcharts present these weaknesses:

- They are not applicable to nonprocedural or object-oriented languages.

- They cannot easily model some situations, such as recursive processes (processes that invoke themselves).

> ## TERMS: **Procedural language**
>
> A *procedural language* is a programming language by which the programmer must describe the process steps required to do something, as opposed to a *non-procedural language*, such as SQL, with which the programmer merely describes the desired results.

The Function Hierarchy Diagram

The *function hierarchy diagram*, as the name suggests, shows all the functions of a particular application system or business process, organized into a hierarchical tree. Figure 7-11 shows this type of process model diagram from our sample order-fulfillment process.

Because the function hierarchy for a single process makes little sense out of context, two other processes have been added to the hierarchy: Order Entry and History Management. To be effective, a function hierarchy must contain *all* the processes required to carry out the function it describes. Figure 7-11 attempts to show all the processes required for the Order Management function at Acme Industries. Order entry is intended to cover all the process steps involved in a customer placing an order and having it recorded in Acme's database. History Management is intended to cover all the steps required to archive

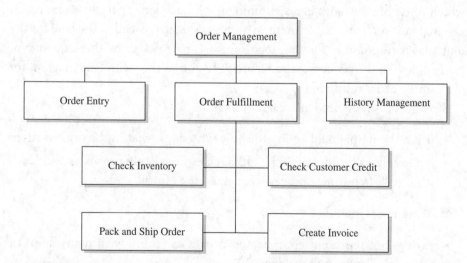

FIGURE 7-11 · Function hierarchy of the Acme order-fulfillment process

and purge old (historical) orders and any required reporting on order history. Both of these processes need to be expanded by adding process steps below them (as was done with Order Fulfillment) to make this a complete diagram. Under Order Fulfillment, the four main process steps involved in fulfilling orders have been added.

The strengths of function hierarchy diagrams are as follows:

- They are quick and easy to learn and use.
- They can quickly document the bulk of the function (they get to 80 percent of the processes quickly).
- They provide a good overview at high and medium levels of detail.

And here are the weaknesses of function hierarchy diagrams:

- Checking quality is difficult and subjective.
- They cannot handle complex interactions between functions.
- They do not clearly show the sequence of process steps or dependencies between steps.
- They are not an effective presentation tool for large hierarchies or at very detailed levels.

The Swim Lane Diagram

The *swim lane diagram* gets its name from the vertical lanes in the diagram, which resemble the lanes in a swimming pool. Each lane represents an organizational unit such as a department, with process steps placed in the lane for the unit that is responsible for the step. Lines with arrows show the sequence or control flow of the process steps. Figure 7-12 shows the swim lane diagram for our sample order-fulfillment process.

Strengths of the swim lane diagram include

- It has the unmatched ability to show who does what in the organization.
- It's excellent for identifying inefficiencies in existing processes and lends itself well to business process reengineering efforts.

Its weaknesses include

- It does not represent complicated processes (those with many steps or with complex step dependencies) well.
- It does not show error and exception handling.

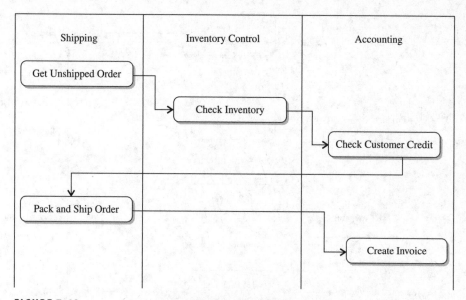

FIGURE 7-12 · Swim lane diagram for the Acme Industries order-fulfillment process

The Data Flow Diagram

The *data flow diagram (DFD)* is the most data-centric of all the process diagrams. Instead of showing a control flow through a series of process steps, it focuses on the data that flows through the process steps. By combining diagrams hierarchically, the DFD combines the best of the flowchart and the function diagram. DFDs became immensely popular in the late 1970s and early 1980s, largely due to the work of Chris Gane and Trish Sarson. Each process on a DFD can be broken down using another complete page until the desired level of detail is reached. Figure 7-13 shows one page of the DFD for the Acme Industries order-fulfillment process.

The components of a DFD are simple:

- Processes are represented with rounded rectangles. Processes are typically numbered hierarchically. The first page of a DFD might have processes numbered 1, 2, 3, and 4. The next page might break down process number 1 and would have processes numbered 1.1, 1.2, and so forth. If process 1.2 were broken down on yet another page, the processes on that page would be numbered 1.2.1, 1.2.2, and so forth.

- Data stores are represented with an open-ended rectangle. A *data store* is a generic representation of data that is made persistent through being

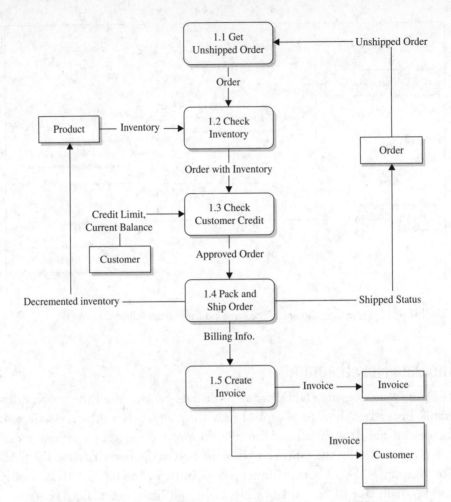

FIGURE 7-13 · Data flow diagram page for the Acme Industries order-fulfillment process

stored somewhere such as a file, database, or even a written document. The term was chosen so that no particular type of storage is implied. Because we already have an ERD for our example, we should closely align the data stores with the entities we have already identified.

- Sources and destinations of data ("external entities" in relational terminology) are shown using squares. Figure 7-13 shows the Customer as the destination of the invoice data flow (in addition to a local data store that will hold the invoice data). Try not to confuse data flows with material flows. Yes, the invoice is printed and mailed to the customer, but the data flow is attempting to show that the *data* is sent to the customer with no regard for the medium used to send it.

- Flows of data are shown using lines with arrowheads indicating the direction of flow. Each flow line is accompanied by a description of the content of the data being sent. Bidirectional flows are permissible but are usually shown as separate flows because the data is seldom exactly the same in both directions.

The strengths of the data flow diagram are as follows:

- It easily shows the overall structure of the system without sacrificing detail (details are shown on subsequent pages that expand on the higher-level processes).
- It's good for top-down design work.
- It's good for presentation of systems designs to management and business users.

And here are the weaknesses of the data flow diagram:

- It's time-consuming and labor-intensive to develop for complex systems.
- Top-down design has proved to be ineffective for situations in which requirements are sketchy and continuously evolving during the life of the project.
- It's poor at showing complex logic, but the lowest level diagrams can easily be supplemented with other documents such as narratives or decision tables.

Process Modeling with UML

UML 2.*x* offers 13 different diagrams, 6 of which are *structure diagrams* that emphasize what things must be in the system being modeled, and 7 of which are *behavior diagrams* that emphasize what must happen in the system being modeled. Of these, the class diagram is covered earlier in this chapter. There's not enough space in this book to cover all the diagrams, but you'll find lots of information on the Internet and in books on the subject. The following table provides a summary description of each UML diagram:

Type	Name	Description
Structure	Class diagram	Shows a collection of static model elements such as classes and types, their contents, and their relationships
Structure	Component diagram	Depicts the components that make up an application, system, or enterprise
Structure	Composite structure diagram	Depicts that internal structure of a classifier (such as a class, component, or use case), including the classifier's interaction points to other parts of the system (added in UML 2.x)
Structure	Deployment diagram	Shows the execution architecture of systems, including nodes, hardware/software environments, and the middleware that connects them
Structure	Object diagram	Depicts objects and their relationships at a point in time
Structure	Package diagram	Shows how model elements are assembled into packages as well as the dependencies between packages
Behavior	Activity diagram	Depicts high-level business processes, including data flow
Behavior	State machine diagram	Describes the states an object or interaction may be in, and the transitions between states
Behavior	Use case diagram	Shows actors, use cases, and their interactions
Behavior	Communication diagram	Shows instances of classes, their interrelationships, and the message flow between them
Behavior	Interaction overview diagram	A variant of an activity diagram that depicts an overview of the control flow within a system or business process (added in UML 2.x)
Behavior	Sequence diagram	Depicts the time ordering of messages between classifiers, essentially showing the sequential logic of the system
Behavior	Timing diagram	Depicts the change in state or condition of a classifier instance or role over time (added in UML 2.x)

Note that some references show a subtype of Interaction diagram under Behavior diagram, containing the Sequence, Interaction Overview, Communication, and Timing diagrams.

Relating Entities and Processes

Once the database designer has completed logical database design and an ERD for the proposed database and, in parallel, the process designers have completed their process model, how can we have any confidence that the two will be able to work together in solving the business problem the new project is supposed to address? Part of the answer lies in a charting technique intended to show how the entities and processes interact, known as the CRUD matrix.

Fortunately, CRUD is not slang for a lousy design but rather an acronym formed from the first letters for the words *Create, Read, Update,* and *Delete,* which are the letters used in the body of the diagram. The concept of the CRUD matrix is very simple:

- One axis of the matrix represents the major processes of the application system.
- The other axis represents the major entities used by the application system.
- In each cell of the matrix, the appropriate combination of letters is written:
  - *C,* if the process creates new occurrences of the entity
  - *R,* if the process reads information about the entity from a data source
  - *U,* if the process updates one or more attributes for the entity
  - *D,* if the process deletes occurrences of the entity

Here is a sample CRUD matrix for the order-management function at Acme Industries, following the major processes shown in the function hierarchy diagram (refer to Figure 7-11). To be effective, only high-level processes and supertype entities should be shown in the matrix. Too much detail clouds the effect of the diagram.

	ENTITY: Product	Order	Customer	Invoice
PROCESS: Order Entry	R	CRU	RU	
Order Fulfillment	RU	RU	R	C
History Management		RD	R	

The CRUD matrix is valuable for verifying the consistency of the process and data (entity) designs. At a glance, we can find the following potential problems:

- Entities that have no Create process
- Entities that have no Delete process
- Entities that are never updated
- Entities that are never read
- Processes that delete or update entities without reading them
- Processes that only read (no Create, Delete, or Update actions)

Our example has multiple problems, which proves only that our process design is incomplete (that is, we are probably missing some key processes for the application system). At the conclusion of the logical design phase of a project, the CRUD matrix is an excellent vehicle for a final review of the work completed.

Summary

In this chapter, we have explored various entity relationship and process modeling techniques that can be used during the logical design step in the database life cycle. The next step in the database life cycle is to complete the physical database design, which is discussed in Chapter 8.

QUIZ

Choose the correct responses to each of the multiple-choice questions. Note that there may be more than one correct response to each question.

1. **Peter Chen's ERD format:**
   A. Shows minimum cardinality with vertical lines
   B. May optionally include attributes
   C. Uses a crow's foot to represent "many"
   D. Represents entities as rectangles or boxes
   E. Was developed in 1976

2. **The diamond in Chen's ERD format:**
   A. Shows the cardinality of the relationship
   B. Contains a word or phrase that describes the relationship
   C. Contains the name of an entity
   D. Represents an attribute
   E. Represents an entity

3. **In the relational ERD format:**
   A. A crow's foot is used to signify "many."
   B. Relationship lines have an arrowhead that points at the "child" entity.
   C. Attributes are shown in ellipses connected to the entity with a line.
   D. Foreign key attributes are marked with "FK" in the margin.
   E. Unique identifier attributes are marked with "PK" in the margin.

4. **The IE ERD format shows**
   A. Minimal cardinality using a combination of small circles and vertical lines shown on the relationship line
   B. Maximum cardinality using a combination of small vertical lines and crow's feet drawn on the relationship line
   C. Independent entities with rounded corners on the rectangle
   D. Identifying relationships with a solid line
   E. Dependent entities with squared corners on the rectangle

5. **In IE notation, subtypes:**
   A. Usually have the same primary key as the supertype
   B. May be shown using a crow's foot
   C. May be shown with a type discriminator attribute name
   D. Have the primary key of the subtype shown as a foreign key in the supertype
   E. May be connected to the supertype via a symbol composed of a circle with a line under it

6. **The basic components of a flowchart are**
   A. Connector symbols for connecting lines on the same page or across pages
   B. Process steps shown as diamonds
   C. Ellipses or rounded rectangles showing starting and ending points
   D. Decision points shown as rectangles
   E. Lines with arrows showing the flow of control

7. **The basic components of a function hierarchy diagram are**
   A. Diamonds to show decision points
   B. Rectangles to show process functions
   C. Ellipses to show attributes
   D. A hierarchy to show which functions are subordinate to others
   E. Lines connecting the processes in order of execution

8. **The basic components of a swim lane diagram are**
   A. Vertical lanes to show the organization units that carry out process steps
   B. Ellipses to show process steps
   C. Lines with arrows to show the sequence of process steps
   D. Open-ended rectangles to show data stores
   E. Diamonds to show decision points

9. **The components of the DFD are**
   A. Lines with arrowheads to show flows of data
   B. Diamonds to show sources and destinations of data
   C. Dotted lines to show the flow of control
   D. Squares to show data stores
   E. Rounded rectangles to show processes

10. **The components of the CRUD matrix are**
    A. Major entities shown on the other axis
    B. Major processes shown on one axis
    C. Letters to show the operations that processes carry out on entities
    D. Ellipses to show attributes
    E. Reference numbers to show the hierarchy of processes

chapter 8

Physical Database Design

As introduced in Chapter 5 in Figure 5-1, once the logical design phase of a project is complete, it is time to move on to physical design. We will focus on the database designer's physical design work, which is transforming the logical database design into one or more physical database designs. The sections that follow cover each of the major steps involved in physical database design.

CHAPTER OBJECTIVES

In this chapter, the reader should:

- Understand the process of designing physical tables, including the alternatives for handling supertypes and subtypes.

- Understand the techniques for integrating business rules and data integrity into physical database designs, including alternatives for implementing constraints.

- Know the basic concepts of designing views and adding indexes to improve performance.

Designing Tables

In situations where an application system is being developed for internal use, it is normal to have only one physical database design for each logical design. However, if the organization is a software vendor, for example, the application system must run on all the various platform and RDBMS versions that the vendor's customers use, and that requires multiple physical designs.

The first step in physical database design is to map the normalized relations shown in the logical design to tables. The importance of this step should be obvious because tables are the primary unit of storage in relational databases. However, if adequate work was put into the logical design, then translation to a physical design is that much easier. As you work through this chapter, keep in mind that Chapter 2 contains an introduction to each component in the physical database model, and Chapter 4 contains the SQL syntax for the DML commands required to create the various physical database components (tables, constraints, indexes, views, and so on). Briefly, the process goes as follows:

1. Each normalized relation becomes a table. A common exception to this is when supertypes and subtypes are involved, a situation we will look at in more detail in the next section.

2. Each attribute within the normalized relation becomes a column in the corresponding table. Keep in mind that the column is the smallest division of meaningful data in the database, so columns should not have subcomponents that make sense by themselves. For each column, the following must be specified:

   - *A unique column name within the table.* Generally, the attribute name from the logical design should be adapted as closely as possible. However, adjustments may be necessary to work around database reserved words and to conform to naming conventions for the particular RDBMS being used. You may notice some column name differences between the Customer relation and the CUSTOMER table in the example that follows. The reason for this change is discussed in the "Naming Conventions" section later in this chapter.

   - *A data type, and for some data types, a length or a precision and scale.* Data types vary from one RDBMS to another, so different physical designs are needed for each RDBMS to be used.

   - *Whether column values are required.* This takes the form of a NULL or NOT NULL clause for each column. Be careful with defaults—they can fool you. For example, when this clause is not specified, Oracle assumes NULL, but Sybase and Microsoft SQL Server might assume NOT NULL depending on the configuration. It's always better to specify such things and to be certain of what you are getting.

- *Check constraints.* These may be added to columns to enforce simple business rules. For example, a business rule requiring that the unit price on an invoice must always be greater than or equal to zero can be implemented with a check constraint, but a business rule requiring the unit price to be lower in certain states cannot be. Generally, a check constraint is limited to a comparison of a column value with a single value, with a range or list of values, or with other column values in the same row of table data. (Constraints are described in detail later in this chapter.)

3. The unique identifier of the relation is defined as the primary key of the table. Columns participating in the primary key must be specified as NOT NULL, and in most RDBMSs, the definition of a primary key constraint causes automatic definition of a unique index on the primary key column(s). Foreign key columns should have a NOT NULL clause if the relationship is mandatory; otherwise, they may have a NULL clause.

4. Any other sets of columns that must be unique within the table may have a unique constraint defined. As with primary key constraints, unique constraints in most RDBMSs cause automatic definition of a unique index on the unique column(s). However, unlike primary key constraints, a table may have *multiple* unique constraints, and the columns in a unique constraint may contain null values (that is, they may be specified with the NULL clause).

5. Relationships among the normalized relations become referential constraints in the physical design. For those rare situations where the logical model contains a one-to-one relationship, you can implement it by placing the primary key of one of the tables as a foreign key in the other (do this for only *one* of the two tables) *and* placing a unique constraint on the foreign key to prevent duplicate values. For example, Figure 2-2 in Chapter 2 shows a one-to-one relationship between Employee and Automobile, and I chose to place EMPLOYEE_ID as a foreign key in the AUTOMOBILE table. We should also place a unique constraint on EMPLOYEE_ID in the AUTOMOBILE table so that an employee may be assigned to only one automobile at any point in time.

6. In most cases, large tables (that is, those that exceed several gigabytes in total size) should be partitioned if the RDBMS being used supports it. *Partitioning* is a database feature that permits a table to be broken into multiple physical components, often with each partition stored in separate data files, in a manner that is transparent to the database user. Typical methods of breaking tables into partitions use a range or list of values for a particular table column (called the *partitioning column*) or use a randomizing method known as *hashing* that evenly distributes table rows across available partitions. The benefits of breaking large tables into partitions are easier administration (particularly for backup and recovery operations) and improved performance, achieved when the RDBMS can run an SQL query in parallel against multiple partitions and then combine the results. Partitioning is solely a physical design issue that is never addressed in logical designs. After all, a partitioned table really is still *one* table. There is wide variation in the way database vendors have implemented partitioning in their products, so you need to consult your RDBMS documentation for more details.

> *Partitioning is a database feature that permits a table to be broken into multiple physical components, often with each partition stored in separate data files, in a manner that is transparent to the database user.*

7. The logical model may be for a complete database system, whereas the current project may be an implementation of a subset of that entire system. When this occurs, the physical database designer will select and implement only the subset of tables required to fulfill current needs.

   Here is the logical design for Acme Industries from Chapter 6:

```
PRODUCT: # Product Number, Product Description,
         List Unit Price

CUSTOMER: # Customer Number, Customer Name,
          Customer Address, Customer City, Customer State,
          Customer Zip Code, Customer Phone

INVOICE: # Invoice Number, Customer Number, Terms,
         Ship Via, Order Date

INVOICE LINE ITEM: # Invoice Number, # Product Number,
                   Quantity, Sale Unit Price
```

And here is the physical table design I created from the logical design, shown in the form of SQL DDL statements. These statements are written for MySQL and may require some modification, mostly of data types, to work on other RDBMSs:

```
CREATE TABLE PRODUCT
  (PRODUCT_NUMBER        VARCHAR(10)   NOT NULL,
   PRODUCT_DESCRIPTION   VARCHAR(100)  NOT NULL,
   LIST_UNIT_PRICE       NUMERIC(7,2)  NOT NULL);

ALTER TABLE PRODUCT
  ADD CONSTRAINT PK_PRODUCT
      PRIMARY KEY (PRODUCT_NUMBER);

CREATE TABLE CUSTOMER
  (CUSTOMER_NUMBER       NUMERIC(5)    NOT NULL,
   NAME                  VARCHAR(25)   NOT NULL,
   ADDRESS               VARCHAR(255)  NOT NULL,
   CITY                  VARCHAR(50)   NOT NULL,
   STATE                 CHAR(2)       NOT NULL,
   ZIP_CODE              VARCHAR(10));

ALTER TABLE CUSTOMER
  ADD CONSTRAINT PK_CUSTOMER
      PRIMARY KEY (CUSTOMER_NUMBER);

CREATE TABLE INVOICE
  (INVOICE_NUMBER        NUMERIC(7)    NOT NULL,
   CUSTOMER_NUMBER       NUMERIC(5)    NOT NULL,
   TERMS                 VARCHAR(20)   NULL,
   SHIP_VIA              VARCHAR(30)   NULL,
   ORDER_DATE            DATE          NOT NULL);

ALTER TABLE INVOICE
  ADD CONSTRAINT PK_INVOICE
      PRIMARY KEY (INVOICE_NUMBER);

ALTER TABLE INVOICE
  ADD CONSTRAINT FK_INVOICE_CUSTOMER
      FOREIGN KEY (CUSTOMER_NUMBER)
      REFERENCES CUSTOMER (CUSTOMER_NUMBER);

CREATE TABLE INVOICE_LINE_ITEM
  (INVOICE_NUMBER   NUMERIC(7)    NOT NULL,
   PRODUCT_NUMBER   VARCHAR(10)   NOT NULL,
   QUANTITY         NUMERIC(5)    NOT NULL,
   SALE_UNIT_PRICE  NUMERIC(7,2)  NOT NULL);
```

```
ALTER TABLE INVOICE_LINE_ITEM
  ADD CONSTRAINT PK_INVOICE_LINE_ITEM
      PRIMARY KEY (INVOICE_NUMBER, PRODUCT_NUMBER);

ALTER TABLE INVOICE_LINE_ITEM
  ADD CONSTRAINT CK_INVOICE_SALE_UNIT_PRICE
      CHECK (SALE_UNIT_PRICE >= 0);

ALTER TABLE INVOICE_LINE_ITEM
  ADD CONSTRAINT FK_INVOICE_LINE_ITEM_INVOICE
      FOREIGN KEY (INVOICE_NUMBER)
      REFERENCES INVOICE (INVOICE_NUMBER);

ALTER TABLE INVOICE_LINE_ITEM
  ADD CONSTRAINT FK_INVOICE_LINE_ITEM_PRODUCT
      FOREIGN KEY (PRODUCT_NUMBER)
      REFERENCES PRODUCT (PRODUCT_NUMBER);
```

Implementing Supertypes and Subtypes

Most data modelers tend to specify every conceivable subtype in the logical data model. This is not really a problem because the logical design is supposed to encompass not only where things currently stand, but also where things are likely to end up in the future. The designer of the physical database therefore has some decisions to make in choosing to implement or not implement the supertypes and subtypes depicted in the logical model. The driving motivators here should be reasonableness and common sense. These, along with input from the application designers about their intended uses of the database, will lead to the best decisions.

From Chapter 7, recall that we ended up with two subtypes for our Customer entity: Individual Customer and Commercial Customer in Figure 7-8, reproduced here as Figure 8-1. There are basically three choices for physically implementing such a logical design, and we will explore each in the subsections that follow.

Implementing Subtypes As Is

This solution involves creating one table for the supertype and one table for each of the subtypes (two in this example). This design is most appropriate when many attributes and/or relationships are particular to individual subtypes. In our example, only two attributes are particular to the Individual Customer subtype (Date of Birth and Annual Household Income), and four are particular to the Commercial Customer subtype. Figure 8-2 shows the physical design for this alternative.

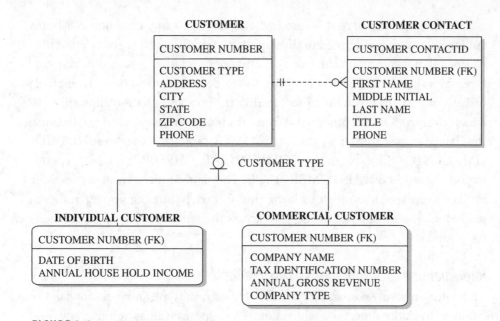

FIGURE 8-1 · Customer subtypes final solution (from Figure 7-8)

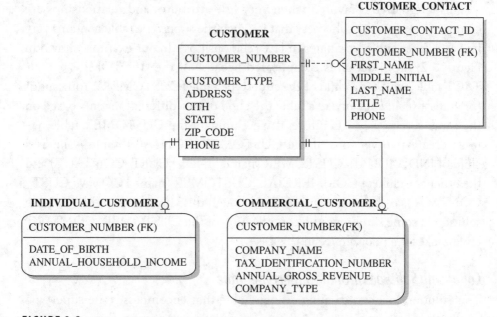

FIGURE 8-2 · Customer subclasses: physical design with subtypes as is

This design alternative is favored when there are many common attributes and/or relationships (defined in the supertype table) as well as many attributes and/or relationships particular to one subtype or another (located in the subtype tables). In one sense, this design is simpler than the other alternatives because no one has to remember which attributes and relationships apply to which subtype. On the other hand, it is also more complicated to use because the database user must join the CUSTOMER table to either the INDIVIDUAL_CUSTOMER table or the COMMERCIAL_CUSTOMER table, depending on the value of CUSTOMER_TYPE. The data-modeling purists on your project team are guaranteed to favor this approach, but the application programmers who must write the SQL to access the tables may likely take a counter position.

Implementing Each Subtype as a Discrete Table

This solution involves creating one table for each subtype and including all the columns from the supertype table in each subtype, as well as defining any relationships from the supertype on each subtype. At first, this may appear to involve redundant data, but there is no redundant storage because a given customer can be only one of the two subtypes. However, some columns are redundantly defined. Figure 8-3 shows the physical design for this alternative.

This alternative is favored when very few attributes and relationships are common between the subtypes (that is, when the supertype table contains very few attributes and participates in few relationships). In our example shown in Figure 8-2, the situation is complicated because of the CUSTOMER_CONTACT table, which is a child of the supertype table (CUSTOMER). You cannot (or at least *should* not) make a table the child of two different parents based on the same foreign key. Therefore, if we eliminate the CUSTOMER table, we must create two versions of the CUSTOMER_CONTACT table—one as a child of INDIVIDUAL_CUSTOMER (named INDV_CUST_CONTACT) and the other as a child of COMMERCIAL_CUSTOMER (named COMM_CUST_CONTACT), as shown in Figure 8-3. Although this alternative may be a viable solution in some situations, the complication of the CUSTOMER_CONTACT table makes it a poor choice in this case.

Collapsing Subtypes into the Supertype Table

This solution involves creating a single table that encompasses the supertype and both subtypes. Figure 8-4 shows the physical design for this alternative. Check constraints are required to enforce the optional columns. For the

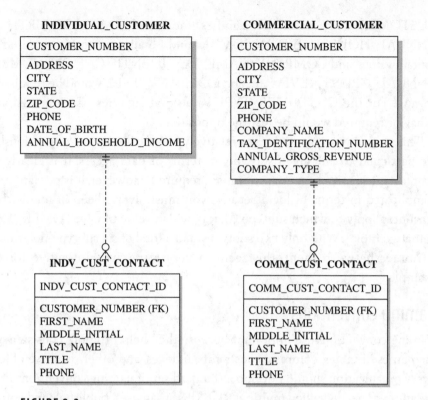

FIGURE 8-3 • Customer subclasses: two-table physical design

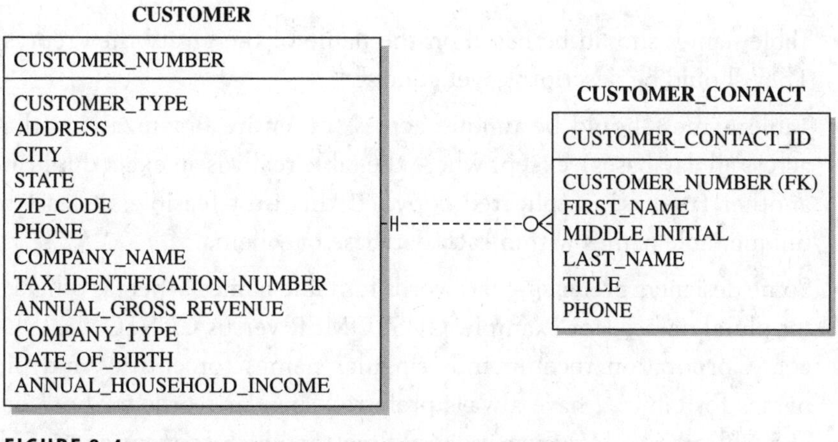

FIGURE 8-4 • Customer subclasses: one-table physical design

CUSTOMER_TYPE value that signifies "Individual," DATE_OF_BIRTH and ANNUAL_HOUSEHOLD_INCOME would be allowed to (or required to) contain values, and COMPANY_NAME, TAX_IDENTIFICATION_NUMBER, ANNUAL_GROSS_REVENUE, and COMPANY_TYPE would be required to be null. For the CUSTOMER_TYPE value that signifies "Commercial," the behavior required would be just the opposite.

This alternative is favored when relatively few attributes and/or relationships are particular to any given subtype. In terms of data access, it is clearly the simplest alternative because no joins are required. However, it is perhaps more complicated in terms of logic because you must always keep in mind which attributes apply to which subtype (that is, which value of CUSTOMER_TYPE in this example). With only two subtypes, and a total of six subtype-determined attributes between them, this seems a very attractive alternative for this example.

Naming Conventions

Naming conventions are important because they help promote consistency in the names of tables, columns, constraints, indexes, and other database objects. Every organization should develop a standard set of naming conventions (with variations as needed when multiple RDBMSs are in use), publish it, and enforce its use. The conventions offered here are suggestions based on current industry best practices.

Table-Naming Conventions

Here are some suggested naming conventions for database tables:

- Table names should be based on the name of the entity they represent. They should be descriptive, yet concise.

- Table names should be unique across the entire organization (that is, across all databases), except where the table really is an exact duplicate of another (that is, a replicated copy). If this isn't feasible, at least have unique table names within each database or schema.

- Some designers prefer singular words for table names, whereas others prefer plural names (for example, CUSTOMER versus CUSTOMERS). Oracle Corporation recommends singular names for entities and plural names for tables. I have always preferred singular words for both entity and table names. However, it doesn't matter which convention you adopt as long as you are *consistent* across *all* your tables, so do set one or the other as your standard.

- Do not include words such as "table" or "file" in table names.

- Use only uppercase letters, and use an underscore to separate words. Not all RDBMSs have case-sensitive object names, so mixed-case names limit applicability across multiple vendors. This is bound to be a controversial topic for organizations using DBMSs, such as MySQL, SQL Server, and Sybase, that fully support mixed-case names. However, mixed-case names present an issue of portability: if you implement a database design with mixed-case names on a DBMS that folds all object names to uppercase, such as Oracle and DB2, then a table named OrderLineItem, for example, instantly becomes ORDERLINEITEM, which clearly isn't easy to read and use.

- Use abbreviations when necessary to shorten names that are longer than the RDBMS maximum (typically 30 characters or so). Actually, it is a good idea to stay a few characters short of the RDBMS maximum to allow for suffixes when necessary. All abbreviations should be placed on a standard list and the use of nonstandard abbreviations discouraged.

- Avoid limiting names such as WEST_SALES. Some organizations add a two- or three-character prefix to table names to denote the part of the organization that owns the data in the table. However, this is not considered a best practice because it can lead to a lack of data sharing. Moreover, placing geographic or organizational unit names in table names plays havoc every time the organization changes.

Column-Naming Conventions

Here are some suggested naming conventions for table columns:

- Column names should be based on the attribute name as shown in the logical data model. They should be descriptive, yet concise.

- Column names must be unique within the table, but where possible, it is best if they are unique across the entire organization. Some conventions make exceptions for common attributes such as City, which might describe several entities such as Customer, Employee, and Company Location.

- Use only uppercase letters, and use an underscore to separate words. Not all RDBMSs have case-sensitive object names, so mixed-case names limit applicability across multiple vendors.

- Prefixing column names with entity names is a controversial issue. Some prefer prefixing names. For example, in the CUSTOMER table, they would use column names such as CUSTOMER_NUMBER, CUSTOMER_ NAME, CUSTOMER_ADDRESS, CUSTOMER_CITY, and so forth. Others (this author included) prefer to prefix *only* the primary key column name (for example, CUSTOMER_NUMBER), which leads easily to primary key and matching foreign key columns having exactly the same names. Still others prefer no prefixes at all and end up with a column name such as ID for the primary key of every single table.

- Use abbreviations when necessary to shorten names that are longer than the RDBMS maximum (typically 30 characters or so). All abbreviations should be placed on a standard list and the use of nonstandard abbreviations discouraged.

- Regardless of any other convention, most experts prefer that foreign key columns always have exactly the same name as their matching primary key column. This helps other database users understand which columns to use when coding joins in SQL.

Constraint-Naming Conventions

In most RDBMSs the error message generated when a constraint is violated contains the constraint name. Unless you want to field questions from database users every time one of these messages shows up, you should name the constraints in a standard way that is easily understood by the database users. Most database designers prefer a convention similar to the one presented here.

Constraint names should be in the format TYPE_TNAME_CNAME, where:

- TYPE is the type of constraint:
  - *PK* for primary key constraints.
  - *FK* for foreign key constraints.
  - *UQ* for unique constraints.
  - *CK* for check constraints.
- TNAME is the name of the table on which the constraint is defined, abbreviated if necessary.
- CNAME is the name of the column on which the constraint is defined, abbreviated if necessary. For constraints defined across multiple columns,

another descriptive word or phrase may be substituted if the column names are too long (even when abbreviated) to make sense. Also, the column name can be omitted for primary key constraints because it is not needed for uniqueness, since each table can have only one such constraint.

Index-Naming Conventions

Indexes that are automatically defined by the RDBMS to support primary key or unique constraints are typically given the same name as the constraint name, so you seldom have to worry about them. For other types of indexes, it is wise to have a naming convention so that you know the table and column(s) on which they are defined without having to look up anything. The following is a suggested convention.

Index names should be in the format TYPE_TNAME_CNAME, where:

- TYPE is the type of index:
  - *UX* for unique indexes.
  - *IX* for non-unique indexes.
- TNAME is the name of the table on which the index is defined, abbreviated if necessary.
- CNAME is the name of the column on which the index is defined, abbreviated if necessary. For indexes defined across multiple columns, another descriptive word or phrase may be substituted if the column names are too long (even when abbreviated) to make sense.

Also, any abbreviations used should be documented in the standard abbreviations list.

View-Naming Conventions

View names present an interesting dilemma. The object names used in the FROM clause of SQL statements can be for tables, views, or synonyms. A *synonym* is an alias (nickname) for a table or view. So how does the DBMS know whether an object name in the FROM clause is a table or view or synonym? It doesn't, until it looks up the name in a metadata table that catalogs all the objects in the database. This means, of course, that the names of tables, views, and synonyms must come from the same *namespace*, or list of possible names. Therefore, a view name must be unique among all table, view, and synonym names.

Because it is useful for some database users to know if they are referencing a table or a view, and as an easy way to ensure that names are unique, it is common practice to give views distinctive names by employing a standard that appends *VW* to the beginning or end of each name, with a separating underscore. Again, the exact convention chosen matters a lot less than picking *one* convention and sticking to it for all your view names. Here is a suggested convention:

- All view names should end with _*VW* so they are easily distinguishable from table names.
- View names should contain the name of the most significant base table included in the view, abbreviated if necessary.
- View names should describe the purpose of the views or the kind of data included in them. For example, CALIFORNIA_CUSTOMERS_VW and CUSTOMERS_BY_ZIP_CODE_VW are both reasonably descriptive view names, whereas CUSTOMER_LIST_VW and CUSTOMER_JOIN_VW are much less meaningful.
- Any abbreviations used should be documented in the standard abbreviations list.

Integrating Business Rules and Data Integrity

Business rules determine how an organization operates and utilizes its data. Business rules exist as a reflection of an organization's policies and operational procedures and because they provide control. *Data integrity* is the process of ensuring that data is protected and stays intact through defined constraints placed on the data. We call these *database constraints* because they prevent changes to the data that would violate one or more business rules. The principal benefit of enforcing business rules using data integrity constraints in the database is that database constraints cannot be circumvented. Unlike business rules enforced by application programs, database constraints are enforced no matter *how* someone connects to the database. The only way around database constraints is for the DBA to remove or disable them.

> A database constraint is a control defined in the database that limits data values in some way.

Business rules are implemented in the database as follows:

- NOT NULL constraints
- Primary key constraints

- Referential (foreign key) constraints
- Unique constraints
- Check constraints
- Data types, precision, and scale
- Triggers

The subsections that follow discuss each of these implementation techniques and the effect the constraints have on database processing. Throughout this topic, we will use the following table definition as an example. A comment (comments in SQL begin with at least two hyphens) has been placed above each component to help you identify it. Note that the INVOICE table used here has a column difference—TERMS is replaced with CUSTOMER_PO_NUMBER, which is needed to illustrate some key concepts. A DROP statement is included to drop the INVOICE table in case you created it when following previous examples.

```sql
--  Drop Tables (in case they already exist)
DROP TABLE INVOICE_LINE_ITEM;
DROP TABLE INVOICE;
DROP TABLE CUSTOMER;
DROP TABLE PRODUCT;

-- Create Customer Table
CREATE TABLE CUSTOMER
  (CUSTOMER_NUMBER      NUMERIC(5)    NOT NULL,
   NAME                 VARCHAR(25)   NOT NULL,
   ADDRESS              VARCHAR(255)  NOT NULL,
   CITY                 VARCHAR(50)   NOT NULL,
   STATE                CHAR(2)       NOT NULL,
   ZIP_CODE             VARCHAR(10));

--  Create Primary Key Constraint
ALTER TABLE CUSTOMER
  ADD CONSTRAINT PK_CUSTOMER
     PRIMARY KEY (CUSTOMER_NUMBER);

--  Create Invoice Table
CREATE TABLE INVOICE
  (INVOICE_NUMBER       NUMERIC(7)    NOT NULL,
   CUSTOMER_NUMBER      NUMERIC(5)    NOT NULL,
   CUSTOMER_PO_NUMBER   VARCHAR(10)   NULL,
   SHIP_VIA             VARCHAR(30)   NULL,
   ORDER_DATE           DATE          NOT NULL);
```

```
-- Create Primary Key Constraint
ALTER TABLE INVOICE
  ADD CONSTRAINT PK_INVOICE
    PRIMARY KEY (INVOICE_NUMBER);

-- Create Referential Constraint
ALTER TABLE INVOICE
  ADD CONSTRAINT FK_INVOICE_CUSTOMER
    FOREIGN KEY (CUSTOMER_NUMBER)
    REFERENCES CUSTOMER (CUSTOMER_NUMBER);

-- Create Unique Constraint
ALTER TABLE INVOICE
  ADD CONSTRAINT UNQ_INVOICE_CUST_NUMB_PO
    UNIQUE (CUSTOMER_NUMBER, CUSTOMER_PO_NUMBER);

-- Create CHECK Constraint
ALTER TABLE INVOICE
  ADD CONSTRAINT INVOICE_CK_TERMS
    CHECK (TERMS IN ('EOM', 'Net 30', 'Cash Account'));
```

NOT NULL Constraints

As you have already seen, business rules that state which attributes are required translate into NOT NULL clauses on the corresponding columns in the table design. In fact, the NOT NULL clause is how we define a NOT NULL constraint on table columns. Primary keys must always be specified as NOT NULL (Oracle will automatically do this for you, but most other RDBMSs will not). And, as already mentioned, any foreign keys that participate in a mandatory relationship should also be specified as NOT NULL.

In our example, if we attempt to insert a row in the INVOICE table and fail to provide a value for any of the columns that have NOT NULL constraints (that is, the INVOICE_NUMBER, CUSTOMER_NUMBER, and ORDER_DATE columns), the insert will fail with an error message indicating the constraint violation. Also, if we attempt to update any existing row and set one of those columns to a NULL value, the update statement will fail.

Primary Key Constraints

Primary key constraints require that the column(s) that make up the primary key contain unique values for every row in the table. In addition, primary key columns must be defined with NOT NULL constraints. A table may have only one primary key constraint. The RDBMS will automatically create an index to assist in enforcing the primary key constraint.

In our sample INVOICE table, if we attempt to insert a row without specifying a value for the INVOICE_NUMBER column, the insert will fail because of the NOT NULL constraint on the column. If we instead try to insert a row with a value for the INVOICE_NUMBER column that already exists in the INVOICE table, the insert will fail with an error message that indicates a violation of the primary key constraint. This message usually contains the constraint name, which is why it is such a good idea to give constraints meaningful names. Finally, assuming the RDBMS in use permits updates to primary key values (some do not), if we attempt to update the INVOICE_NUMBER column for an existing row and we provide a value that is already used by another row in the table, the update will fail.

Referential (Foreign Key) Constraints

The referential constraint on the INVOICE table defines CUSTOMER_NUMBER as a foreign key to the CUSTOMER table. It takes some getting used to, but referential constraints are always defined on the child table (that is, the table on the "many" side of the relationship). The purpose of the referential constraint is to make sure that foreign key values in the rows in the child table *always* have matching primary key values in the parent table.

In our INVOICE table example, if we try to insert a row without providing a value for CUSTOMER_NUMBER, the insert will fail due to the NOT NULL constraint on the column. However, if we try to insert a row and provide a value for CUSTOMER_NUMBER that does not match the primary key of a row in the CUSTOMER table, the insert will fail due to the referential constraint. Also, if we attempt to update the value of CUSTOMER_NUMBER for an existing row in the INVOICE table and the new value does not have a matching row in the CUSTOMER table, the update will fail, again due to the referential constraint.

Unique Constraints

Like primary key constraints, unique constraints ensure that no two rows in the table have duplicate values for the column(s) named in the constraint. However, there are two important differences:

- Although a table may have only one primary key constraint, it may have as many unique constraints as necessary.
- Columns participating in a unique constraint do not have to have NOT NULL constraints on them.

Still Struggling

Always keep in mind that referential constraints work in both directions, so they can prevent a child table row from becoming an "orphan," meaning it has a value that does not match a primary key value in the parent table. Therefore, if we attempt to delete a row in the CUSTOMER table that has INVOICE rows referring to it (or if we attempt to update the primary key value of such a row), the statement will fail because it would cause child table rows to violate the constraint. However, many RDBMSs provide a feature with referential constraints written as ON DELETE CASCADE, which causes referencing child table rows to be *automatically* deleted when the parent row is deleted. Of course, this option is not appropriate in all situations, but it is nice to have when you need it.

As with a primary key constraint, an index is automatically created to assist the DBMS in efficiently enforcing the constraint.

As with the primary key constraint, if we attempt to insert a row with values for the CUSTOMER_NUMBER and PO_NUMBER columns that are already in use by another row, the insert will fail. Similarly, we cannot update a row in the INVOICE table if the update would result in the row having a duplicate combination of CUSTOMER_NUMBER and PO_NUMBER.

Still Struggling

In our example, a unique constraint is defined on the CUSTOMER_NUMBER and CUSTOMER_PO_NUMBER columns, to enforce a business rule that states that customers may only use a PO (purchase order) number once. It is important to understand that it is the *combination* of the values in the two columns that must be unique. There can be many invoices for any given CUSTOMER_NUMBER, and there can be multiple rows in the INVOICE table with the same PO_NUMBER (we cannot prevent two customers from using the same PO number, nor do we wish to). However, no two rows for the same customer number may have the same PO number.

Check Constraints

Check constraints are used to enforce business rules that restrict a column to a list or range of values or to some condition that can be verified using a simple comparison to a constant, calculation, or a value of another column in the same row. Check constraints may *not* be used to compare column values between different rows, whether in the same table or not. Check constraints are written as conditional statements that must always be true. The term comes from the fact that the database must always "check" the condition to make sure it evaluates to true before allowing an insert or update to a row in the table.

In our example, we have a check constraint that requires the TERMS to be one of the following values: EOM, Net 30, or Cash Account. This enforces a business rule that restricts the invoice terms to a finite list of values. Alternatively, we could accomplish the same thing (perhaps more flexibly) with a lookup table and referential constraint. Keep in mind that the condition is only checked when we insert or update a row in the INVOICE table, so it will not be applied to existing rows as the terms change. With the constraint in force, if we attempt to insert or update a row with TERMS set to a value not included in the list, the statement will fail.

Data Types, Precision, and Scale

The data type assigned to the table columns automatically constrains the data to values that match the data type. For example, anything placed in a column with a date format must be a valid date. You cannot put nonnumeric characters in numeric columns. However, you can put just about anything in a character column.

For numeric data types that support the specification of the precision (maximum size) and scale (positions to the right of the decimal point), these specifications also constrain the data. You cannot put a number larger than the maximum size for the column into the database. Nor can you specify decimal positions beyond those allowed for in the scale of a number. For character data types, the length prevents character data that is too long from being placed into the column.

In our example, CUSTOMER_NUMBER must contain only numeric digits and cannot be larger than 99,999 (five digits) or smaller than –99,999 (again, five digits). Also, because the scale is 0, it cannot have decimal digits (that is, it must be an integer). It may seem silly to allow negative values for CUSTOMER_ NUMBER, but there is no SQL data type that restricts a column to only positive integers. However, it is easy enough to restrict a column to only positive numbers by using a check constraint if needed.

Triggers

As you may recall, a *trigger* is a unit of program code that executes automatically based on some event that takes place in the database, such as inserting, updating, or deleting data in a particular table. Triggers must be written in a language supported by the RDBMS. For Oracle, this is either a proprietary extension to SQL called PL/SQL (Procedural Language/SQL) or Java (available in Oracle8*i* or later). For Sybase and Microsoft SQL Server, the supported language is Transact-SQL. Some RDBMSs have no support for triggers, whereas others support a more general programming language such as C. Trigger code must either end normally, which lets the SQL statement that caused the trigger to fire end normally, or must raise a database error, which lets the SQL statement that caused the trigger to fire fail.

Triggers can enforce business rules that cannot be enforced via database constraints. Because they are written using a full-fledged programming language, they can do just about anything that can be done with a database and a program (some RDBMSs do place some restrictions on triggers). Whether a business rule should be enforced in normal application code or through the use of a trigger is not always an easy decision. Application developers typically want control of such things, but on the other hand, the main benefit of triggers is that they run automatically and cannot be circumvented (unless the DBA removes or disables them), even if someone connects directly to the database, bypassing the application.

A common use of triggers in RDBMSs that do not support ON DELETE CASCADE in referential constraints is to carry out the cascading delete. For example, if we want invoice line items to be automatically removed from the INVOICE_LINE_ITEM table when the corresponding invoice in the INVOICE table is deleted, we could write a trigger that carries that out. The trigger would be set to fire when a delete from the INVOICE table takes place. It would then issue a delete for all the child rows related to the parent invoice (those matching the primary key value of the invoice being deleted) and then end normally, which would permit the original invoice delete to complete. (Because the referencing child rows will be done by this time, the delete will not violate the referential constraint.)

Designing Views

As covered in Chapter 2, views can be thought of as virtual tables. They are, however, merely stored SQL statements that do not themselves contain any data. Data can be selected from views just as it can from tables, and with some restrictions, data can be inserted into, updated in, and deleted from views. Here are the restrictions:

- For views containing joins, any DML (that is, insert, update, or delete) statement issued against the view must reference only one table.

- Inserts are not possible using views where any required (NOT NULL) column has been omitted.

- Any update against a view may reference only columns that directly map to base table columns. Calculated and derived columns may not be updated.

- Appropriate privileges are required (just as with base tables).

- There are various other product-specific restrictions to using views, so always consult the RDBMS documentation.

Views can be designed to provide the following advantages:

- In some RDBMSs, views provide a performance advantage over ordinary SQL statements. Views are precompiled, so the resources required to parse and bind the statement are saved when views are repeatedly referenced. However, there is no such advantage with RDBMSs that provide an automatic SQL statement cache, as Oracle does. Moreover, poorly written SQL can be included in a view, so putting SQL in a view is not a magic answer to performance issues.

- Views may be tailored to individual department needs, providing only the rows and columns needed, and perhaps renaming columns using terms more readily understood by the particular audience.

- Because views hide the real table and column names from their users, they insulate users from changes to those names in the base tables.

- Data usage can be greatly simplified by hiding complicated joins and calculations from the database users. For example, views can easily calculate ages based on birth dates, and they can summarize data in nearly any way imaginable.

- Security needs can be met by filtering rows and columns that users are not supposed to see. Some RDBMS products permit column-level security, where users are granted privileges by column as well as by table, but using views is far easier to implement and maintain. Moreover, a WHERE clause in the view can filter rows easily.

Once created, views must be managed like any other database object. If many members of a database project are creating and updating views, it is very easy to lose control. Moreover, views can become invalid as maintenance is carried out on the database, so their status must be reviewed periodically. Finally, while views can be referenced in additional views, if views are nested in too many layers, there can be significant performance consequences because the DBMS has to peel back all the layers when the view is referenced.

Adding Indexes for Performance

Indexes provide a fast and efficient means of finding data rows in tables, much like the index at the back of a book helps you in quickly finding specific references. Although the implementation in the database is more complicated than this, it's easiest to visualize an index as a table with one column containing the key value and another containing a pointer to where the row with that key value physically resides in the table, in the form of a row ID or a relative block address (RBA). For non-unique indexes, the second column contains a list of matching pointers.

Indexes provide faster searches than scanning tables for two reasons. First, index entries are considerably shorter than typical table rows, so many more index entries fit per physical file block than the corresponding table rows. Therefore, when the database must scan the index sequentially looking for matching rows, it can get a lot more index entries with a single read to the file on disk than with a corresponding read to the file holding the table. Second, unlike table rows, index entries are always maintained in key sequence, often with a hierarchical tree structure to organize the entries. The RDBMS software can take advantage of this by using binary search techniques that remarkably reduce search times and the resources required for searching.

There are no free lunches, however—indexes take up space and must be maintained. Storage space seems less of an issue with every passing day because storage devices keep getting cheaper. However, they still cost something, and they require maintenance and must be backed up. Most RDBMS vendors provide tools to help calculate the storage space required for indexes. These will assist you in estimating storage requirements. The more important consideration is maintenance of the index. Whenever a row is inserted into a table, every index defined on that table must have a new entry inserted as well. As rows are deleted, index entries must also be removed. And when columns that have an index defined on them are updated, the index must be updated as well. It's easy to forget this point because the RDBMS does this work automatically, but every index has a detrimental effect on the performance of inserts, updates, and deletes to table data. In essence, this is a typical trade-off, sacrificing a bit of DML statement performance for considerable gains in SELECT statement performance.

Here are some general guidelines regarding the use of indexes:

- Keep in mind that primary key constraints and unique constraints automatically create indexes on the key columns.

- Indexes on foreign keys can markedly improve the performance of joins.

- Consider using indexes on columns that are frequently referenced in WHERE clauses.

- The larger the table, the less you want any database query to have to scan the entire table (in other words, the more you want *every* query to use an index).

- The more a table is updated, the fewer the number of indexes you should have on the table, particularly on the columns that are updated most often.

- For relatively small tables (less than 1,000 rows or so), sequential table scans are probably more efficient than indexes. Most RDBMSs have optimizers that decide when an index should be used when processing a particular SQL statement, and typically they will choose a table scan over an index until there are at least a few hundred rows in the table.

- For tables with relatively short rows that are most often accessed using the primary key, consider the use of an *index organized table* (on RDBMSs that support such a table), where all the table data is stored in the index. This can be a highly efficient structure for lookup tables (tables containing little more than code and description columns).

- Consider the performance consequences carefully before you define more than two or three indexes on a single table.

Summary

In this chapter, we covered the essentials of physical database design, including designing tables, alternatives for handling supertypes and subtypes, techniques for integrating business rules and data integrity using constraints, designing views, and adding indexes for performance. In Chapter 9, we'll look at how databases can be connected to the outside world.

QUIZ

Choose the correct responses to each of the multiple-choice questions. Note that there may be more than one correct response to each question.

1. **When you're designing tables:**
   A. Unique identifiers become triggers.
   B. Each attribute in the relation becomes a table column.
   C. Each normalized relation becomes a table.
   D. Primary key columns must be defined as NOT NULL.
   E. Relationships become check constraints.

2. **Physical database design:**
   A. Immediately follows the logical design stage
   B. Immediately follows the requirements-gathering stage
   C. Is done in parallel with the definition of the hardware and system software required for the application system
   D. Can be done without a corresponding logical design
   E. Includes the design of application programs

3. **Supertypes and subtypes:**
   A. Only apply to the logical design
   B. Usually have the same primary key in the physical tables
   C. Must be implemented exactly as specified in the logical design
   D. May have the supertype columns folded into each subtype in the physical design
   E. May be collapsed in the physical database design

4. **Relationships in the logical model:**
   A. Are enforced with triggers in the physical design
   B. Require a NOT NULL constraint in the physical model
   C. Become check constraints in the physical model
   D. Become a primary key in the parent table and a foreign key in the child table
   E. Become referential constraints in the physical model

5. **Unique constraints:**
   A. May only be defined once per table
   B. Force column values to be unique within the table
   C. Are usually implemented using an index
   D. Are identical to primary key constraints
   E. Require columns that have NOT NULL constraints

6. **Check constraints:**
   A. May be used to force a column to match another column in the same row
   B. May be used to force a column to match a list of values
   C. May be used to force a column to match a range of values
   D. May be used to enforce a foreign key constraint
   E. May be used to force a column to match a column in another table

7. **Referential constraints:**
   A. Should have descriptive names
   B. Are always defined on the parent table
   C. Define relationships identified in the logical model
   D. Name the parent and child tables and the foreign key column
   E. Require that foreign keys be defined as NOT NULL

8. **Precision and scale:**
   A. Apply to all data types
   B. Can be used to prevent negative numbers in numeric columns
   C. Can be used to prevent decimal digits in columns that should contain only integers
   D. Can be used to prevent numbers that are too small from being stored in a column
   E. Can be used to prevent numbers that are too large from being stored in a column

9. **View restrictions include**
   A. If a view omits a mandatory column that has no default, inserts to the view are not possible.
   B. Any update involving a view may only reference columns from one table.
   C. Privileges are required in order to update data using views.
   D. Views containing joins can never be updated.
   E. Updates to calculated columns in views are prohibited.

10. **Indexes:**
    A. Are slower to sequentially scan than corresponding tables
    B. Are usually smaller than the tables they reference
    C. May be used to assist with primary key constraints
    D. May be used to improve insert, update, and delete performance
    E. May be used to improve query performance

chapter 9

Connecting Databases to the Outside World

We begin this chapter with a look at the evolution of database deployment models. We see the ways databases have been connected with their users and with the other computer systems within the enterprise computing *infrastructure* (the internal structure of all the computing resources of an enterprise). We then explore the methods used to connect databases to applications that use a web browser as the primary user interface, which is the way many modern application systems are constructed. Finally, we look at current methods for connecting databases to applications, namely using ODBC connections (for most programming languages) and various methods for connecting databases to applications written in Java.

CHAPTER OBJECTIVES

In this chapter, the reader should:

- Learn database deployment models.
- Understand how to connect databases to the outside world.
- Understand how to connect databases to applications.

Deployment Models

The history of the information technology (IT) industry is interesting because it clearly proves the old adage that history repeats itself. Nowhere is this truer than in the ways that we have deployed databases, and computer systems in general, on enterprise networks. The subsections that follow outline the major deployment models that have been used. Most of these models are still in active use.

Centralized Model

The centralized model, shown in Figure 9-1, was the original method used to connect databases to the enterprise computing infrastructure. Database users were equipped with what are now called "dumb" terminals, meaning that there was very little processing power or intelligent programming in the device. The only functions the terminals had were to present screens of data that came across the network, move the cursor about the screen, and capture user keystrokes, sending those back across the network. On the other end of the network was a mainframe or other large, centralized server that housed all the other functions, including the business logic (in application programs), the database, and any advanced presentation features, such as composing graphs and charts and selecting colors to display (if color terminals were connected).

> *The infrastructure is the internal structure of all the computing resources of an enterprise, including databases, applications, computer hardware, and the network.*

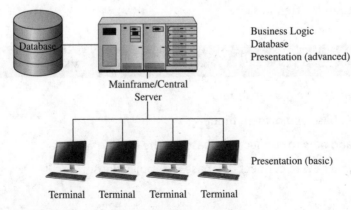

FIGURE 9-1 · The centralized deployment model

Today, people often scoff at this seemingly primitive arrangement. Keep in mind, however, that personal computers had not been invented yet. When they came on the scene, some of their first uses were to replace the dumb terminals, thereby giving computer users a desktop device that they could at least use for other purposes, such as word processing (or perhaps playing those early computer games). Programs called *terminal emulators* on the early personal computers took care of the network connection in such a way that the mainframe still thought it was connected to the original dumb terminal.

The benefits of the centralized model are as follows:

- **Very easy administration**   Upgrades and maintenance were straightforward because all the application logic and the database were centralized.

- **Lower development labor costs**   Fewer specialists were required because everything ran on one platform.

- **Potentially higher data input productivity**   Studies have shown that the fancy GUI screens that appeared later actually slowed down experienced users who were performing repetitive tasks. Many an experienced Windows user can perform some tasks much more quickly using the command prompt (DOS command window) instead of the available GUI tools. Much of this is due to the time required to move one hand between keys used for typing and the pointing device (mouse, trackball, and so on). If we all had a third hand, or if we could somehow use something else to control the pointing device (for example, our feet or eye movements), perhaps this could be overcome.

Here are the drawbacks:

- The mainframe or centralized server is a single point of failure.
- Graphical displays were quite primitive, limiting the user interface.
- Until the advent of the personal computer, the dumb terminal took a lot of desktop space for the purpose it served.

Distributed Model

As computer networks became more readily available in the late 1970s and early 1980s, the IT industry became enamored with the concept of distributed databases and distributed applications. In this case, *distributed* means the partitioning (dividing up) of the application and/or database into parts and the placement of different parts on different computing devices, all connected by

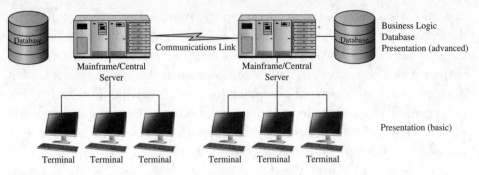

FIGURE 9-2 • The distributed deployment model

a network. Done correctly, the distribution is *transparent* to the users, meaning that the system hides the distribution details from the users, making everything appear to be from a single source. Figure 9-2 shows a simple distributed model, using two centralized servers.

> *A distributed database is a database with processing or data or both divided into different parts that are deployed on multiple computing devices.*

Unfortunately, the marketing hype attached to the initial appearance of the distributed model never played out due to high costs, along with performance and reliability issues. Among other things, network technology was not mature enough to reliably handle the load. In many ways, the early versions were solutions in need of problems to solve. Much like the Ford Edsel, the implementation of the new ideas was simply ahead of its time. This architecture has reappeared since the advent of more advanced networks, including the Internet, and is now successfully used for backup data centers, data warehouses, departmental computer systems, and much more. In some object-oriented architectures, an agent known as an *object request broker* manages objects distributed across a network so applications can access objects without regard to their location. Moreover, the current trends in grid computing can be easily seen as extensions to the original distributed model. History really does repeat itself.

The benefits of the distributed deployment model are as follows:

- Improved fault tolerance, because any component deployed on more than one device is no longer a single point of failure

- Potential performance improvement by placing data and application logic closer to the users that need them (that is, departmental computer systems)

Here are the drawbacks:

- Much more complicated
- Potential performance issues related to synchronizing data updates for any redundantly stored data
- More expensive than the centralized model
- Lack of guidelines and best practices for how to partition data and applications across the available computing devices

Client/Server Model

The client/server model involves one or more shared computers, called *servers*, that are connected by a network to the individual users' workstations, called *clients*. Client/server computing arrived in the 1980s, riding a wave of marketing hype from hardware and software vendors the likes of which had never been seen in the IT industry. The original model used is now called the *two-tier client/ server model*, which later evolved into what we call the *three-tier client/server model*, and finally into the *N-tier client/server model*, which is also known as the *Internet computing model*. Each of these models is discussed in the following subsections.

Two-Tier Client/Server Model

The two-tier client/server model, shown in Figure 9-3, is almost the opposite of the centralized model in that all the business and presentation logic is placed on the client workstation, which typically is a high-powered personal computer system. The only thing remaining on a centralized server is the database.

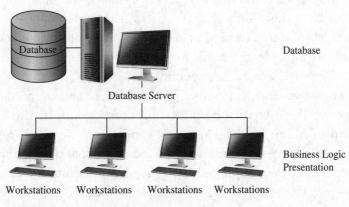

FIGURE 9-3 • The two-tier client/server deployment model

? Still Struggling

Among the variables of delivery time, number of defects, and cost, you can minimize only *two* of the three. If you think of the three as the legs of a triangle and the area inside the triangle as the amount of work required to complete the system, it becomes clear that you cannot shrink all three legs of the triangle and hold the area inside the triangle the same.

The notion was to take advantage of the superior presentation and user interface capabilities of the modern workstation. However, the marketing hype of the day promised *faster* development of *better* application systems at a *lower* cost. It didn't pan out this way, nor is it ever likely to do so. However, the vendors were offering a "silver bullet" solution, and business managers of the day were far too willing to believe them.

The white lie of the time was in cost comparisons between mainframes and central servers and workstations. The vendors typically showed cost comparisons in dollars per millions of instructions per second (MIPS). The problem was that a given instruction on the personal computers of the day did far less than a given instruction on a mainframe or high-powered server. So it really was comparing apples and oranges. Cynics of the day defined MIPS as "meaningless indicator of processor speed," and they were not far wrong. The other factor that was largely ignored was that at that time personal computers did not read from and write to their disks at anywhere near the rates achieved by mainframes and high-powered servers. So although moving all the application programs (business logic) to the client workstations appeared to be a much less expensive solution, it was a false economy.

Nearly every two-tier client/server project finished late and well over budget. Moreover, there were sobering failures. For example, the California Department of Motor Vehicles spent $44 million on a vehicle-registration system that ended up being far slower and less functional than the centralized model system that it was supposed to replace. It was eventually scrapped at a total loss—even the hardware was so specialized that it could not be used for any other purpose, so it went on the junk pile. There were some successes, however. For example, PeopleSoft built a two-tier client/server human resources system that was successfully deployed by many large enterprises. Incidentally, PeopleSoft subsequently migrated their applications to the N-tier client/server model with no code running on the client workstations aside from a standard web browser. (PeopleSoft was acquired by Oracle Corporation in December 2004.)

The benefits of the two-tier client/server model include the following:

- It greatly improved the user interface compared with systems using dumb terminals.
- It offered the potential for improved performance because the workstation processor did all the work and did not have to be shared with anyone else.

Here are the drawbacks:

- Very expensive client workstations were required because all the application logic ran on the client. Client workstation costs in the $10,000–$20,000 range were not unusual.
- Administrative nightmares mounted because the application was installed on every client workstation, and all had to be updated with a new software release at the same time.
- Much more complicated (and often more expensive) development resulted because the database server and the client workstation were almost always completely different platforms that required a different set of skills.

Three-Tier Client/Server Model

The many failures of the two-tier client/server model led to some serious rethinking. The result was the three-tier client/server model, which essentially moved the application logic from the client workstation back to a centralized server, now dubbed the *application server*. Figure 9-4 shows this architecture, which proved very workable.

An application server is a computing device devoted to running application logic.

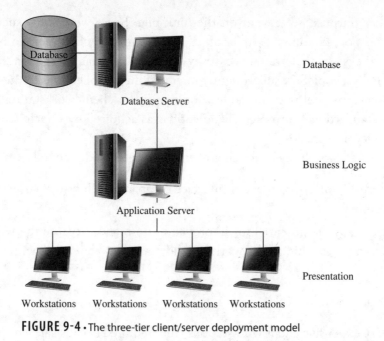

FIGURE 9-4 · The three-tier client/server deployment model

The benefits of the three-tier client/server model include the following:

- It solved the administrative issues of the two-tier model by centralizing application logic on the application server.
- It improved scalability because multiple application servers can be added as needed. (The same can be done with database servers, but that requires distributed database technology to synchronize any data updates across all copies of the data.)
- It retained the user interface advantages of the two-tier model.
- The client workstations were far less expensive (standard personal computers could easily do the job).

Here are the drawbacks:

- It was still more complicated compared with the centralized model.
- Custom presentation methods and logic added to expense and limited portability across client platforms.

The N-Tier Client/Server (Internet Computing) Model

As web browsers became ubiquitous, business computer systems migrated to using web pages as the primary presentation method. The N-tier client/server model (which some call the *Internet computing model*) is shown in Figure 9-5.

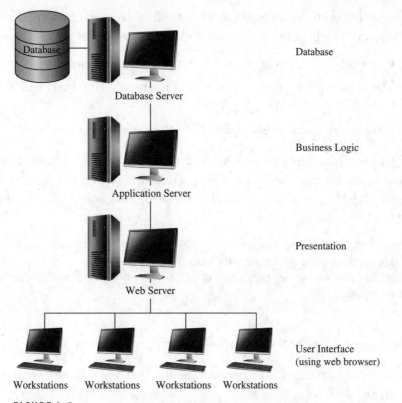

Database

Database Server

Business Logic

Application Server

Presentation

Web Server

User Interface
(using web browser)

Workstations   Workstations   Workstations   Workstations

FIGURE 9-5 • The N-tier client/server (Internet computing) deployment model

The evolution from three-tier to N-tier involved adding a web server to handle responding to client requests and the rendering (composing) of web pages, as well as swapping proprietary display logic on the workstation to a standard web browser. The interaction between the client and the web server goes something like this:

1. Using the web browser, the client submits a request in the form of a URL (Uniform Resource Locator).

2. The web server processes the request, renders the requested web page, and sends it to the client.

3. The user at the client workstation works with the web page and eventually submits a new request to the web server, and then the cycle repeats.

This architecture has been wildly successful in deployment of modern business systems. The benefits of the N-tier client/server model are as follows:

- It offers an industry-standard presentation method using web pages.
- The same architecture can be used for internal (intranet) and external (Internet) applications.
- It retains all the benefits of the three-tier client/server model.

Client workstations can be scaled all the way down to so-called *network computing devices* that do not even have a disk drive—a "smart" version of the original "dumb" terminals, if you will. Is this evolution or is it history repeating itself?

> *A network computing device is a small scale desktop system, usually without any disc drives, that is designed to function as a client workstation in the N-tier client/server model.*

Here are the drawbacks of the N-tier client/server model:

- Security challenges exist because the Internet and the Web were not designed with security in mind.
- The N-tier client/server model potentially necessitates larger development project teams because each layer requires a specialist.
- The model potentially requires more hardware (at a higher overall cost). It is possible to combine some of the servers onto common devices, but this is seldom a recommended approach because separation by function improves security.
- Increased cost to administer the larger technology stack.

Connecting Databases to the Web

The "technology stack" required to deploy an application system and corresponding database on the Internet is extensive. The basic components are shown in Figure 9-6. For completeness, we'll review each component. However, our focus is on the database, so you may wish to consult other publications for more detail on other components.

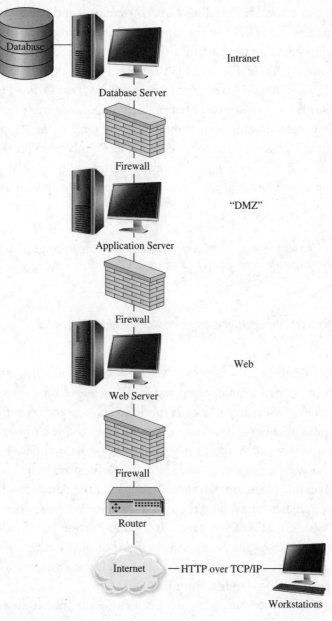

FIGURE 9-6 • Web-connected databases

Introduction to the Internet and the Web

The *Internet* is a worldwide collection of interconnected computer networks. It began in the late 1960s and early 1970s as the U.S. Department of Defense (DoD) ARPANET (Advanced Research Projects Agency Network), intended as a way of connecting DoD facilities with the colleges and universities that had DoD research grants. TCP/IP (Transmission Control Protocol/Internet Protocol) was adopted as a standard in 1982. Other protocols include FTP (File Transfer Protocol), SMTP (Simple Mail Transfer Protocol), Telnet (remote login protocol), DNS (Domain Name System), and POP (Post Office Protocol).

An *intranet* is a segment of a network, including a web site or group of web sites, that is accessible only to members of an organization. An *extranet* is an intranet that is accessible to authorized outsiders. Both are typically protected by a *firewall*, which is a dedicated gateway that applies security precautions such that only network traffic that meets certain criteria is allowed to pass through.

> An intranet is a segment of a network, including a web site or group of web sites, that is accessible only to members of an organization.

> An extranet is an intranet that is accessible to authorized outsiders.

The *Web* (formerly known as the *World Wide Web*) is a hypermedia-based system that provides a simple "point and click" means of browsing information on the Internet by using hyperlinks. Hyperlinks allow users to navigate pages in a nonsequential manner. Clients use a web browser to present pages. The web server *hosts* (stores and renders) pages and responds to client requests. Web pages may be *static* (always the same) or *dynamic* (custom built for a particular request). Dynamic pages are of a special interest in the database world because they are the vehicles for sending requested data from the database to the business user. Typically, a dynamic page has a static portion (title, help text, data field labels) and a dynamic portion in the form of placeholders where current and applicable data content (customer number, customer name) will be placed when serving a specific request from the client.

A *URL* (Uniform Resource Locator) is a string of alphanumeric characters that represents the location or address of a resource on the Internet and how the resource should be accessed. It ultimately must translate to an IP address, port, and a protocol (for example, HTTP). The general format of a URL is

```
<protocol>://<host>[:<port>]/<absolute path> [?arguments]
```

> *A URL (Uniform Resource Locator) is a string of alphanumeric characters that represents the location or address of a resource on the Internet and how the resource should be accessed.*

In most browsers, the protocol is understood to be HTTP if omitted. The host can be an IP address, but is more commonly a host name (for example, www.MySQL.com) that is resolved by looking up the corresponding IP address for the host using the Domain Name System (DNS). If the port is omitted, it takes the default for the protocol (80 for HTML). The absolute path identifies the specific page (or other resource) requested, and the web server selects a default if it is omitted. Arguments are variables passed to the web server and are considered optional.

HTTP (Hypertext Transfer Protocol) is the protocol used to transfer web pages through the Internet. It uses a request-based paradigm that is "stateless," meaning that each request is treated as an independent transaction. Statelessness makes it difficult to support the concept of a session, which is essential to basic DBMS transactions. Typically, data must be hidden in the web page or in arguments in the URL for the page to assist the web and application servers in distinguishing between pages from one user session versus another.

HTML (Hypertext Markup Language) is the document-formatting language used to design most web pages. The HTML system for marking up or tagging a

Still Struggling

Various RDBMS vendors now directly support XML as a data type, and there are also several proprietary XML databases on the market. However, businesses have been reluctant to abandon relational databases and undergo a major paradigm shift in the way they organize and store data. So, thus far, XML is most widely used for exchanging data between organizations in industry-standard XML formats. Standards committees are working on standard XML vocabularies (that is, data tags, schema structures, and conventions for using them) for specific data areas; for example, HR-XML Consortium, Inc., works solely on human resources (HR) data.

document for publication on the Web was derived from the Standard Generalized Markup Language (SGML), a 1986 ISO standard.

XML (Extensible Markup Language) is a general-purpose specification for creating custom markup languages for use in creating documents. While HTML describes presentation using a fixed set of tags, XML describes content and allows developers to create their own tags. Although XML and HTML are not at all the same language, some refer to XML as "HTML on steroids." Among the features XML offers is the ability to define an XML schema, which allows data to be stored in a hierarchical tree of XML tags within the XML document.

Components of the Web "Technology Stack"

Here's a list of the components shown in Figure 9-6 (starting at the bottom of the figure) and what they do:

- The client *workstation* runs a web browser and communicates on the *Internet* using *HTTP over TCP/IP*.
- The *web server* (site) sits behind a *router*, which forwards packets between networks, and a *firewall*. The router makes decisions on which packets are transferred between the Internet and the subnetwork on which the web server resides. Although some routers do rudimentary filtering, the additional firewall protection is considered the best way to protect the web server from intruders.

A router is specialized software, often running on a dedicated hardware device, that inconnects two or more computer networks and selectively exchanges packets between them.

- The web server is responsible for hosting and rendering web pages.
- URLs handled by the web server may cause transactions to be run on the application server. There is more on web transactions, in the following Invoking Transactions from Web Pages topic. The *application server* typically resides between a pair of firewalls to isolate it from both the web server and the *intranet*, where the *database* server typically resides. This area is commonly called the *DMZ*, a term borrowed from buffer zones between two countries in dispute.
- The application server submits SQL (or similar language) requests to the database server when data from the database is required.

Invoking Transactions from Web Pages

Information in a web request received by the web server can invoke a transaction on the application server in several ways. These methods are detailed in the following subsections.

CGI (Common Gateway Interface)

CGI (Common Gateway Interface) is a specification for transferring information between a web server and a CGI program. The CGI script (sometimes called a "CGI program") runs on either the web server or application server. CGI defines how scripts communicate with web servers. The URL points to the CGI script, and the server launches it. The actual script can be written in a variety of languages, such as Perl, PHP, and Visual Basic. In essence, instead of the URL in the incoming request pointing directly to an HTML document, it points to a script. This script is run, and the output from the script is an HTML document that is then returned to the client in response to the request.

The advantages of CGI include the following:

- Simplicity
- Language and web server independence
- Wide acceptance

Here are the disadvantages:

- The web server is always between the client and the database.
- No transaction support (stateless).
- Not intended for long exchanges.
- Each CGI execution spawns a new process (or thread), which presents resource issues.
- CGI is not inherently secure.

Server-Side Includes

Server-Side Includes (SSI) are commands embedded in a document that cause the web server to execute a program (as with CGI) and to incorporate the output into the document. Essentially, an SSI is an HTML macro. The URL in the request points to an HTML document, but the web server parses the document and handles any SSI commands before returning the document to the requesting client. SSI solves some of the CGI performance issues, but it offers few other advantages or disadvantages.

Non-CGI Gateways

Non-CGI gateways work like CGI gateways, except that each is a proprietary extension to a specific vendor's web server. The two most popular choices during the "dot-com" era were the Netscape Server API and Active Server Pages (ASP), part of the Microsoft Internet Information Server (IIS) API. The Netscape Server API was subsequently acquired by Sun Microsystems and incorporated into their product line. Since 2002, Microsoft has offered a gateway within its .NET framework.

The advantages of non-CGI gateways include the following:

- Improved performance over CGI.
- Additional features and functions.
- They run in the server address space instead of as new processes or threads.

Here are the disadvantages:

- Proprietary solution that is not portable to another vendor's web server
- Potential instability
- Much more complex compared with CGI

Connecting Databases to Applications

Now that you have seen how the web layer interacts with the application server layer, you need to understand how applications on the application server connect to and interact with the database. Most connections between the application server and remote databases (that is, those running on another server) use a standard API.

An *API (application programming interface)* is a set of calling conventions by which an application program accesses services. Such services can be provided by the operating system or by other software products such as the DBMS. The API provides a level of abstraction that allows the application to be portable across various operating systems and vendors.

> *An* API (application programming interface) *is a set of calling conventions by which an application program accesses services.*

Connecting Databases via ODBC

ODBC (Open Database Connectivity) is a standard API for connecting application programs to DBMSs. ODBC is based on a Call Level Interface (CLI, a convention that defines the way calls to services are made), which was first defined by the SQL Access Group and released in September 1992. Although Microsoft was the first company to release a commercial product based on ODBC, it is not a Microsoft standard, and versions are now available for Unix, Macintosh, and other platforms.

ODBC is independent of any particular language, operating system, or database system. An application written to the ODBC API can be ported to another database or operating system merely by changing the ODBC driver. It is the ODBC driver that binds the API to the particular database and platform, and a definition known as the *ODBC data source* contains the information necessary for a particular application to connect with a database service. On Windows systems, the most popular ODBC drivers are shipped with the operating system, as is a utility program to define ODBC data sources (found on the Control Panel or Administrative Tools Panel, depending on the version of Windows).

Most commercial software products and most commercial databases support ODBC, which makes it far easier for software vendors to market and support products across a wide variety of database systems. One notable exception is applications written in Java. They use a different API known as JDBC, which is covered in the next section.

PROBLEM 9-1

A common dilemma is that relational database vendors do not handle advanced functions in the same way.

SOLUTION

This problem can be circumvented using an escape clause that tells the ODBC driver to pass the proprietary SQL statements through the ODBC API untouched. The downside of this approach, of course, is that applications written this way are not portable to a different vendor's database (and sometimes not even to a different version of the same vendor's database).

Connecting Databases to Java Applications

Java started as a proprietary programming language (originally named Oak) that was developed by Sun Microsystems. It rapidly became the de facto standard programming language for web computing, at least in non-Microsoft environments. Java is a type-safe, object-oriented programming language that can be used to build client components (*applets*) as well as server components (*servlets*). It has a machine-independent architecture, making it highly portable across hardware and operating system platforms.

You may also run across the terms *JavaScript* and *JScript*. These are scripting languages with a Java-like syntax that are intended to perform simple functions on client systems, such as editing dates. They are not full-fledged implementations of Java and are not designed to handle database interactions, but they can perform the same function as a CGI script if desired.

JDBC (Java Database Connectivity)

JDBC (Java Database Connectivity) is an API, modeled after ODBC, for connecting Java applications to a wide variety of relational DBMS products. Some JDBC drivers translate the JDBC API to corresponding ODBC calls and thus connect to the database via an ODBC data source. Other drivers translate directly to the proprietary client API of the particular relational database, such as the Oracle Call Interface (OCI). As with ODBC, an escape clause is available for passing proprietary SQL statements through the interface. The JDBC API offers the following features:

- **Embedded SQL for Java** The Java programmer codes SQL statements as string variables, the strings are passed to Java methods, and an embedded SQL processor translates the Java SQL to JDBC calls.

- **Direct mapping of RDBMS tables to Java classes** The results of SQL calls are automatically mapped to variables in Java classes. The Java programmer may then operate on the returned data as native Java objects.

JSQL (Java SQL)

JSQL (Java SQL) is a method of embedding SQL statements in Java without having to do special coding to put the statements into Java strings. It is an extension of the ISO/ANSI standard for SQL embedded in other host languages, such as C. A special program called a *precompiler* is run on the source program that automatically translates the SQL statements written by the Java programmer into pure Java. This method can save a considerable amount of development effort.

Middleware Solutions

Middleware can be thought of as software that mediates the differences between an application program and the services available on a network, or between two disparate application programs. In the case of Java database connections, middleware products such as JRB (Java Relational Binding) from Unidata can make the RDBMS look as if it is an object-oriented database running on a remote server. The Java programmer then accesses the database using standard Java methods, and the middleware product takes care of the translation between objects and relational database components.

> *Middleware can be thought of as software that mediates the differences between an application program and the services available on a network, or between two disparate application programs.*

Summary

In this chapter, you learned about database implementation details, including database deployment models, connecting databases to the outside world, and connecting databases to applications. In Chapter 10, we'll take a detailed look at how to secure database environments.

QUIZ

Choose the correct responses to each of the multiple-choice questions. Note that there may be more than one correct response to each question.

1. In the three-tier client/server model:
   A. A web server hosts the web pages.
   B. The client workstation handles all presentation logic.
   C. The database is hosted on a centralized server.
   D. All application logic runs on an application server.
   E. Client workstations must be high-powered systems.

2. In the N-tier client/server model:
   A. Client workstations must be high-powered systems.
   B. All application logic runs on an application server.
   C. The client workstation handles all presentation logic.
   D. A web server hosts the web pages.
   E. The database is hosted on a centralized server.

3. In the centralized deployment model:
   A. There are no single points of failure.
   B. A "dumb" terminal is used as the client workstation.
   C. Administration is quite easy because everything is centralized.
   D. Develop costs are often very high.
   E. A web server hosts all web pages.

4. The Internet:
   A. Supports multiple protocols, including HTTP, FTP, and Telnet
   B. Is a worldwide collection of interconnected computer networks
   C. Always used TCP/IP as a standard
   D. Began as the U.S. Department of Education's ARPANET
   E. Dates back to the late 1960s and early 1970s

5. An extranet is
   A. Available to authorized outsiders
   B. Available to anyone on the Internet
   C. Available to authorized (internal) members of an organization
   D. Typically connected to the Internet
   E. Protected by a firewall

6. **HTTP is**

    A. A document-formatting language
    B. A protocol used to transfer web pages
    C. The Hypertext Transmission Protocol
    D. A stateless protocol
    E. Used for remote database connections

7. **The advantages of CGI are**

    A. Language and server independent
    B. Statelessness
    C. Simplicity
    D. Widely accepted
    E. Inherently secure

8. **The advantages of a non-CGI gateway are**

    A. Simpler than CGI
    B. Proprietary solution
    C. Known for stability
    D. Runs in server address space
    E. Improved security over CGI solutions

9. **Server-Side Includes (SSI):**

    A. Are commands embedded in a web document
    B. Are inherently secure
    C. Are non-CGI gateways
    D. Solve some of the CGI performance issues
    E. Are HTML macros

10. **JSQL is**

    A. A middleware solution
    B. Independent of any particular language, operating system, or DBMS
    C. A Sun Microsystems standard
    D. An extension of an ISO/ANSI standard
    E. A method of embedding SQL statements in Java

chapter 10

Database Security

Security has become an essential consideration in modern systems. In addition to the potential damage from database security breaches, nothing can be more embarrassing to an organization than a media story regarding sensitive data or trade secrets that were electronically stolen from their computer systems. In this chapter, we will discuss the need for security, the security considerations for deploying database servers and clients that access those servers, and methods for implementing database access security. We conclude with a discussion of security monitoring and auditing.

CHAPTER OBJECTIVES

In this chapter, the reader should:

- Know why security is necessary.

- Understand database server security issues and precautions, including physical security, network security, and server-level security.

- Understand database client and application security issues and precautions, including login credentials and data encryption.

- Understand the database security architectures of MySQL, Microsoft SQL Server, Sybase, and Oracle.

- Know how system and object privileges are implemented in most relational DBMS products.

Why Is Security Necessary?

Murphy's Law states that anything that can go wrong will go wrong. Seasoned IT security professionals will tell you that Murphy was an optimist. Servers placed on the Internet with default configurations and passwords have been compromised within *minutes*. Default database passwords and common security vulnerabilities are widely known. In early 2003, the Slammer worm infected tens of thousands of Microsoft SQL Server databases that had been set up with a default SA (System Administrator) account that had no password. Oddly, thanks to a software defect in the payload that the Slammer worm carried, the worst damage done by this worm was in loss of service when infected computers sent out hundreds of thousands of packets on the network in search of other computers to infect. If you think this cannot happen to you, think again. Here are some reasons why security must be designed into your computer systems:

- Databases connected to the Internet, or to any other network, are vulnerable to hackers and other criminals who are determined to damage or steal the data. These include the following:

  - Spies from competitors who are after your secrets.

  - Hackers seeking notoriety from penetrating your systems.

  - Individuals interested in whatever they can obtain that has economic value.

  - Disgruntled employees. It seems odd that we never hear of gruntled employees ("gruntle" means "to make happy"), but only of disgruntled ones.

  - Zealots interested in making a political statement at the expense of your organization.

  - The emotionally unbalanced, and just plain evil people.

- Fraud attempts. Any bank auditor will tell you that 80 percent of fraud is committed by employees. So, don't assume your system is immune just because the database is not accessible from the Internet.

- Honest mistakes by authorized users can cause security exposures, loss of data, and processing errors.

- Security controls keep people honest in the same way that locks on homes and offices do.

Database Server Security

This section focuses on the security considerations for the database server. When you're considering security, it is best to start at one end of the network or the other (that is, at either the database user's client workstation or at the database server) and to work systematically through all the components in the path. This is the only way you can be sure you don't miss something. In this case, we'll start with the database server and work out from there.

Physical Security

Physically securing the server to prevent theft of the server or the disk drives is an essential ingredient. The server and other components should be in a locked room where only authorized personnel have access. Once thieves make off with the hardware, they have all the time and privacy they need to hack away at the system until they are finally able to access the data. Moreover, systems are easier to compromise using the server console than remotely; therefore, "hands-on" access to servers must be tightly controlled. Depending on the sensitivity of the data in the database, the following additional measures might be needed:

- Video surveillance system.
- *Token* security devices, where administrators must possess the device in order to gain access. Tokens range from cards or keys that must be inserted into the server in order to gain access, to crypto devices where a PIN must be entered in order to obtain a password. Some of these devices are synchronized with satellites and change the encryption key used for generating passwords every minute or so.
- Biometric devices, where administrators must pass a fingerprint or retinal scan in order to obtain access.
- Policy provisions that always require at least two employees in the room whenever anyone is directly working on the server.
- Policy provisions regarding removal of hardware and software from the workplace. I once worked at a financial institution where employees were searched whenever they left the premises. The removal of any hardware or materials, for example, computer listings, microfilmed documents, or media such as tapes and disks was strictly prohibited. However, there was a laughable loophole. A person could put *anything* in an envelope addressed

to their home (or anywhere else) and drop it in the outbound mail bins. Not only would the envelope go out without inspection, the firm would even *pay the postage*, no questions asked. Before you get the wrong idea, the only time I saw this technique used was to send some home-grown computer games offsite, but the security exposure was enormous.

Network Security

It should be obvious that physical security is not enough when the database server is accessible via a network. Intruders who manage to obtain a network connection to the server can work from outside the server room or, for servers connected to the Internet, from anywhere in the world. Moreover, because clients or other servers (such as the application server) are able to connect to the database server, we must take a holistic approach to network security and not only ensure that the network is secure, but also that *every* computer system attached to that network is equally secure.

Complete details in how to secure a network are well outside the scope of this book. However, the sections that follow compose a summary of the network security issues that must be considered. Note that the term *enterprise network* is used to mean the private network that connects the computing resources for the business enterprise.

> *An enterprise network is a private network that connects the computing resources for the business enterprise.*

Isolate the Enterprise Network from the Internet

If the enterprise network is connected to the Internet, it must be isolated so that hackers on the Internet cannot see the internals of the enterprise network or easily gain access to it. Measures to consider include the following:

- The router that connects the enterprise network to the Internet must be properly configured. Recall that a *router* is a device that forwards data packets between networks using rules contained in a *routing table*. A *packet* is merely a piece of a message that is transmitted over a network. Network devices divide messages into uniformly sized packets for efficient handling. The router must be configured so that only appropriate packets of data are routed from the Internet to the local network. Some routers can do limited filtering of packets, but typically they do not look at the contents of data packets beyond the destination IP address, contained in the packet header, making decisions on the best way to route the packet based on the destination address and the routing table.

- Each layer in the enterprise network should be protected by a firewall, with the security rules applied by the firewall getting progressively tighter with each layer. In Chapter 9, Figure 9-6 shows this arrangement. A *firewall* can be implemented using software on a general-purpose computer or using a specialized hardware device that comes with its own operating system and filtering software. The purpose of the firewall is to prevent unauthorized access to the network segment that it protects (that is, computer resources connected to the part of the network that is *inside* the firewall). All data packets passing from the network outside the firewall to the network segment (often called a *subnet*) inside the firewall must pass the security criteria imposed by the firewall, or they are simply rejected. Here are some of the methods the firewall may use:

  - **Packet filtering**   The contents of each packet entering or leaving the network are inspected to make sure user-defined rules are met. Although packet filtering is effective, it is subject to *IP spoofing*, where a hacker masquerades as a legitimate user by planting a legitimate IP address that is acceptable to the firewall in an otherwise illegitimate message. To prevent your network from being used to launch so-called *zombie attacks*, your firewall should always be configured to reject outbound packets that have a return IP address that is not a legitimate address for the enterprise network. A zombie attack occurs when an intruder plants a rogue program on one or more of your servers, which at an appointed time, wakes up and starts sending hundreds or thousands of packets per second at a target system—typically the web browser of an enterprise that the attacker has some grudge against—in an attempt to clog their system, rendering it useless. This type of attack (that is, flooding the target with useless packets) is called a *denial of service (DOS)* attack.

IP spoofing is a security breach attempt where the hacker masquerades as a legitimate user by planting a legitimate IP address that is acceptable to the firewall in an otherwise illegitimate message.

A denial of service (DOS) attack is an attempt to clog an enterprise network by sending hundreds or thousands of useless data packets per second to a target system.

- **Application gateway**   Different network applications (HTTP, FTP, Telnet, and so on) use different default ports. For example, HTTP uses port 80 as a default. Ports that are not needed should be shut down. *Always* configure firewalls to open *only* the ports that are *absolutely required* for your normal business.

- **Circuit-level gateway**   For efficiency, this feature applies security mechanisms when a connection is established; then, after the connection is established, it allows packets to flow freely for that established connection. A firewall should normally be configured so that connections can *only* be established from *inside* the firewall—attempts made from outside the firewall to establish connections with resources inside the firewall should be rejected.

- **Proxy server**   Firewalls can translate all the IP addresses used in the protected network into different addresses as packets pass through, typically assigning each a different port so that any responses to those packets can be sorted out and passed back to the originator. This feature, known as *network address translation (NAT)*, hides the internal network from the outside world.

Network address translation (NAT) is a process that translates IP addresses in packet headers as the packets are moved from one network to another by a routing device.

- Consider using a secure network connection such as secure sockets layer (SSL) for all connections between user client systems and database servers, and also between application servers and database servers.

PROBLEM 10-1

Employees working from home present a special risk. If they are connected to a broadband Internet service such as DSL or cable, they essentially reside on a local area network (LAN) with many other users of that particular service. Therefore, if these employees merely plug their personal computers directly into the DSL or cable modem without other precautions, any shared devices they may have (disk drives, printers, and so forth) are now automatically shared by all their *neighbors* on the same LAN. All the intruder has to know is how to click Network Neighborhood and then Entire Network, and all the unprotected systems on the LAN will be there ripe for picking.

✔ SOLUTION

Two precautions can circumvent the problem:

- A security device, typically a combination router/hub/firewall, should be placed between the DSL or cable modem and any computers used in the home. A side benefit here is that the user can hook multiple computers to the high-speed service while only paying for one IP address with their ISP. The device automatically "NATs" any IP address inside the home network to the single IP address assigned by the ISP for the broadband connection, using different ports to differentiate between different connections. I have such a device on my home Internet cable service and have seen firsthand the attempts by hackers to scan ports and to ping resources inside the home network. A *port scan* is a technique commonly used to by hackers where they launch a special program that tries every conceivable port on an IP address, recording which ones are active so they can try to use the active ports to break into the target system. Intrusion attempts happen with *alarming* frequency, sometimes several times in a single hour. If you install an unprotected home network, your network will likely be penetrated within *hours* of it being activated. Note that all Microsoft Windows versions from XP on come with a built-in configurable software firewall. However, most security experts prefer an external firewall on a dedicated hardware device because it offers better protection.
- A secure network technique known as a *virtual private network (VPN)* can be used when connecting from the Internet to the enterprise network. This approach encrypts all data packets and applies other measures to make sure that the packets are useless to any unauthorized party that intercepts them, and that they cannot be altered and retransmitted by hackers. Usually, this technique is implemented using special software from a commercial software vendor in concert with a small device that the remote user employs to generate a unique

password each time they connect remotely to the enterprise network. Without the device in their possession (and typically a PIN that goes with the device), the would-be hacker has no chance of penetrating the enterprise network using the VPN.

Secure Any Wireless Network Access

Wireless access points are network devices that receive radio signals from computer devices equipped with wireless network adapters, connecting them to the wired network in the office. Most wireless networks adhere to a version of the network standard protocol known as 802.11. Wireless access points have become inexpensive (prices as low as $30) and therefore prolific because people like to be able to freely move around their home or office without having to drag a network cable with them. However, wireless access points require special attention because an intruder can access your network from outside your premises without going through the routers and firewalls that you have carefully set up to prevent such an intrusion. Horror stories abound in IT trade publications about an unknowing user bringing an unauthorized wireless access point into an office, plugging it into the nearest network jack, and giving everyone within 75 to 150 feet open access to the network. By default, many of these devices, particularly the older ones, have *absolutely no* encryption or other access controls enabled, thus providing access to anyone with a wireless-capable computer in a neighboring office, out in the parking lot, or even in a building across the street. Worst of all is that once intruders connect, they are on the intranet, completely *inside* all the firewalls and other controls you so carefully implemented to protect your network from intruders.

If you think this cannot happen to you, here are just a few real-life examples:

- On a recent trip to a medical office, I found that my laptop, which is equipped with an 802.11g wireless network adapter, *automatically* connected to a wireless network in an adjoining doctor's office from the waiting room. I didn't look to see what I might have been able to access in terms of computers, shared disks, files, and the like, but the office staff was totally unaware that anyone could connect to their wireless network. They didn't understand that walls don't stop wireless networks. Incidentally, a quick look at the wireless adapter's site survey showed two other vulnerable networks accessible from the same waiting room. One of those even had the default network name that comes with the wireless access point, so we can easily assume that the password to the router would also be the factory default. An intruder could reconfigure their entire network before they knew what happened.

- On a recent drive down Market Street in San Francisco, I discovered that the wireless adapter in the same laptop detected at least three wireless networks in every block, a surprising number of them wide open to anyone who would want to connect.

- An IT manager once told me that after they discovered that an unauthorized wireless access point was connected to their company's network, they went hunting for it, failing to find it in several attempts. Finally, they brought in a consultant who had a device to track down the rogue signal. (Believe it or not, an antenna inside a potato chip tube covered with aluminum foil makes an excellent directional antenna for "sniffing out" wireless access points.) They found it hidden in the suspended ceiling of a conference room. The person who installed it knew it was against the rules, but just didn't want to bother to cable-connect their laptop to a nearby outlet. Needless to say, that person lost their job, but who knows what the intruders got before the unauthorized access point was shut down?

Here are some countermeasures you can put in place to help secure your wireless network:

- **Policy**   Your organization's security policy should address wireless connections, forbidding anyone other than trained network administrators from installing them, and setting standards for their proper installation.

- **Mandatory encryption**   Standards should mandate that encryption be enabled on every wireless access point. All the access points on the market have encryption capability built into them, and it only takes a few minutes to enable the feature and to input a passphrase that any device trying to connect must supply in order to gain access to the network.

- **Disable SSID broadcasting**   Each wireless network access point is assigned an SSID (Service Set Identifier) when it is configured. It is the SSID that is displayed on client systems when users are given the list of wireless networks that have been detected within range. If the SSID is not broadcast, then (at least in theory) the user must know it and input it in order to connect to the wireless network. However, this is a controversial security measure. Some experts say that disabling the SSID broadcast does nothing to enhance security and may actually increase network vulnerability. For example, in Windows XP and Windows Server 2003, clients send probes that include the SSIDs in the preferred network client list even when the network is not in range, so those SSIDs are easily detectable. This situation has been remedied with a new option in subsequent versions of Windows, but keep in mind that obfuscation is not the same as security. I recommend you read up on this topic on the Web before you decide to disable SSID broadcasting.

- **MAC address list**   Every network device currently manufactured has a unique MAC (Media Access Control) address assigned to it by the manufacturer. Most wireless access points permit the entry of a MAC address list that restricts network access to *only* the devices that appear in the list. Alternatively, the MAC address list can list devices that are *not* allowed to connect. However, MAC addresses are sent over the wireless network in plain text (they aren't encrypted), so it is not all that difficult to counter this precaution.

System-Level Security

Once the network is as secure as we can make it, the next area of focus is the system that will run the DBMS. A poorly secured database server can provide many unchecked paths for intruders to use. Here are some measures worth considering:

- **Installing minimal operating system software**   Particularly on a production server, install only the minimal software components to get the job done. Avoid default or "typical" installation options, and use the "custom" installation option to choose only the components needed. For example, on production Unix servers, you should be in the habit of removing the "make" utility and C language compilers after you complete an installation. Hackers have a very difficult time installing things when the tools needed to perform software installations do not exist on the server.

- **Using minimal operating system services**   Shut down or remove operating system services that are not required. In particular, communications services such as FTP (File Transfer Protocol) should not be running unless they are expressly required. On Windows systems, it's a good idea to set Startup Type to "Disabled" for services that are not required. This makes it impossible to start these services unless you have Administrator privileges.

- **Installing minimal DBMS software**   The fewer the features of the DBMS that you have installed, the less exposure you'll have to problems such as buffer overflow vulnerabilities. The DBA should work with the application developers to create a consolidated list of the DBMS functions needed. Once you have the list, use the custom installation option for the DBMS and perform only minimal installations.

- **Run the DBMS using an account with appropriate privileges**   It is most unwise to use a superuser account, such as root in Unix or Administrator in Windows, to run the database software. Doing so gives hackers full access to the server should they manage to compromise the DBMS security system. Also, require all user accounts that can access the database to have passwords.

- **Applying security patches in a timely manner**   Establish a program where security alerts are reviewed as they are announced and where countermeasures, including patches and workarounds, are applied in a timely manner. Patches should be shaken down in a development environment for a finite period before being applied to a production environment.

- **Changing all default passwords**   These should be changed to new ones that are difficult to guess or discover via *brute force*, a method that repeatedly tries possibilities until access is finally achieved.

Database Client and Application Security

A *database client* is any computer system that signs on directly to the database server. Therefore, the application server is nearly always a database client, along with the client workstation of any person in the organization who has sign-on privileges with the database. Typically, the DBMS requires installation of client software on these systems to facilitate communication between the database client and the DBMS using any specialized communications mechanisms required by the DBMS.

Login Credentials

Every database user who connects to the database must supply appropriate credentials to establish the connection. Typically, this is in the form of a user ID (or login ID) and a password. Care must be taken to establish credentials that are not easily compromised. Here are some considerations:

- Credentials must not be shared by multiple database users.

- Passwords should not be easy to guess. A security policy should establish minimum standards for password security, including minimum length, the mixture of upper/lowercase letters, numbers and special characters required, avoiding words that can be found in a dictionary, and the like.

- Passwords should be changed on a regular basis, such as every 30 or 45 days.

- Any exposed password should be immediately changed.

- Passwords should never be written down and must be encrypted whenever they are electronically stored.

Data Encryption

Encryption is the translation of data into a secret code that cannot be read without the use of a password or secret key. Unencrypted data is called *plain text*, whereas encrypted data is called *cipher text*.

Some encryption schemes use a *symmetric key*, which means that a single key is used to both encrypt plain text and to decrypt cipher text. This form is considered less secure compared with the use of *asymmetric keys*, where a pair of keys is used—one called the *public* key and the other the *private* key. What the public key encrypts, the private key can decrypt, and vice versa. The names come from the expected use of the keys—the public key is given to anyone an enterprise does business with, and the private key remains confidential and internal to the enterprise.

Here are some guidelines to follow regarding encryption:

- Encryption keys should be a minimum of 128 bits in length. The longer the key, the more secure it is considered to be.

- The loss of an encryption key should be treated with the same seriousness as the loss of the data that it was used to encrypt.

- Sensitive data should be encrypted whenever permanently stored. Which data is considered sensitive is a judgment call that should be made by the businesspeople who own the data, not by the DBA. In general, however, any personal data (such as social security numbers) that can be used for identity theft should be considered sensitive.

- All data not considered public knowledge should be encrypted whenever transported electronically across network connections that are not otherwise encrypted. For example, if a company sends a purchase order file to a trading partner via FTP, the file should be encrypted. There is no guarantee that the bad guys are not monitoring public networks.

- E-mail is not considered secure, so any sensitive information to be sent via e-mail should be in an encrypted attachment instead of in the main body of the e-mail message.

Other Client Considerations

Database clients require special scrutiny in terms of security precautions because, if compromised, they provide an easy pathway for the intruder to gain access to data in the database. Here are some additional client considerations:

- **Web browser security level**   Modern web browsers allow the setting of a security level for the browser. For Microsoft Internet Explorer, the security settings are controlled using the Security tab on the Internet Options panel, which is accessible using the Tools option on the main toolbar. This security level should be set to the highest possible level that still permits normal use of the database applications. Here are two considerations related to the web browser:

  - *Cookies* provide the ability for the web browser to store textual information on the client, which can be automatically retrieved later by the web browser and sent to the web server that requested them. Cookies are not very secure and can be used to spy on users of the client system. Furthermore, there is no guarantee that unauthorized persons and software will have no access to information in cookies. The organization's security policy should address this issue and set a clear standard for cookie use, which is one of the facilities controlled by the web browser's security level. Also, it is not wise to design application systems that require cookies because they are not supported by all web browsers and not permitted by all users. In Microsoft Internet Explorer, options for cookies are controlled using the Privacy tab on the Internet Options panel.

  - Scripting languages such as VBScript, JavaScript, and JScript provide nice features for assisting with a user's interaction with a web page. However, they can be and have been used for injecting malicious code into systems, so take care when allowing such languages to be used on the client. VBScript is especially notorious for its misuse and has been used to transport viruses in e-mail attachments.

- **Minimal use of other software**   Software that is not required for the normal functioning of the client should not be installed. Security policy should forbid employees from installing unauthorized software.

- **Virus scanner**   All computer systems running operating systems that are susceptible to computer viruses should have appropriate virus-scanning software installed. Virus scanners that automatically update their virus profiles on a regular basis offer the most effective protection.

- **Test application exposures**   Web-based applications should be thoroughly tested using a client configured just the way your real business users' client workstations will be configured. Hacker tricks such as the following should be attempted to verify that the exposures do not exist:

  - **SQL injection**   SQL statements can be entered along with data in one or more web page data fields in such a way that the application server or web server hands them off to the database for processing. For example, if there is a web page field that allows entry of an employee ID that is placed directly in an SQL statement, if the user enters only employee ID *1234*, the result is an SQL statement as the developer intended it to be:

    ```
    SELECT * FROM EMPLOYEE
      WHERE  EMPLOYEE_ID = 1234;
    ```

    However, if the user enters 1234 OR 1=1, the additional predicate shown in the following SQL statement makes the search condition true for all rows (1 is always equal to 1, so the predicate is always true), and the user sees every employee row instead of just one.

    ```
    SELECT * FROM EMPLOYEE
      WHERE  EMPLOYEE_ID = 1234 OR 1=1;
    ```

  - **URL spoofing**   The URL in the web browser is manually overtyped in such a way that unauthorized data is revealed. Designs where session IDs are assigned sequentially by the application server and then passed back to the web browser as an argument in the URL are especially susceptible to this approach. If you can guess another user's session ID, you can hijack their session just by overtyping the session ID in the URL.

- **Buffer overflows**   Published exposures such as buffer overflows should be thoroughly tested once the vendor's patch has been installed to ensure that the problem really was corrected.

?
Still Struggling

Those skilled at SQL injection can add entirely new SQL statements and compromise a database in just minutes. There are several techniques available for making sure user input is not interpreted as SQL, but their effectiveness varies across DBMSs and operating systems. The best thing to do is to always test for the vulnerability in all fields where users can enter data.

Database Access Security

With the confidence that our clients, servers, and network are now secure, we can focus on database access. The goal here is to determine precisely the data that each database user needs to conduct their business, and what they are permitted to do with the data (that is, select, insert, update, or delete). Each database user should be given *exactly* the privileges they need—nothing more and nothing less. Recall that an application program with database access is a database user just as an employee who directly queries the database is. In terms of database security, all database users should be treated in the same way (that is, the same standards should be applied to all), whether the database user is software or "liveware." In this section, we will explore the options and challenges related to securing access to the database and its data.

Database Security Architectures

For DBAs who support databases from multiple vendors, one of the challenges is that, with the exception of Microsoft SQL Server and Sybase, no two databases have the same architecture for database security. And of course, this is a side effect of the overall database architectures being different. The only reason that Microsoft SQL Server and Sybase have such similar architectures is that the former was derived from the latter. Because MySQL, Microsoft SQL Server, and Oracle are among the most popular databases today, let's have a quick look at how each implements database security.

Database Security in MySQL

With MySQL, once the DBMS software is installed on the server (or on a personal computer), a database server is created. This is a confusing term, of course, because we call the hardware a "server." In this case, the term *server* is a copy of the DBMS software running in memory as a set of processes (also called "services" in Windows environments) with related control information that is stored in special catalog tables in a database named mysql. In this architecture, each server manages many databases, with each database representing a logical grouping of data as determined by the database designer. Figure 10-1 shows a simplified view of the security architecture for MySQL, including the following:

- **User**   This is a user account defined in the MySQL server's User table. MySQL identifies a user with the combination of the user identifier (login) from the user's host system and the name of the host system. This arrangement allows the same user account name to be used to connect to the MySQL server from different host systems, even if those account names belong to different individuals. However, the MySQL user name does not have to be the same as the user's account name on their host Windows, Linux, or Unix system. Note that once a login is defined in the MySQL server, the database user may connect to the server, but a login

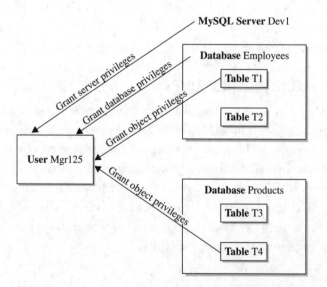

FIGURE 10-1 · Security in MySQL

alone does *not* give them access to any database information. The user account must be granted privileges at the server, database, or database object level before it can be used to perform any sort of operation on the database. However, a root user is automatically created when the server is installed, and like the Unix root user, it has full privileges across the server and all the databases and objects therein. For all other user accounts, MySQL supports a CREATE USER statement to set up new user accounts, but user accounts may also be implicitly created when they are referenced in a GRANT statement. In addition, MySQL offers a most unusual alternative: users with administrator privileges, such as the MySQL root user, can use SQL INSERT, UPDATE, and DELETE statements to directly modify the User table and other tables that control user access and privileges. Figure 10-1 shows only one user login, called Mgr125.

- **Database**   A database is a logical collection of database objects (tables, views, indexes, and so on) as defined by the database designer. Figure 10-1 shows two databases: Employees and Products. It is important to understand that a user is allowed to connect to a database only after the user has been granted that privilege by an administrator. In addition to databases holding user data, a special database named mysql is created (not shown in Figure 10-1) and is used by the DBMS to manage the MySQL server. Among the tables in the mysql database, the ones that control security are

  - **user**   Contains one row for each user and host system combination allowed to access the MySQL server

  - **db**   Contains one row for each database privilege granted to a MySQL user

  - **tables_priv**   Contains one row for each table privilege granted to a MySQL user

  - **columns_priv**   Contains one row for each column privilege granted to a MySQL user

  - **procs_priv**   Contains one row for each stored routine privilege granted to a MySQL user

- **Server privileges**   These are general privileges applied across the entire MySQL server, such as CREATE USER, SHOW DATABASES, and

SHUTDOWN. Each server privilege is represented as a column in the users table that contains a *Y* if the user is granted the privilege or an *N* if not.

- **Database privileges**   These privileges, such as CREATE and DROP, are applied across a particular database. Each database privilege is implemented as a row in the db table. Database privileges and server privileges are often collectively known as *system privileges*. System privileges work in a similar manner across all relational databases and are therefore covered in the "System Privileges" section that follows a little later in this chapter.

- **Object privileges**   These privileges allow specific actions on a specific object, such as allowing select and update on Table T1. Figure 10-1 contains arrows that show the granting of object privileges on Table T1 in the Employees database, and on Table T4 in the Products database to user Mgr125. These privileges work in much the same way across all relational databases, thanks to ANSI standards, and are therefore covered in the "Object Privileges" section that follows a little later in this chapter.

Database Security in Microsoft SQL Server and Sybase

With Microsoft SQL Server and Sybase, once the DBMS software is installed on the server, a database server is created. As with MySQL, the term *server* or *SQL server* is a copy of the DBMS software running in memory as a set of processes (also called "services" in Windows environments) with related control information that is stored in a special database on the SQL server. In this architecture, each SQL server manages many databases, with each database representing a logical grouping of data as determined by the database designer. Figure 10-2 shows a simplified view of the security architecture for Microsoft SQL Server and Sybase.

- **Login**   This is a user account on the SQL server, also called a *user login*. This is not the same as any operating system account the user may have on the database server. However, on database servers running Microsoft Windows, the login can use Windows authentication, meaning the Windows operating system stores the credentials (login name and password) and authenticates users when they connect to the SQL server. An obvious advantage to Windows authentication is that user access to the various SQL servers in the enterprise can be centrally managed through the Windows account, rather than locally managed on each SQL server. Note that

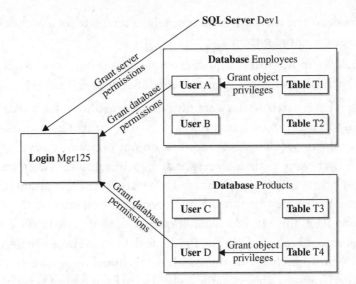

FIGURE 10-2 • Security in Microsoft SQL Server and Sybase

once a login is defined in the SQL server, the database user may connect to the SQL server, but a login alone does *not* give them access to any database information. There is, however, a master login called "sa" (system administrator) that, similar to root in Unix and Administrator in Microsoft Windows, has full privileges to everything in the SQL Server environment. Figure 10-2 shows only one user login, called Mgr125.

- **Database**   A database is a logical collection of database objects (tables, views, indexes, and so on) as defined by the database designer. Figure 10-2 shows two databases: Employees and Products. It is important to understand that a login is allowed to connect to a database only after it has been granted that privilege by an administrator (discussed next). In addition to databases holding system data, some special databases are created when the SQL server is created (not shown in Figure 10-2) and are used by the DBMS to manage the SQL server. Among these are the following databases:

  - **master**   The master database contains system-level information, initialization settings, configuration settings, login accounts, the list of databases configured in the SQL server, and the location of primary database data files.

  - **tempdb**   The tempdb database contains temporary tables and temporary stored procedures.

- **model** The model database contains a template for all other databases created on the system.
- **msdb** In Microsoft SQL Server databases only, the msdb database contains information used for scheduling jobs and alerts.

- **User** Each database has a set of users assigned to it. Each database user maps to a login, so each user is a pseudo-account that is an alias to an SQL Server login account. User accounts do not necessarily have to have the same user name as their corresponding login accounts. When an administrator grants access to a database for a particular login account, the user account corresponding to the login account is created by the DBMS. In Figure 10-2, the Mgr125 login corresponds to user A in the Employees database and to user D in the Products database. These privileges permit the login to connect to the database(s), but do not give the user any privileges against objects in those databases. Each user may be granted any number of permissions (described next). (While most DBMS vendors use the term *privileges*, Microsoft seems to prefer the term *permissions*.)

- **Server permissions** These are privileges that can be applied at the server level. Microsoft SQL Server divides these into *server privileges*, which include such permissions as starting up, shutting down, and backing up the SQL server, and *statement privileges*, which include such permissions as creating a database and creating a table.

- **System permissions** These are privileges that can be applied at the database level. Many of these overlap with server permissions. (A general discussion of system privileges appears in a topic later in this chapter.)

- **Object privileges** These allow specific actions on a specific object, such as allowing select and update on Table T1. Figure 10-2 contains arrows that show the granting of object privileges on Table T1 to user A in the Employees database, and on Table T4 to user D in the Products database. These privileges work in much the same way across all relational databases, thanks to ANSI standards. (A general discussion of object privileges appears in a topic later in this chapter.)

Database Security in Oracle

Oracle's security architecture, shown in Figure 10-3, is markedly different compared with that of SQL Server. The differences between the two are highlighted as each component is introduced:

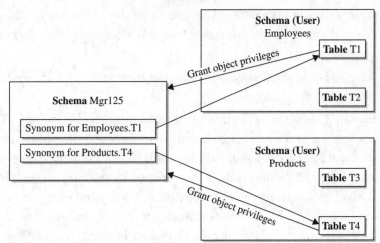

Database Dev1

FIGURE 10-3 · Database security in Oracle

- **Instance**   This is a copy of the Oracle DBMS software running in memory. Each instance manages only *one* database.

- **Database**   This is the collection of files managed by a single Oracle instance (or cluster of instances in the case of Oracle Real Application Clusters, a configuration that enhances scalability and availability). Taken together, the Oracle instance and database compose what MySQL, Microsoft SQL Server, and Sybase call the *SQL server*. Figure 10-3 depicts the Dev1 database.

- **User**   Each database account is called a *user*. As with MySQL, Microsoft SQL Server, and Sybase, the user account may be authenticated externally (that is, by the operating system) or internally (by the DBMS). Each user is automatically allocated a schema (defined next), and this user is the *owner* of that schema, meaning it automatically has full privileges over any object in the schema. The following predefined users are created automatically when the database is created (not shown in Figure 10-3):

  - The SYS user is the owner of the Oracle instance and database and contains objects that Oracle uses to manage them. This user is equivalent to the root user in MySQL and the "sa" user in Microsoft SQL Server and Sybase.

- The SYSTEM user is automatically created and assigned the DBA role during Oracle installation. This user is similar to the mysql database in MySQL and the master database in Microsoft SQL Server and Sybase.

- Many Oracle database options create their own user accounts when those options are installed.

- **Schema**   This is the collection of database objects that belong to a specific Oracle user. The Oracle schema is equivalent to what Microsoft SQL Server and Sybase call a *database*. Figure 10-3 shows the Employees, Products, and Mgr125 schemas, which are owned by the Employees, Products, and Mgr125 users, respectively. Schema and user names are *always* identical in Oracle. Mgr125 is a workaround to a special challenge we face with Oracle's security architecture, as discussed in the "Schema Owner Accounts" section that follows.

- **Privileges**   As with MySQL, Microsoft SQL Server, and Sybase, privileges are divided into system and object privileges. These are covered in the "System Privileges" section later in this chapter.

Schema Owner Accounts

With all databases, we want to avoid giving database users more privileges than they need to do their job. This not only prevents errors made by humans (including those contained in the application programs and database queries they write) from becoming data disasters, but it also keeps people honest.

In Microsoft SQL Server and Sybase, we want to avoid having database users connect as the "sa" user. We want to create database logins that have the minimal privileges required. Sadly, this is often not done, and applications connect as "sa" or to a database with a user account that has the DBO (database owner) or DBA (database administrator) role. Roles are a collection of privileges and are discussed in the upcoming "Roles" section. Whether done out of lack of understanding or out of laziness, using highly privileged user accounts for application and business user connections represents a *huge* security exposure that should be forbidden as a matter of policy.

In Figure 10-3, note that the Mgr125 user owns no tables but does have some privileges granted to it by the Employees and Products users. This is to work around a fundamental challenge with Oracle's security architecture. If we allowed a database user to connect to the database using a user such as

Employees or Products, the user would automatically have full privileges to every object in the schema, including insert, delete, and update against any table, and also the ability to create and alter tables without restriction. This is fundamentally the same issue as allowing use of the "sa" user or the DBO and DBA roles in Microsoft SQL Server and Sybase. The Mgr125 user mimics the behavior of the login with the same name, as shown in Figure 10-1. With the right system privileges, we can prevent the Mgr125 user in Oracle from being able to create any tables of its own.

You may have noticed the synonyms for user Mgr125 in Figure 10-3. A *synonym* is merely an alias or nickname for a database object. The synonyms are for the convenience of the user so that names do not have to be qualified with their schema name. To select from the T1 tables in the Employees schema directly, user Mgr125 would have to refer to the table name as Employees.T1 in the SQL statement. This not only is inconvenient, but also can cause no end of problems if we ever decide to change the name of the Employees user. By creating a synonym called T1 in the Mgr125 schema that points to Employees. T1, the user may now refer to the table as just T1. Incidentally, you may recall that all user and object names in Oracle are case insensitive, so the use of mixed case here is only for illustration. The syntax for creating this synonym is as follows:

```
CREATE SYNONYM T1 FOR EMPLOYEES.T1;
```

System Privileges

As stated earlier, system privileges are general permissions to perform functions in managing the server and the database(s). Hundreds of permissions are supported by each database vendor, with most of those being system privileges. As with object privileges, system privileges are granted using the SQL GRANT statement and rescinded using the SQL REVOKE statement. Some of the most commonly used ones are listed in the sections that follow. Complete details may be found in vendor-supplied documentation.

MySQL System (Server and Database) Privilege Examples

Here are some commonly used MySQL system privileges:

- **CREATE USER**   Provides the ability to create new user accounts
- **RELOAD**   Provides the ability to reload privileges, which causes changes made directly in the security tables to take immediate effect

- **SHOW DATABASES**   Provides the ability to show (display) all databases
- **SHUTDOWN**   Provides the ability to shut down the server
- **CREATE**   Provides the ability to create databases, tables, and indexes
- **DROP**   Provides the ability to drop databases, tables, and indexes

Microsoft SQL Server System (Server and Statement) Privilege Examples

Here are some commonly used Microsoft SQL Server system privileges:

- **SHUTDOWN**   Provides the ability to issue the server shutdown command
- **CREATE DATABASE**   Provides the ability to create new databases on the SQL server
- **BACKUP DATABASE**   Provides the ability to run backups of the databases on the SQL server

Oracle System Privilege Examples

Here are some commonly used Oracle system privileges:

- **CREATE SESSION**   Provides the ability to connect to the database.
- **CREATE TABLE**   Provides the ability to create tables in your own schema. Similar privileges exist for other object types, such as indexes, synonyms, procedures, and so on.
- **CREATE ANY TABLE**   Provides the ability to create tables in *any* user's schema. Similar privileges are available for other object types, such as indexes, synonyms, procedures, and so on.
- **CREATE USER**   Provides the ability to create new users in the database.

Object Privileges

Object privileges are granted to users with the SQL GRANT statement and revoked with the REVOKE statement. The database user (login) who receives the privileges is called the *grantee*. These statements are also covered in Chapter 6. The GRANT statement may include a WITH GRANT OPTION clause that allows the recipient to then grant the privilege to others. If the privilege is subsequently revoked, a cascading revoke takes place if this user has, in turn, granted the permission to anyone else. I do *not* recommend use of the WITH GRANT OPTION clause because it is far too easy to lose control over who has which privileges.

The general syntax of the GRANT statement is shown here, along with some examples:

```
GRANT <privilege list> ON <object> TO <grantee list>
   [WITH GRANT OPTION];

GRANT SELECT, UPDATE, INSERT ON T1 TO Mgr125;

GRANT SELECT ON T2 TO User1, User2, User3;


REVOKE <privilege list> ON <object> FROM <grantee list>;

REVOKE SELECT, UPDATE, INSERT ON T1 FROM Mgr125;

REVOKE SELECT ON T2 FROM User1, User2, User3;
```

Roles

A *role* is a named collection of privileges that can, in turn, be granted to one or more users. Most RDBMS systems, including SQL Server, Sybase, and Oracle, have predefined roles that come with the system, and database users with the CREATE ROLE privilege may create their own. However, as of version 5.2, MySQL does not support roles.

> *A role is a named collection of database privileges.*

Roles have the following advantages:

- *Roles may exist before user accounts do.* For example, we can create a role that contains all the privileges required to work on a particular development project. When a new hire joins the project team, one GRANT statement gives their new user account all the permissions they need.

- *Roles relieve the administrator of a lot of tedium.* Many privileges may be granted with a single command when a role is used.

- *Roles survive when user accounts are dropped.* In cases where the DBA must drop and re-create a user account, it can be a lot of work to reinstate all the privileges, which is simplified if all the privileges are assembled into one role.

For administrators, a common role is DBA, which conveys a lot of powerful privileges (over 125 separate privileges in Oracle). Obviously, such a high-powered privilege must be granted judiciously.

Views

One of the common security issues to be addressed is how to allow database users access to some rows and columns in a table while preventing access to other rows and columns. Views are an excellent way to accomplish this. Here are some of the benefits of using views to accomplish security objectives:

- *Columns that a database user does not require may be omitted from the view.* Assuming the user has been granted access to the view rather than the underlying table, this method totally prevents them from seeing the information in the columns that were omitted from the view.

- *A WHERE clause may be included in the view to limit returned rows.* Joins may be included to match to other tables as a way of limiting rows. For example, the view could limit Product table rows to only those products for a Division ID that matches the division in which the employee works.

- *Joins to "lookup" tables can be used to replace code values in a table with their corresponding descriptions.* A lookup table typically contains a list of code values (for example, department codes, transaction codes, status codes) and their descriptions, and it's used to "look up" the descriptions for the codes. Although this is a minor point, employees trying to hack database records during fraud attempts have a much more difficult time if they cannot see the codes used to categorize the transactions. Furthermore, employees trying to do their best usually have a better time reading and understanding code descriptions than the corresponding code values.

Security Monitoring and Auditing

Security policies and controls are typically not enough to ensure compliance. There must be a monitoring system to detect security breaches so that corrective measures can be taken. Multiple intrusion-detection tools are on the market that are capable of monitoring a server and detecting unauthorized changes to files stored in the file system. Also, most of the major RDBMS products have provisions for setting up auditing so that selected actions in the database are silently logged, typically into audit tables that may subsequently be used for reporting. Consult your RDBMS documentation for a full description of these auditing features.

It is also a good idea to have an independent auditor review your organization's security policies and procedures when they are initially written, and at periodic intervals thereafter. Furthermore, it is wise to have your auditors, or a consultant who specializes in information systems security, perform an onsite audit, including testing the site for vulnerabilities that have not yet been addressed. System intrusions, including fraud, can cost you many times more than a system audit, which may also save you any embarrassment before your employees and customers.

Summary

In this chapter, you have learned about the need for security, database server security issues and precautions, database client and application security issues and precautions, database access security, including the security architectures of MySQL, Microsoft SQL Server, Sybase, and Oracle, and an overview of security monitoring and auditing. In Chapter 11, we look at implementing databases.

QUIZ

Choose the correct responses to each of the multiple-choice questions. Note that there may be more than one correct response to each question.

1. **In MySQL, Microsoft SQL Server, and Sybase, a login (user login):**
   A. Can be authenticated by the operating system
   B. Can be authenticated by the DBMS
   C. Can connect to any number of databases
   D. Owns a database schema
   E. Automatically has database access privileges

2. **In MySQL, Microsoft SQL Server, and Sybase, a database:**
   A. May have one or more users assigned to it
   B. Is owned by a login
   C. Is a logical collection of database objects
   D. May be granted privileges
   E. May contain system data (for example, master data) or user (application) data

3. **In Oracle, a user account:**
   A. Can connect to (log into) any number of databases
   B. Can use operating system authentication
   C. Can be authenticated by the Oracle DBMS
   D. Owns a database schema
   E. Automatically has database privileges

4. **In Oracle, a database:**
   A. Is the same as a schema
   B. Is owned by a user
   C. Is managed by an Oracle instance
   D. May contain system data (for example, system schema) and user (application) data
   E. May have one or more user accounts defined in it

5. **Security is necessary because:**
   A. 80 percent of fraud is committed by outside hackers.
   B. Honest people make mistakes.
   C. Security controls keep people honest.
   D. Application security controls alone are inadequate.
   E. Databases connected to the Internet are vulnerable to hackers.

6. **Wireless networks need to be secured because:**
   A. Employees may use the wireless network to secretly communicate with hackers.
   B. Inexpensive wireless access points are readily available.
   C. Radio waves may carry to public roads outside the building.
   D. Radio waves penetrate walls to adjoining offices.
   E. Anyone with a wireless network adapter can connect to an unprotected network.

7. **Client security considerations include:**
   A. Granting only database table privileges that are absolutely necessary
   B. Web browser security level
   C. MAC address lists
   D. Testing of application exposures
   E. Use of a virus scanner

8. **Object privileges:**
   A. Are granted using the SQL GRANT statement
   B. Are granted in a similar way in Oracle, Sybase, and Microsoft SQL Server
   C. Are specific to a database object
   D. Allow the grantee to perform certain administrative functions on the server, such as shutting it down
   E. Are rescinded using the SQL REMOVE statement

9. **Roles:**
   A. May contain any number of object privileges
   B. May contain only one object privilege
   C. May exist before users do
   D. May be assigned to only one user
   E. May be shared by many users

10. **Using the WITH GRANT OPTION when granting object privileges:**
    A. Gives the grantee DBA privileges on the entire database
    B. Can lead to security issues
    C. Allows the grantee to grant the privilege to others
    D. Will cascade if the privilege is subsequently revoked
    E. Is a highly recommended practice because it is so convenient to use

Database Implementation

In this chapter, we cover some considerations regarding the implementation of a database system. These include cursor processing, transaction management, performance tuning, and change control.

CHAPTER OBJECTIVES

In this chapter, the reader should:

- Know how to use cursors in database applications.
- Understand database transactions and how to implement them.
- Understand database performance-tuning concepts.

Cursor Processing

Before we embark on transaction management, which includes a discussion of the locking mechanisms required to support concurrent updates of the database, we must explore the way application programs handle database queries. The collection of rows returned by the execution of a database query is called the *result set*. When you're selecting data from the database, application programming languages such as C and Java present a dilemma when the result set contains multiple rows of data. These programming languages are designed to handle one record at a time (one object instance at a time in the case of Java). So there is a mismatch that must be addressed.

> A result set is the collection of rows returned by the DBMS when a database query has been executed.

To overcome the mismatch, most relational databases support the concept of a *cursor*, which is merely a pointer to a single row in the result set. In Oracle, cursor support is included in a procedural language SQL extension called PL/SQL (Procedural Language/SQL) and similarly is included in Transact-SQL in Sybase and Microsoft SQL Server. For MySQL, cursors are only supported within stored procedures and functions. The examples in this chapter use MySQL, which closely follows the ANSI/ISO SQL standard syntax; however, some of them may require minor modification before they will work on other RDBMS products. The use of a cursor parallels the use of a traditional flat file in that the cursor must be defined and opened before it may be used, it may be read from by fetching rows in a programming loop, and it should be closed when the program no longer needs it.

Following is an example of a cursor declaration. For clarity, all the keywords are shown in uppercase and database object names in lowercase.

```
DECLARE ny_customers CURSOR FOR
   SELECT customer_number, name, address, city, zip_code
     FROM customer
    WHERE state = 'NY';
```

Again, there are dialect differences between various SQL implementations. For example, in Oracle PL/SQL, the first line of the preceding declaration must be changed to:

```
DECLARE CURSOR ny_customers IS
```

You may recognize the customer table from Chapter 8. If you ignore the first line, the statement looks like any ordinary SQL query—it selects some columns from a table, and in this case, has a WHERE clause to limit the rows returned to only those from New York state. This is very nice because it means we can test the query using any interactive SQL client tool before we paste it into a program and turn it into a cursor declaration. The DECLARE CURSOR clause defines the cursor for us, which we have named ny_customers. Cursor declarations are not executable statements, meaning that when they are processed by the RDBMS, they do nothing but set up a definition that may be subsequently referenced. The declaration is checked for syntax and some other internal details, but the database does not need to access any table rows until the cursor is opened.

The cursor must be opened before it can be used. In this example, the RDBMS may not have to retrieve any rows when we open the cursor, but for efficiency, it might decide to retrieve some number of rows and place them in a buffer for us. A *buffer* is merely an area of computer memory used to temporarily hold data. It is far more efficient to use a buffer to hold some number of prefetched rows rather than going to the database files for every single row, because computers can access memory so much faster than files in the file system. In some cases, however, the RDBMS *must* fetch all the rows matching a query and sort them before the first row may be returned to the application program. You may have guessed that these are queries containing an ORDER BY to sequence the returned rows for us. If there is no index on the column(s) we use for sequencing, then the RDBMS must find and sort all of them before it knows which one is the correct one to return as the *first* row (the one that sorts first in the requested sequence). Although a lot goes on when we open a cursor, the statement itself is quite simple. Here is the OPEN statement for our example:

```
OPEN ny_customers;
```

Each time our program requires a new row from the result set, we simply issue a FETCH command against the cursor. This is very much like reading the next record from a file in an older flat file system. Remember that the cursor is merely a pointer into the result set. Every time a fetch is issued, the row currently pointed to is returned to the calling program (that is, the program that issued the FETCH), and the cursor is advanced one row to point to the next row to be returned. If there are no more rows in the result set, a code is returned to the calling program to indicate this. Another detail handled by the fetch is mapping the columns returned to programming language variables (called *host language variables*, or just *host variables*). This is done with the INTO clause, and naturally the syntax of the variable names will vary from one programming language to another. Our example uses very simple names to stay away from programming language issues, but in real life you would want the names to be as descriptive as possible. It's also good programming practice to use names that are *not* exactly the same as the database column names, so as to avoid confusion when someone else reads the program. The variable names in this example are prefixed with *v_* (for *variable*) for this reason. Here is the fetch of the ny_customers cursor:

```
FETCH ny_customers
 INTO v_customer_number, v_name, v_address, v_city,
     v_zip_code;
```

Notice that the FETCH statement refers only to the cursor name and the host variables. The cursor declaration ties the cursor to the table(s) and column(s) being referenced. As stated, we should always close the cursor when the program no longer needs it because this frees up any resources the cursor has used, including memory for buffers. The CLOSE statement is as simple as the OPEN statement:

```
CLOSE my_customers;
```

The topic of cursor processing has been introduced before the discussion of transaction management because cursors play a key role in some transaction events.

Transaction Management

To successfully support the database users, the DBMS must include provisions to manage the transactions carried out by the application systems using the database.

What Is a Transaction?

A *transaction* is a discrete series of actions that must be either completely processed or not processed at all. Some call a transaction a *unit of work* as a way of further emphasizing its all-or-nothing nature.

A transaction, also known as a unit of work, is a discrete series of actions that must be either completely processed or not processed at all.

Transactions have properties that can be easily remembered using the acronym ACID (Atomicity, Consistency, Isolation, Durability):

- **Atomicity**   A transaction must remain whole. That is, it must completely succeed or completely fail. When it succeeds, all changes that were made by the transaction must be preserved by the system. Should a transaction fail, all changes that were made by it must be completely undone. In database systems, we use the term *rollback* for the process that backs out any changes made by a failed transaction, and we use the term *commit* for the process that makes transaction changes permanent.

- **Consistency**   A transaction should transform the database from one consistent state to another. For example, a transaction that creates an invoice for an order transforms the order from a *shipped* order to an *invoiced* order, including all the appropriate database changes.

- **Isolation**   Each transaction should carry out its work independently of any other transaction that might occur at the same time.

- **Durability**   Changes made by completed transactions should remain permanent, even after a subsequent shutdown or failure of the database or other critical system component. In object terminology, the term *persistence* is used for permanently stored data.

? Still Struggling

"Permanent" here can be confusing because nothing seems to ever stand still for long in an OLTP (online transaction processing) database. Just keep in mind that *permanent* (persistent) means the change will not disappear when the database is shut down or fails—it does *not* mean that the data is in a permanent state that can never be changed again.

DBMS Support for Transactions

Aside from personal computer database systems, most DBMSs provide transaction support. This includes provisions in SQL for identifying the beginning and end of each transaction, along with a facility for logging all changes made by transactions so that a rollback may be performed when necessary. As you might guess, standards lagged behind the need for transaction support, so support for transactions varies a bit across RDBMS vendors. As examples, let's look at transaction support in MySQL, Microsoft SQL Server, and Oracle, followed by discussion of transaction logs.

Transaction Support in MySQL

MySQL supports transactions with its InnoDB storage engine. MySQL offers several choices for storage engines that can be selected during table creation. Tables using different storage engines can be mixed and matched within a MySQL database. (The differences among the various MySQL storage engines are beyond the scope of this book. Consult your MySQL documentation for details. The MySQL 5.5 manual has conflicting information about which storage engine is the default, so it's best to explicitly specify InnoDB if you need transaction support.)

InnoDB provides ACID-compliant transaction support with commit, rollback, and crash recovery capabilities. Locking is at the row level, with select statements performing a consistent non-locking read similar to what Oracle provides. MySQL supports three transaction modes: autocommit, explicit, and implicit. Here is a description of each:

- **Autocommit mode**   By default, MySQL runs with the autocommit mode enabled. In autocommit mode, each SQL statement is automatically committed as it completes. Essentially, this makes every SQL statement a discrete transaction.

- **Explicit mode**   In explicit mode, each transaction is started with a START TRANSACTION statement and ended with either a COMMIT statement (for successful completion) or a ROLLBACK statement (for unsuccessful completion). This mode is used most often in application programs, stored procedures, and scripts. The syntax for the very simple SQL statements that control explicit transactions in MySQL is

```
START TRANSACTION [WITH CONSISTENT SNAPSHOT];
COMMIT;
ROLLBACK;
```

The WITH CONSISTENT SNAPSHOT clause starts a consistent read for storage engines that are capable of it (currently only InnoDB). The effect is the same as issuing a START TRANSACTION statement followed by a SELECT from any InnoDB table.

- **Implicit mode**   If you are using transaction-safe tables, such as those provided by the InnoDB and BDB storage engines, you can disable autocommit mode. Although MySQL does not use the term, most DBAs refer to this as implicit mode. In implicit mode, a new transaction is started whenever an SQL statement that modifies table data is executed, including DELETE, INSERT, and UPDATE, among others. Once a transaction is implicitly started, it continues until the transaction is either committed or rolled back. If the database user disconnects before submitting a transaction-ending statement, the transaction is automatically rolled back. The following statement disables autocommit mode:

```
SET AUTOCOMMIT=0;
```

Transaction Support in Microsoft SQL Server

Microsoft SQL Server supports transactions in three modes: autocommit, explicit, and implicit. All three modes are available when you're connected directly to the database using a client tool designed for this purpose. However, if you plan to use an ODBC or JDBC driver, you should consult the driver's documentation for information on the transaction support it provides. Here's a description of the three modes:

- **Autocommit mode**   In autocommit mode, each SQL statement is automatically committed as it completes. Essentially, this makes every SQL statement a discrete transaction. Every connection to Microsoft SQL Server uses autocommit until either an explicit transaction is started or the implicit transaction mode is set. In other words, autocommit is the default transaction mode for each SQL Server connection.

- **Explicit mode**   In explicit mode, each transaction is started with a BEGIN TRANSACTION statement and ended with either a COMMIT TRANSACTION statement (for successful completion) or a ROLLBACK TRANSACTION statement (for unsuccessful completion). Savepoints provide a mechanism for rolling back portions of transactions. The SAVE TRANSACTION statement creates the savepoint, and the ROLLBACK TRANSACTION statement can then reference the savepoint to roll back the transaction to the specific savepoint.

Explicit mode is used most often in application programs, stored procedures, triggers, and scripts. The general syntax of these SQL statements follows:

```
BEGIN TRAN[SACTION] [tran_name | @tran_name_variable]
SAVE TRAN[SACTION] (savepoint name | @savepoint_name_variable)
COMMIT [TRAN[SACTION] [tran_name | @tran_name_variable]]
ROLLBACK [TRAN[SACTION] [tran_name | @tran_name_variable |
         savepoint_name | @savepoint_name_variable]]
```

- **Implicit mode**   Implicit transaction mode is toggled on or off with the command SET IMPLICIT_TRANSACTIONS {ON | OFF}. When implicit mode is on, a new transaction is started whenever any of a list of specific SQL statements is executed, including DELETE, INSERT, SELECT, and UPDATE, among others. Once a transaction is implicitly started, it continues until the transaction is either committed or rolled back. If the database user disconnects before submitting a transaction-ending statement, the transaction is automatically rolled back.

Microsoft SQL Server records all transactions and the modifications made by them in the *transaction log*. The before-and-after image of each database modification made by a transaction is recorded in the transaction log. This facilitates any necessary rollback because the before images can be used to reverse the database changes made by the transaction. A transaction commit is not complete until the commit record has been written to the transaction log. Because database changes are not always written to disk immediately, the transaction log is sometimes the only means of recovery when there is a system failure.

Transaction Support in Oracle

Oracle supports only two transaction modes: autocommit and implicit. As with Microsoft SQL Server, support varies when ODBC and JDBC drivers are used, so the driver vendor's documentation should be consulted in those cases. Here's a description of these two modes in Oracle:

- **Autocommit mode**   As with Microsoft SQL Server, each SQL statement is automatically committed as it completes. Autocommit mode is toggled on and off using the SET AUTOCOMMIT command, as shown here, and is off by default:

```
SET AUTOCOMMIT ON
SET AUTOCOMMIT OFF
```

- **Implicit mode**   A transaction is implicitly started when the database user connects to the database (that is, when a new database session begins). This is the default transaction mode in Oracle. When a transaction ends with a commit or rollback, a new transaction is automatically started. Unlike in Microsoft SQL Server, nested transactions (transactions within transactions) are not permitted. A transaction ends with a *commit* when any of the following occurs: (1) the database user issues the SQL COMMIT statement; (2) the database session ends normally (that is, the user issues an EXIT or DISCONNECT command); (3) the database user issues an SQL DDL statement (that is, a CREATE, DROP, or ALTER statement). A transaction ends with a *rollback* when either of the following occurs: (1) the database user issues the SQL ROLLBACK statement; (2) the database sessions ends abnormally (that is, the client connection is canceled, or the database crashes or is shut down using one of the shutdown options that aborts client connections instead of waiting for them to complete).

Locking and Transaction Deadlock

Although the simultaneous sharing of data among many database users has significant benefits, a serious drawback also can cause updates to be lost. Fortunately, the database vendors have worked out solutions to the problem. This section presents the concurrent update problem and various solutions.

The Concurrent Update Problem

Figure 11-1 illustrates the concurrent update problem that can occur when multiple database sessions are allowed to concurrently update the same data. Recall that a session is created every time a database user connects to the

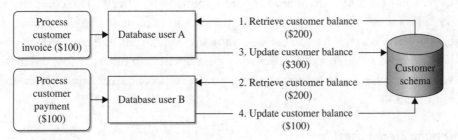

FIGURE 11-1 · The concurrent update problem

database, which includes the same user connecting to the database multiple times. The concurrent update problem happens most often between two different database users who are unaware that they are making conflicting updates to the same data. However, database users with multiple connections can trip themselves up if they apply updates using more than one of their database sessions.

The scenario presented uses a fictitious company that sells products and creates an invoice for each order shipped, similar to Acme Industries in the normalization examples from earlier chapters. Figure 11-1 illustrates User A, a clerk in the Shipping department who is preparing an invoice for a customer, which requires updating the customer's data by adding to the customer's balance due. At the same time, User B, a clerk in the Accounts Receivable department, is processing a payment from the very same customer, which requires updating the customer's balance due by subtracting the amount they paid. Here is the exact sequence of events, as illustrated in Figure 11-1:

1. User A queries the database and retrieves the customer's balance due, which is $200.

2. A few seconds later, User B queries the database and retrieves the same customer's balance, which is still $200.

3. In a few more seconds, User A applies her update, adding the $100 invoice to the balance due, which makes the new balance $300 in the database.

4. Finally, User B applies his update, subtracting the $100 payment from the balance due he retrieved from the database ($200), resulting in a new balance due of $100. He is unaware of the update made by User A and thus sets the balance due (incorrectly) to $100.

The balance due for this customer should be $200, but the update made by User A has been overwritten by the update made by User B. The company is out $100 that either will be lost revenue or will take significant staff time to uncover and correct. As you can see, allowing concurrent updates to the database without some sort of control can cause updates to be lost. Most database vendors implement a locking strategy to prevent concurrent updates to the same data.

Locking Mechanisms

A *lock* is a control placed in the database to reserve data so that only one database session may update it. When data is locked, no other database session can update the data until the lock is released, which is usually done with a COMMIT or ROLLBACK SQL statement. Any other session that attempts to update locked data will be placed in a *lock wait* state, and the session will stall until the lock is released. Some database products, such as IBM's DB2, will time out a session that waits too long and return an error instead of completing the requested update. Others, such as Oracle, will leave a session in a lock wait state for an indefinite period.

> *A lock is a control placed in the database to reserve data so that only one database session may update it.*

By now it should be no surprise that how locks are handled by different database products varies significantly. A general overview is presented here with the recommendation that you consult your database vendor's documentation for details on how locks are supported. Locks may be placed at various levels (often called *lock granularity*), and some database products, including Sybase, Microsoft SQL Server, and IBM's DB2, support multiple levels with automatic *lock escalation*, which raises locks to higher levels as a database session places more and more locks on the same database objects. Locking and unlocking small amounts of data requires significant overhead, so escalating locks to higher levels can substantially improve performance. Typical lock levels are as follows:

- **Database**   The entire database is locked so that only one database session may apply updates. This is obviously an extreme situation that should not happen very often, but it can be useful when significant maintenance is being performed, such as upgrading to a new version of the database software. Oracle supports this level indirectly when the database is opened in exclusive mode, which restricts the database to only one user session.

- **File**   An entire database file is locked. Recall that a file can contain part of a table, an entire table, or parts of many tables. This level is less favored in modern databases because the data locked can be so diverse.

- **Table**   An entire table is locked. This level is useful when you're performing a table-wide change such as reloading all the data in the table, updating every row, or altering the table to add or remove columns. Oracle calls this level a *DDL lock*, and it is used when DDL statements (CREATE, DROP, and ALTER) are submitted against a table or other database object.

- **Block or page** A block or page within a database file is locked. A *block* is the smallest unit of data that the operating system can read from or write to a file. On most personal computers, the block size is called the *sector size*. Some operating systems use pages instead of blocks. A *page* is a virtual block of fixed size, typically 2K or 4K, which is used to simplify processing when multiple storage devices support different block sizes. The operating system can read and write pages and let hardware drivers translate the pages to appropriate blocks. As with file locking, block (page) locking is less favored in modern database systems because of the diversity of the data that may happen to be written to the same block in the file.

- **Row** A row in a table is locked. This is the most common locking level, with virtually all modern database systems supporting it.

- **Column** Some columns within a row in the table are locked. This method sounds terrific in theory, but it's not very practical because of the resources required to place and release locks at this level of granularity. Very sparse support for it exists in modern commercial database systems.

Locks are always placed when data is updated or deleted. Most RDBMSs also support the use of a FOR UPDATE OF clause on a SELECT statement to allow locks to be placed when the database user declares their *intent* to update something. Some locks may be considered *read-exclusive*, which prevents other sessions from even reading the locked data. Many RDBMSs have session parameters that can be set to help control locking behavior. One of the locking behaviors to consider is whether all rows fetched using a cursor are locked until the next COMMIT or ROLLBACK, or whether previously read rows are released when the next row is fetched. Consult your DBMS documentation for more details.

The main problem with locking mechanisms is that locks cause *contention*, meaning that the placement of locks to prevent loss of data from concurrent updates has the side effect of causing concurrent sessions to compete for the right to apply updates. At the least, lock contention slows user processes as sessions wait for locks. At the worst, competing lock requests can stall sessions indefinitely, as you will see in the next section.

Deadlocks

A *deadlock* is a situation where two or more database sessions have locked some data, and then each has requested a lock on data that another session has locked. Figure 11-2 illustrates this situation.

> *A deadlock is a situation where two or more database sessions have locked some data, and then each has requested a lock on data that another session has locked.*

This example again uses two users, cleverly named A and B, from our fictitious company. User A is a customer representative in the Customer Service department and is attempting to correct a payment that was credited to the wrong customer account. He needs to subtract (debit) the payment from Customer 1 and add (credit) it to Customer 2. User B is a database specialist in the IT department, and she has written an SQL statement to update some of the customer phone numbers with one area code to a new area code in response to a recent area code split by the phone company. The statement has a WHERE clause that limits the update to only those customers having a phone number with certain prefixes in area code 510 and updates those phone numbers to the new area code. User B submits her SQL UPDATE statement while User A is working on his payment credit problem. Customers 1 and 2 both have phone numbers that need to be updated. The sequence of events (all happening within seconds of each other), as illustrated in Figure 11-2, takes place as follows:

1. User A selects the data from Customer 1 and applies an update to debit the balance due. No commit is issued yet because this is only part of the transaction that must take place. The row for Customer 1 now has a lock on it due to the update.

2. The statement submitted by User B updates the phone number for Customer 2. The entire SQL statement must run as a single transaction, so there is no commit at this point, and thus User B holds a lock on the row for Customer 2.

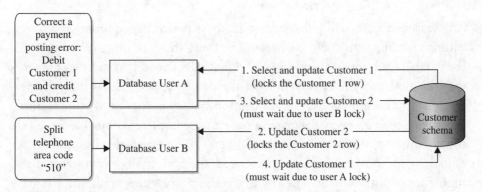

FIGURE 11-2 · The deadlock

3. User A selects the balance for Customer 2 and then submits an update to credit the balance due (same amount as debited from Customer 1). The request must wait because User B holds a lock on the row to be updated.

4. The statement submitted by User B now attempts to update the phone number for Customer 1. The update must wait because User A holds a lock on the row to be updated.

These two database sessions are now in deadlock. User A cannot continue due to a lock held by User B, and vice versa. In theory, these two database sessions will be stalled forever. Fortunately, modern DBMSs contain provisions to handle this situation. One method is to prevent deadlocks. Few DBMSs have this capability due to the considerable overhead this approach requires and the virtual impossibility of predicting what an interactive database user will do next. However, the theory is to inspect each lock request for the potential to cause contention and not permit the lock to take place if a deadlock is possible. The more common approach is *deadlock detection*, which aborts one of the requests that caused the deadlock. This can be done either by timing lock waits and giving up after a preset time interval, or by periodically inspecting all locks to find two sessions that have each other locked out. In either case, one of the requests must be terminated and the transaction's changes rolled back in order to allow the other request to proceed.

> Deadlock detection is a technique that proactively finds deadlocks and automatically resolves them by terminating one of the deadlocked transactions.

Performance Tuning

Any seasoned DBA will tell you that database performance tuning is a never-ending task. It seems there is always something that can be tweaked to make the database run more quickly and/or efficiently. The key to success is managing your time and the expectations of the database users, and setting the performance requirements for an application before it is even written. Simple statements such as "every database update must complete within 4 seconds" are usually the best. With that done, performance tuning becomes a simple matter of looking for things that do not conform to the performance requirement and tuning them until they do. The law of diminishing returns applies to database tuning, and you can put lots of effort into tuning a database process for little or no gain. The beauty of having a standard performance requirement is that you can stop when the process meets the requirement and then move on to the next problem.

Although components other than SQL statements can be tuned, these other components are so specific to a particular DBMS that it is best not to attempt to cover them here. Suffice it to say that memory usage, CPU utilization, and file system I/O all must be tuned along with the SQL statements that access the database. The tuning of SQL statements is addressed in the sections that follow.

Tuning Database Queries

About 80 percent of database query performance problems can be solved by adjusting the SQL statement. However, you must understand how the particular DBMS being used processes SQL statements in order to know what to tweak. For example, placing SQL statements inside stored procedures can yield remarkable performance improvement in Microsoft SQL Server and Sybase, but the same is not true in Oracle.

A query *execution plan* is a description of how an RDBMS will process a particular query, including index usage, join logic, and estimated resource cost. It is important to learn how to use the "explain plan" utility in your DBMS, if one is available, because it will show you exactly how the DBMS will process the SQL statement you are attempting to tune. In Oracle, the EXPLAIN PLAN statement analyzes an SQL statement and posts analysis results to a special plan table. The plan table must be created exactly as specified by Oracle, so it is best to use the script they provide for this purpose. After running the EXPLAIN PLAN statement, you must then retrieve the results from the plan table using a SELECT statement. Fortunately, Oracle's Enterprise Manager has a GUI version available that makes query tuning a lot easier. The Microsoft SQL Server Management Studio tool has a button labeled "Display Estimated Execution Plan" that graphically displays how the SQL statement will be executed. This feature is also accessible from the Query menu item as the option Show Execution Plan. In versions prior to SQL Server 2005, this feature is included in the Query Analyzer tool.

> *A query execution plan is a description of how an RDBMS will process a particular query, including index usage, join logic, and estimated resource cost.*

Following are some general tuning tips for SQL. You should consult a tuning guide for the particular DBMS you are using because techniques, tips, and other considerations vary by DBMS product.

- Avoid table scans of large tables. For tables over 5,000 rows or so, scanning all the rows in the table instead of using an index can be expensive in terms of resources required. And, of course, the larger the table, the more expensive a table scan becomes. Full table scans typically occur in the following situations:

  - The query does not contain a WHERE clause to limit rows.

  - None of the columns referenced in the WHERE clause match the leading column of an index on the table.

  - Index and table statistics have not been updated. Most RDBMS query optimizers use statistics to evaluate available indexes, and without statistics, a table scan may be seen as more efficient than using an index.

  - At least one column in the WHERE clause does match the first column of an available index, but the comparison used obviates the use of an index. These cases include the following:

    - Use of the NOT operator (for example, WHERE NOT CITY = 'New York'). In general, indexes can be used to find what *is* in a table, but cannot be used to find what is *not* in a table.

    - Use of the NOT EQUAL operator (for example, WHERE CITY <> 'New York').

    - Use of a wildcard in the first position of a comparison string (for example, WHERE CITY LIKE '%York%').

    - Use of an SQL function in the comparison (for example, WHERE UPPER(CITY) = 'NEW YORK').

- Create indexes that are selective. *Index selectivity* is a ratio of the number of distinct values a column has, divided by the number of rows in a table. For example, if a table has 1,000 rows and a column has 800 distinct values, the selectivity of the index is 0.8, which is considered good. However, a column such as gender that only has two distinct values (M and F) has very poor selectivity (.002 in this case). Unique indexes always have a selectivity ratio of 1.0, which is the best possible. With some RDBMSs such as DB2, unique indexes are so superior that DBAs often add otherwise unnecessary columns to an index just to make the index unique. However, always keep in mind that indexes take storage space and must be maintained, so they are never a free lunch.

- Evaluate join techniques carefully. Most RDBMSs offer multiple methods for joining tables, with the query optimizer in the RDBMS selecting the one that appears best based on table statistics. In general, creating indexes on foreign key columns gives the optimizer more options from which to choose, which is always a good thing. Run an explain plan and consult your RDBMS documentation when tuning joins.

- Pay attention to views. Because views are stored SQL queries, they can present performance problems just like any other query.

- Tune subqueries in accordance with your RDBMS vendor's recommendations.

- Limit use of remote tables. Tables connected remotely via database links never perform as well as local tables.

? Still Struggling

Very large tables require special attention. When tables grow to millions of rows in size, any query can be a performance nightmare. Evaluate every query carefully, and consider partitioning the table to improve query performance. Table partitioning is addressed in Chapter 8. Your RDBMS may offer other special features for very large tables that will improve query performance.

Tuning DML Statements

DML (Data Manipulation Language) statements generally produce fewer performance problems than query statements. However, if they contain a WHERE clause with search predicates that specify the row(s) to be updated or deleted, all of the query-tuning guidelines in the previous topic apply. Other considerations are covered in this topic.

For INSERT statements, there are two main considerations:

- *Ensuring that there is adequate free space in the tablespaces to hold new rows.* Tablespaces that are short on space present problems as the DBMS searches for free space to hold rows being inserted. Moreover, inserts do not usually put rows into the table in primary key sequence because free space usually isn't available in exactly the right places. Therefore, reorganizing the table, which is essentially a process of unloading the rows to a flat file, re-creating the table, and then reloading the table, can improve both insert and query performance.

- *Index maintenance.* Every time a row is inserted into a table, a corresponding entry must be inserted into every index built on the table (except that null values are never indexed). The more indexes there are, the more overhead every insert will require. Index free space can usually be tuned just as table free space can.

UPDATE statements have the following considerations:

- *Index maintenance.* If indexed columns are updated, the corresponding index entries must also be updated. In general, updating primary key values has particularly bad performance implications because foreign key values that reference the primary key must also be updated, so much so that some RDBMSs prohibit it.

- *Row expansion.* When columns are updated in such a way that the row grows significantly in size, the row may no longer fit in its original location, and there may not be free space around the row for it to expand in place (other rows might be right up against the one just updated). When this occurs, the row must either be moved to another location in the data file where it will fit, or be split with the expanded part of the row placed in a new location, connected to the original location by a pointer. Both of these situations are not only expensive when they occur, but are also detrimental to the performance of subsequent queries that touch those rows. Table reorganizations can resolve the issue, but it is better to prevent the problem by designing the application so that rows tend not to grow in size after they are inserted.

DELETE statements are the least likely to present performance issues. However, a table that participates as a parent in a relationship that is defined with the ON DELETE CASCADE option can perform poorly if there are many child rows to delete.

Change Control

Change control (also known as *change management*) is the process used to manage the changes that occur after a system is implemented. A change control process has the following benefits:

- It helps you understand when it is acceptable to make changes and when it is not.
- It provides a log of all changes that have been made to assist with troubleshooting when problems occur.
- It can manage versions of software components so that a defective version can be smoothly backed out.

Change is inevitable. Not only do business requirements change, but also new versions of database and operating system software and new hardware devices eventually must be incorporated. Technologists should devise a change control method suitable to the organization, and management should approve it as a standard. Anything less leads to chaos when changes are made without the proper coordination and communication. Although terminology varies among standard methods, they all have common features:

- **Version numbering**   Components of an application system are assigned version numbers, usually starting with 1 and advancing sequentially every time the component is changed. Usually a revision date and the identifier of the person making the change are carried with the version number.
- **Release (build) numbering**   A *release* is a point in time at which all components of an application system (including database components) are promoted to the next environment (for example, from development to system test) as a bundle that can be tested and deployed together. Some organizations use the term *build* instead. Database environments are discussed in Chapter 5. As releases are formed, it is important to label each component included with the release (or build) number. This allows us to tell which version of each component was included in a particular release.
- **Prioritization**   Changes may be assigned priorities to allow them to be scheduled accordingly.

- **Change request tracking** Change requests can be placed into the change control system, routed through channels for approval, and marked with the applicable release number when the change is completed.

- **Check-out and check-in** When a developer or DBA is ready to apply changes to a component, they should be able to check it out (reserve it), which prevents others from making potentially conflicting changes to the same component at the same time. When work is complete, the developer or DBA checks the component back in, which essentially releases the reservation.

? Still Struggling

A number of commercial and freeware software products can be deployed to assist with change control. However, it is important to establish the process *before* choosing tools. In this way, the organization can establish the best process for their needs and find the tool that best fits that process rather than trying to retrofit a tool to the process.

From the database perspective, the DBA should develop DDL statements to implement all the database components of an application system and a script that can be used to invoke all the changes, including any required conversions. This deployment script and all the DDL statements should be checked into the change control system and managed just like all the other software components of the system.

Summary

In this chapter, we explored some considerations regarding the implementation of a database system, including cursor processing, transaction management, performance tuning, and change control. In Chapter 12, we take a detailed look at databases for analytical procession, including data warehouses and data marts.

QUIZ

Choose the correct responses to each of the multiple-choice questions. Note that there may be more than one correct response to each question.

1. **A cursor is**
   A. The same as a result set
   B. A pointer into a result set
   C. The collection of rows returned by a database query
   D. A method to analyze the performance of SQL statements
   E. A buffer that holds rows retrieved from the database

2. **The / in the ACID acronym stands for:**
   A. Iconic
   B. Informational
   C. Immediate
   D. Integrated
   E. Isolation

3. **Microsoft SQL Server supports the following transaction modes:**
   A. Explicit
   B. Implicit
   C. Autocommit
   D. Durable
   E. Automatic

4. **Oracle supports the following transaction modes:**
   A. Explicit
   B. Implicit
   C. Autocommit
   D. Durable
   E. Automatic

5. **The SQL statements (commands) that end a transaction are**
   A. `SAVEPOINT`
   B. `BEGIN TRANSACTION` (in SQL Server)
   C. `SET AUTOCOMMIT`
   D. `COMMIT`
   E. `ROLLBACK`

6. **A deadlock:**
   A. Can theoretically put two or more users in an endless lock wait state
   B. Occurs when two database users each request a lock on data that is locked by the other
   C. May be resolved by lock timeouts on some RDBMSs
   D. May be resolved by deadlock detection on some RDBMSs
   E. Is a lock that has timed out and is therefore no longer needed

7. **SQL query tuning:**
   A. Usually involves using an explain plan facility
   B. Only applies to SQL SELECT statements
   C. Can be done in the same way for all relational database systems
   D. Requires detailed knowledge of the RDBMS on which the query is to be run
   E. Always involves placing SQL statements in a stored procedure

8. **SQL practices that obviate the use of an index are**
   A. Use of table joins
   B. Use of the NOT EQUAL operator
   C. Use of a WHERE clause
   D. Use of wildcards in the first column of LIKE comparison strings
   E. Use of a NOT operator

9. **The main performance considerations for INSERT statements are**
   A. Free space usage
   B. Any very large tables that are involved
   C. Row expansion
   D. Subquery tuning
   E. Index maintenance

10. **The main performance considerations for UPDATE statements are**
   A. Subquery tuning
   B. Index maintenance
   C. Any very large tables that are involved
   D. Row expansion
   E. Free space usage

chapter 12

Databases for Online Analytical Processing

Starting in the 1980s, businesses recognized the need for keeping historical data and using it for analysis to assist in decision making. It was soon apparent that storing significant amounts of history in an *operational* database (a database designed to support the day-to-day transactions of an organization) could have serious detrimental effects on performance. William H. (Bill) Inmon participated in pioneering work in a concept known as *data warehousing,* where historical data is periodically trimmed from the operational database and moved to a database specifically designed for analysis. It was Bill Inmon's dedicated promotion of the concept that earned him the title "father of data warehousing." E.F. (Ted) Codd added his endorsement to the data warehouse approach and coined two important terms in 1993:

- **Online transaction processing (OLTP)**   Systems designed to handle high volumes of transactions that carry out the day-to-day activities of an organization

- **Online analytical processing (OLAP)**   Analysis of data (often historical) to identify trends that assist in making strategic decisions regarding the business

CHAPTER OBJECTIVES

In this chapter, the reader should:

- Understand how online transaction processing (OLTP) databases differ from online analytical processing (OLAP) databases.

- Know the basic architectures used for OLAP databases, including data warehouses and data marts.

- Understand the concept of data mining.

Data Warehouses

Inmon defines a *data warehouse (DW)* as a subject-oriented, integrated, time-variant, and nonvolatile collection of data intended to support management decision making. Up to this point, the chapters of this book have dealt almost exclusively with OLTP databases. This chapter, on the other hand, is devoted exclusively to OLAP database concepts.

> *A data warehouse is a subject-oriented, integrated, time-variant, and nonvolatile collection of data intended to support management decision making.*

The popularity of the data warehouse approach grew with each success story. In addition to Bill Inmon, others made significant contributions, notably Ralph Kimball, who developed specialized database architectures for data warehouses (covered in the "Data Warehouse Architecture" section, later in this chapter).

Here are some important properties of a data warehouse:

- Organized around major subject areas of an organization, such as sales, customers, suppliers, and products. OLTP systems, on the other hand, are typically organized around major processes, such as payroll, order entry, billing, and so forth.

- Integrated from multiple operational (OLTP) data sources.

- Not updated in real time, but periodically, based on an established schedule. Data is pulled from operational sources as often as needed, such as daily, weekly, monthly, and so forth. Recent years have shown a trend toward near real-time reporting of business analytics. Several approaches are emerging, ranging from using a data warehouse staging area such as an Operational Data Store (ODS) for reporting, to updating the data warehouse in near real-time using high-speed data movement between disk storage systems or using messaging systems that send changes as they occur in the OLTP data sources.

The potential benefits of a well-constructed data warehouse are significant, including the following:

- Competitive advantage
- Increased productivity of corporate decision makers
- Potential high return on investment as the organization finds the best ways to improve efficiency and/or profitability

However, there are significant challenges to creating an enterprise-wide data warehouse, including the following:

- Underestimation of the resources required to load the data
- Hidden data integrity problems in the source data
- Omitting data later found to be required
- Ever-increasing end user demands (each new feature spawns ideas for even more features)
- Consolidating data from disparate data sources
- High resource demands (huge amounts of storage; queries that process millions of rows)
- Ownership of the data
- Difficulty in determining what the business really wants or needs to analyze
- "Big bang" projects that seem never-ending

? Still Struggling

Data warehouse systems and OLTP systems are fundamentally different. Here is a comparison:

OLTP Systems	Data Warehouse Systems
Hold current data.	Hold historic data.
Store detailed data only.	Store detailed data along with lightly and highly summarized data.
Data is dynamic.	Data is static, except for periodic additions.
Database queries are short-running and access relatively few rows of data.	Database queries are long-running and access many rows of data.
High transaction volume.	Medium to low transaction volume.
Repetitive processing; predictable usage pattern.	Ad hoc and unstructured processing; unpredictable usage pattern.
Transaction driven; support day-to-day operations.	Analysis driven; support strategic decision making.
Process oriented.	Subject oriented.
Serve a large number of concurrent users.	Serve a relatively low number of managerial users (decision makers).

Data Warehouse Architecture

Most data warehouses are implemented using general-purpose hardware and DBMS components. However, specialized data warehouse appliances (combinations of specialized hardware and software) have had some success in the marketplace, including Teradata, Exdata, Neteeza, and others.

The two primary schools of thought as to the best way to organize OLTP data into a data warehouse are the summary table approach and the star schema approach. The following subsections take a look at each approach, along with the benefits and drawbacks of each.

Summary Table Architecture

Bill Inmon originally developed the summary table data warehouse architecture. This data warehouse approach involves storing data not only in detail form, but also in summary tables so that analysis processes do not have to continually summarize the same data. This is an obvious violation of the principles of normalization, but because the data is historical—and therefore is never changed after it is stored—the data anomalies (insert, update, and delete) that drive the need for normalization simply don't exist. Figure 12-1 shows the summary table data warehouse architecture.

Data from one or more operational data sources (databases or flat file systems) is periodically moved into the data warehouse database. A major key to success is determining the right level of detail that must be carried in the database and anticipating the levels of summarization necessary. Using Acme Industries as an example, if the subject of the data warehouse is sales, it may be necessary to keep every single invoice; or it may be necessary to only keep invoices that exceed a certain amount; or perhaps only those that contain certain products. If requirements are not understood, then it is unlikely that the data warehouse project will be successful. Failure rates of data warehouse

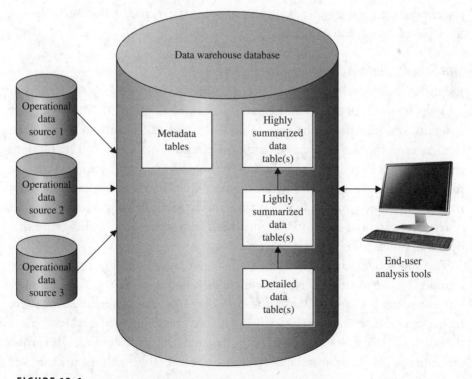

FIGURE 12-1 • Summary table data warehouse architecture

projects are higher than most other types of IT projects, and the most common cause of failure is poorly defined requirements.

In terms of summarization, we might summarize the transactions by month in one summary table and by product in another. At the next level of summarization, we might summarize the months by quarter in one table and the products by department in another. An *end user* (the person using the analysis tools to obtain results from the OLAP database) might look at sales by quarter and notice that one particular quarter doesn't look quite right. The user can expand the quarter of concern and look at the months within it. This process is known as "drilling down" to more detailed levels. The user may then pick out a particular month of interest and drill down to the detailed transactions for that month.

The metadata (data about data) shown in Figure 12-1 is very important, and unfortunately, often a missing link. Ideally, the metadata defines every data item in the data warehouse, along with sufficient information so its source can be tracked all the way back to the original record in the operational database. The biggest challenge with metadata is that, lacking standards, each vendor of data warehouse tools has stored metadata in their own way. When multiple analysis tools are in use, metadata must usually be loaded into each one of them using proprietary formats. For end user analysis tools (also called *OLAP tools*), you can choose among dozens of commercial products, including Business Objects, SAS, IBM Cognos, and Actuate.

Star Schema Data Warehouse Architecture

Ralph Kimball developed a specialized database structure known as the *star schema* for storing data warehouse data. His contribution to OLAP data storage is significant. Red Brick, the first DBMS devoted exclusively to OLAP data storage, used the star schema. In addition, Red Brick offered SQL extensions specifically for data analysis, including moving averages, this year vs. last year, market share, and ranking. Informix acquired Red Brick's technology, and later IBM acquired Informix, so IBM now markets the Red Brick technology as part of its data warehouse solution. Figure 12-2 shows the basic architecture of a data warehouse using the star schema.

The star schema uses a single detailed data table, called a *fact table*, surrounded by supporting reference data tables called *dimension tables*, forming a star-like pattern. Compared with the summary table data warehouse architecture, a fact table replaces each detailed data table, and dimension tables replace the summary tables. A star schema is constructed for each fact table. Dimension tables have a one-to-many relationship with the fact table, with the primary key

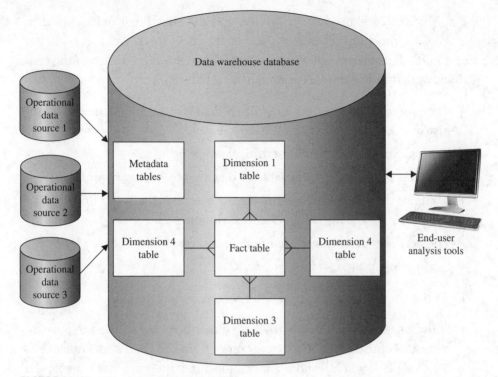

FIGURE 12-2 • Star schema data warehouse architecture

of the dimension table appearing as a foreign key in the fact table. However, dimension tables are not necessarily normalized because they may have an entire hierarchy, such as layers of an organization or different subcomponents of time, compressed into a single table. The dimension tables may or may not contain summary information such as totals. Star schemas can be represented in popular spreadsheet tools by using pivot tables.

> *A fact table in a dimensional model contains the measurements, metrics, and facts for a business process.*

> *A dimension table is one of a set of companion tables to the fact table in a dimensional model that contains reference data.*

Using our prior Acme Industries sales example, the fact table would be the invoice table, and typical dimension tables would be time (months, quarters, and perhaps years), products, and organizational units (departments, divisions, and so forth). Time, product or service, and organizational units appear as dimensions in most star schemas. As you might guess, the key to success in star schema OLAP databases is getting the fact table right. Here's a list of the considerations that influence the design of the fact table:

- The required time period (how often data will be added and how long history must remain in the OLAP database)
- Storing every transaction vs. statistical sampling
- Columns in the source data table(s) that are not necessary for OLAP
- Columns that can be reduced in size, such as taking only the first 25 characters of a 200-character product description
- The best uses of intelligent (natural) and surrogate (dumb) keys
- Partitioning of the fact table

Over time, some variations to the star schema emerged:

- **Snowflake schema**   A variant where dimensions are allowed to have dimensions of their own. The name comes from the ERD's resemblance to a snowflake. If you fully normalize all the dimensions of a star schema, you end up with a snowflake schema. For example, the time dimension at the first level could track weeks, with a dimension table above it to track months, and one above that one to track quarters. Similar arrangements could be used to depict the hierarchy of an organization (departments, divisions, and so forth).
- **Starflake schema**   A hybrid arrangement containing a mixture of (denormalized) star and (normalized) snowflake dimensions.

Multidimensional Databases

Multidimensional databases evolved from star schemas. They are sometimes called *multidimensional OLAP (MOLAP)* databases. A number of specialized multidimensional database systems are on the market, including Oracle Express (acquired from IRI in 1995), Oracle Essbase (acquired from Hyperion in 2007), MicroStrategy, and Cognos PowerPlay. MOLAP databases are best visualized as cubes, where each dimension forms a side of the cube. To accommodate additional dimensions, the cube (or set of cubes) is simply repeated for each one.

Product Line	Sales Department	Quarter	Quantity
Helmets	Corporate Sales	1	2250
Helmets	Corporate Sales	2	2107
Helmets	Corporate Sales	3	5203
Helmets	Corporate Sales	4	5806
Helmets	Internet Sales	1	1607
Helmets	Internet Sales	2	1812
Helmets	Internet Sales	3	4834
Helmets	Internet Sales	4	5150
Springs	Corporate Sales	1	16283
Springs	Corporate Sales	2	17422
Springs	Corporate Sales	3	21288
Springs	Corporate Sales	4	32768
Springs	Internet Sales	1	12
Springs	Internet Sales	2	24
Springs	Internet Sales	3	48
Springs	Internet Sales	4	48
Rockets	Corporate Sales	1	65
Rockets	Corporate Sales	2	38
Rockets	Corporate Sales	3	47
Rockets	Corporate Sales	4	52
Rockets	Internet Sales	1	2
Rockets	Internet Sales	2	1
Rockets	Internet Sales	3	6
Rockets	Internet Sales	4	9

FIGURE 12-3 · Four-column fact table for Acme Industries

Figure 12-3 shows a four-column fact table for Acme Industries. Product Line, Sales Department, and Quarter are dimensions, and they would be foreign keys to a dimension table in a star schema. Quantity contains the number of units sold for each combination of Product Line, Sales Department, and Quarter. In most star schemas, fact tables contain only facts (columns that can be easily accumulated) and foreign keys to dimension tables.

Figure 12-4 shows the multidimensional equivalent of the table shown in Figure 12-3. Note that Sales Department, Product Line, and Quarter all become edges of the cube, with the single fact Quantity stored in each grid square. The dimensions displayed may be changed by simply rotating the cube.

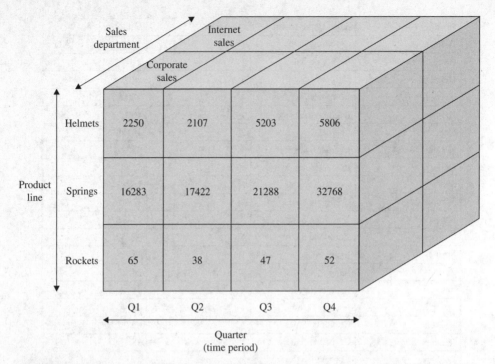

FIGURE 12-4 · Three-dimensional cube for Acme Industries

Data Marts

A *data mart* is a subset of a data warehouse that supports the requirements of a particular department or business function. In part, data marts evolved in response to some highly visible multimillion-dollar data warehouse project failures. When an organization has little experience building OLTP systems and databases, or when requirements are very sketchy, a scaled-down project such as a data mart is a far less risky approach.

> *A data mart is a subset of a data warehouse that supports the requirements of a particular department or business function.*

Here are a few characteristics of data marts:

• Focus on one department or business process

• Do not normally contain any operational data

- Contain much less information than a data warehouse
- Typically implemented using star schemas

Here are some reasons for creating a data mart:

- Data can be tailored to a particular department or business function.
- Lower overall cost than a full data warehouse.
- Lower-risk project than a full data warehouse project.
- Limited (usually only one) end user analysis tool, allowing data to be tailored to the particular tool to be used.
- For departmental data marts, the database may be placed physically near the department, reducing network delays.

There are three basic strategies for building data marts:

- *Build the enterprise-wide data warehouse first, and use it to populate data marts.* The problem with this approach is that you will never get to build the data marts if the data warehouse project ends up being cancelled or put on indefinite hold.
- *Build several data marts and build the data warehouse later, integrating the data marts into the enterprise-wide data warehouse at that time.* This is a lower-risk strategy because the data marts do not depend on completion of a major data warehouse project. However, it may cost more because of the rework required to integrate the data marts after they have been implemented. Moreover, if several data marts are built containing similar data without a common data warehouse to integrate all the data, the same query may yield different results depending on the data mart used. Imagine the Finance Department quoting one revenue number and the Sales Department another, only to find they are both correctly quoting their data sources.
- *Build the data warehouse and data marts simultaneously.* This sounds great on paper, but when you consider that the already complex and large data warehouse project now has the data marts added to its scope, you appreciate the enormity of the project. In fact, this strategy practically *guarantees* that the data warehouse effort will be the never-ending project from hell.

Data Mining

Data mining is the process of extracting valid, previously unknown, comprehensible, and actionable information from large databases and using it to make crucial business decisions. The biggest benefit is that it can uncover correlations in the data that were never suspected. The caveat is that it normally requires very large data volumes in order to produce accurate results. Most commercial OLAP tools include some data-mining features.

> *Data mining is the process of extracting valid, previously unknown, comprehensible, and actionable information from large databases and using it to make crucial business decisions.*

One of the commonly cited stories of an early success with data mining involves an NCR Corporation employee who produced a study for American Stores' Osco Drugs in 1992. The study noted that there was a correlation between beer sales and diaper sales between 5 P.M. and 7 P.M., meaning that the two items were found together in a single purchase more often than pure randomness would suggest. This correlation was subsequently mentioned in a speech, and the "beer and diapers" story quickly became a bit of an urban legend in data warehouse circles. Countless conference speakers have related the story, often embellished well beyond the facts, of young fathers sent out for diapers who grab a six-pack at the same time. However, the story remains an excellent example of how unexpected the results of data mining can be.

Once you discover a correlation, the organization must decide what action to take to best capitalize on the new information. In the "beer and diapers" example, the company could either place a stack of beer next to the diapers display for that quick impulse sale, or perhaps strategically locate beer and diapers at opposite corners of the store in hopes of more impulse buys as the shopper picks up one item and heads across the store for the other. For the newly found information to be of benefit, the organization must be agile enough to take some action, so data mining itself isn't a silver bullet by any measure.

Summary

In this chapter, you learned about the differences between OLAP and OLTP databases, the architectures used for OLAP databases, including data warehouses and data marts, and the concept of data mining. In Chapter 13, we will explore integrating XML documents and objects into databases.

QUIZ

Choose the correct responses to each of the multiple-choice questions. Note that there may be more than one correct response to each question.

1. **OLAP:**
   A. Was coined by Ralph Kimball
   B. Was coined by E.F. Codd
   C. May use data stored in a data warehouse database
   D. May use data stored in an operational database
   E. Handles high volumes of transactions

2. **A data warehouse is**
   A. Updated in real time
   B. Organized around one department or business function
   C. Subject oriented
   D. Integrated from multiple data sources
   E. Time variant

3. **Challenges with the data warehouse approach include**
   A. Underestimation of required resources
   B. Updating operational data from the data warehouse
   C. Diminishing user demands
   D. High resource demands
   E. Large, complex projects

4. **The summary table architecture:**
   A. Includes lightly and highly summarized tables
   B. Should include metadata
   C. Includes a fact table
   D. Was originally developed by Bill Inmon
   E. Includes dimension tables

5. **The process of moving from more summarized data to more detailed data is known as:**
   A. Data mining
   B. Normalization
   C. Denormalization
   D. Drilling up
   E. Drilling down

6. **Factors to consider in designing the fact table include**

   A. Partitioning the fact table
   B. How long history must remain in it
   C. How often it must be updated
   D. Reducing column sizes between the source and fact tables
   E. Adding columns to the fact table

7. **The starflake schema:**

   A. Can be designed by fully normalizing all the dimension tables
   B. Allows dimensions to have dimensions of their own
   C. Does not use a fact table
   D. Was developed by Bill Inmon
   E. Is a hybrid containing both normalized and denormalized tables

8. **Multidimensional databases:**

   A. Use a fully normalized fact table
   B. Are sometimes called MOLAP databases
   C. Accommodate dimensions beyond the third by repeating cubes for each additional dimension
   D. Have fully normalized dimension tables
   E. Are best visualized as cubes

9. **Reasons to create a data mart include**

   A. It is more comprehensive than a data warehouse.
   B. Data may be tailored to a particular department or business function.
   C. It contains more data than a data warehouse.
   D. It is a potentially lower-risk project.
   E. The project has a lower overall cost than a data warehouse project.

10. **Data mining:**

   A. Can be successful with small amounts of data
   B. Usually requires large data volumes in order to produce accurate results
   C. Extracts previously unknown data correlations from the data warehouse
   D. Is most useful when the organization is agile enough to take action based on the information
   E. Is a scaled-down data warehouse

13

Integrating XML Documents and Objects into Databases

Along with the explosive growth in the use of databases, particularly relational databases, the need to store more complex data types has increased sharply. This is especially true for databases that support web sites that render images and formatted documents as well as sound and video clips. Furthermore, as the use of object-oriented programming languages such as C++ and Java has grown, so has the need to store the objects that these languages manipulate. (Objects were briefly introduced in Chapter 1.) In this chapter, we'll look at a number of ways to integrate such content into databases.

CHAPTER OBJECTIVES

In this chapter, the reader should:

- Understand the basics of XML and SQL/XML.

- Understand object-oriented applications and object-relational databases.

The Basics of XML

The Extensible Markup Language (XML) is a general-purpose markup language used to describe data in a format that is convenient for display on web pages and for exchanging data between different parties. In 2003, the specifications for storing XML data in SQL (relational) databases were added to the ANSI/ISO SQL Standard as Part 14, named SQL/XML. Part 14 was expanded further in 2006.

> **TERMS: XML**
>
> Extensible Markup Language (XML) is a general-purpose markup language used to describe data in a format that is convenient for display on web pages and for exchanging data between different parties.

NOTE *SQL/XML is not at all the same as Microsoft's SQLXML, which is a proprietary technology used in SQL Server. As you can imagine, the unfortunately similar names have caused much confusion. Microsoft participated in the standards proceedings for SQL/XML, but then chose not to implement the standard.*

To understand SQL/XML, you must first understand the basics of XML. While a complete explanation of XML is well beyond the scope of this book, I'll provide a brief overview. You can find a lot more information by searching on the Internet.

You may already be familiar with HTML, the markup language used to define web pages. If so, the syntax of XML will look familiar. This is because both are based on the Standard Generalized Markup Language (SGML), which itself is based on Generalized Markup Language (GML), developed by IBM in the 1960s. A *markup language* is a set of annotations, often called *tags*, that are used to describe how text is to be structured, formatted, or laid out. The tagged text is intended to be human-readable. One of the fundamental differences between HTML and XML is that HTML provides a predefined set of tags, while XML lets authors create their own tags.

> *A markup language is a set of annotations, often called tags, that are used to describe how text is to be structured, formatted, or laid out.*

DEPARTMENT

DEPT_ID	DEPT_NAME
BUS	Business
IT	Information Technology

COURSE

COURSE_ID	COURSE_TITLE	DEPT_ID
101	Accounting 101	BUS
102	Concepts of Marketing	BUS
400	Introduction to Computer Systems	IT
401	C Programming I	IT
402	C Programming II	IT

FIGURE 13-1 · The DEPARTMENT and COURSE tables

Let's look at a sample XML document that contains the results of an SQL query. Figure 13-1 shows a DEPARTMENT table containing two departments and a COURSE table containing five educational courses offered by those departments. As you learned in Chapter 4, the two tables can be easily joined using an SQL SELECT statement like this one:

```
SELECT a.DEPT_NAME, b.COURSE_TITLE, b.COURSE_ID
  FROM DEPARTMENT a JOIN COURSE b
       ON a.DEPT_ID = b.DEPT_ID
 ORDER BY a.DEPT_NAME, b.COURSE_TITLE;
```

Note that I used the ORDER BY clause to specify the order of the rows in the result set. The query results should look something like this:

```
DEPT_NAME                COURSE_TITLE                       COURSE_ID
--------------------     --------------------------------   ---------
Business                 Accounting 101                     101
Business                 Concepts of Marketing              102
Information Technology   C Programming I                    401
Information Technology   C Programming II                   402
Information Technology   Introduction to Computer Systems   400
```

The query results are well suited for display or printing, but they are not in a form that would be easy to display on a web page or to pass to another computer application for further processing. One way to make this easier is to convert the query results into XML, as shown here:

```
<departments>
  <department name="Business">
    <courses>
      <course title="Accounting 101"><id>101</id></course>
      <course title ="Concepts of Marketing">
        <id>102</id></course>
```

```
        </courses>
      </department>
      <department name="Information Technology">
        <courses>
          <course title="C Programming I"><id>401</id></course>
          <course title="C Programming II"><id>402</id></course>
          <course title="Introduction to Computer Systems">
            <id>400</id></course>
        </courses>
      </department>
      <!-- Additional departments available soon -->
</departments>
```

As you can see in the code listing, tags are enclosed in angle brackets (<>), and each start tag has a matching end tag that is identical, except for the slash (/) used in the end tag. (HTML uses an identical convention; however, HTML is a lot more forgiving if you do something like omit an end tag.) For example, the tag **<departments>** starts the list of academic departments, while the end tag **</departments>** ends it. Within the list of departments, the information for each individual department begins with the **<department>** tag, which includes a data value for the name attribute, and ends with the **</department>** tag. It is customary (and considered a best practice) to name a list using the plural of the tag name used for each item in the list. Comments can be added using a special tag that begins with **<!--** and ends with **-->**, as shown in the next to last line of the example.

Data items and values, such as those that would be stored in a relational table column, can be coded as name and value pairs in one of two ways. The first way is by using an XML *attribute*, by naming the attribute inside another tag, followed by the equal sign and the data value enclosed in double quotation marks, such as I did with the name and title attributes. The second way is by using an XML *element*, creating a separate tag for the data item with the data value sandwiched between the start and end tags, such as I did with the **id** attribute within the **course** tag. The question of which form to use has been the subject of much debate among XML developers. However, the general consensus is to use elements whenever the data item might later be broken down into additional elements, such as splitting a person's name into first name and last name, or dividing a single data element containing a comma-separated list of prerequisite course names into a list of elements. An additional consideration is whether you want to allow the XML processor to ignore insignificant whitespace, as it would do for attributes but not for elements.

You probably noticed that, unlike the SQL result set, XML can show the hierarchy of the data. In this case, the list of courses offered by each department is nested within the information about the department. I have indented the XML statements to make the nesting more obvious. While indentation of nested tags is a best practice, it is not significant because whitespace between tags is ignored when the XML is processed.

XML coding can be quite tedious. Fortunately, tools are available to help you convert between XML and plain text, and SQL/XML functions (covered later in this chapter) can be used to convert relational database data into XML. For a time, specialized databases for storing and retrieving XML were gaining popularity, but the major relational database vendors added features to permit native XML to be stored directly in their databases. At the same time, the SQL standard was expanded to include provisions for XML data, as I discuss in the next section of this chapter.

SQL/XML

As mentioned, XML is commonly used to represent data on web pages, and that data often comes from relational databases. However, as you have seen, the two models in use are quite different, in that relational data is stored in tables where neither hierarchy nor sequence have any significance, while XML is based on hierarchical trees in which order is considered significant. The term *forest* is often used to refer to a collection of XML tree structures. XML is used for web pages because its structure so closely matches the structure that would be used to display the same data in HTML. In fact, many web pages are a mixture of HTML for the static portions and XML for the dynamic data. It is perhaps this widespread implementation that has led many of the major vendors, including Oracle, Microsoft, and IBM, to support XML extensions. However, only Oracle and IBM's DB2 UDB support the SQL/XML commands covered in this topic. The Microsoft SQL Server XML extension is markedly different, and I have not included it in this book because it is proprietary.

> *In XML, a forest is a collection of XML tree structures.*

SQL/XML can be divided into three main parts: the XML data type, SQL/ XML functions, and SQL/XML mapping rules. I cover the XML data type and

SQL/XML functions as the major topics in the remainder of this chapter. The SQL/XML mapping rules are too advanced a topic to include here.

The XML Data Type

The XML data type is handled in the same general way as all the other data types discussed in Chapter 2. Storing data in XML format directly in the database is not the only way to use SQL and XML together. However, it's a very simple way to get started because it's a logical extension of the earliest implementations, where SQL developers simply stored the XML text in a column defined with a general character data type such as CHARACTER VARYING (VARCHAR). It is far better to tell the DBMS that the column contains XML and the particular way the XML is coded, so that the DBMS can provide additional features tailored to the XML format.

The specification for the XML data type has this general format:

XML (<type modifier> {(<secondary type modifier>)})

The type modifier is required and must be enclosed in a pair of parentheses as shown, while the secondary type modifier is optional and is not supported for all type modifiers. The standard is not specific about how a particular SQL implementation should treat the various types, but some conventions and syntax rules are specified. The valid type modifiers are as follows:

- **DOCUMENT** The DOCUMENT type is intended for storage of text documents formatted using XML. In general, the data values are expected to be composed of human-readable characters such as letters, numbers, and symbols as they would appear in an unstructured text document.

- **CONTENT** The CONTENT type is intended for more complex data that can include binary data such as images and sound clips.

- **SEQUENCE** The SEQUENCE type is intended for XQuery documents, which are often called XQuery sequences. XQuery is an advanced topic that is beyond the scope of this book.

The secondary type modifier, used only with the DOCUMENT and CONTENT primary type modifiers, can have one of these values:

- **UNTYPED** The XML data is not of a particular type.

- **ANY** The XML data is of any of the types supported by the SQL implementation.

- **XMLSCHEMA** The XMLSCHEMA type refers to a registered XML schema that has been made known to the database server. The three most common are shown in the following table:

Common Prefix	Target Namespace URI (Uniform Resource Identifier)
Xs	www.w3.org/2001/XMLSchema
Xsi	www.w3.org/2001/XMLSchema-instance
Sqlxml	standards.iso.org/iso/9075/2003/sqlxml

For SQL implementations that do not support the secondary type modifier, ANY is assumed as a default.

NOTE *Because SQL/XML is a relatively new standard, vendor implementation support varies. Instead of the XML type, Oracle supports an XMLType data type, which can be used on a column in a regular table or at the table level so that the entire table is stored as XML. IBM's DB2 UDB supports an XML type, but without the type modifiers. As mentioned, Microsoft SQL Server supports XML and an XML data type, but in a manner a bit different from the SQL/XML standard. As of version 5.1, MySQL provides no support for XML, but it is expected to be included in a future release.*

Suppose we want to add the course syllabus to our course table that can be displayed on a web page. If the syllabus could come from several different sources, and thus be formatted differently depending on the source, XML might be a good way to store the data in our course table. In the following example, I have added the column to the definition of the COURSE table that appears in Figure 13-1:

```
CREATE TABLE COURSE
( COURSE_ID        INT,
  COURSE_TITLE     VARCHAR(60),
  DEPT_ID          CHAR(3),
  COURSE_SYLLABUS  XML(DOCUMENT(UNTYPED)) );
```

NOTE *Although the ISO/ANSI SQL Standard specifies an XML data type in the form shown here, no major SQL implementations seem to support this exact syntax. However, the standard is quite new, so hopefully this syntax will be supported in the near future.*

SQL/XML Functions

An SQL/XML function (also called an XML value function) is simply a function that returns a value as an XML type. For example, a query can be written that selects non-XML data (that is, data stored in data types other than XML) and formats the query results into XML suitable for inclusion in an XML document that can be displayed on a web page or transmitted to some other party. In other words, SQL/XML does not always format complete documents—sometimes additional elements must be added to wrap the XML returned by the DBMS into a complete document. Table 13-1 shows the basic SQL/XML functions.

More functions exist than are listed here, and all these SQL/XML functions can be used in combinations to form extremely powerful (if not complicated) queries. Also, the functions available vary across SQL implementations. Let's

TABLE 13-1   SQL/XML Functions

Function	Value Returned
XMLAGG	A single XML value containing an XML forest formed by combining (aggregating) a collection of rows, each of which contains a single XML value
XMLATTRIBUTES	An attribute in the form *name=value* within an XMLELEMENT
XMLCOMMENT	An XML comment
XMLCONCAT	A concatenated list of XML values, creating a single value containing an XML forest
XMLDOCUMENT	An XML value containing a single document node
XMLELEMENT	An XML element, which can be a child of a document node, with the name specified in the name parameter
XMLFOREST	An XML element containing a sequence of XML elements formed from table columns, using the name of each column as the corresponding element name
XMLPARSE	An XML value formed by parsing the supplied string without validating it
XMLPI	An XML value containing an XML processing instruction
XMLQUERY	The result of an XQuery expression (XQuery is a sublanguage used to search XML stored in the database; it is beyond the scope of this book)
XMLTEXT	An XML value containing a single XML text node, which can be a child of a document node
XMLVALIDATE	An XML sequence that is the result of validating an XML value

look at a simple example to clarify how these functions can be used. This example lists the courses for the Business Department using the DEPART-MENT and COURSE tables shown in Figure 13-1. Here is the SQL statement, using the XMLELEMENT and XMLFOREST functions:

```
SELECT XMLELEMENT("DepartmentCourse",
       XMLFOREST(a.DEPT_NAME as Department, a.DEPT_ID, b.COURSE_ID,
                 b.COURSE_TITLE))
  FROM DEPARTMENT a JOIN COURSE b
       ON a.DEPT_ID = b.DEPT_ID
 WHERE a.DEPT_ID = 'BUS'
 ORDER BY b.COURSE_ID;
```

The results returned should look something like this:

```
<DepartmentCourse>
  <Department>Business</Department>
  <DEPT_ID>BUS</DEPT_ID>
  <COURSE_ID>101</COURSE_ID>
  <COURSE_TITLE>Accounting 101</COURSE_TITLE>
</DepartmentCourse>
<DepartmentCourse>
  <Department>Business</Department>
  <DEPT_ID>BUS</DEPT_ID>
  <COURSE_ID>102</COURSE_ID>
  <COURSE_TITLE>Concepts of Marketing</COURSE_TITLE>
</DepartmentCourse>
```

Notice that the XML element names are taken from the column names, in uppercase with underscores as is customary in SQL. However, using the column alias, as I did for the DEPT_NAME column, you can change the column names to just about anything you want.

PROBLEM 13-1

The result set in the previous example is not a complete document (an XML developer would say the XML may not be "well formed").

SOLUTION

To turn the XML in the last example into a complete document, at the very least a root element is needed, along with its corresponding end tag. If we were to add the element **<DepartmentCourses>** at the beginning of the results and **</DepartmentCourses>** at the end of the results, we would have a well-formed document.

Object-Oriented Applications

This section assumes that you have read and understood the section "The Object-Oriented Model" in Chapter 1. You may want to review it before continuing.

Object-oriented (OO) applications are written in an object-oriented programming language. These OO languages usually come with a predefined object class structure and predefined methods—but, of course, the developers can create their own classes and methods. Some applications come with a complete development environment that includes not only the language elements, but also an integrated OO database. It is important for you to understand that OO applications can be created without an OO database, and an OO database can exist (at least in theory) without an OO application to access it.

Object-Oriented Programming

Object-oriented programming uses *messages* as the vehicle for object interaction. A *message* in the OO context is composed of the identifier of the object that is to receive the message, the name of the method to be invoked by the receiving object, and optionally, one or more parameters. You will recall from Chapter 1 that a *method* is a piece of application program logic that operates on a particular object and provides a finite function. The notion that all access to an object's variables is done via its methods is essential to the OO paradigm. Therefore, OO programming involves writing methods that encompass the *behavior* of the object (that is, what the object does) and crafting messages within those methods whenever an object must interact with other objects. OO application development includes object and class design in addition to the aforementioned programming tasks.

The OO paradigm also supports *complex* objects, which are objects composed of one or more other objects. Usually, this is implemented by using an object *reference*, where one object contains the identifier for one or more other objects. For example, a Customer object might contain a list of Order objects that the customer has placed, and each Order object might contain the identifier of the customer who placed the order. The unique identifier for an object is called the *object identifier* (*OID*), the value of which is automatically assigned to each object as it is created and is then invariant (that is, the value never changes).

Object-Oriented Languages

Let's have a look at four of the most popular OO programming languages: Smalltalk, C++, Java, and C#.

Smalltalk

The pioneering OO system was Smalltalk, developed in 1972 by the Software Concepts Group at the Xerox Palo Alto Research Center (PARC), led by Alan Kay. It was Kay who coined the term *object-oriented*. Smalltalk includes a language, a programming environment, an "image file system" to store objects and methods (more or less a database), and an extensive object library. Smalltalk's innovations include a bitmap display, a windowing system, and the use of a mouse. In an interesting twist of history, Xerox funded and owned the first commercial OO programming environment, the original windowing system, the mouse, and many other technical computing innovations. Yet Xerox never figured out how to market any of them, so the company's innovations fell into other hands over time and were eventually "introduced" into the market by other companies. Although not nearly as popular as it once was, Smalltalk is still around today, and you can find much more about it at www.smalltalk.org.

C++

As the name suggests, C++ is based on the C programming language. In fact, ++ is the operator in C that increments a variable by 1, so C++ literally means "C plus 1." This superset of C was developed primarily by Bjarne Stroustrup at AT&T Bell Laboratories in 1986. Classes are implemented as user-defined types—a *struct* (structure) in C syntax. Methods are implemented as member functions of a struct. Object purists frown upon C++, claiming it's not an OO language because programmers can ignore the object paradigm when they choose to and can do such things as manipulate data directly using C language commands. C++ aficionados, on the other hand, see this as a huge benefit because it gives them a great deal of flexibility.

Java

Java is a simple, portable, general-purpose OO language that was developed by Sun Microsystems around 1995. It took the market by storm immediately after its introduction, largely because of its support for Internet programming in the form of platform-independent "applets." Another advantage of Java is that it can run on very small computers due to the small size of its interpreter. Unlike Smalltalk and C++, Java is an *interpretive* language, which means that each statement is evaluated at runtime instead of being compiled ahead of time. A *compiler* is a program that converts a computer program from the source language the programmer wrote with to the machine language of the computer on which it is to be run. Initially, the interpreter hampered performance compared with compiled languages, but recent innovations, such as *just-in-time* compilers, which compile statements just prior to their execution, have helped performance enormously.

> *A compiler is a program that converts a computer program from the source language the programmer wrote with to the machine language of the computer on which it is to be run.*

C#

Microsoft began development of C# ("C sharp") in late 1999, when it chose not to directly support Java. The initial language specification was released in December 2001 with the first compiler available in January 2002. Like C++, C# is a superset of C, with the name taken from the musical term *sharp* that raises a pitch by one half step. Some view C# as a superset of C++, but the underlying architecture and implementation is different enough that many think of it as a separate language.

Like C++ and Java, C# is a general-purpose object-oriented language. However, it was developed within the .NET initiative to fit within the .NET framework and is thus designed to comply with the Common Language Infrastructure (CLI). C# is intended to be suitable for hosted and embedded systems, ranging from highly sophisticated operating systems all the way down to very small dedicated functions.

Object Persistence

Persistence is the OO property that preserves the state of an object between executions of an application and across the shutdown and startup of the computer system itself. In most cases, a database is used to store objects permanently, so it is the database that implements persistence. Objects must be loaded into memory for an application to access them, and any changes must be saved back to persistent storage when they are no longer required. Object loading into memory is an *indirect* process, which means the application does not specifically request that an object be loaded—the application environment works with the database environment to load objects into memory automatically whenever they are accessed by an application. This access is usually in the form of a message that is sent to the object, but as discussed in the next subsection, it may also occur when an object contains a reference to another object.

Let's look at two methods for implementing object persistence using a database—the OO database and the relational database. In the next section, we explore a hybrid approach that combines features of both object-oriented and relational databases.

Persistence Using an OO Database

Figure 13-2 shows the retrieval of an object from persistent storage in an OO database. For the purposes of illustration, the specific components that execute each of the illustrated steps have been omitted, thereby showing what happens without worrying about how it happens. This is actually a very good way to think about OO databases, because a common property of OO systems is to hide implementation details. As shown in Figure 13-2, the database contains persistent copies of objects A1, A2, A3, B1, and C1. Assume that the first letter denotes the object class to which the objects belong. Note that object B1 references object C1, as illustrated using a broken line to connect them. This is a typical arrangement in which one object, such as an order, contains the object

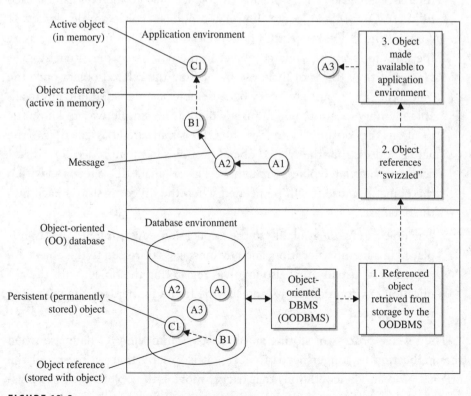

FIGURE 13-2 · Persistence using an OO database

ID (OID) of a related object, such as the customer who placed the order. In an equivalent relational database, this relationship would be implemented using a foreign key in the order.

As shown in Figure 13-2, the sequence of events when an object is first referenced by the application is as follows:

1. A request to retrieve the object is sent to the OO database, typically because a message in the application environment referenced the object. The OODBMS retrieves the object from persistent storage and passes it to the application environment. If the object contains references to other objects, the OODBMS may also automatically retrieve those objects, depending on the architecture of the OODBMS.

2. If an object contains references to other objects, those references must be changed into memory addresses when the objects are loaded into memory. This process is known as *swizzling* the references. (The origin of the term *swizzle* is unknown, but it may have been derived from swizzle sticks that are used to stir drinks.) In persistent storage, the OID can be used as the reference because other storage structures similar to indexes can be used by the OODBMS to locate the related objects. For example, object B1 contains the OID of object C1, and the OODBMS has no difficulty using the OID to locate the related object in the database's persistent storage. However, the OID is of little use in locating the related object once the objects are loaded into memory because objects are loaded into any available memory location, which means there is no simple way to know the locations they occupy. Therefore, the OID is translated (swizzled) into the actual address that the related object occupies in memory to allow direct access of the related object in memory. The original OID is retained within the object because it will be needed when the object is stored back into the database.

3. The object is made available to the application environment. That is, it is placed in a memory location, and any messages addressed to the object are routed to it. Usually, this also involves registering the object with the application environment so it can easily be found in memory the next time it is referenced.

The reverse process of storing an object back into the OO database when the application no longer needs to access it is exactly that—a *reverse* of the original process. The conditions that trigger moving the object back to persistent storage vary from one OODBMS to another, but typically involve a *least recently used* (*LRU*) algorithm. The LRU algorithm is a process that is invoked when space must be freed up for the loading of more objects into memory locations. The algorithm finds the objects that were accessed the longest time ago (that is, least recently), and it removes those objects from memory. And, of course, a request to shut down the database requires that every object in memory be made persistent before the database is shut down. The sequence of events to move an object from memory to persistent storage is as follows:

1. The object is removed from its memory location, and any registration of the object in the application environment is deleted.

2. Any memory addresses added to the object when references were swizzled are removed.

3. If the object was modified while it was in memory, it is sent back to the OODBMS, which stores the new version.

Persistence Using a Relational Database

When the object data is stored in a relational database, some important differences should be noted. First, everything in a relational database must be stored in a table. Therefore, objects must be translated to and from relational tables. Typically, each class is stored in a different relational table, with the rows in the tables representing object instances for the corresponding classes. Second, relational tables cannot store objects in their native format because objects are composed of methods and a class hierarchy along with the data itself. The methods and class hierarchy are usually not stored in the relational database at all, but rather are maintained in a file system location (directory) that is managed by the application environment. Figure 13-3 illustrates this arrangement.

Take note of the differences between Figures 13-2 and 13-3. First, in the latter figure, the object data is stored in the database in tables. Second, an additional step is required when retrieving objects and making them available in memory—the data from the relational database must be mapped to object classes and variables. This can be accomplished in many different ways. A common approach with applications written in Java is to issue the relational SQL directly from a Java method using a Java Database Connectivity (JDBC) driver (introduced in Chapter 9), and within the same method, to relate the results returned by the JDBC driver to one or more objects. This is a manual and very labor-intensive approach for Java programmers. Fortunately, more automated solutions are available, wherein an application server or middleware product handles all the details of persistently storing objects in the relational database,

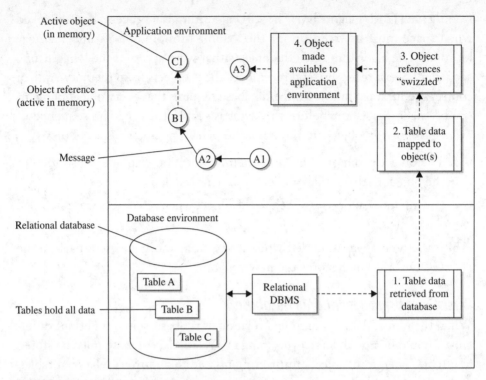

FIGURE 13-3 · Persistence using a relational database

including the translation between relational tables and objects. Figure 13-3 has been simplified to show the steps required to assemble an object stored in a relational database and to make it available in the application environment without any details as to which components handle the various steps.

As illustrated in Figure 13-3, here is the sequence of events required to assemble an object from data stored in a relational database:

1. An SQL query is sent to the RDBMS to retrieve the table data (typically one row) from the database. The query is executed by the RDBMS and the resultant data sent to the application environment.

2. The table data is mapped to the object. Typically, this involves assigning the table data to a class and the individual columns to variables within that class, along with retrieving the methods defined for the class from wherever they are stored in the file system. This mapping step is the proverbial Achilles heel of this architecture—it is expensive in terms of resources, and it requires design compromises because object data cannot always be perfectly represented in relational database tables.

3. As with Figure 13-2, any object references are swizzled.

4. As with Figure 13-2, the object is placed in a memory location and registered with the application environment, making it available to the application.

When an object is no longer needed in memory, it must be placed back into persistent storage. The sequence of events is as follows:

1. The object is removed from memory, and any registration with the application environment deleted. If the object was not modified while it was in memory, no other action is necessary; otherwise, the sequence continues with the next step.

2. Any memory addresses added for object references are removed.

3. The data in the object is mapped back to the relational table row(s) from which it came. One or more SQL statements (INSERT, UPDATE, or DELETE) are formed to change the relational database data to match the object data. For efficiency, this often involves comparing before and after versions of the object (if available) so that only variables that changed in some way need to be referenced in the generated SQL statement(s). You need not do anything with the class structure or methods because they do not change when the object is used in the application environment. These components change only when a new version of the application is installed.

4. The SQL statement(s) is (are) passed to the relational DBMS to be processed. If the object was not changed while it was in memory, this step is not required.

Object-Relational Databases

This section assumes you have read and understood the section "The Object-Relational Model" in Chapter 1. You may wish to review it before continuing. The object-relational DBMS (ORDBMS) evolved in response to the difficulties of mapping objects to relational databases and to market pressure from OODBMS vendors. Relational database vendors such as Informix (subsequently acquired by IBM) and Oracle added object extensions in hopes of preventing any loss of market share to the OODBMS vendors. To a large degree, this tactic appears to have worked, with pure OO databases gaining ground only in niche markets. Moreover, the lack of ad-hoc query capability in pure OO databases has certainly not helped them in the marketplace. The ORDBMS provides a blend of desirable features from the object world, such as the storage of complex data types, with the relative simplicity and ease of using the relational model. Most industry experts believe that object-relational technology will continue to gain market share.

The advantages of an object-relational database are as follows:

- Complex data types (that is, data types formed by combining other data types) are directly supported while preserving ad-hoc query capability.
- The DBMS may be extended to perform common functions (methods) centrally, which improves program logic reuse compared with a pure relational DBMS.
- Storing object functions (methods) in the database makes them available to all applications, which improves object sharing compared with a pure relational DBMS.
- Ad-hoc query capability is fully supported, which is a feature that is not supported in pure OO databases.

Here are the disadvantages of the object-relational approach:

- The combination is more complex than either pure relational or pure OO databases, leading to increased development costs.
- Objects are *table-centric*, meaning that all persistent objects must be stored within a table.
- Relational purists argue that the essential simplicity of the relational model is clouded by the object extensions.
- Object purists are not attracted to the extension of objects into relational databases, arguing that the ORDBMS is little more than a relational database with user-defined data types added.
- Current ORDBMSs lack the class structure and inheritance that are at the foundation of OODBMSs.
- Object applications are not as data-centric as relational applications, and therefore pure OO databases may better serve the needs of object applications.

In terms of deciding which database model is the best fit for a given application, consider the following points:

- Simple data with no requirement for ad-hoc query capability, such as static web pages, can be adequately stored in ordinary file system files.

- Simple data that requires ad-hoc query capability, such as customer data, fits well into a relational database.

- Complex data that does not require ad-hoc query capability, such as images, maps, and drawings, fits well into an object-oriented database.

- Complex data that requires ad-hoc query capability, such as purchase orders stored as composite data types, fits well into an object-relational database.

Summary

In this chapter, we looked at the basics of XML and SQL/XML along with the architecture of object-oriented applications and object-relational databases. This concludes our introduction to database management systems. The best way to learn more about databases is to get out there and use them. I hope you find databases as fun and rewarding as I have.

QUIZ

Choose the correct responses to each of the multiple-choice questions. Note that there may be more than one correct response to each question.

1. Which of the following are valid type modifiers for the XML data type?
   A. DOCUMENT
   B. SEQUENCE
   C. SQLXML
   D. CONTENT
   E. QUERY

2. Which of the following SQL/XML functions creates an element based on a table column?
   A. XMLQUERY
   B. XMLELEMENT
   C. XMLFOREST
   D. XMLDOCUMENT
   E. XMLPARSE

3. Object-oriented (OO) applications:
   A. Require the use of an OO database
   B. Are written in an OO language
   C. Use development environments that usually come with predefined classes
   D. Use development environments that usually come with predefined methods
   E. May be written in the C programming language

4. Smalltalk:
   A. Was developed in 1972
   B. Was developed by Linus Torvalds
   C. Was developed at the Xerox PARC facility
   D. Is based on the C programming language
   E. Was the first OO programming language to include a windowing system and use of a mouse

5. C++:
   A. Was developed by Alan Kay
   B. Was developed at AT&T Bell Laboratories
   C. Was developed in 1976
   D. Is based on the Java programming language
   E. Allows programmers to ignore the object paradigm if they wish

6. **Java:**
    A. Was developed by Sun Microsystems
    B. May be run only on large systems with lots of memory
    C. Was developed around 1995
    D. Is an interpretive language
    E. Is a general-purpose OO language

7. **Object persistence:**
    A. Preserves the state of an object between executions of an application
    B. Preserves the state of an object across the shutdown and startup of the computer system
    C. Loads objects into memory to preserve them permanently
    D. Occurs when the application requests that an object be saved
    E. Can be accomplished only with an OO database

8. **The events necessary to retrieve an object from an OO database include**
    A. A message is sent to the object, so the object must be loaded into memory.
    B. A request to retrieve the object is sent to the OO database.
    C. Object references are swizzled into memory addresses.
    D. Relational data is assigned to an object class.
    E. The object is made available to the application environment.

9. **The disadvantages of object-relational databases include**
    A. The combination is more complex than either pure object-oriented or pure relational databases.
    B. Ad-hoc query capability is limited.
    C. Objects are table-centric.
    D. Neither relational purists nor object purists are enamored with this combination.
    E. Object applications are not as data-centric as relational ones.

10. **When considering the selection of a database model, which of the following facts should be taken into account?**
    A. Ordinary file system files can handle simple data, provided there are no ad-hoc query requirements.
    B. Relational databases can handle simple data that has ad-hoc query requirements.
    C. Object-oriented databases are best at handling complex data.
    D. Object-relational databases can handle complex data that has ad-hoc query requirements.
    E. Object-oriented databases can handle complex data, provided there are no ad-hoc query requirements.

Final Exam

Choose the correct responses to each of the multiple-choice questions. Note that there may be more than one correct response to each question.

1. **Examples of logical changes that can be safely made in a system that has a high degree of logical data independence are**

    A. Adding data items to existing database objects

    B. Adding new database objects

    C. Deleting database objects

    D. Deleting data items from existing database objects

    E. Moving a database object from one physical file to another

2. **Examples of physical changes that can be safely made in a system that has a high degree of physical data independence are**

    A. Adding new user views

    B. Adding new data files

    C. Moving a file from one disk device to another

    D. Splitting or combining database objects

    E. Renaming a data file

3. **The main reasons that the relational model became so popular are**

   A. The network model saw no commercial success.

   B. Computer systems became less expensive, so flexibility became more important than efficiency.

   C. Products were developed that were reasonably efficient.

   D. Simple-to-use query languages such as SQL emerged.

   E. Relational calculus was invented.

4. **Logical data independence:**

   A. Allows database objects to be freely added to the physical database files without disrupting existing database users and processes

   B. Allows data to be freely deleted from the physical database files without disrupting existing database users and processes

   C. Is a property that all modern computer systems have to some degree

   D. Is achieved through the separation of the physical and logical layers of the ANSI/SPARC model

   E. Is achieved through the separation of the logical and external layers of the ANSI/SPARC model

5. **Physical data independence:**

   A. Is something a database either has or does not have

   B. Is achieved through the separation of the physical and logical layers of the ANSI/SPARC model

   C. Is achieved through the separation of the logical and external layers of the ANSI/SPARC model

   D. Is a property that all modern computer systems have to some degree

   E. Allows nondisruptive changes to be made to the physical layer in the ANSI/SPARC model

6. **The relational database model:**

   A. Provides superior flexibility for ad hoc queries

   B. Is difficult to understand and use

   C. Was first proposed by Dr. E.F. Codd

   D. Presents data as two-dimensional tables

   E. Does not use physical pointers to connect database records

7. **User views are important because:**

    A. Application programs reference them.

    B. Data updates are shown in a delayed fashion.

    C. They provide physical data independence.

    D. They can be tailored to the needs of the database user.

    E. People querying the database reference them.

8. **Currently available relational databases include**

    A. Oracle

    B. MySQL

    C. Microsoft SQL Server

    D. System R

    E. IDS

9. **The object-relational model:**

    A. Overcomes the ad hoc query restrictions found in the relational model

    B. Overcomes the ad hoc query restrictions found in the object-oriented model

    C. Combines concepts from the relational and object models in an attempt to get the best from each

    D. Is not supported by the mainstream (bestselling) DBMS products

    E. Was first proposed by Charles Bachman

10. **The external layer of the ANSI/SPARC model:**

    A. Is directly referenced by database users

    B. Contains the database subschema

    C. Lies between the physical and logical layers

    D. Provides physical data independence

    E. Contains all the user views for the database

11. A relationship in the conceptual design becomes which object in the logical design?

A. Referential constraint

B. Index

C. View

D. Table

E. Column

12. An entity in the conceptual design becomes which object in the logical/ physical design?

A. Table

B. Column

C. View

D. Referential constraint

E. Index

13. An attribute in the conceptual design becomes which object in the logical/ physical design?

A. Table

B. Column

C. View

D. Referential constraint

E. Index

14. A column in a relational table:

A. Is derived from an entity in the conceptual design

B. May be composed of other columns

C. Must be assigned a data type

D. Must be assigned a unique name within the table

E. Is the smallest named unit of storage in a relational database

15. **If a product can be manufactured in many plants and a plant can manu-facture many products, this is an example of which type of relationship?**

    A. One-to-one

    B. One-to-many

    C. Many-to-one

    D. Many-to-many

    E. Recursive

16. **A referential constraint:**

    A. Must have primary key and foreign key columns that have identical names

    B. Is derived from a user view in the conceptual model

    C. Ensures that a foreign key value always refers to an existing primary key value in the parent table

    D. Defines a many-to-many relationship between two tables

    E. Ensures that a primary key does not have duplicate values in a table

17. **Examples of an entity are**

    A. A customer order

    B. A customer

    C. An alphabetical listing of products

    D. An employee's paycheck

    E. A customer's name

18. **Examples of an attribute are**

    A. An alphabetical listing of employees

    B. An employee

    C. An employee's name

    D. An employee's paycheck

    E. An employee's birth date

19. **Which of the following are examples of recursive relationships?**
    A. An employee who manages a department
    B. An organizational unit made up of other organizational units
    C. An organizational unit made up of departments
    D. An employee who manages other employees
    E. An employee who has many dependents

20. **Intersection tables:**
    A. Are used to provide users with a customized view of their data
    B. Resolve a one-to-many relationship
    C. May contain intersection data
    D. Resolve a many-to-many relationship
    E. Appear only in the conceptual database design

21. **When a query with no criteria included is executed, the result is**
    A. An error message
    B. A Cartesian product
    C. No rows being displayed
    D. All the rows in the table being displayed
    E. None of the above

22. **Self-joins in a query are a method of resolving**
    A. Recursive relationships
    B. NULL values
    C. Cartesian products
    D. Many-to-many relationships
    E. Aggregate functions

23. **When sequencing (sorting) of rows is not included in a database query, the rows returned by the query are in:**
    A. Ascending sequence by the first column in the query results
    B. No particular sequence
    C. The order in which the rows were added to the tables
    D. By the first column in the table
    E. Ascending sequence by the primary key

24. **Tables may be joined**

    A. Using only the primary key in one table and a foreign key in another

    B. Only using the Cartesian product formula

    C. Only to other tables

    D. Only to themselves

    E. Using any column in either table (theoretically)

25. **An aggregate function:**

    A. May be applied to table columns but not to calculated columns

    B. Combines data from multiple columns together

    C. Requires that every column in a query be either an aggregate function or named in the GROUP BY list for the query

    D. Combines data from multiple rows together

    E. All of the above

26. **In SQL, row order in query results:**

    A. May be specified only for columns in the query results

    B. Defaults to descending when sequence is not specified

    C. Is specified using the SORTED BY clause

    D. Is unpredictable unless specified in the query

    E. May be either descending or ascending for any column

27. **A check constraint:**

    A. Restricts a database user's privileges

    B. Enforces a business rule

    C. Validates data in an index

    D. Creates an index to assist with the constraint

    E. Enforces referential integrity

28. **In SQL, an outer join:**

    A. Has proprietary syntax in older RDBMS products

    B. Always results in a Cartesian product

    C. Can be a left, right, or full outer join

    D. Always returns all rows in at least one of the two tables

    E. Always returns all rows in both of the tables

29. **SQL may be divided into the following subsets:**

    A. Data Replication Language (DRL)

    B. Data Control Language (DCL)

    C. Data Selection Language (DSL)

    D. Data Query Language (DQL)

    E. Data Purge Language (DPL)

30. **An SQL CREATE statement:**

    A. May be reversed later using a DROP statement

    B. Is a form of DML

    C. May be corrected later using an ALTER statement

    D. Creates new user privileges

    E. Creates a database object

31. **A subselect in SQL:**

    A. Is a powerful way of calculating columns

    B. Allows for the flexible selection of rows

    C. May be corrugated or noncorrugated

    D. Must not be enclosed in parentheses

    E. May be used to select values to be applied to WHERE clause conditions

32. **The SQL BETWEEN operator:**

    A. Can be rewritten using the <= and NOT = operators

    B. Can be rewritten using the <= and >= operators

    C. Includes the endpoint values

    D. Is an Oracle extension to SQL

    E. Selects rows added to a table during a time interval

33. **Database privileges:**

    A. Are managed using an SQL GRANT and REVOKE statement

    B. May be either system or object privileges

    C. Must be granted using roles

    D. May be changed with an SQL ALTER PRIVILEGE statement

    E. Are best managed when assembled into groups using the SQL GROUP BY clause

34. **An SQL DELETE statement with a column list:**

    A. Can be used to delete from a view

    B. Deletes every column in the table

    C. Deletes every row in the table

    D. Results in an error message

    E. Results in a Cartesian product

35. **An SQL ALTER statement:**

    A. May be used to add a view

    B. May be used to add a constraint

    C. May be used to drop a view

    D. May be used to drop a table column

    E. May be used to drop a constraint

36. **E.F. Codd invented:**

    A. Normalization

    B. Rapid Application Development (RAD)

    C. The SDLC methodology

    D. The relational database

    E. Quality assurance testing

37. **In an SDLC methodology, normalization takes place during:**

    A. Logical design

    B. Physical design

    C. Construction

    D. Implementation and rollout

    E. Ongoing support

38. **Prototyping:**

    A. Is an integral part of most SDLC methodologies

    B. Works well when requirements are sketchy

    C. May be used as a technique for gathering requirements

    D. May be used to create complete systems

    E. Helps in setting user expectations

39. **In the N-tier client/server model:**

    A. Client workstations must be high-powered systems.

    B. All application logic runs on an application server.

    C. The client workstation handles all presentation logic.

    D. A web server hosts the web pages.

    E. The database is hosted on a centralized server.

40. **The phases of the traditional system development life cycle (SDLC) methodology include**

    A. Requirements gathering

    B. Logical design

    C. Prototyping

    D. Physical design

    E. Ongoing support

41. **User views are analyzed during:**

    A. Requirements gathering

    B. Logical design

    C. Physical design

    D. Construction

    E. Quality assurance testing

42. **The database is initially constructed in the:**

    A. System test environment

    B. Development environment

    C. Quality assurance environment

    D. Staging environment

    E. Production environment

43. **The advantages of document reviews during requirements gathering are**

    A. Documents will always reflect current practices.

    B. Document reviews can be done relatively quickly.

    C. Pictures and diagrams are valuable tools for understanding systems.

    D. Documents will always be up to date.

    E. Documents often present overviews better than other techniques can.

44. **The advantages of observation during requirements gathering are**

    A. The Hawthorne effect enhances your results.

    B. You may see the way things really are instead of the way management and/or documentation presents them.

    C. You are likely to see lots of situations where exceptions are handled.

    D. You may observe events that would not be described to you by anyone.

    E. You always see people acting normally.

45. **The advantages of conducting surveys during requirements gathering include**

    A. Surveys are simple to develop.

    B. Most survey recipients respond.

    C. A lot of ground can be covered quickly.

    D. Nonverbal responses are excluded.

    E. Prototyping of requirements is unnecessary.

46. **Most business systems require that you normalize only as far as:**

    A. First normal form

    B. Second normal form

    C. Boyce-Codd normal form

    D. Third normal form

    E. Fourth normal form

47. **A foreign key in a normalized relation may be**

    A. A multivalued attribute

    B. A repeating group

    C. The entire primary key of the relation

    D. A non-key attribute in the relation

    E. Part of the primary key of the relation

48. **In general, violations of a normalization rule are resolved by:**

    A. Moving attributes or groups of attributes to a new relation

    B. Creating summary tables

    C. Combining relations

    D. Combining attributes

    E. Denormalization

49. **Criteria useful in selecting a primary key from among several candidate keys are**

   A. Invent a surrogate key if that is the best possible key.

   B. Choose concatenated keys over single attribute keys.

   C. Choose the simplest candidate.

   D. Choose the shortest candidate.

   E. Choose the candidate most likely to have its value change.

50. **The roles of unique identifiers in normalization are**

   A. You cannot choose a primary key until relations are normalized.

   B. They are unnecessary.

   C. All normalized forms require designation of a primary key.

   D. They are required once you reach third normal form.

   E. You cannot normalize relations without first choosing a primary key.

51. **The Web:**

   A. Uses hyperlinks to navigate pages

   B. Uses the Telnet protocol

   C. Is a hypermedia-based system

   D. Uses a web browser to present pages

   E. Supports only static web pages

52. **The purpose of normalization is**

   A. To optimize data-retrieval performance

   B. To optimize data for inserts, updates, and deletes

   C. To eliminate redundant data

   D. To remove certain anomalies from the relations

   E. To provide a reason to denormalize the database

53. **Second normal form resolves anomalies caused by:**

   A. Transitive dependencies

   B. Repeating groups

   C. Multivalued attributes

   D. Join dependencies

   E. Partial dependency on the primary key

54. **Proper handling of multivalued attributes when converting relations to first normal form usually prevents subsequent problems with:**

    A. First normal form

    B. Second normal form

    C. Third normal form

    D. Fourth normal form

    E. Boyce-Codd normal form

55. **The delete anomaly refers to a situation where:**

    A. Data deletion causes unintentional loss of another entity's data.

    B. Data must be deleted before it can be inserted.

    C. Data must be inserted before it can be deleted.

    D. A required delete cannot be done due to referential constraints.

    E. A required delete cannot be done due to a check constraint.

56. **It is important for a database designer to understand process modeling because:**

    A. The database design must support the intended process model.

    B. Process design is a primary responsibility of the DBA.

    C. The process model must be completed before the data model.

    D. The data model must be completed before the process model.

    E. The database designer must work closely with the process designer.

57. **The IDEF1X ERD format:**

    A. Covers both data and process models

    B. Has many variants

    C. Was first released in 1983

    D. Has been adopted as a U.S. federal government standard

    E. Follows a standard developed by the National Institute of Standards and Technology

58. **A subtype:**

    A. Shows various states of the supertype

    B. Is a subset of the supertype

    C. Is a superset of the supertype

    D. Has a conditional one-to-one relationship with the supertype

    E. Has a one-to-many relationship with the supertype

59. **Examples of possible subtypes for an Order entity supertype include**

    A. Approved order, pending order, canceled order

    B. Office supplies order, professional services order

    C. Auto parts order, aircraft parts order, truck parts order

    D. Shipped order, unshipped order, invoiced order

    E. Order line items

60. **When subtypes are being considered in a database design:**

    A. There is a trade-off between generalization and specialization.

    B. The more subtypes that can be found, the better.

    C. They should be avoided as much as possible because they complicate the design.

    D. There are multiple correct designs—the challenge is to find the one that best fits the organization's intended use of the database.

    E. There is one correct design—the challenge is to find it.

61. **The strengths of flowcharts are**

    A. They are specific to application programming only.

    B. They are useful for spotting reusable components.

    C. They can be easily modified as requirements change.

    D. They are natural and easy to use for procedural language programmers.

    E. They are equally useful for nonprocedural and object-oriented languages.

62. **The CRUD matrix helps find the following problems:**

    A. Entities that are never updated

    B. Entities that are never read

    C. Processes that only read

    D. Processes that have no create entity

    E. Processes that are never deleted

63. **The strengths of the DFD are**

    A. It shows complex logic easily.

    B. It's quick and easy to develop, even for complex systems.

    C. It's great for presentation to management.

    D. It's good for top-down design work.

    E. It shows overall structure without sacrificing detail.

64. **The data flow diagram (DFD):**

    A. Is the most data centric of all process models

    B. Was first developed by E.F. Codd

    C. Was first developed in the 1980s

    D. Combines the best of the flowchart and the function diagram

    E. Combines diagram pages together hierarchically

65. **The strengths of the function hierarchy diagram are**

    A. It provides a good overview at high and medium levels of detail.

    B. It is quick and easy to learn and use.

    C. It clearly shows the sequence of process steps.

    D. Checking quality is easy and straightforward.

    E. Complex interactions between functions are easily modeled.

66. **Physical security of the database server:**

    A. Requires both physical devices and policies

    B. Is unnecessary if the server is connected to the Internet

    C. Should include a locked room to contain the server

    D. May include biometric controls

    E. May include surveillance equipment

67. **Network security:**

    A. Must include provisions for remotely located employees

    B. Is mandatory for all computer systems connected to any network

    C. Can be handled by routers alone

    D. Can be handled by encryption alone

    E. Can be handled by firewalls alone

68. **The web "technology stack" includes**

    A. An application server

    B. A database server

    C. A web server

    D. A client workstation running a web browser

    E. Network hardware (firewalls, routers, and so on)

69. **Employees connecting to the enterprise network from home or from another remote work location:**

    A. Should have a firewall between their computer and a cable or DSL modem

    B. Are best protected by a software firewall such as is available in Microsoft Windows

    C. Are better protected when a VPN is used

    D. Should not use network address translation

    E. Should have IP spoofing implemented

70. **Components of wireless access point security include**

    A. Virtual private networks

    B. MAC address lists

    C. Network address translation

    D. Encryption

    E. The organization's security policy

71. **System-level security precautions include**

    A. Using simple passwords that are easy to remember

    B. Applying security patches in a timely manner

    C. Installing the minimal software components necessary

    D. Changing all default passwords

    E. Granting only table privileges that users require

72. **Login credentials:**

    A. Should be difficult to guess

    B. Should have passwords changed periodically

    C. Need not be encrypted

    D. May be shared by multiple users provided all of them are trustworthy

    E. Should be governed by security policy

73. **Encryption:**

    A. Should use keys of at least 28 bits in length

    B. Should be used for sensitive data sent over a network

    C. Should be used for all sensitive data

    D. Should never be used for login credentials

    E. Can use symmetric or asymmetric keys

74. **System privileges:**

    A. Allow the grantee to perform certain administrative functions on the server, such as shutting it down

    B. Are rescinded using the SQL REMOVE statement

    C. Are specific to a database object

    D. Are granted in a similar way in Oracle, Sybase, and Microsoft SQL Server

    E. Vary across databases from different vendors

75. **Views may assist with security policy implementation by:**

    A. Storing database audit results

    B. Restricting the table columns to which a user has access

    C. Restricting table rows to which a user has access

    D. Restricting the databases to which a user has access

    E. Monitoring for database intruders

76. **A result set is**

    A. A pointer into a cursor

    B. The collection of rows returned by a database query

    C. A method to analyze the performance of SQL statements

    D. The same as a cursor

    E. A buffer that holds rows retrieved from the database

77. **A transaction:**

    A. May not be partially processed and committed

    B. May be partially processed and committed

    C. Is sometimes called a *unit of work*

    D. Changes the database from one consistent state to another

    E. Has properties described by the ACID acronym

78. **ODBC is**

    A. A Microsoft standard

    B. Flexible in handling proprietary SQL

    C. Independent of any particular language, operating system, or DBMS

    D. A standard API for connecting to DBMSs

    E. Used by Java programs

79. **A lock:**

    A. Is usually released when a COMMIT or ROLLBACK takes place

    B. May cause contention when other users attempt to update locked data

    C. Is a control placed on data to reserve it so that the user may update it

    D. May have levels and an escalation protocol in some RDBMS products

    E. Has a timeout set in DB2 and some other RDBMS products

80. **The concurrent update problem:**
    A. Is the reason that transaction locking must be supported
    B. Cannot occur when AUTOCOMMIT is set to ON
    C. Occurs when two database users make conflicting updates to the same data
    D. Occurs when two database users submit conflicting SELECT statements
    E. Is a consequence of simultaneous data sharing

81. **Indexes work well at filtering rows when:**
    A. The selectivity ratio is very high.
    B. They are unique.
    C. The selectivity ratio is very low.
    D. They are very selective.
    E. They are not unique.

82. **Performance tuning:**
    A. Should be requirements based
    B. Is a never-ending process
    C. Should be used only on queries that fail to conform to performance requirements
    D. Should be used on each query until no more improvement can be realized
    E. Involves not only SQL tuning but also CPU, file system I/O, and memory usage tuning

83. **General SQL tuning tips include**
    A. Use an ORDER BY clause whenever possible.
    B. Use a WHERE clause to filter rows whenever possible.
    C. Use an index whenever possible.
    D. Use views whenever possible.
    E. Avoid table scans on large tables.

84. **Common features of change control processes are**

   A. Release numbering

   B. Prioritization

   C. Deadlock prevention

   D. Transaction support

   E. Version numbering

85. **Before rows may be fetched from a cursor, the cursor must first be**

   A. Declared

   B. Opened

   C. Committed

   D. Purged

   E. Closed

86. **XML is**

   A. Extensible because custom tags may be defined

   B. A subset of HTML

   C. Used for remote database connections

   D. A document-formatting language

   E. A protocol used to transfer web pages

87. **Data warehousing:**

   A. Involves storing data for day-to-day operations

   B. May involve one or more data marts

   C. Is a form of OLAP database

   D. Was pioneered by Bill Inmon

   E. Involves storing historical data for analysis

88. **Properties of data warehouse systems include**

   A. Medium to low transaction volume

   B. Process orientation

   C. Support for day-to-day operations

   D. Holding historic rather than current information

   E. Long-running queries that process many rows of data

89. **Compared with OLTP systems, data warehouse systems:**

    A. Have a relatively smaller number of users

    B. Have data that is not normalized

    C. Store data that is more static

    D. Have higher transaction volumes

    E. Tend to have shorter running queries

90. **The star schema:**

    A. Always has fully normalized dimension tables

    B. Was developed by Ralph Kimball

    C. Involves multiple levels of dimension tables

    D. Includes a dimension table and one or more fact tables

    E. Was a key feature of the Red Brick DBMS

91. **The snowflake schema:**

    A. Does not use a fact table

    B. Can be designed by fully normalizing all the dimension tables

    C. Allows dimensions to have dimensions of their own

    D. Was developed by Bill Inmon

    E. Is a hybrid containing both normalized and denormalized tables

92. **A data mart:**

    A. Can be a good starting point for organizations with no data warehouse experience

    B. Can be a good starting point when requirements are sketchy

    C. Is a shop that sells data to individuals and businesses

    D. Is a subset of a data warehouse

    E. Supports the requirements of a particular department or business function

93. **Object-oriented programming:**

    A. Uses messages as a vehicle for object interaction

    B. Allows an object to directly access the variables in a related object

    C. Uses methods to define the behavior of an object

    D. Requires objects to have a primary key

    E. Supports the use of complex objects

94. **The advantages of object-relational databases include**

    A. Objects are stored within tables.

    B. Complex data types are supported.

    C. Ad-hoc query capability is fully supported.

    D. Class structures and inheritance are fully supported.

    E. Centrally stored functions (methods) improve reuse.

95. **Which of the following are common uses of XML?**

    A. Display database data on a web page

    B. Create static web pages

    C. Store objects in a relational database

    D. Transmit database data to another party

    E. Enforce business rules on documents

96. **General rules to follow regarding indexes include**

    A. Indexes on very small tables tend not to be very useful.

    B. The more a table is updated, the more indexes will help performance.

    C. Columns that are frequently updated should always be indexed.

    D. The larger the table, the more important indexes become.

    E. Indexing foreign key columns often helps join performance.

97. **An intranet is**

    A. Available to authorized outsiders

    B. Available to anyone on the Internet

    C. Available to authorized (internal) members of an organization

    D. Typically connected to the Internet

    E. Protected by a firewall

98. **Data types:**

    A. Require that precision and scale be specified also

    B. Can be used to prevent numeric characters from being stored in character format columns

    C. Can be used to prevent alphabetic characters from being stored in numeric columns

    D. Can be used to prevent invalid dates from being stored in date columns

    E. Prevent incorrect data from being inserted into a table

99. **Primary key constraints:**

    A. Require column values to be unique within the table

    B. Require column values to be unique within the database

    C. Require columns that have check constraints

    D. Require columns that have NOT NULL constraints

    E. Are required on foreign key columns

100. **Business rules are implemented in the database using:**

    A. Primary key constraints

    B. Unique constraints

    C. Check constraints

    D. Referential constraints

    E. Abbreviations

Answers to Quizzes and Final Exam

Chapter 1	Chapter 2	Chapter 3	Chapter 4
1. B, D, E	1. C	1. B, E	1. A, C
2. A, B, C, D, E	2. E	2. D, E	2. D
3. C, D	3. B	3. B	3. E
4. B, E	4. A, B, E	4. E	4. B
5. B, C, E	5. A, B, C	5. D	5. A, D
6. B, D, E	6. B, C, D	6. A, B, D	6. C, E
7. A, B, C, E	7. A, B, D	7. C	7. A, B, C
8. A, D	8. B, C	8. C	8. B, D
9. A, B, E	9. B, C, E	9. A, C, D	9. A, B, C, D, E
10. A, B, D, E	10. A, B, D, E	10. D	10. B, C, D

Chapter 5	Chapter 6	Chapter 7	Chapter 8
1. B, D	1. A, B, C, D	1. B, D, E	1. B, C, D
2. C, E	2. E	2. B	2. A, C
3. A, B, C	3. D	3. D, E	3. B, D, E
4. B, C, E	4. A, B, E	4. A, B, D	4. D, E
5. A, B, D	5. B	5. A, C, D, E	5. B, C
6. C, D	6. E	6. A, C, E	6. A, B, C
7. B, D, E	7. C	7. B, D	7. A, C
8. B, C, E	8. B	8. A, B, C	8. C, D, E
9. A	9. E	9. A, E	9. A, B, C, E
10. B, D	10. D	10. A, B, C	10. B, C, E

Chapter 9	Chapter 10	Chapter 11	Chapter 12	Chapter 13
1. B, C, D	1. A, B, C	1. B	1. B, C	1. A, B, D
2. B, D, E	2. A, C, E	2. E	2. C, D, E	2. C
3. B, C	3. B, C, D	3. A, B, C	3. A, D, E	3. B, C, D
4. A, B, E	4. C, D, E	4. B, C	4. A, B, D	4. A, C, E
5. A, C, D, E	5. B, C, D, E	5. D, E	5. E	5. B, E
6. B, D	6. B, C, D, E	6. A, B, C, D	6. A, B, C, D	6. A, C, D, E
7. A, C, D	7. B, D, E	7. A, D	7. B, E	7. A, B, D
8. D, E	8. A, B, C	8. B, D, E	8. B, C, E	8. A, B, C, E
9. A, B, E	9. A, C, E	9. A, E	9. B, D, E	9. A, C, D, E
10. D, E	10. B, C, D	10. B, D	10. B, C, D	10. A, B, C, D, E

Answers to Final Exam

1. A, B	26. D, E	51. A, C, D	76. B
2. B, C, E	27. B	52. B, D	77. A, C, D, E
3. B, C, D	28. A, C, D	53. E	78. B, C, D
4. A, E	29. B, D	54. D	79. A, B, C, D, E
5. B, D, E	30. A, C, E	55. A	80. A, C, E
6. A, C, D, E	31. A, B, E	56. A, E	81. A, B, D
7. A, D, E	32. B, C	57. D, E	82. A, B, C, E
8. A, B, C	33. A, B	58. B, D	83. B, C, E
9. B, C	34. D	59. B, C	84. A, B, E
10. A, B, E	35. B, D, E	60. A, D	85. A, B
11. A	36. A, D	61. B, C, D	86. A, D
12. A	37. A	62. A, B	87. B, C, D, E
13. B	38. B, C, D	63. C, D, E	88. A, D, E
14. C, D, E	39. B, D, E	64. A, D, E	89. A, B, C
15. D	40. A, B, D, E	65. A, B	90. B, E
16. C	41. A	66. A, C, D, E	91. B, C
17. A, B, D	42. B	67. A, B	92. A, B, D, E
18. C, E	43. B, C, E	68. A, B, C, D, E	93. A, C, E
19. B, D	44. B, D	69. A, C	94. B, C, E
20. C, D	45. C	70. B, D, E	95. A, D
21. D	46. D	71. B, C, D	96. A, D, E
22. A	47. C, D, E	72. A, B, E	97. C, D, E
23. B	48. A	73. B, C, E	98. C, D
24. E	49. A, C, D	74. A, D, E	99. A, D
25. C, D	50. C, E	75. B, C	100. A, B, C, D

Video Store Sample Database

This appendix contains an overview of the video store sample database used in this book along with instructions for downloading and installing it so you can follow along as you read.

Overview of the Video Store Sample Database

The SQL and forms-based query examples used in this book are based on a database for a fictitious video store. The next section provides instructions for downloading a ZIP file that contains a Microsoft Access 2000 database for the video store as well as the SQL statements required to create the database objects and populate them with data using MySQL, Oracle, Microsoft SQL Server, and other SQL-based databases.

The following illustration presents the entity relationship diagram (ERD) for the entire video store database. A PDF of this ERD is included in the ZIP file that can be downloaded from the web site.

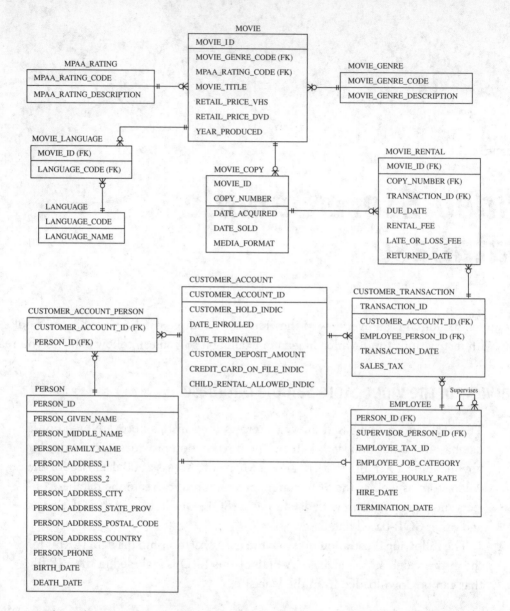

The video store for which the sample database was designed is a small family-owned and -operated store that rents videos in both VHS and DVD formats. However, the VHS format is being discontinued. The store manager expects to expand into selling videos as well as other product lines, such as snack foods, but the plans to do so were not firm enough to be included in the current database design.

Table A-1 gives some information about each table included in the design.

TABLE A-1 Video Store Database Tables

Table Name	Description	Primary Key	Parent Table(s)
CUSTOMER_ ACCOUNT	Contains one row for each customer account opened with the video store.	CUSTOMER_ ACCOUNT_ID	None
CUSTOMER_ ACCOUNT_PERSON	Intersection table that shows which people are associated with each customer account.	CUSTOMER_ ACCOUNT_ID, PERSON_ID	CUSTOMER_ ACCOUNT, PERSON
CUSTOMER_ TRANSACTION	Contains one row for each transaction initiated by a customer. Each transaction may contain one or more movie rentals.	TRANSACTION_ID	CUSTOMER_ ACCOUNT, EMPLOYEE
EMPLOYEE	Contains one row for each employee of the video store. This table is a subclass of Person (each Employee will have a matching row with the same primary key value in the PERSON table).	PERSON_ID	PERSON
LANGUAGE	Lookup table of language codes and names (used to show language options for movies).	LANGUAGE_CODE	None
MOVIE	Contains one row for each movie title. Child table MOVIE_COPY shows copies of the movie owned by the store.	MOVIE_ID	MPAA_RATING, MOVIE_GENRE
MOVIE_COPY	Contains one row for each movie copy available for rent.	MOVIE_ID, COPY_NUMBER	MOVIE
MOVIE_GENRE	Lookup table of genre codes and descriptions (used to categorize movies).	MOVIE_GENRE_CODE	None
MOVIE_LANGUAGE	Intersection table that shows languages available for each movie.	MOVIE_ID, LANGUAGE_CODE	MOVIE, LANGUAGE
MOVIE_RENTAL	Contains one row for each time the movie was rented.	MOVIE_ID, COPY_NUMBER, TRANSACTION_ID	MOVIE_COPY, CUSTOMER_ TRANSACTION
MPAA_RATING	Lookup table of MPAA rating codes and descriptions.	MPAA_RATING_CODE	None
PERSON	Contains one row for each individual associated with the video store. Each person may be a customer (associated with a Customer Account), an Employee, or both.	PERSON_ID	None

Table A-2 gives some information about the columns in the database tables.

TABLE A-2 Video Store Database Table Columns		
Table Name	**Column Name**	**Description**
CUSTOMER_ACCOUNT	CHILD_RENTAL_ALLOWED_INDIC	Yes/No indicator as to whether persons under 18 are permitted to check out movies using this account
CUSTOMER_ACCOUNT	CREDIT_CARD_ON_FILE_INDIC	Yes/No indicator as to whether the customer left a credit card imprint on file to guarantee payment of their account
CUSTOMER_ACCOUNT	CUSTOMER_ACCOUNT_ID	Primary key—sequential number assigned to each customer account
CUSTOMER_ACCOUNT	CUSTOMER_DEPOSIT_AMOUNT	For customers who did not provide a credit card, the amount of the cash deposit they provided to the store
CUSTOMER_ACCOUNT	CUSTOMER_HOLD_INDIC	Yes/No indicator as to whether customer account is on hold; rentals are not permitted against accounts on hold
CUSTOMER_ACCOUNT	DATE_ENROLLED	The date the account with the store was opened
CUSTOMER_ACCOUNT	DATE_TERMINATED	If account was closed, the date of closure (null for active accounts)
CUSTOMER_ACCOUNT_PERSON	CUSTOMER_ACCOUNT_ID	Part of primary key—foreign key to CUSTOMER_ACCOUNT table
CUSTOMER_ACCOUNT_PERSON	PERSON_ID	Part of primary key—foreign key to PERSON table
CUSTOMER_TRANSACTION	CUSTOMER_ACCOUNT_ID	Foreign key to CUSTOMER_ACCOUNT table
CUSTOMER_TRANSACTION	EMPLOYEE_PERSON_ID	Foreign key (PERSON_ID) to EMPLOYEE table
CUSTOMER_TRANSACTION	SALES_TAX	Sales tax charged for the transaction
CUSTOMER_TRANSACTION	TRANSACTION_DATE	Date of the transaction
CUSTOMER_TRANSACTION	TRANSACTION_ID	Primary key—sequential number assigned to each new transaction
EMPLOYEE	EMPLOYEE_HOURLY_RATE	Pay rate per hour for the employee
EMPLOYEE	EMPLOYEE_JOB_CATEGORY	Job category for the employee (manager or clerk)

TABLE A-2 Video Store Database Table Columns (*continued*)

Table Name	Column Name	Description
EMPLOYEE	EMPLOYEE_TAX_ID	ID used for reporting payroll taxes for the employee (usually a social security number)
EMPLOYEE	HIRE_DATE	Date the employee was hired by the store
EMPLOYEE	PERSON_ID	Primary key—foreign key to the PERSON table
EMPLOYEE	SUPERVISOR_PERSON_ID	Foreign key to the EMPLOYEE table (to show the person to whom they report)
EMPLOYEE	TERMINATION_DATE	For former employees, the date their employment was terminated
LANGUAGE	LANGUAGE_CODE	Primary key—ISO (International Organization for Standardization) standard two-character code for a language
LANGUAGE	LANGUAGE_NAME	Name (in English) for the language
MOVIE	MOVIE_GENRE_CODE	Foreign key to MOVIE_GENRE table
MOVIE	MOVIE_ID	Primary key—values are assigned sequentially as new movies become available
MOVIE	MOVIE_TITLE	Official title of the movie (movie titles are not necessarily unique)
MOVIE	MPAA_RATING_CODE	Foreign key to MPAA_RATING table
MOVIE	RETAIL_PRICE_DVD	Retail list price for DVD copies of the movie
MOVIE	RETAIL_PRICE_VHS	Retail list price for VHS copies of the movie
MOVIE	YEAR_PRODUCED	The year the movie completed production; year released by studio
MOVIE_COPY	COPY_NUMBER	Part of primary key—sequential number assigned to each copy of a movie (number unique only within a given movie)
MOVIE_COPY	DATE_ACQUIRED	Date movie copy was acquired by the video store
MOVIE_COPY	DATE_SOLD	Date movie copy was sold (null if movie has not been sold); lost rentals are considered sold when customer pays for them

TABLE A-2 Video Store Database Table Columns (*continued*)

Table Name	Column Name	Description
MOVIE_COPY	MEDIA_FORMAT	Recording format of the movie copy (DVD or VHS)
MOVIE_COPY	MOVIE_ID	Part of primary key—foreign key to MOVIE table
MOVIE_GENRE	MOVIE_GENRE_CODE	Primary key—a code used to place movies into categories such as Comedy, Drama, Action–Adventure, and so forth
MOVIE_GENRE	MOVIE_GENRE_DESCRIPTION	Text description of a movie category (see MOVIE_GENRE_CODE)
MOVIE_LANGUAGE	LANGUAGE_CODE	Part of primary key—foreign key to LANGUAGE table
MOVIE_LANGUAGE	MOVIE_ID	Part of primary key—foreign key to MOVIE table
MOVIE_RENTAL	COPY_NUMBER	Part of primary key—foreign key to MOVIE_COPY table
MOVIE_RENTAL	DUE_DATE	The date a rented movie is due to be returned to the store
MOVIE_RENTAL	LATE_OR_LOSS_FEE	Fee charged (if any) because the movie copy was returned late or was permanently lost
MOVIE_RENTAL	MOVIE_ID	Part of primary key—foreign key to MOVIE_COPY table
MOVIE_RENTAL	RENTAL_FEE	Fee charged for the rental (adjusted for any coupons or discounts)
MOVIE_RENTAL	RETURNED_DATE	Date movie copy was returned (null until movie is checked in as returned)
MOVIE_RENTAL	TRANSACTION_ID	Part of primary key—foreign key to CUSTOMER_ TRANSACTION table
MPAA_RATING	MPAA_RATING_CODE	Primary key—movie rating code supplied by Motion Picture Association of America (MPAA), including G, PG, PG–13, R, NC–17, and NR (not rated)
MPAA_RATING	MPAA_RATING_DESCRIPTION	Text description of rating, as supplied by the MPAA
PERSON	BIRTH_DATE	The person's date of birth
PERSON	DEATH_DATE	The person's date of death (if person reported as deceased)
PERSON	PERSON_ADDRESS_1	First line of the person's street address

TABLE A-2 Video Store Database Table Columns (*continued*)

Table Name	Column Name	Description
PERSON	PERSON_ADDRESS_2	Optional second line of the person's street address
PERSON	PERSON_ADDRESS_CITY	The municipality for the person's mailing address
PERSON	PERSON_ADDRESS_COUNTRY	The ISO abbreviation for the country for the person's mailing address
PERSON	PERSON_ADDRESS_POSTAL_CODE	The postal code (ZIP code in the U.S.) for the person's mailing address
PERSON	PERSON_ADDRESS_STATE_PROV	The state or province for the person's mailing address
PERSON	PERSON_FAMILY_NAME	The last name of the person
PERSON	PERSON_GIVEN_NAME	The first name of the person
PERSON	PERSON_ID	Primary key—sequential number assigned to each person who has an affiliation with the video store
PERSON	PERSON_MIDDLE_NAME	The middle name (or initial) of the person
PERSON	PERSON_PHONE	The person's primary phone number

Instructions for Downloading and Installing the Sample Database

To enhance your learning of database concepts and SQL, I have provided a Microsoft Access 2000 database containing the video store sample database as well as scripts containing SQL statements tailored for MySQL (version 5.1), Oracle (version 7.0 and above), and SQL Server (version 2000 and above) in a ZIP file that is available for download from the McGraw-Hill web site. The SQL scripts include not only the statements required to create the database tables and other objects, but also the INSERT statements required to load sample data rows into the tables. The ZIP file also includes a PDF of the ERD for the sample database that you can print as a reference. To access the downloads page, follow these steps:

1. Open your web browser and go to www.mhprofessional.com.
2. On the banner across the top of the page, click COMPUTING.

3. Along the left margin about halfway down the page, click DOWN-LOADS.

4. Scroll down the page to the line for this title (*Databases Demystified*, 2nd Edition).

5. Click the title and your browser will open a dialog box with options for opening or saving the ZIP file. Choose the option that opens the file immediately after it is downloaded.

6. When the ZIP file opens, extract the files to a local directory where you can run the files. On Windows systems, I highly recommend that you put the files in a simply named directory that is immediately below your root directory, such as C:\sql. In most DBMS products, you must type in the path to the file in order to run it from within the database, and some of the products do not deal well with file paths such as "My Documents" that contain spaces.

7. Follow the instructions in the topic for your DBMS product.

Using the Microsoft Access Sample Database

In Microsoft Access 2000 or higher, follow these steps:

1. Double-click the file video_store_Access_2000.mdb.

2. If you see a yellow security warning on the startup screen, enable the content as follows:

    a. In Access 2000 and 2007, click the Options button next to the security warning, and select the option that enables the content.

    b. In Access 2010, simply click the Enable Content button next to the security warning.

3. Follow the examples in Chapter 3 to run forms-based or SQL queries.

Installing the Sample Database in MySQL

MySQL is an attractive choice because versions are available for Microsoft Windows, Mac OS X, several versions of Linux, and several versions of Unix. To install the sample database on MySQL, follow these steps:

1. If you have not yet installed MySQL, you can download the Community Server edition free of charge from www.mysql.com/downloads.

2. Launch the MySQL Command Line Client. On Windows systems you will find it on the Start menu under MySQL and then MySQL Server *x.y*

(*x.y* being the version number, such as 5.1). You will be prompted for the MySQL root password in order to connect. You should see a window like the one shown in the following illustration. (Note that the default window is a black background with white letters on most systems—I reversed mine so it shows up better in print.)

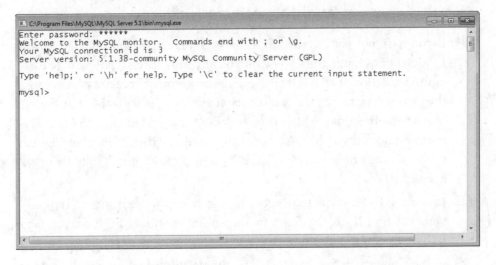

3. Enter the **source** command followed by the full path name of the video_store_MySQL.sql file that you extracted from the downloaded ZIP file. For example, if you placed the file in a directory named sql under the C: root directory on a Windows system, the command would be

```
source c:\sql\video_store_MySQL.sql
```

4. The file is written so you can rerun it should you need to start over. Therefore it contains a DROP DATABASE command that will fail the first time you run the script because the database to be deleted (VIDEO_STORE) won't exist. For all other statements in the file, you should see a message that starts with "Query OK", which of course means the statement was successfully processed.

5. Should you wish to close your database session and return to it later, you can just close the command-line window. When you relaunch the Command Line Client later and successfully enter the MySQL root password, simply enter this command at the mysql> prompt to reconnect to the database:

```
use VIDEO_STORE
```

Installing the Sample Database in SQL Server

To install the sample database on SQL Server, follow the steps in this section. If you intend to use a database other than one installed on your personal computer, you should solicit the help of a database administrator (DBA) who can help you set up the database and permissions on an appropriate server. The following steps assume installation on a personal computer:

1. If you have not yet installed SQL Server, you can download the Express Edition at no charge from www.microsoft.com/express/Database. The default installation option (Database and Management Tools) is best because the easiest way to run the sample database script is with the SQL Server Management Studio, which is one of the tools included in the management toolset. (If you have SQL Server installed without the management tools, you can choose an installation option that will install only the management tools.)

2. Launch SQL Server Management Studio from the Start menu. Typically, you will find it on the Start menu under Microsoft SQL Server *xxxx* (where *xxxx* is the version).

3. In the Connect To Server dialog box, the default values are usually correct for the server installed on your personal computer, but you may correct them if you are using a different server. Click Connect to connect to the database server. Once connected, you should see a screen like the following:

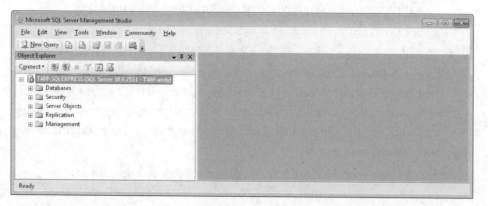

4. A database must be created to hold the video store objects. To create the database:

   a. In the hierarchical list along the left margin, right-click Databases and then click New Database.

b. In the New Database dialog box, enter the Database Name **video_store**, and let all the other values default as shown in the following illustration. Click OK to create the database. (If you accidentally click Add, which adds a line for another data file, click Remove to back up to where you were.)

5. Expand the Databases list along the left margin by clicking the plus sign. You should see the video_store database you just added. If not, try right-clicking Databases and selecting Refresh.

6. Click the video_store database to make sure it is selected. Otherwise, it is easy to accidentally run the script in the wrong database.

7. On the toolbar, select File | Open | File, or click the Open File icon. In the Open File dialog box, navigate to where you placed the video_store_SqlServer.sql file you extracted from the ZIP file you downloaded and

double-click it. The script should be loaded into Management Studio as shown next:

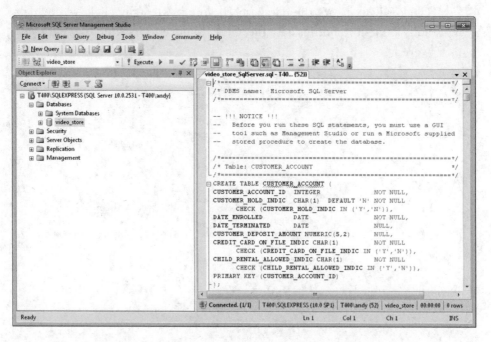

8. Click the Execute icon on the toolbar (the one with the red exclamation point) to run the script. Messages appear as shown in the following

illustration. If there are no errors, a green checkmark appears on the status line just below the messages.

9. Close the script file by clicking the small black *X* just above the script along the right margin. Be careful not to click the white *X* on the red button at the top of the window because that will close Management Studio instead of just the script file.

10. To begin writing and running your own SQL, click the New Query button on the toolbar. Should you need to close Management Studio and return later, just close the window, and when you relaunch Management Studio, expand the Databases list, select video_store, and click the New Query button to get back to where you left off.

11. If you need to start over from the beginning, you should drop and re-create the database using Management Studio before rerunning the script.

Installing the Sample Database Schema in Oracle

To install the sample database schema in an Oracle database, follow the steps in this topic to install the sample database. If you intend to use a database other than one on your own personal computer, you should solicit the help of a database administrator (DBA) who can help you set up the database and permissions on an appropriate server. The following steps assume installation on a personal computer:

1. If you do not have Oracle installed on your personal computer, you can download and install Oracle XE (Express Edition) at no charge from www .oracle.com/technology/products/database/xe.

2. You will need the SYSTEM user password in order to add a new user schema to your Oracle database. Make sure you have it available.

3. Launch the Oracle command-line window. For Oracle 10*g* XE, you will find it on the Start menu as Oracle Database 10*g* Express Edition | Run SQL Command Line. (Although Oracle 11*g* is available as of this writing, the most recent version of XE is 10*g*.)

4. Enter the @ command followed by the full path to the video_store_ Oracle.sql file you extracted from the ZIP file you downloaded. If the file is in the C:\sql directory, the command would look like this:

   ```
   @C:\sql\video_store_Oracle.sql
   ```

5. Enter the SYSTEM user password when prompted. The following illustration shows the command from step 4 and the password prompt. (Note that the default configuration is a black background with white text, which I reversed so it shows up better in print.)

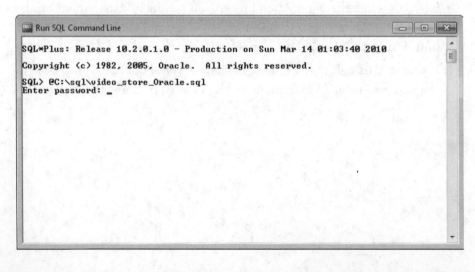

6. You will see a series of messages. The script is written so it can rerun, so you will see an error caused by the `DROP USER` command the first time you run it (the user will not exist prior to the first run).

7. You may begin entering your own SQL statements into the command-line tool. If you need to exit and return later, you may close the window at any time. When you relaunch the command-line tool, use the following command to connect to the video_store schema. When prompted for it, the password will be **video**. (For versions prior to 11g, Oracle user IDs and passwords are not case-sensitive.)

```
connect video_store
```

Installing the Sample Database in Other SQL-Based DBMS Products

Support for data types and syntax across available SQL products varies significantly. The statements may require modification to run them on an SQL-based DBMS product other than the ones previously listed. I suggest that you start with the MySQL script because MySQL is the most compliant with the current ISO/ANSI SQL standard. You might start out copying and pasting small batches of statements at first to avoid being overwhelmed with error messages. Consult an SQL guide for the DBMS you are using to correct any syntax errors reported when you run the statements.

Index